D1567723

Greater Cincinnati
Bicentennial History Series

Board of Editors
Zane L. Miller
Gene D. Lewis

Books in the Series

Making Better Citizens: Housing Reform and the Community
Development Strategy in Cincinnati, 1890–1960
  Robert B. Fairbanks

Ethnic Diversity and Civic Identity: Patterns of Conflict and
Cohesion in Cincinnati since 1820
  Edited by Henry D. Shapiro and Jonathan D. Sarna

Race and the City: Work, Community, and Protest in
Cincinnati, 1820–1970
  Edited by Henry Louis Taylor, Jr.

Going to Cincinnati: A History of the Blues in the Queen City
  Steven C. Tracy

Going to Cincinnati

Going to Cincinnati

A History of the Blues
in the Queen City

Steven C. Tracy

University of Illinois Press
Urbana and Chicago

To Cathy, Michelle, and Michael

Publication of this work was supported in part by a grant from the Cincinnati Historical Society.

© 1993 by the Board of Trustees of the University of Illinois
Manufactured in the United States of America
C 5 4 3 2

This book is printed on acid-free paper.

Library of Congress Cataloging-in-Publication Data

Tracy, Steven C. (Steven Carl), 1954–
    Going to Cincinnati : a history of the blues in the queen city /
Steven C. Tracy.
        p.   cm. — (Greater Cincinnati bicentennial history series)
    Discography:
    Includes bibliographical references and index.
    ISBN 0–252–01999–7
    1. Blues (Music)—Ohio—Cincinnati—History and criticism.
I. Title. II. Series.
ML3521.T7   1993
781.643'09771'78—dc20   92–39111
                                                              CIP
                                                              MN

Contents

Steve Tracy is not only a talented blues musician with a national and international reputation as a player/singer and writer for blues magazines but also a sophisticated student of the blues as a developing musical form in changing urban contexts. In this book he deals with the definition of the urban blues (as opposed to the rural variety), the relationship of the blues to the first and second ghettoes between the 1920s and 1950s, and with the blues revival of the 1960s and 1970s. Tracy is interested in the blues as both a form of music and a lifestyle. Consequently, this volume contains descriptions and analyses of what and how blues players played and sang as well as biographical material about the musicians, much of it gleaned from interviews conducted by Tracy.

This book deals with many of the major blues figures in America. Some of them still live and play in Cincinnati. Some of them played but did not live in Cincinnati. Some of them cut recordings at King Records in Cincinnati, one of the major producers and distributors of what we used to call "race" music. Some of them neither lived nor played in Cincinnati but appear in the recollections of blues performers. We think this is a very interesting book, often poignant, often funny, and always well written, about one of the most distinctive aspects of American civilization.

Going to Cincinnati is the third volume in the Greater Cincinnati Bicentennial History Series, which focuses on a broad range of historical topics relating to the Cincinnati region. The series is a joint venture of the Cincinnati Historical Society and the Department of History and Center for Neighborhood and Community Studies at the University of Cincinnati.

Zane L. Miller
Gene D. Lewis

Acknowledgments

Over the years as I have worked on the articles, interviews, and research that culminated in this book, I have always been aware that this was a book that I especially wanted to write. However, the scholarly work has always been secondary: people, friendships, and the desire to help, to right a thousand wrongs, from deliberate neglect and exploitation to errors of omission, have been my foremost concerns. I hope it will always be so. It has been painfully clear to me in my life that as a white male, even when I was only a teenager wandering about haphazardly on the blues scene here in Cincinnati, I had more access to the upper echelons, the officials, of the system than African-Americans three times my age. That awareness led me to commit myself to assisting the African-American blues singers I knew to gain the access and recognition they deserved. The dividends have been many—and not just the performing experience and the admitted recognition I gained from my writing. What I found when I found the blues was not a genre, not a pile of brittle Paramount 78s, not a career—it was people: kind, loving, talented, and, yes, sometimes maddening and unreasonable but always *real,* people. We have celebrated and commiserated together, have sung and swung as well as suffered, sacrificed, and sweated through these years of low pay and high pathos—but always we have had each other, the sweetest reward of an enriching twenty years. To all of those people whom I interviewed for this book I extend my deepest thanks; to Albert Washington, Big Joe Duskin, Pigmeat Jarrett, James Mays, Lonnie Bennett, Russell Givens, Jr., and Big Ed Thompson I add to these thanks my gratitude and love for the times that helped make these eventful years so fruitful, and especially so happy.

Without the generous support of a Taft Postdoctoral Fellowship from the University of Cincinnati this book might never have been written. Without the encouragement and assistance of Zane Miller and Gene Lewis of the University of Cincinnati and the Greater Cincinnati Bicentennial History Series the book might never have been published. My thanks to these people for their generosity and support, and to Dick Wentworth, Karen Hewitt, Patricia Hollahan, and the support staff at the University of Illinois Press for their time and effort.

Special thanks also go to Dudley Radcliff, Gary Fortine, and Cliff Warnken for their support and assistance. Having three such knowledgeable and willing blues fans to talk with and consult has been a pleasure and a boon over the years. Dudley in particular has read the manuscript and made useful suggestions, and I thank him for his diligent and unselfish efforts, and for the camaraderie as well.

I owe a debt of gratitude to two other musicians and special friends with whom I've played over the years in many different settings. Hudson Rivers III and Phil Buscema are both consummate musicians and devoted friends who have given me more than I can ever express through their marvelous friendship. The gigs would have been much less exciting, less fun, without them. Perhaps I would not have come to this point at all without their enthusiasm and effort. They have been constants through the jobs with Pigmeat, James Mays, Big Joe, Albert, and now the Crawling Kingsnakes, important contributors to the blues scene in Cincinnati and to my life. And I hope to be with them for gigs and years to come. Brothers.

A number of blues collectors/aficionados have also provided information and support: special thanks to Ray Funk in Alaska, Roger Misiewicz and Per Mathews in Canada, Dave Moore in The Netherlands, Jonas Bernholm of Route 66 Records in Sweden, and Bob Eagle in Australia. Discographical details often derive from the work of R. M. W. Dixon and John Godrich (pre–World War II) and Mike Leadbitter and Neil Slaven (post–World War II). I also owe a great debt to Bruce Bastin and David Evans, both of whom read the manuscript of this book and made a number of useful corrections and suggestions. Their expertise in the field has been an inspiration to me, and their assistance with this text was invaluable. Another great inspiration for my work has been Paul Oliver, who, though I only met him recently at a conference in Belgium, has been a constant and most welcome guide and companion to me, as well as to two generations of blues fans. Intelligent, meticulous, graceful, passionate about the blues and the people who create them, his work has been, and will continue to be, I'm sure, exemplary. And I cannot let this occasion pass without recognizing again one of the great champions of the blues, Mike Leadbitter, whose encouragement meant so much to a sixteen-year-old kid who had the audacity to believe that he might have something to contribute to the literature on the blues. A less patient or thoughtful person might have demeaned my efforts, green as I was, but Mr. Leadbitter always treated me as if I had something to offer, and welcomed my correspondence so cordially and warmly that I always felt buoyed enough by his letters to redouble my efforts. Truly a great man.

Mr. Leadbitter, of course, was a long-time editor of the pioneering blues magazine *Blues Unlimited,* a publication to which so many of us owe a great deal. Not only did the magazine provide fascinating and groundbreaking research but it also provided valuable record reviews and news to read, as well as a place for both fledgling and veteran writers to publish their findings. Other magazines like *Blues World; Alley Music; Living Blues; Jefferson; Block; Whiskey, Women And; Blues and Rhythm;* and *Juke Blues* have provided blues fans and researchers with essential information unavailable elsewhere as well. I salute them all and acknowledge their contributions to my work. Blues lovers owe them a tremendous debt.

I was also particularly fortunate to have encountered a number of teachers during my career who encouraged me in my endeavors, modeling for me an intelligence, diligence, meticulousness, and passion that I hope I have been able to achieve and communicate. Because they recognized the value of ethnic literature and folklore, I never felt pressured to turn aside from my pursuits to some theoretically more "legitimate" subjects. To Amy Elder, Angelene Jamison-Hall, Wayne Miller, and Edgar Slotkin, my sincerest gratitude. And to Jon Hughes, who provided me with much useful material by Lafcadio Hearn, many thanks.

This is also a special occasion on which I can recognize a long overdue debt to two people whose love and support and understanding made me what I am and allowed me to do whatever I have done. Not all parents would allow their sixteen-year-old to go to a black ghetto bar at the height of the riots in Cincinnati around the time of Martin Luther King's death, nor allow him to walk the streets of black neighborhoods researching a subject it seemed hardly anyone else cared about. I'm sure they worried—agonized—over my choice of avocation, but they never discouraged, *always* encouraged, my interest because they knew it was part of me. It was a part of me they fostered, this love of Cincinnati, this love of people, this love of music, this love of justice and equality. My parents, Edward R. and Jean Tracy, are in every line of this book as they are in every breath of my life. Breathing in their atmosphere was inspiring; if this book breathes, its life, like mine, originated with them.

Finally I acknowledge the great sacrifice and support of my wife Cathy, who has endured my often obsessive pursuit of my interest in the blues. Certainly there have been many trying times, many sacrifices that she has made on account of my performing and researching. Her comments, criticisms, typing, proofreading, and technical support have all been essential to my success; but most of all, her love and the love of my children, Michelle and Michael, have gotten me through. You turn my blue days into gold.

Introduction

Imagine, for a moment, the following: a small brownskin man spreading tar on his feet and then sticking bottle caps on them, proceeding to tap dance to the music of guitar, mandolin, and harmonica, driven by the sound of a man half spitting, half blowing into an empty bootleg liquor jug; an old black man standing, still as a cigar-store Indian, in front of a pawn shop in the sweltering August heat wearing a full-length coat and horned Viking's helmet and leaning on a long shepherd's staff; men named Psycheye Willie and Jesse James pounding pianos into a rollicking submission, not facing each other down in a gunfight in the old West; two men standing on top of each other's Cadillacs, sledgehammering the cars gleefully; a recording engineer carefully kneeling and placing a studio microphone to pick up the tapping of a worn leather shoe on a two-by-four; a fire-eating female impersonator named Connie silencing hecklers with retorts like "I'm more man than you'll ever be and more woman than you'll ever get"; a man named H-Bomb in a multicolored fright wig dancing with a woman who hasn't yet realized that his pet boa constrictor Boo Boo is wrapped around his neck. And then realize that you don't have to imagine: you are following a succession of the sometimes bizarre moments of a long and notable history of the blues in Cincinnati.

Of course, the history of Cincinnati's blues is not distinguished because it had its odd or outlandish moments. Rather, it is a history of fine and interesting, and sometimes outstanding, performers, recordings, and occasionally record labels that has sadly not been reported in any detail—in fact, rarely mentioned at all—in most accounts of the city. And if many Cincinnatians are not aware of the significant recordings made by performers resident in their city through the years, if they undervalue the contributions of African-Americans living in Cincinnati, they might take some lessons from blues historians and aficionados and researchers from around the world who have tracked down details about the life of Stovepipe No. 1, transcribed the lyrics of Bob Coleman, reissued the recordings of Albert Washington, and sent for Big Joe Duskin to undertake a tour of West Germany. West Germany! When Walter Coleman sang about how you can "shake, rattle, and roll" your dice in a 1936 recording, little could he have guessed that nearly forty years later the German MCA Coral label would be reissuing two of his recordings, one the remarkable "I'm Going to Cincinnati," or that his recordings would give impetus to research that would focus attention on Cincinnati blues performers of his time and, as a bonus, bring the music of contemporary blues artists like Pigmeat Jarrett, James Mays, Big Joe Duskin, and many other performers to a new and broader audience, an audience Coleman never had the chance to know—indeed never would have dreamed of.

The number of people who remember and are willing to talk about Cincinnati blues performers of the twenties and thirties is small—most are dead, and those who are left either never knew much or don't remember much about their old cronies, or they don't care to talk about the subject with a white man—so information concerning those artists is a bit sketchy; but their recorded legacy is, as is the music of those performers who followed them from the forties to the present, an important part of the history of Cincinnati. An old blues song goes, "I been down so long, down don't worry me," but another chimes in just as surely, "I'll be up someday." Let's hope that for Cincinnati's largely unsung blues performers someday has come. It is way past time.

One of the reasons for the strong presence of blues music in Cincinnati was the settlement, from near the city's beginning, of African-Americans around the area now called Cincinnati. A major reason for this was the Continental Congress's passage of the Northwest Ordinance prohibiting slavery northwest of the Ohio River, which halted further importation of slaves into the region but did not free slaves already there. As a result of this antislavery proviso, Ohio began attracting Southern slaves anxious to escape from their masters and to "freedom," as well as freedmen seeking the opportunities they might have assumed to be available to them in this area. In addition, some Ohioans discovered ways to circumvent the ordinance to serve their own economic purposes: Thomas Worthington, for example, imported his ex-slaves as farm tenants; and long-term indentured servitude, combined with white racist attitudes toward African-

Americans, created in many cases a de facto condition of bondage, if not a de jure one.

Although it is reported that three African-Americans were punished for theft in Cincinnati in 1794, none were reported to be residents in the city in 1801. Legislation passed in 1803 and 1804 made it clear that slaves were to be closely watched as they passed from the neighboring slave state of Kentucky to Cincinnati, and Black Laws requiring that African-Americans provide certificates of freedom to verify their status and post five hundred dollar bonds in order to settle in Ohio were obviously intended to discourage migration.[1] However, sporadic enforcement of those laws resulted in the presence in Ohio by the late 1820s of several thousand African-Americans who had neither registered or posted bond.[2] Encountering such white hostility caused African-Americans to turn "to their own communities for support";[3] and as Cincinnati's African-American population grew, from 80 in 1810 to 690 in 1826, not only were African-American institutions such as the first church (which probably served as a station on the Underground Railroad), the Cincinnati Lancaster Seminary's segregated black school, prayer groups, benevolent societies, and Sunday schools established, sometimes with help from whites,[4] but an atmosphere of grudging—truly grudging—toleration had developed.

This toleration gave way, according to Carter G. Woodson, to a period of persecution from 1826 to 1841.[5] African-American manual laborers and domestics were crowded into frighteningly run-down structures in the areas known as "Little Africa" (later Bucktown), the Levee, and the Swamp. Wendell P. Dabney, a black man who served as city paymaster of Cincinnati and was owner and editor of the weekly newspaper *The Union*, wrote in his history *Cincinnati's Colored Citizens* that the "Negroes took refuge in the swamps and forest, now the region comprising the West End"[6]—an area that would figure prominently in the history of Cincinnati blues. Indeed these areas were the most run-down in the city, where famine and disease were rampant and vice flourished. In fact, the perception of a problem with the number of blacks in the city was so great that in 1828 the Cincinnati City Council sought to "prevent the increase of the negro population within our city,"[7] not only because many white citizens were outraged (though not wealthy whites who charged exorbitant prices to blacks for the shanties the whites owned) but also because of pressure from Southerners who wished Cincinnatians to discourage black labor from coming to the city. In addition, there were pleas from European immigrants and poor whites for preferential treatment in the competition for local employment. The atmosphere was clearly far from congenial, to say the least. Carol V. R. George reports that between 1100 and 2200 African-Americans, hounded out of their homes by revitalized black codes and menaced by mobs of whites, emigrated from the area in and around Cincinnati to western Canada around 1827;[8] and Henry Bibb described how he was captured by "a mob of ruffians who were willing to become the watchdogs of slaveholders for a dram in connection with a few slave-hunting petty constables" in the city in 1837.[9] One can imagine that there were a number of stories, too, like the one involving deception and kidnapping related by Cincinnatian Henrietta Woods to famed journalist Lafcadio Hearn and reported in the *Cincinnati Commercial* on April 2, 1876.[10] Riots in 1829, 1836, and 1841, reflecting white anger directed at African-Americans and their sympathizers, caused the situation to deteriorate even further.

But despite continuing violence and glaring inequities, African-Americans nonetheless made gains in establishing religious, educational, business, and social institutions, spearheaded by leaders like Peter Clark and W. H. Parham, while artists like daguerreotype photographer Robert S. Duncanson were making solid artistic contributions as well. Cincinnati, the pork-packing and manufacturing center situated on a booming river port, which benefited from increased canal traffic and the expanding railroad industry as well, provided employment opportunities for African-Americans not only in these industries but also in various trades. African-Americans were still crowded into several squalid areas of the city, most prominently Bucktown, in the vicinity of Sixth and Seventh streets east of Broadway, the demise of which Lafcadio Hearn described in the *Cincinnati Commercial* of August 22, 1875:

> Lying in the great noisome hollow, then untraversed by a single fill, the congregation of dingy and dilapidated frames, hideous huts, and shapeless dwellings, often rotten with the moisture of a thousand petty inundations, or filthy with the dirt accumulated by vice-begotten laziness, and inhabited only by the poorest poor or the vilest of the vicious, impressed one with the fancy that Bucktown was striving, through conscious shame, to bury itself under the earth. Today we find much of the horrible hollow filled up; and the ancient Bucktown is gradually but surely disappearing, not as though by reason of a *fiat* from the Board of Improvements, but as though the earth were devouring, swallowing, engulfing this little Gomorrah.[11]

Hearn's is a picture of shattered windows and shattered lives, of boarded-up entrances symbolic of boarded-up exits, where the "gurgling gutter-water seems blacker than ink with the filth it is vainly

trying to carry away; the air is foul with the breath of nameless nar-
row alleys; and the more distant lights seem to own a phosporescent
glow suggesting foul miasmal exhalation and ancient decay."[12] It is a
picture of foul dens of prostitution and dissipation, where houses formerly set above the streets and entered by ladders have descended underground, roofs level with the street, to be entered by crawling on
hands and knees into the horrifying dens of iniquity. And a place
where violence is a casual part of life: "People can still remember
how, in a certain low brothel there, masked by a bar, a negro levee
hand blew a brother roustabout's brains all over the bar; and how the
waiter girl related the occurrence with a smile to divers breathless po-
licemen and reporters, at the same time wiping the blood and white
brains off the counter with a cloth—like so much spilt beer."[13]

Life on the levee, the area between the Ohio River and Third Street
east of Sycamore, where transient roustabouts dominated, was little
better, with its "Desperate and drunk levee hands and dusky-skinned,
tigerish, half-famished courtesans, who mingle in groups at the en-
trance of a villainous looking grog holes that look out upon the
riverfront,"[14] its knifings and shootings, and its prostitution and
drug-related problems. But Hearn includes, too, some of Rat Row's
tender moments, even happy moments, to which an outsider such as
he was not always privy, in the touching and ultimately tragic tale of
Dolly, who doted upon an orphaned child,[15] and in "Black Varieties:
The Minstrels of the Row," where athletic dancers, minstrel performers, comedians, and musicians performed in front of a wildly entertained crowd at Pickett's.[16] These were areas that fascinated Hearn,
and indeed he reported that "It was not uncommon to find white men
of respectable appearance" in the foul underground dens,[17] but it
was a fascination that was Dantesque in description, a revulsed
fascination.

Several other areas, such as "Little Bucktown" around West Fifth
and Sixth and, for the wealthier, McAllister Street in Walnut Hills,
were also developing. Harriet Beecher Stowe reported using a number of incidents remembered from her eighteen years' residence in
Cincinnati in her landmark novel Uncle Tom's Cabin, but even with
the end of the Civil War a local newspaper of this progressive city in
a long time "free" state could lament: "Slavery is dead, the negro is
not, there is the misfortune. For the sake of all parties, would that he
were."[18] Luckily, the convention of African-American newspaper editors meeting in Cincinnati in 1875 did not agree. They "stressed racial self-confidence and self-reliance, the need for intelligence and
wealth, and called for united action to advance the welfare of the

race."[19] Unfortunately, the great majority of the nearly 8200 African-Americans in Cincinnati in 1880 were not in a position to gather the wealth or the education necessary to make the strides suggested by that group. The Black Laws were gone, public accommodations bills were enacted, and African-American children were now allowed to attend white schools, but the color line definitely remained.[20]

As Boss Cox's political machine brought Cincinnati into the twentieth century, the city's 14,482 African-Americans still found themselves living with poverty and injustice, now increasingly in the section of the city known as the West End. Late in the nineteenth century wealthier white families had moved out of the West End, bounded on the west by Central Avenue, to the suburbs, prompting an influx of Slavic immigrants and, around the time of World War I, African-Americans who settled in the area. In fact, in 1917 there was an influx of Southern Negroes, as a result of economic inequities, lynchings, and political disenfranchisement, that prompted great alarm in both the black and white communities of Cincinnati, in part because of health concerns expressed by J. H. Landis. However, newspaper articles with headlines like "1500 Negroes," "Influx of Negroes from South," "Appeal to State to Stop Negro," and "Groan Comes from South" suggest that there were deeper concerns as well, including a suggestion that German propaganda was responsible.[21] Many of these Southern blacks sought housing in the already over-crowded West End, compounding an already serious problem. By the 1920s and 1930s increasing numbers of whites left the West End, and "the entire West End became homogenous—rough, tough, and squalid."[22]

There were still, as always, those who were able to champion the cause of their people through educational, editorial, political, and artistic activities, people such as the educator Jennie D. Porter, Wendell P. Dabney, Garveyite William Ware, and the poet Raymond G. Dandridge; and organizations such as the National Progressive League, the Douglass League, and the Colored Citizens' Labor League continued efforts to improve the lives of African-Americans in the city. Indeed, the *Cincinnati Times Star* of May 4, 1928, reported in an article entitled "Studio for Negro Films Being Established Here" that the Eureka Film Corporation, housed in the Provident Bank Building and directed by a number of white men and W. P. Dabney and A. A. Schomburg, would have as its objective "to present the negro in a light that will help his own brother and will remove the white man's prejudice against him."[23] Their desire to avoid all "objectionable" and "controversial topics" in favor of sentimental plots and positive images aimed at improving, under their definition, the lives of African-Americans through the medium of motion pictures. The following year a group of concerned black citizens, including Reverend Wilbur A. Page and the "Black Chief" of the West End, policeman John Toney, petitioned Governor Cooper to have the state of Ohio purchase the home of Harriet Beecher Stowe and turn the house at 2950 Gilbert Avenue into a social center for blacks.[24] Clearly there was an active black middle class whose efforts on behalf of the betterment of their race were persistent and heroic. But the problem of the twentieth century, in Cincinnati as elsewhere, was, as W. E. B. Du Bois proclaimed, the problem of the color line, and out of such eighteenth- and nineteenth-century backgrounds and that twentieth-century milieu emerged the blues musicians who distinguished Cincinnati's street corners, speakeasies, bars, nightclubs, record players, radios, and televisions with their music—not of the middle but lower class.

Cincinnati's African-American music, of course, didn't spring suddenly fully formed from the head of some washboard player out front at Hog Head Joe's in the twenties. Ike Simond recalled clearly a thriving minstrel scene here: he remembered a concert company at New Street Church in 1864; the formation of a minstrel troupe, "Davis' Alabamas" in 1874; the first pairing of Jim Bland and Billy Kersands at Huick's Opera House in 1877; a gigantic minstrel festival with two hundred performers in 1883; and a show "given in honor of the Colored Knight Templars in 1886."[25] Several sources also trace the source of the "Jump Jim Crow" song and dance, from which the infamous phrase derives, to the performance of a crippled black Cincinnatian as well. The turn of the twentieth century saw Cole and Johnson (performing "Coon Songs by Real Coons") appearing at the Lyceum on Central Avenue between Fourth and Fifth;[26] one year later, in 1901, a production of *Uncle Tom's Cabin* with "A Carload of Beautiful Scenery" and "A Pack of Genuine Bloodhounds" played at the same theater.[27] Of course, minstrel shows and traveling vaudeville and stage shows did not provide the only African-American music in Cincinnati. Lafcadio Hearn wrote of life on the levee in 1876 for the *Cincinnati Commercial,* articles in which he describes the life and music of the blacks and mulattoes "from all parts of the States, but chiefly from Kentucky and Eastern Virginia"[28] who crowded into Bucktown and Rat Row and Sausage Row: the songs of the roustabouts, some of which were "not of a character to admit of publication in the columns of a daily newspaper" (150), others "low, and melancholy" with "a strange, sad sweetness" in their unison

performance (151); the singer and song "Limber Jim," a profane creation often accompanied by patting Juba (157); and the songs of separation, work, and sadness. Hearn calls attention to a number of bars
and brothels in the area, describing one in some detail:

> With its unplastered and windowless limestone walls; sanded floor; ru-
> ined ceiling; half plank, half cracked plaster; a dingy black counter in one
> corner, and rude benches ranged along the walls, this dancing room pre-
> sented rather an outlandish aspect when we visited it. At the corner of the
> room opposite "the bar," a long bench was placed, with its face to the
> wall; and upon the back of this bench, with their feet inwardly reclining
> upon the seat, sat the musicians. A well-dressed, neatly-built mulatto
> picked the banjo, and a somewhat lighter colored musican led the music
> with a fiddle, which he played remarkably well and with great spirit. A
> short, stout negress, illy dressed, with a rather good-natured face and a
> bad shawl tied about her head, played the bass viol, and that with no ex-
> perienced hand. This woman is known to the police as Anna Nun. (162)

All of the inhabitants, according to a local policeman, Patrolman
Tighe, carried knives, razors, and/or guns, and most were well
schooled in the art of thievery (163), and, according to Hearn, the
women were all "morphine eaters" (169). The white prostitutes, and
there were a number of them like those who were kept by Mary Pearl
on Sausage Row (167), generally did not last beyond two or three
years, though, because such a dissolute life was too much for them
(169). Hearn overstates his conclusions about life on the levee, particularly in his assertion that this is purely an "animal" existence, yet
there is something of the fascinated disgust, oversimplified, romanti-
cized, amplified, that overwhelms the sensibilities of the outsider
looking in on a world he doesn't quite understand:

> Their whole existence is one version of anticipated animal pleasure or of
> animal misery; of giant toil under the fervid summer sun; of toil under the
> icy glare of the winter moon; of fiery drinks and drunken dreams; of the
> madness of music and the intoxication of fantastic dances; of white and
> dark mistresses awaiting their coming at the levees, with waving of
> brightly colored garments; of the deep music of the great steam whistles;
> of the torch-basket fires redly dancing upon the purple water, the white
> stars sailing over-head, the passing lights of well known cabins along the
> dark river banks, and the mighty panting of the iron heart of the great
> vessel, bearing them day after day and night after night to fresh scenes of
> human frailty, and nearer to that Dim Levee slope, where weird boats ever
> discharge ghostly freight, and depart empty. (169–70)

Indeed, the river should be credited with bringing much fine
African-American music to Cincinnati, another of the precious car-
goes it carried and one that attracted a young African-American

named Tom Fletcher, who wrote in his book of reminiscences *100 Years of the Negro in Show Business:* "When I was older I used to go down on the levee in Cincinnati and watch them and listen to their songs,"[29] perhaps in much the way Stephen Foster did, eventually to incorporate their songs into his minstrel productions. Fletcher also reports that famed African-American Tin Pan Alley songwriter Gussie Lord Davis, born in Cincinnati on December 3, 1863, wrote the lyrics to his immensely popular "In the Baggage Coach Ahead" on Fletcher's mother's kitchen table in Cincinnati.[30] Given that Davis was educated in Cincinnati, instructed privately at the Nelson Musical College because he was barred by race from attending, and began writing his songs while still a resident of the city, it is likely that the music of the levee was known to him. Known as a songwriter who "did more than his share to open up the tear ducts of America,"[31] he credited his knowledge of songwriting to his association with James E. Stewart, who authored "Only to See Her Face Again," "Cricket on the Hearth," and "Jenny, the Flower of Kildare." Stewart died in the Cincinnati workhouse.[32] Happily Davis escaped that fate, remaining one of the country's most successful songwriters until his untimely death in 1899, some fourteen years before Artie Matthews published the first of his musically advanced and modernistic "Pastime Rags Nos. 1–5."

Praised by Jelly Roll Morton, Matthews nevertheless gave up ragtime around the year 1915, first becoming a church organist and then moving to Cincinnati in 1918, opening his Cosmopolitan Conservatory of Music in 1921, where he "taught classical theory. . . , made symphonic arrangements for the Cincinnati Symphony, and would hardly allow talk about ragtime in his presence, preferring to be associated only with the music of the classical masters such as Beethoven and Bach."[33] In fact, Matthews was in Cincinnati at the time Morton made his thirteen piano rolls for Vocalstyle Music Roll Co. at 412 East Sixth Street in 1924, but there is no evidence that the two met at that time. And although Matthews apparently disassociated himself from ragtime, he did participate in a number of Negro Folk Music Festivals as director, assistant to Clarence Cameron White, and chorus master when they were held in Cincinnati in the late thirties and forties, rehearsing at times at Harriet Beecher Stowe School and holding performances at the Eden Park Ampitheatre and the U.C. Outdoor Theatre, with Paul Robeson on occasion as featured soloist.[34]

But out on the streets, characters like "Whistling Charlie," who "whistled 'The Mocking Bird' between bites at a half fried pork chop" and "never missed a note," incessantly whistling as he pushed "that old hand cart down Vine Street"[35] provided daily music, while at parties given by whites who "wanted amusement rather than music," according to W. P. Dabney, "Pork Chops" and his band held forth.[36] The city was, all things considered, well situated to host a variety of African-American musical styles and genres including, of course, the blues.

Define the blues.

That directive has confounded the efforts of many blues scholars who have sought a restricted definition for a genre of such vast potential and variety. To generalize about the blues can be difficult because the individuals who create and perform blues music have often been (and are) varied in their approaches and philosophies about their lives and art, so that sociopolitical and aesthetic pigeonholing can be extremely difficult and unduly limiting. "See, blues is a living thing," stated blues singer Big Chief Ellis,[37] attempting to indicate its vastness and its sometimes organic nature. It is large, it contains multitudes; therefore, attempting to capture the complexities of nearly one hundred years of blues performed by millions of performers without acknowledging conflicts, contradictions, and paradoxes would be a significant error. And failing to identify the various approaches that the term "blues" encompasses would result in only a partial definition as well. "Blues Everywhere," recorded by the Yas Yas Girl in 1937, reflects the truth about the subject: blues can be, and sometimes are, everywhere, "from the roof to the ground,"[38] so any definition must be necessarily broad and open in order to avoid any reduction of the actual scope of the blues.

The term "blues" can be divided into four parts: the blues as an emotion, as a musical or lyric structure, as a technique, and as a "way of life."[39] The four do not always accompany each other, though it is true that the best blues performances often combine them to create the transcendent art of the blues. It is at that point that the art of the blues is fully and truly defined, that definition by example that eschews the distant, third-person, pseudo-objectivity of a descendant of Noah Webster for the personal subjectivity of a Ma Rainey.

The blues as an emotion, a feeling of sadness or isolation, derives its name from the proverbial phrase "to have a fit of the blue devils,"[40] which means to experience a mood of despondency. These are the blues that can be experienced by everyone. Son House sang:

> You know the blues ain't nothin but a low-down shakin achin chill,
> I say the blues is a low-down and a achin chill.
> Well if you ain't had 'em, honey, I hope you never will.[41]

And numerous blues singers attempt to define this emotion with words like "the blues ain't nothin but a botheration on your mind" or "The blues ain't nothin but a woman lovin a married man" as they wake in the morning with the blues all around their beds or wander a symbolic landscape where the blues falls down like showers of rain or walks just like a man or drives away religious spirit or just won't let you take your rest. This is the kind of blues that anyone can have for any reason that makes one feel sad, the type of blues that Albert King sings about in "Blues Power": "Everybody understands the blues; everybody from one day to another have the blues," King intones, citing for his predominantly white, middle-class, youthful crowd "The little baby that's layin in the cradle, he can't get that milk bottle fast enough" and the girl whose mother tells her, "daughter, you was just out last night, you can't go out tonight, that's too many nights in a row."[42] His words are obviously meant to attract a new audience, one by whom and for whom blues music was not created, as he attempts to cross over into a market of broader record sales. As King well knows, everybody has the generic emotion known as the blues, but not everyone does or can express them in the manner known as performing the blues.

The sung or instrumentally performed music known as the blues is an African-American creation. Inevitably, people transported from their homeland, in this case violently against their will, will carry elements of their heritage with them to their new "home," retaining or abandoning them in proportion to the way they immigrate, the access they have to the mainstream, and their ability and desire to mainstream themselves. Since African-Americans were captives, often isolated as a group and given few chances for social advancement, much less mainstreaming, we would expect some amount of carryover of Africanisms into African-American life. Dena J. Epstein identifies many survivals of African instrumental, vocal, and music techniques in the music of African-American slaves through 1867, and Alan Lomax has established a system of analysis called cantometrics that finds through its thirty-seven rating scales that "the song styles of black communities in . . . the United States . . . adhere closely to the core Black African model."[43] However, the sometimes vague or impressionistic nature of Lomax's categories and criteria has caused some concern, sometimes forcing the individual rater to the conclusion that in fact Africanisms are in the ear of the behearer, a thought which may contain a modicum of truth.

Certainly the extent to which Africanisms carry over into African-American music is arguable; given that written records by the earliest

African-American musicians discussing the subject do not exist to explain the influence, scholars are left to theorize, as they have about the influence on the blues. Paul Oliver's *Savannah Syncopators: African Retentions in the Blues* is still the most significant work on the subject, supplemented by responses to that work by Richard Alan Waterman and David Evans in the pages of *Living Blues* magazine and Janheinz Jahn's *Muntu* and *A History of Neo-African Literature.* Oliver's exploration of nonblues vocal traditions on race records, *Songsters and Saints,* also makes an important contribution to our understanding of blues, pointing out the influence of ragtime, dance songs, ballads, and other genres on the work of blues singers.

What is clear is that despite all of these influences, the blues was created on American soil and is distinctly different from those other genres from which it drew. Drawing from African roots, field hollers, work songs, and various sacred and secular, professional and nonprofessional material, it developed slowly into a distinctive and varied idiom. The blues encountered in the field by folklorists and interested parties such as Ma Rainey, W. C. Handy, Gates Thomas, Howard W. Odum, Will Thomas, W. Prescott Webb, and John A. Lomax in the years before the existence of blues on phonograph recordings took a variety of structural forms, but by the twenties, in the first decade of commercial blues recording, the musical and lyric structure tended to become more fixed and standardized into what eventually became the most common pattern: a musical stanza of roughly twelve bars in 4/4 time, with a harmonic sequence of tonic (I), subdominant (IV), and dominant (V) chords arranged in the following manner (one chord per bar):

I	I	I	I
IV	IV	I	I
V	IV	I	I

The IV in bar ten can be replaced by either V or I in this sequence. Thus, a twelve-bar blues performed in the key of C would progress basically as follows:

C	C	C	C
F	F	C	C
G	F	C	C

It should be emphasized that the designation of twelve bars is often a very loose one, depending upon the individual performer and that performer's technical or emotional sense of timing, so that stanzas of ten and a half or fourteen bars are certainly possible and more than acceptable, sometimes almost necessary, for a successful blues performance, to give it that vital, extemporaneous, involved edge.

The most common blues lyric pattern is designated AAB—one thought or "line" sung twice, the repeat line a rough or not necessarily exact repetition of the line as initially sung, followed by a third line that end rhymes and somehow completes or modifies the thought of the first two lines:

> Now it's run here, sweet mama, I'm goin to get you told, Lordy Lord,
> And it's run here, sweet mama, I'm certainly goin to get you told,
> You ain't the onliest woman in Cincinnati strut your lovin jelly roll.[44]

Although this AAB pattern became the most common twelve-bar pattern, other patterns such as AAA (three roughly identical lines), ABB (the second line, different from the first, is the line that is repeated), AB Refrain (two different lines followed by a refrain in each verse), and other combinations seem to have been common as well, appearing in material collected by folklorists and on phonograph records. Additionally, there were and are other musical structures, such as those tending toward eight-bar, sixteen-bar, and thirty-two-bar stanzas that require various lyric patterns as well, a number of which will be discussed as the lyrics of Cincinnati blues performers are explored. The point is that the blues is not a harshly restrictive and limiting musical form but one with the possibility of great flexibility and variety—a form of guided liberation.

One can speak of the blues as a technique, a way of playing, as well, since the combination of the distinctive twelve-bar structure and AAB lyric, for example, does not guarantee that the performance will sound like the blues when sung. There have been, of course, over the years and in various geographical locations, a variety of ways of singing and playing the blues, often drawing from an African way of performing and sharing at times certain core characteristics with other secular and sacred African-American music. Those ways of attacking a note, anticipating it, delaying it, stretching it, twisting it, and cutting it off, the intonation, and the spirit and feeling with which those things are done are all part of the technique of the blues performer, a technique, again, that is varied and changing. Jeff Titon suggests that the blues " is best understood as a feeling (the blues) and a musical form, whereas jazz is a technique, a *way* of forming,"[45] but the blues performer's technique is often very different, more basic and earthy and gritty, than the jazz singer's, and is often but not always less professionally schooled. Of course, it is not lack of skill or professional training that makes blues singers sing the way they do, but very often "lack of school" in the sense of professional training in music contributes to the bedrock power and directness of their music.

In fact, blues performers sometimes even play up their lack of professional training on an instrument by creating legendary scenarios in which they sell their souls to the devil in exchange for the ability to play or sing, or receive an instrument tuned by the devil, or simply describe their talent not as a result of long practice and hard work but as the result of a "gift." Such a romantic story is clearly aimed at mythologizing the performer, whether the gift is from the devil—an association often made with the blues because of its secular nature and often frank and unexpurgated manner—or God, but it at least partially undermines the idea of the blues performer as a craftsperson, albeit one who is not always so decorative or flashy as the jazz musician, or so interested in exploring a plethora of chordal or melodic changes. Technically advanced blues performers there have been, like Lonnie Johnson, Blind Blake, and Robert Lockwood, each of whom also played either ragtime or jazz at some time in their careers, but their best performances result from a very careful balance of their advanced technique and their emotional commitment, and their ability to reach into the core of passion that enlivens the blues. In other words, when they wanted to get down home, they knew the way to get there. Put another way, there may be those who can play the notes of blues music, but it takes something special to PLAY the blues.

And finally the blues can be seen as a way of life. When Leroi Jones wrote of "blues people" in his book of the same name, he was writing of those people whose existence had been circumscribed in some way—in many ways—by the conditions to which African-Americans have been subjected in this country, the common background and the necessity of dealing with a system of institutionalized racism in this country which ties together African-Americans, whether they wish to be tied together or not.[46] "They comes from back in slavery times," says James Butch Cage when asked about the blues;[47] Wild Child Butler describes the neighborhood: "I'm from the lowland, the swamp. I'm from where the blues came from, and that's where I'm going before it ends up and something happens to me. I'm going back to the lowlands—that's where the blues came right off, that old country farm."[48] And, as Butler makes clear, it is not a neighborhood of which he is ashamed, for one thing because it was thrust upon him, for another because of what he has made of it with his culture and his music. If being black, poor, beaten, lynched, and forced both literally and figuratively into the bottom is part of what was or is always on the horizon for African-Americans, the blues can often see the sun that will shine in the back door someday, and as Johnny Shines articulates, a great deal more:

> (Everybody think of) the bluesman as bein' stupid, illiterate, not able to think for himself, that's why he's singin' these dirty, lowdown songs. They don't realize that THEY'RE the one that's STUPID because they've been taught that these songs was dirty, they was filthy, they was no good. The younger white audience is catering to the blues because they understand the blues moreso. Because you reads a lot about the conditions in which the blues came about. And your parents probably didn't read about it and didn't care about it. They didn't want to hear anything about that nigger because he's just a dirty, lowdown, nasty, filthy, diseased NIGGER. And if you don't do somethin' for him, he's gonna starve. They didn't realize this nigger was takin' care of HIM. It's twisted all the way around . . . I AM the privileged character. I'm the one wearin' the crown, even though it don't show. I'M the king, see.[49]

In other words, it is a world where through sheer power of will, the bottom is not only the bottom but the top. Certainly one can find there the faults and follies of the world at large, but it is a very special haven as well. It is a place to return to, a place of roots and renewal, a place where the white world with all its bitterness and oppression is unwelcome, almost irrelevant, in the wake of what beauty can be found there.

So the blues is not all sadness. Although the blues arose out of socioeconomic conditions that rank among the most inhumane in the history of the world, and often describe the harshness of that life in a range of complexity, they can just as quickly be celebratory—of a mate, a feat, sexual prowess, perhaps even of the power of the blues themselves to, as Janheinz Jahn says, create a desired mood.[50] They can put the singer or the audience or both into a happier mood because the expression performs a catharsis of emotions or affirms the legitimacy, even primacy, of the blues as an artistic expression in the face of denial in the white world. Whether the singer is singing his own blues, a first-person autobiographical creation, or the blues of his audience, expressing a kind of common group experience, or the blues of some persona created by the performer to fit into the accepted notions of what the blues performer is "supposed" to be, the singer must be communicating someone's literal or psychological truth with an urgency born of having been there, not collecting the rent but scraping it together. The isolated, illiterate, rural man, battered guitar strings wound on pencil nubs rigged to the top of his guitar, huddled in the corner of a one-room country shack wailing a teary-eyed blues about the departure of his woman with his last thin dime and half-empty bottle of Jake liquor may exist, but he is not the sole representative of the blues and, as Johnny Shines posits, we may not see him for what he is. The blues is, indeed, about life, and life is more complicated than stereotypes. Life is social, political, spiritual, artistic—and so is the blues.

The history of the blues in Cincinnati is, musically, largely a history of individual performers or record labels rather than of a distinct regional blues style identified with the city, such as the styles identified generally with Mississippi, Texas, Chicago, and sections of the Southeast. The often intense, rhythmic music of many (but not all) Mississippi blues performers reflects, it is said, the harsh, crowded life of the Mississippi Delta plantation; in Texas, in an environment less crowded and thus, according to Sam Charters, less musically competitive, the music was less insistently rhythmic and more traditional because competition had not worked to displace earlier elements of slave songs and work songs.[51] There is by no means a consensus on this issue among blues scholars. The blues of the Southeast contrasts with the styles of these two regions as well:

> The melancholy of the Deep South is lacking in the more buoyant Southeast and this feeling expresses itself in its music. One would naturally expect the folk music of a region to reflect the moods of that region: if the powerful, jagged music of the Mississippi Delta and the heavy, sensual, pulsating sounds of the post-war Chicago blues bands reflect their respective environments, so, too, does the delicate, sensitive music of the Southeast reflect an environment; not necessarily one that is itself delicate and sensitive (as I think no one would lay claim), but an environment that lacks, by its very easy-going, day-to-day existence, the pace and tension of the claustrophobic, densely-packed cities.[52]

The blues of Chicago, fed by the migration of Mississippi blacks aboard the Illinois Central, adapted the blues of Mississippi to the brash, urban, industrialized environment. Of course, blues scholars recognize that these designations are certainly broad, too broad to be totally accurate. To define a blues style, we must consider not only the location and milieu but also the time, the dominance of a local figure or local figures who help establish a certain sound or sounds, the accessibility of the area to outside influences either via transportation or, after 1920, blues records over the phonograph, radio, and, later, television. All of these elements are likely to influence the style of a particular region, and because many different performers may be playing in that region, there is room for a great deal of variety, even dissent: "What should be apparent is that no large geographical area had absolutely and exclusively one style, though there might be some common characteristics; the styles were often dynamic and in transitional phrases, and were forged out of a complex interaction of elements."[53]

Traveling back to the beginning of the recorded history of the blues in Cincinnati, we can see various rural and urban factors at work in the music of the blues performers in the city.[54] And variety is, in fact, what we encounter in the blues music of Cincinnati in the twenties and thirties.

Because the river and railroad traffic brought African-Americans from a variety of areas, Cincinnati did not develop a single homogeneous blues style that was an urban updating and altering of a single rural blues style, the way Chicago blues developed from the Mississippi migration. Rather, Cincinnati's known blues performers seem to draw from a number of different sources, including minstrel and folk songs, vaudeville tunes, jug band music, hokum, and Southeastern, Alabama, and stomping Deep South piano traditions. The fact that there were so many blues musicians around; that they likely came from such a variety of geographical locations; that none of those who recorded achieved any commercial success; and that the city was not a center for the recording of blues singers (though Roosevelt Sykes and Walter Davis recorded in Cincinnati at the Sinton Hotel in 1930, Baby Bonnie may have recorded here in 1924, and a number of other recordings were done for Victor in Louisville and Gennett in Richmond, Indiana) likely prevented a single Cincinnati blues style from emerging. Additionally, since many of the Cincinnati blues musicians worked as street musicians who depended on their versatility in pleasing both black and white crowds in order to make a living, the formation of a highly individual and personal blues style was probably not foremost in their minds, and they were influenced to adopt a kind of generic songster approach to performing rather than fashioning an individual style like Blind Lemon Jefferson, Skip James, or Walter Davis did.

Tony Russell's comments on an LP featuring New York blues sounds of the fifties are pertinent to Cincinnati as well:

the album is best seen not as a collection of the rare and hot but as evidence in the case for, or against, New York as a significant center of postwar blues. It seems to me to confirm the standard view that Chicago and L.A. blues drew their strength from having specific regional roots and from the continuity of rural forms into urban, whereas New York drew its musicians from a population that was more widely spread, possessed a more varied musical culture and represented a different and probably larger selection of occupations and castes. . . . Consequently the New York "sound" of this era, so far as there is one, is based more in the sophistication of the musicians . . . than in a homogeneous root form.[55]

Save for the reference to the diversity of occupations and castes, Russell could be describing Cincinnati's blues milieu in the twenties. Nonetheless, although Cincinnati was not a major blues center in the twenties and thirties, there were a number of interesting and significant performers whose work deserves attention in histories of the blues and of Cincinnati. Blowing into a stovepipe isn't just a novelty: it is a way of life.

Going to Cincinnati

1

Backgrounds

I run into Stovepipe around in the sixties . . . . Yeah, I seen
Stovepipe on Sixth Street. With a guitar on his shoulder.
Yeah. Walkin' down Sixth Street.
  —James Mays, 23 Nov. 1988

It is significant that the last time James Mays saw Sam Jones—*nom
du disque* Stovepipe No. 1—Stovepipe was walking on Sixth Street in
Cincinnati's West End. Some forty years earlier Stovepipe sat down
in front of a recording studio microphone for the first time and recorded his very first tune, "Six Street Blues," at the Gennett facilities
in Richmond, Indiana. In the early seventies, septuagenarian Patfoot
Charlie Collins, a member of one incarnation of the Cincinnati Jug
Band, told me that although he lived in Walnut Hills, he made a daily
trek down to the West End to see what was left of his old friends and
haunts. Pianist Pigmeat Jarrett still lives by the West End, and on any
given day you stand a decent chance of finding him at some hour sitting in his car in a vacant lot on the corner of Wade and Central,
across the street from a makeshift shelter that serves as a gathering
place for a number of neighborhood old-timers, block watchers who
see the block slowly slipping away, who attempt to stave off the inevitable by seeing to it that their rickety structure maintains its (fragile) presence. They are filled with kidding, cajoling, and memories of
their friends and neighbors, an exclusive club for which no outsiders
learn the "secret handshake." Strong and enduring friendships have
outlasted the years and circumvented the geographical dispersal that
came with the expressways that replaced part of the West End neighborhood and were supposed to revitalize it, to help rebuild it—but
didn't.

The West End has, since the beginning of Cincinnati's history,
been a particularly important part of town for African-Americans.

Cincinnati Enquirer reporter William Collins discussed its signifi-cance and milieu in a series of articles in 1956:

> Historically, the Negro begins in the West End. He comes from the South to join relatives or to make out on his own, but he's heard that things are better for his race north of the Mason-Dixon line.
> He becomes a laborer or a domestic, doing the city's muscle work, shining its shoes, washing its dishes.
> In the deep West End, he will be reminded of home by the watermelon stands and barbecue joints, by the free, sensual speech and accents of the people, by their easy way with conventions.
> If he's so inclined, he can hock a piece of clothing on Central Avenue, take the money to any one of a dozen basement crap games, and, possibly, see it confiscated by police in a raid. . . .
> Some time or other he will be offered the chance to try a fix of heroin or play the numbers.[1]

It is the now-familiar story of the black migration to the promised land in the North, and the equally familiar story of the land that doesn't deliver on its promises. There have been other traditionally African-American areas in Cincinnati, but the West End is centrally important in this work because of its prominence for masses of poor blacks, from whom traditionally come the ranks of blues performers. Where they lived, what they experienced, provides a context for the songs they performed and sometimes recorded, a number of which made references to West End locations, landmarks, and people oth-erwise not commemorated in the "official" civic histories written by those born and raised outside the West End or Cincinnati's other ghettoes. When Walter Coleman tells his guitar-playing partner on his recording of "Mama Let Me Lay It on You" to "play it like you did back to George Street," he is evoking a scene which increasingly fewer people know or remember, though the impression to be gained from the music has both its good-timing and hard time connotations.

In the twenties and thirties, the West End had its share of problems with the health and welfare of its residents, problems which were common to the slum areas into which African-Americans were sep-arated and crowded in the major cities of an America that had just fought purportedly to make the world safe for democracy. The Shoe-maker Health and Welfare Center, which opened in early 1926 at 667 West Fourth Street in the West End and moved around 1930 to 1041 Cutter Street, attempted to identify and deal with those prob-lems in the community. The problems were discussed in the center's annual reports, beginning with the first in a 1927 report entitled *This West End Problem:*

The opening of the Shoemaker Health and Welfare Center early in 1926 marked the beginning of a program to meet one of our most serious social problems. What we speak of as the West End of Cincinnati, consists of the fifteenth, sixteenth, seventeenth, and eighteenth wards in which about 25,000 of our colored population live. This has for some time been one of the problem sections of the city. Here congestion, bad housing, poor sanitation, lack of recreation facilities, have produced an environment that falls far short of giving the Negro citizens, compelled by fate to live there, a fair opportunity to get forward in the struggle for normal life and decency.

There are some 11,500 Negroes living in Cincinnati outside of the West End district. Certain of these other Negro residential areas are on a very satisfactory plane, demonstrating that bad environment is certainly to be blamed for many short comings that some of us ascribe to the Negro himself. The problem in the West End has been aggravated by the large increase in the Negro population in recent years. Back in 1910 the total population of these wards was 59,000—less than 15 per cent of whom were colored. By 1920 migrations from the South had increased the Negro population of these wards by nearly 100 per cent. We now estimate that there are some 25,000 Negroes in this one district and that they constitute approximately 32 per cent of the West End population. Prostitution, gambling, bootlegging, and book making have thrived there in the past. White promoters preying upon the credulity and ignorance of the erstwhile workers in the cotton field of the South have not made the problem any easier. The homes in the West End were practically all formerly the private residences of white families in fair circumstances. Most of them have been converted into tenement houses with only makeshift alterations, producing the most baffling kind of housing problem.[2]

The report is accurate about this switch from a neighborhood of wealth to one of poverty. Alfred Segal, who wrote a column under the name Cincinnatus for the *Cincinnati Post* in the fifties and sixties, wrote nostalgically about the West End of his youth: "These old timers recall the quiet West End streets they knew when they were orderly kids playing hide-and-seek on the sidewalks there. They could run safely across the streets then . . . no vehicular traffic except for the occasional milkman's wagon, or a carriage of one of the West End's rich of that time. The carriage was drawn by a team of stately looking horses."[3] In 1965 Segal described the West End of 1902 as "a community of loveliness and neighborly kindness" where "Sixth Street's rich inhabitants accepted their poorer neighbors."[4] But by the twenties conditions had clearly deteriorated, and the center's report was fully justified in placing a large part of the blame on institutional racism and individual rapacity. In their 1928 annual report, the Shoemaker center praises the Building Department for its achievements in compelling William P. Devou, "probably the largest tenement house owner in Cincinnati," to keep his buildings in better repair. The city extracted a promise from Devou that he would "improve his buildings at the rate of fifteen every two months, until all of the 170 properties involved were repaired to comply with the requirements of the building codes," though the city declined to use legal means for enforcement.[5]

Additionally, in 1931 the Shoemaker center reported that in its ten-year history it had 94,684 visits to its venereal disease clinic, increasing from a low of 1055 visits in 1926–27 to a high of 10,516, ten times the number of visits in 1926–27, in 1935–36.[6] Despite the dimensions of the problem, the surgeon general of the United States Public Health Service reported that people in the United States were "doing little to check the spread of syphilis," and this may have been due in part to the fact that, according to the United States Public Health Service in 1936, syphilis was "six times as prevalent among negroes as among whites."[7]

Another part of the problem, of course, was that Cincinnati's restricted district had been located in the West End. Articles from the *Cincinnati Enquirer* in November of 1917 detail the efforts by the federal government to force Cincinnati to eliminate its restricted district because it was located within five miles of an army post in Fort Thomas, Kentucky, proving to be too accessible to military personnel. Chairman of the Committee on Training Camp Activities Raymond B. Fosdick called for the abolition of the district, naming specifically George Street, Longworth Street, Carlisle Avenue, West Sixth Street, Plum Street, John Street (a great name for a street in a restricted district), Mound Street, and Smith Street as target areas where he had found "40 'parlor houses' and 20 'assignation houses,' " though police estimated the number of houses at seventy.[8] One end result of the closing of the district was reflected in a 1918 *Cincinnati Enquirer* headline: "Soliciting on Streets Is Rampant."[9]

As with any restricted district, gambling and violence were prevalent as well. One example reported in the *Cincinnati Enquirer* as a " 'Hard Game' of Dice" illustrates:

> A dispute over 50 cents caused the murder of William Young, negro, 1 Barnes Alley, according to witnesses at the Coroner's inquest yesterday. They alleged Archie Wheeler, Columbia Road, Oakley, charged with the murder, was playing a "hard game" at a craps game in Barnes Alley.
> According to the negroes, a "hard game" is played when a man insists he be paid all the money he wins, and refuses by force of arms to pay any money he loses.

Young won 50 cents, they alleged, and when he demanded payment was stabbed to death. Patrolman Lawrence Klump captured Wheeler after running nine blocks at top speed. Wheeler declined to testify.[10]

Here in Barnes Alley, which was located between Mill and Cutter running from Mill to Sweeney, we see the interplay of poverty, vice, and casual violence that was clearly an integral part of the milieu of the West End. Others who lived in the West End in the twenties and thirties remember more than that: they remember also friends, good times, music, and humane people, a neighborhood full of people who wouldn't approach the violence and nastiness we see in contemporary society. The "truth," if we can approach it, lies somewhere in between, or rather in a mixture of memories. We can read in the newspapers and official reports about vice and violence; we can now turn to the blues performers like Walter Coleman, who, in "I'm Going to Cincinnati," sang that in Cincinnati "the times is good," for their stories and insights.

The truth is, sometimes the "official" record is entirely inadequate when it comes to mining information about Cincinnati's blues artists—African-Americans were simply not kept track of, partly because of their race, partly because of their economic status. As a result, a number of blues performers in this city remain obscure to us because official records, especially birth certificates but also death certificates and census data, were sometimes only casually kept for them. For example, no birth certificate or census record yields a clue to the birthplace or life of one of the most significant of all blues singers, Mamie Smith.

The first of the blues performers associated with Cincinnati to make recordings is often cited as the first black woman to record a vocal blues. Mamie Smith was reputedly born in Cincinnati on May 26, 1883.[11] However, this fact cannot be corroborated by any living residents of Cincinnati nor by city directories from the years 1883–93, around which time she left Cincinnati to tour as a dancer with the Four Dancing Mitchells. Birth records show only one "Female Colored" baby born in Cincinnati in 1883 with the name of Smith. This one was delivered by a midwife named F. Brunning on December 3, but not all babies were necessarily listed, so this may or may not be Mamie. There are a number of Mamie Smith listings for those years in the city directories, including West End listings on Longworth, Baymiller, and George streets, but someone Smith's age would not have been listed under her own name, so unless her mother was also named Mamie, there is no connection between those listings and the blues singer.

Regardless, Mamie, sometimes billed "Queen of the Blues," opened up the field for all other blues singers. Through the dogged efforts of bandleader, singer, and composer Perry Bradford, who tirelessly struggled to get the music of his people onto recordings and lobbied the various recording studios vigorously to give him and Mamie a chance, and the courage of Fred Hager of Okeh, who gave Bradford and Smith that chance when no one else would (not unlike the efforts of Branch Rickey on behalf of Jackie Robinson), Mamie secured a recording date on February 14, 1920. Hager had initially wanted cabaret artist Sophie Tucker to record Bradford's "That Thing Called Love" and "You Can't Keep a Good Man Down," but with Bradford's persuasion it was Mamie who made history that Saturday in the New York studios and upon release of Okeh 4113.[12]

With hindsight we can say that Mamie was more of a pop-blues singer: researcher Derrick Stewart-Baxter, author of *Ma Rainey and the Classic Blues Singers,* judged her "an artist of only moderate ability" whose "voice lacked the richness of the truly great women artists who were to follow her into the recording studios in the years to come."[13] Stewart-Baxter's judgment that she was seldom "really involved in what she was singing"[14] is a bit harsh, though. Clearly she was not, and did not intend to be, a low-down back porch Saturday night blues moaner, but she was a mature, blues-inflected singer of some power and depth, and though her singing would be out of place in juke joints, cotton fields, and chain gangs, certainly it was far closer to them than to Victorian parlors. A listen to "Goin' Crazy with the Blues" and "What Have You Done to Make Me Feel This Way," both from 1926, reveals a confident, full-voiced singer with an occasional trombonelike edge to her voice. She was, in fact, an ideal singer to throw the coming-out party for the blues.

The pop market, after all, requires of its music a certain smoothness around the edges, a certain staginess and decorum, a calculated dilution of traditional and nonmainstream elements before granting admission, and Mamie, with her good looks, experience, and honest talent, was capable of bringing to the eighty-five blues and pop tunes she recorded a certain flair that helped keep her popular and extravagantly wealthy until the Wall Street Crash of 1929. In fact, Okeh had even proclaimed a Mamie Smith Week in the spring of 1922 to recognize the sales and popularity of Mamie and her records. Her fame was enduring enough to keep her working sporadically in the thirties, including a European tour around 1936 and appearances in five films from 1939 to 1943. Besides Willie "The Lion" Smith she could count Johnny Dunn, Porter Grainger, Coleman Hawkins, Bubber Miley, Joe Smith, Clarence Williams, Sidney Bechet, and Lucky Millinder (later with Cincinnati's King Records) among her accompanists, and her record sales, from her first "real" blues record, "Crazy Blues" and "It's Right Here for You (If You Don't Get It . . . 'T'aint' No Fault of Mine)," which reputedly sold 75,000 copies in the first month, and beyond, made it clear that Mamie had her following of fans.

Unfortunately, after some unsuccessful films her health began to fail and, after two years' residence in Harlem Hospital, "her health failing her fortune gone,"[15] she died penniless. There is some poetic justice in the fact that Mamie was buried in Frederick Douglass Memorial Park Cemetery in Staten Island, New York: she was, it must be admitted, regardless of opinions of her talent, a pioneer like Douglass, a person whose success made success possible for many others who followed, and a person whose fusion of African-American background and popular techniques and sophistication helped drive the accomplishments of her people toward the mainstream.

So when the era of blues recording, an era fraught with possibilities for this "new" music to dazzle a popular audience, started, a part of Cincinnati was there in the studio; but unlike Mamie, the blues did not leave Cincinnati. There was too much to be blue about, and too many people to sing about it. Those who remained behind continued to sing, in their varied ways, blues that reflected different geographical backgrounds, even if Cincinnati was their current residence and the locale for the good and bad times they described in their songs.

2

Stovepipe

The man who appears on Gennett, Columbia, and Okeh record labels and in company files as Stovepipe No. 1, Stovepipe Jazz Band, Stovepipe Jones, Samuel Jones, Sam Jones, Stovepipe No. 1 and David Crockett, and King David's Jug Band, cannot be accurately described as a bluesman. Howard W. Odum, in his important 1911 article "Folk-Song and Folk-Poetry as Found in the Secular Songs of the Southern Negroes," discusses the existence of "musicianers" (experts with banjo or fiddle), "music physicianers" (traveling singers and banjo and fiddle specialists), and "songsters" (semiprofessional musicians whose wide repertoire of popular songs, folk songs, individual reworkings of popular and folk songs, and original material made them ideally suited to perform music for special occasions).[1] In some cases, these songsters were permanent fixtures in a single community, but in other cases you might find the songsters traveling across the countryside performing for whatever occasion might arise and, incidentally, participating in the spread of various songs across a wider geographical area by transmitting their songs to other performers through their own performances.

David Evans points out that the distinctions between the "songster" and the "bluesman" are not always clear:

> Almost all writers on blues have made a distinction between the "songster" and the "bluesman." The former is generally described as someone who performs a broad variety of song types, such as ragtime pieces, popular songs, blues, and church songs, while the latter is someone who performs blues almost exclusively. Although these terms admittedly can be useful for some purposes, in this study I will try to avoid them for several reasons. One of the main reasons is that "songster" is used by other writers in a different sense than black folksingers themselves use the word. Howard W. Odum reported the correct meaning in 1911 as "any negro who regularly sings or makes songs." This is how I have always heard the

term used by black audiences and folksingers. Thus, those who perform blues exclusively are called "songsters," as are all other people who have a reputation for being good singers, no matter what kinds of songs they sing. "Bluesman," on the other hand, often carries with it the implication of a greater commitment to the blues and a more intense performance style than others with wider repertoires have.[2]

Paul Oliver emphasized the social importance of the songster:

Songsters were the entertainers, providing music for every kind of social occasion in the decades before phonographs and radio. They were receptive to a wide variety of songs and music; priding themselves on their range, versatility, and capacity to pick up a tune, they played not only for the black communities, but for the whites too, when the opportunities arose. Whatever else the songster had to provide in the way of entertainment, he was always expected to sing and play for dances. This overriding function bound many forms of black secular song together. Social songs, comic songs, the blues and ballads, minstrel tunes and popular ditties all had this in common, and whether it set the time for spirited lindy-hopping or for low-down slow dragging across a pungeon floor, the music of black secular song could always be made to serve this purpose.[3]

Stovepipe No. 1 was a songster in the broad sense. He sang and recorded square dance sets, minstrel tunes, religious tunes, folk songs, vaudeville tunes, hokum songs, and blues, primarily on the streets but also occasionally in speakeasies, for both blacks and whites in various neighborhoods in and around Cincinnati, though the West End was both his playing base and his home. His real name was Sam Jones, as listed in the Columbia Records files and verified independently by Pigmeat Jarrett and James Mays, both of whom knew and performed with him. Stovepipe was a central figure on the black music scene in the West End in the twenties and thirties especially, though he reportedly remained in the city and continued to perform here into the sixties. James Mays recalled Stovepipe as the most popular performer in the West End in the twenties and thirties—a time when there certainly was an abundance of street music to be heard in the area, and when the competition would have been fierce. Vocalist/trumpeter/personal manager Roosevelt Lee remembered Stovepipe still playing and pleasing audiences in the forties.

Doubtless Stovepipe was remembered not only for his versatility in terms of material but for his novelty as well. As a multi-instumentalist one-man band, Stovepipe was certainly a sight to be reckoned with, a figure very early on in the long tradition of one-man bands in the blues, a tradition which includes Daddy Stovepipe, Jesse Fuller, Doctor Ross, Joe Hill Louis, Wilbert Harrison, Juke Boy

Bonner, Harmonica Frank Floyd, Buddy Folks, and Blind Joe Hill. He was instantly identifiable and recognizable, although unfortunately not many people got to know him close enough in the sense of learning about his background.

Concrete biographical information on Stovepipe is practically non-existent. Pigmeat Jarrett suggested that if Stovepipe were alive in 1989 he would be around ninety years old—roughly Pigmeat's age. But certainly Stovepipe was at least ten years older than that. He surely sounds older than the twenty-four or twenty-five years of age that he would have been, if Pigmeat's estimation were right, when he entered the studios in Richmond, Indiana, for the Gennett label in 1924. It may be that his choice of material—archaic to say the least—contributes to the sense that he is an older man, but his delivery and sound suggest more a man who saw the turn of the century while he was in his twenties. Both Jarrett and Mays recall Stovepipe's appearance similarly: he was about 6'1", they report, and though Mays had earlier suggested that Stovepipe weighed about 185 pounds, both he and Jarrett later remembered Stovepipe as being heavier, over 200 pounds, and being, in Mays's words, "real big in the waist."[4] When the two were shown a picture of a one-man band wearing a stovepipe hat who was later correctly identified as Daddy Stovepipe, Jarrett falsely identified the photo as being Stovepipe No. 1, but Mays stated that Stovepipe No. 1 was heavier than the man in the picture, though the man in the picture did favor Stovepipe No. 1 a bit. Perhaps seeing that stovepipe hat in the picture made the two different "Stovepipes" look more alike to Jarrett and Mays.

And, of course, one of the reasons Jones was called "Stovepipe" was that he wore a stovepipe hat, so called because it was elongated and the color of the often black metal stovepipes that were used to channel off smoke and fumes from a stove to some outside location. It was formal attire, albeit somewhat battered in Stovepipe's case, that lent an air of hilarity to Stovepipe's appearance and performances as he stepped among the prostitutes and ragpickers—and, it should be said, the more legitimately employed residents of the area—singing "Lord Don't You Know I Have No Friend like You," chapeaued with what Pigmeat laughingly referred to as a "funeral hat" and clad in a formal suit. There was, perhaps, something of what Sterling Brown lovingly immortalized in his lines from the poem of the same name as "puttin' on dog" in Stovepipe's attire, a sense of style, ostentation, showmanship, and individuality that made him attempt to stand out in this way. But whatever it was, it was a successful public relations ploy. Indeed, the hat served not only that purpose but a very practical, useful second purpose as well. "That's all he wore," Pigmeat chuckled about the stovepipe hat. "Boy he had that motherfucker full. Them old great big paper dollar bills."[5] And so, with his image maker and money carrier in position on his head—and need we mention that it also kept his head warm and his eyes shaded?—Stovepipe cut quite a figure as he played the streets, beer gardens, restaurants, and even funeral parlors of Cincinnati and environs.

Of course, as he walked he toted his guitar along with him, slung over his shoulder, and kept his neck rack holding his harmonica and kazoo resting on his chest but ever ready to swing up into action. But in addition to being called "Stovepipe" because of the hat he wore, Stovepipe also had the name because of another instrument he played: the stovepipe![6] Although James Mays never saw him play one, Pigmeat remembers vividly that he did, and a listen to Stovepipe's recordings confirms that the droning instrument being played in addition to guitar and harmonica is very likely not a kazoo, jug, or comb—though it can occasionally sound like them—but a metal pipe of some kind, in this case a stovepipe. The sound is often tinnier, more hollow than a jug, a nice, driving bass instrument that sometimes takes the swooping jug part on the recordings and at other times alternates carrying the melody with Stovepipe's harmonica playing. It is another perfect example of the "found art" of the folk musician, testifying to the ability to find and make music, fine music, out of everyday, supposedly nonmusical objects. The presence of the stovepipe as an instrument on Stovepipe's recordings make them even more unique, interesting, and lively, so one can only imagine the effect out on the streets. Stovepipe must have been even more of a sight when he took to strapping an amplification speaker around his head with a belt in order to make himself better heard!

And heard he should be. Pigmeat Jarrett had a particularly high opinion of Stovepipe's harmonica playing and singing: "Stovepipe would play anything. Yeah. And sing his ass off! Stovepipe could play harp now. He could blow harp. Don't let nobody fool you. Shit, boy, Stovepipe was somethin else, boy. Yeah. That old man could play."[7] While Jarrett remembered him as having a varied repertoire, James Mays remembers him as a friendly rival whose repertoire was more limited: "We run upon one another lots of times. They would come to parties where we would be playing and they would play a piece to show us up. He'd play things like 'M and O Blues.' I believe he played that 'Mama Blues' too . . . . 'Tuxedo Junction.' Mostly blues."[8] If, as other West End residents recall, Stovepipe did play mostly for whites on Central Avenue, he probably did not play mostly blues, but more minstrel and pop tunes.[9] Mays probably has a better recollection of Stovepipe's performances at parties for blacks, which might account for the differing ideas about Stovepipe's repertoire. Additionally, it should be pointed out that Mays is assigning songs to Stovepipe's repertoire that Mays himself plays. Mays is, then, perhaps recalling only those songs he still plays himself, that have stuck with Mays the performer. Certainly Stovepipe's recorded repertoire is not so heavily blues oriented.

Interestingly, although Stovepipe recorded in 1924 as a one-man band, he seems rarely to have performed as a one-man band on the street. Pigmeat remembers him playing at various times on Court and Cutter and Sixth and Mound (site of the Cotton Club in Cincinnati), at the back of a funeral home on Sixth Street, and at Mom's Restaurant at Ninth and Linn. At the last location, Pigmeat joined him on piano as they played inside, but usually on the street Stovepipe had at least one other guitar player, particularly Charlie Red, accompanying him. Along with Charlie Red, harmonica player Little Joe, a jug player, and a comb player were also present, and James Mays reminisces that a man named Bob would be with the group to go around and collect money in a hat while the group performed. Strangely, Mays is the only person with any memory of David Crockett, who was a guitar player who played several times with Stovepipe during his near ten-year residence. Crockett was, says Mays, around 5'11", 150 pounds, a likeable guy and a good guitar player who left the area inexplicably after his decade-long stay. Indeed, Crockett played at times with Stovepipe, but must not have been a regular member of his band, since he is recalled by no one else. The personnel in the various groups that hustled money on the streets in the West End—and there was music on every corner, according to local residents—was very changeable, so that Stovepipe might be playing inside with Pigmeat one day, at the funeral home with Charlie Red or Little Joe the next, and with a five-piece group on Sixth and Mound the next day with Crockett aboard but without, perhaps, either Charlie Red or Little Joe. What you could count on was that when Stovepipe was there the music was lively and fine and the coins and bills were overflowing the hat—even the stovepipe hat.

Still, though Stovepipe must have made a fair amount of money, and was not, to James Mays's recollection, ever married, he continued to reside in the West End. There he lived among the people he knew and the people who knew and loved his music, people who provided him with a ready and steady source of income. His residence has been placed by James Mays as being on George Street, a street that figures prominently in Cincinnati blues history, and it seems appropriate that Stovepipe would have lived on this major blues thoroughfare, even if only for a short time—apparently he changed residences frequently. The city directories for 1917–19 list a laborer, Samuel Jones, residing at 545 or 546 George Street during those three years, and this may indeed be our man. However, because Sam Jones is such a common name, it is impossible to determine which of the several Sam Joneses listed as living in the West End during the years before Stovepipe's death was the performer under discussion. Many of those residences are gone, and urban renewal helped to scatter what West Enders remain from that era. This is true for Stovepipe's address in the thirties, forties, and fifties as well, when he lived, according to Pigmeat Jarrett, in residences on Carlisle and Gest streets. There are in fact several Sam Joneses listed in the city directories on Carlisle Street between 1927 and 1933; from 1941 through 1944 a Samuel J. Jones, with a wife Pasty (misspelled, I think) in 1941 and Mary in 1942, lived at either 417 or 427 Carlisle. The occupation of the Sam J. Jones at 417 Carlisle in 1943 is listed as "musician," but Sam Jones at that address disappears from 1945 to 1950, only to turn up again at that address in 1951. The last possibility of a listing for Stovepipe comes from 1956—Sam Jones, musician, with his wife Ada, is listed as living at 1105 Dayton Street, apartment 6. If any of these women was the wife of the Sam Jones listed and James Mays is correct about Stovepipe's marital status, then this is not our Sam Jones. However, given that different "spouse" names appear for the same Sam Jones at the 417 Carlisle address, it also seems possible that what was listed as a spouse in the directories was a living companion and not a wife in the legal sense. If Pigmeat is right about the Carlisle Street address for Stovepipe, then this could conceivably be the man. However, Pigmeat also insisted on a Gest Street address for Stovepipe, too, and no Sam Jones is listed in the city directories on Gest. However, given the plastic nature of living arrangements in this economically depressed area and the difficulties of attaining 100 percent accuracy in such directory endeavors, it is entirely possible that Stovepipe may have lived on Gest Street undetected by official reports. Official reports don't always report what they should about the black and poor. And so it is to the recordings of Stovepipe that we must turn to get a concrete sense of the man as reflected in his musical style, ability, and influences, and we should be thankful that he got into the studio as often as he did, to record as much as he did, and that his music has survived, even if only on the fragile, very breakable 78 rpm discs in whose grooves, thankfully, reside the spirit of Stovepipe.

Stovepipe first went into the studio for the Gennett label in Richmond, Indiana, on Friday, May 16, 1924.[10] It was a solo session for Stovepipe, who accompanied his singing with harmonica, guitar, and stovepipe playing an interesting variety of tunes:

11869-A	Six Street Blues	Ge Special
11870-A	Them Pitiful Blues	Ge Special
11871	Dixie Barn Dance	Ge Special
11872	Spanish Rag	Ge Special
11873	Hummin' Blues	Ge Special
11874	In Dey Go	Ge Special

Three of the six tunes from this first session, it is interesting to note, are blues, including Stovepipe's inaugural recording, which should likely read "Sixth Street Blues," referring to a Cincinnati thoroughfare that ran parallel to and one block from George Street in the West End and a place where prostitutes, according to James Mays, were very much in evidence. "Dixie Barn Dance" is most likely a series of barn dance set calls, the first of a small number of such pieces recorded by Stovepipe that he probably played to entertain whites or accompany their dances. "Spanish Rag" may refer to the tuning of the guitar on this piece rather than any Spanish melody or flavor to this tune. Spanish tuning, the most widespread nonstandard folk guitar tuning, consisted of open strings tuned to the G major triad (D-G-D-G-B-D). The tuning was "similar to banjo G tuning and may have gotten its name from a piece often called 'Spanish Fandango' which employed it."[11] Songs with the title "Hummin' Blues" or "Humming Blues" were recorded subsequent to Stovepipe's version by Laura Smith in 1925, Elzadie Robinson in 1926, Joe Linthecombe in 1929, and John Brim in 1952.[12] The employment of a mournful, wordless hum can very effectively convey a great feeling of sadness, as indeed it does in Brim's "Humming Blues," and the technique is certainly a common one in black folk music, not merely limited to songs with that title, so in fact Stovepipe's song may have little save the humming that is probably present in common with these other tunes.

Unfortunately, no copies of these sides have turned up so any speculation about their contents must remain just that unless copies are located. It is also interesting to note that the first five titles from this session were listed in the Gennett files as being by the Stovepipe Jazz Band, while the final title, "In Dey Go," which sounds like a minstrel tune from its title, was listed as being by Stovepipe Jones. Although Stovepipe was the only person listed as performing on the sessions, perhaps the distinction in file credits indicates the presence of other band members on the first five cuts; or perhaps Gennett was simply trying to cash in on the jazz craze by referring to Stovepipe as a jazz band. Whatever the case, this first session remains a mystery to us except in that it provides us with our first tantalizing glimpse of Stovepipe's varied repertoire.

A scant three months later, on Monday, August 18, 1924, Stovepipe had again found his way to New York City. This time he recorded four titles for Columbia Records, which had begun manufacturing discs in 1902 and, with Okeh and Paramount, dominated the blues and gospel record market between 1923 and 1926, primarily due to the success of female "vaudeville" blues singers Bessie Smith and Clara Smith.[13] Unfortunately, once again Stovepipe's recordings are unavailable to us, this time because they were not issued and, according to Tina McCarthy of the CBS archives, no metal parts for the recordings exist.[14] Neither do any advertisements, contracts, or any other pertinent information that might shed some light on Stovepipe's sessions for Columbia or Okeh, save for session details listed in the Columbia files.

Of the unissued recordings from August 18, 1924, two songs are likely rerecordings of songs performed at his Gennett session, and two are new. Oddly, Stovepipe accompanies his vocals on this session with only guitar, harmonica, and kazoo, apparently using no stovepipe according to the files—not even on his "Stovepipe Blues." He is named in the files as Samuel Jones, and his four unissued titles are this time predominantly blues songs, two indicating clear Cincinnati ties:

81920-2	Stovepipe Blues	Columbia unissued
81921-2	Spanish Rag	Columbia unissued
81922-2	Sixth Street Blues	Columbia unissued
81923-2	Loveland Blues	Columbia unissued

Here the incorrectly titled "Six Street Blues" of the Gennett session is corrected to "Sixth Street Blues," and another local reference to a nearby city turns up in the title of his "Loveland Blues."

David Pritchard, director of Loveland's Historical Museum, states that Loveland had quite a large black community of about five hundred or so in the early twenties. The community was located on the western side of the city, although occasional floods caused the people in the community to shift from place to place at various times.[15] Wilamae Minegan, who lived in Loveland at that time, has no recollection of Stovepipe or, indeed, any street musicians being present during the twenties. She recalled that most of the younger people were playing pianos at the time, and the Fry brothers, who were guitarists, always played in their home and not on the streets.[16] However, Chris Perkins, another resident of Loveland in the twenties, did remember Stovepipe Jones. Stovepipe, he stated, looked something like B. B. King before King gained weight. It was on Loveland's west side street corners that Stovepipe played, usually alone but sometimes with a jug band, and it was there that he got the title for his "Loveland Blues."[17] The song does not necessarily make any references to Loveland people or landmarks. However, this is not the only instance where a blues song that names a location in its title makes no reference to the location in the song: Stovepipe's recording of "Court Street Blues" from 1927 makes no mention of the street in the body of the song. The titles might stem from the popularity of the song at a certain location (a song popular in Loveland is the "Loveland Blues"); they also might stem from an attempt to get people in a certain location to respond more warmly to the performer by naming the song after that location. Whatever the reason, the city whose postmark is popular with sweethearts on Valentine's Day had certainly been visited by Stovepipe, but his song, because it is unavailable, cannot give us any clues to his involvement there.

The following day, Tuesday, August 19, 1924, Stovepipe returned to the same studio to record nine titles, two-thirds of which were religious tunes. Columbia only issued two of the titles, which were also issued on the Harmony label, so Stovepipe No. 1, as he was called on the label,[18] left seven titles in the can, so to speak, that have never been—and won't be—heard:

81925-2	Lord Don't You Know I Have No Friend like You	Co 210-D, Ha 5102-H
81926-2	When The Saints Go Marching Through	Co unissued
81927-2	I've Got Salvation in My Heart	Co 210-D, Ha 5102-H
81928-2	Soon One Morning Death Came Creeping in the Room	Co unissued
81929-2	I'm Going to Wait on the Lord	Co unissued
81930-2	Bye and Bye When the Morning Came	Co unissued
81933-3	Pitiful Blues	Co unissued
81934-2	Sundown Blues	Co unissued
81935-3	Dan Tucker	Co unissued

The two issued titles from this session feature only Stovepipe's vocals, guitar, and harmonica, as is apparently the case with his other religious titles. Possibly the kazoo and stovepipe were deemed inappropriate, since Stovepipe did apparently add kazoo to the final three songs from the session; perhaps it was felt that they were a bit too rough and raucous to carry a spiritual message—though recording artists like Elder Richard Bryant and Brother Williams would later record sacred tunes with a jug player among the instrumentalists. On the first of the two issued sides from the session, Stovepipe lays down a basic strumming backing, sometimes barely making chord changes, as a backdrop for his simple and effective harmonica melody line. The lyrics to the song seem to draw from the common motif in religious songs dealing with being bound for some land, be it named as Canaan or simply referred to as the promised land, which may be seen not only as a Christian land of deliverance from enemies but as the land of deliverance from slavery as well. Henry M. Belden and Arthur Palmer Hudson reprint a text in *North Carolina Folklore*, volume 3: *Folk Songs from North Carolina* that was said to be "a favorite of the blackface minstrels" entitled "I Am Bound for the Promised Land" with a text by Samuel Stennett (1727–95), the chorus of which goes:

> I am bound for the promised land
> I am bound for the promised land
> Oh, who will come and go with me?
> I am bound for the promised land.[19]

A version of this song was recorded in 1926 for the Library of Congress by a singer named John Williams. The melody of this tune, as sung by Alfred G. Karnes in 1928, is substantially different from Jones's song, as are the melodies to Blind Willie Johnson's "Go with Me to That Land" (1930); Bo Weavil Jackson's "I'm on My Way to the Kingdom Land" (1926); and the New Gospel Keys' "I'm on My Way to the Kingdom Land"; and songs like "Old Ship of Zion" and "Roll Jordan Roll"; but the sentiment of reaching a promised land of rest is common to them and a host of other tunes that were spiritually, psychologically, and socially significant to African-Americans.[20] Stovepipe's text is fragmentary, almost patchwork-like, and he shifts with a very offhand nonchalance from vocals to harmonica playing in midstream on the second verse:

> Well come on think of me, heaven when I'm dyin
> I'm on the way back to the promised land.
> Oh lord don't you know I have no friend like you?
> If heaven's not my home Lord what shall I do?
> Harmonica break.

> You've got a quivering mind, your father's tears and cryin
> I am the way back to the promised land.
>
> Harmonica break.
>
> Oh Lord don't you know I have no friend like you?
> Heaven's not my home. Lord what shall I do?
> Someone's takin me heaven when I die
> I'm on the way back to the promised land.

In verse two here Stovepipe changes the line "I'm on my way," which he repeats in the final stanza, to "I am the way back to the promised land," a notable alteration of the lyrics. It could be, of course, that Stovepipe stumbles over his lyrics at this point—he certainly seems to do that in several other tunes he recorded. It is also possible that he has taken on the persona of Christ at this point, not in any serious way, but singing as Christ would that the example of Christ that the singer is following is the way, something like, perhaps, the titles to Reverend Gary Davis's "I Am the Light of the World" or "I Am the True Vine."[21] Whatever the reason is finally for the change, Stovepipe clearly does sing "I am the way" in verse two, but not out of any sense that he *is* Christ and thus "the way to heaven."

"I've Got Salvation in My Heart" is performed in the same key and in a similar manner:

> Aw in my heart in my heart
> I have got a little wheel turning in my heart
> Aw in my heart in my heart
> I have got a little wheel turning in my heart.
>
> Aw in my heart in my heart
> I have got salvation in my heart.
> I have got salvation in my heart.
> Well in my heart aw in my heart
> I have got salvation in my heart.

The "little wheel" in the song apparently refers to the salvation which keeps his heart pumping and his blood flowing—which keeps him alive, possibly a reference to the wheels described in Ezekiel 1:15–16 and 10:10–11. Unfortunately, neither this nor the other songs are particularly lively, and Stovepipe deserves for these songs Tony Russell's judgment that he "played in a somewhat pedestrian fashion,"[22] though their looseness and simplicity make them, perhaps, pleasing.

The following three items, plus "When the Saints Go Marching Through," are all unissued sacred songs from the session. "Saints" is by now internationally famous, and in Stovepipe's time the song was recorded by such artists as Sam Butler (1926) and Blind Willie Davis

(1928). "Soon One Morning" was used by Willie McTell in 1933 as part of his "Death Room Blues," and Rev. Edward W. Clayborn recorded "Bye and Bye When the Morning Comes" (1927).[23] It seems that Stovepipe was drawing on a pool of sacred songs for the session, probably prompted by the company for some old sacred tunes in addition to the old secular ones they wanted for that market. Unfortunately, they were not issued, as most of this day's work was not, but the titles certainly suggest a familiarity with traditional sacred material to go along with his knowledge of secular folk songs.

Stovepipe's "Pitiful Blues" is perhaps a reworking of his early recording for Gennett, while "Sundown Blues" may have some relation to Daddy Stovepipe's earlier recording of a tune by the same title.[24] It should surely be pointed out that Daddy Stovepipe, whose real name was Johnny Watson, recorded for the same company for which Stovepipe No. 1 first recorded, Gennett, and just six days earlier (on May 10, 1924) in Richmond, Indiana. Two of the songs he recorded at that session, "Sun Down Blues" and "Stove Pipe Blues," share titles, though perhaps not lyrics, with two recorded by Stovepipe No. 1 at sessions just three months later. This is, perhaps, coincidence: there have been other songs with the title "Sun Down Blues," and someone called Stovepipe might be expected to have a "Stove Pipe Blues" available for performance. The two men are clearly not the same person. Daddy Stovepipe is a livelier performer and a sweeter and smoother harmonica player. Still, one might wonder whether some type of exchange took place between the two men, or whether Gennett encouraged the exchange.

The final tune from this date is a blackface minstrel piece, though the music apparently predates the days of blackface minstrelsy. The words to "Dan Tucker," often called "Old Dan Tucker," have been attributed to Henry Russell, J. R. Jenkins, and most often to Southern Ohioan Dan Emmett, one of the Virginia Minstrels whose 1843 performances in New York City helped to popularize blackface minstrelsy.[25] John A. and Alan Lomax printed a description of the nature of performances of the song:

> Ole Dan Tucker was adjustable—you began singing it where you chose and could play both against the middle, or sing it backward, or forward, or improvise topical stanzas according to your mind and skill. It was a fine dancing tune, and the black fiddlers often sang it as they fiddled, the prompter meanwhile racking his wits to find new figures yet to keep the proper rhythms. . . . Let me say further the singing was commonly in negro dialect, but not invariably so. That rested with singers who, singing for their own joy, neither knew nor cared if they sang in key.[26]

Stovepipe, of course, sang in key on his records, but the description of this song as a dance piece, sometimes a square dance piece, emphasizes Stovepipe's role as an entertainer who would pay more attention to the demands of the dancer than any demand for a consistent coherent song. That is, as long as the music continued and favorite verses cropped up occasionally, even more than once, as long as the "proper rhythms" continued, the audience was satisfied. The looseness on a number of Stovepipe's recordings likely stems from this type of performance aesthetic, with the aim to keep 'em dancing and keep 'em smiling:

> Old Daniel Tucker wuz a mighty man,
> He washed his face in a fryin' pan;
> Combed his hair wid a wagon wheel
> And died wid de toofache in his heel.[27]

Wednesday, August 20, 1924, seemed to shape up as traditional secular folk song day for Stovepipe, in contrast to the predominance of religious songs recorded the previous day and the concentration on blues tunes the day before that.

81936-3	John Henry	Co unissued
81937-3	Lonesome John	Co 15011-D, Ha 5137-H
81938-1,-3	Cripple Creek and Sourwood Mountain	Co 201-D, Ha 5100-H
81939-1	Turkey in the Straw	Co 201-D, Ha 5100-H
81940-3	Arkansas Traveler	Co unissued
81941-1	Fisher's Hornpipe	Co unissued
81941-2	Fisher's Hornpipe	Co 15011-D, Ha 5137-H

Stovepipe opened this day's recording session with a version, sadly unissued, of the famous blues ballad "John Henry." The ballad had first surfaced in E. C. Perrow's 1905 collection of songs gathered from east Tennessee mountain whites, though it wasn't until Perrow's collection of songs from Kentucky mountain whites in 1913 that John Henry was linked with the steam drill with which he did battle at Big Bend. Of course, the ballad was widespread, and the story of the black hero who waged war against advancing industrialization and died with his hammer in his hand (similar to dying with one's boots on) was not only widely performed but widely recorded as well, including versions of the song recorded before Stovepipe's, by the New Orleans Blue Nine in 1921, and after, like the justly famous two-part version by Furry Lewis recorded in 1929.[28] "John Henry" was, indeed, like most of the tunes recorded by Stovepipe on this day, part of "the traditional music of the countryman . . . shared by black and white; a common stock."[29] That is, black and white musicians would have repertoires of music which overlapped, sharing common tunes that both blacks and whites played for both black and white audiences, and which might often be described by the musician "according to the kind of dance it accompanies,"[30] emphasizing the social and recreational nature of the song.

Stovepipe's second recording at the session, "Lonesome John," is seemingly related to other songs variously titled "Lost John," "Long John," and "Long Gone Lost John," which deal with the slave or convict one step ahead of the pack of bloodhounds sent to capture him; though the version collected by Odum and Johnson makes no reference to such a chase,[31] the version Alan Lomax collected from "Lightning" at Darrington Farm was sung by a prisoner who could and did duplicate the feats of escape described in his version of "Long John Green."[32] Stovepipe's version, which includes no more than forty seconds worth of singing, is extremely sketchy lyrically, but it is spiritually evocative. Following a harmonica introduction and a chorus on the stovepipe, he enters singing not of "Lonesome John" but of "Lost John":

> Lost John you move
> Lost John in town
> Lost John got out of town this day.
>
> Lost John in the woods
> Lost John in town
> Lost John got out of town this day.

It is notable that on this secular recording Stovepipe is a great deal livelier, with spirited harmonica playing and pumping stovepipe playing driving along over a basic, hard-strummed guitar accompaniment. Perhaps, at this point, he was most comfortable with older traditional secular tunes which he may have heard and been playing longer. At any rate, despite the dearth of lyrics, it is an attractively played song.

"Cripple Creek," a common banjo and fiddle tune in the South and West and popular as a square dance song in the Middle West, is also given lively treatment by Stovepipe, particularly when he weds it to another southern Appalachian fiddle piece, "Sourwood Mountain," during which he calls sets for square dancers and provides directions for the dancers to follow as he plays:

> Me and my wife and bobtail hound
> Goin' away to Bagentown
> Me and my wife and a bobtail hound
> Take a little ride and we go to town.
>
> Man in his britches pants rolled to his knees
> Wade over Cripple Creek much as I please.
>
> I found Sal in Sourwood Mountain
> Swing your partners all the way around
> Eight hands up circle to the right
> Promenade all the way around.
>
> Stick your hands up circle to the right
> Promenade all the way 'round
> Swing your girl let mine alone.

"Eight hands up" is an admonition by the singer for each two couple group to put their hands in the air, as reported in Jensen's *Square Dancing:* "Eight hands up and 'round and 'round and 'round you go."[33] However, at various times when Stovepipe repeats this line, including in his next recorded song, "Turkey in the Straw," he sounds as if he might be saying "pick y'hands up" or "stick y'hands up." At other times he is clearly using the number eight.

Stovepipe's version of "Turkey in the Straw," a song which derived from the old blackface minstrel favorite, "Old Zip Coon," contains none of the sung verses from the song, concentrating instead on the melody, which was popular with fiddlers, calling sets and playing harmonica and stovepipe interludes:

> Eight hands up circle to the right
> Promenade all the way around
> Swing the gal you love the best
> Please let mine alone.
>
> All to your places pick up your paces
> Then trade partners swing tomcat.

The line "Please let mine alone" is a jocular reference to the practice in some square dances, as reported for "Old Dan Tucker" by Margot Mays in *American Square Dance,* to have someone "steal" someone else's partner, thereby leaving a different dancer stranded.[34] Of course, the implications of the stealing in the song extend beyond the end of the dance and proceedings.

The next recording, "The Arkansas Traveler," was based presumably on the old Southwest fiddle tune that dealt with the meeting of a traveler with the proprieter of a rural tavern, or some other figure, and included a comic dialogue like this section from Thomas

Wilson's *The Arkansas Traveller* quoted in the Lomaxes' *American Ballads and Folk Songs:*

Traveller: Why don't you put a new roof on your house?
Squatter: Because it's rainin' and I can't.
                (Plays)
Traveller: Why don't you do it when it is not raining?
Squatter: It don't leak then (Plays).[35]

Columbia files indicate that Stovepipe did not sing but spoke on this title, so he may have in fact reproduced some jokes like this in his version of the old tune. He also took a spoken part on the first take of "Fisher's Hornpipe," which was not issued, but by the second take he had cut the song back to an instrumental version. An old Irish dance tune probably composed by one J. Fishar and published in 1780,[36] it was used by William Hauser in his "Methodist and Formalist" to defend "the institution, the stamping, the jumping, and dancing of those in religious ecstasy," for which purpose George Pullen Jackson deemed the tune entirely appropriate.[37]

The name hornpipe referred originally to a musical instrument, mentioned in works by Chaucer, Spenser, and Ben Jonson, which most often took the form of "double pipes played with an inflated bag of goatskin, cow's stomach, etc."[38] Later the term was applied to a jiglike dance with a meter of 3/2, 2/4, or 4/4 that is distinct from the jig, and not necessarily related to the instrument or hornpipe at all. Eventually, the term came to refer to the music that accompanied the dance, such as the one Stovepipe performed at this particular session. Regardless, Stovepipe's version of the hornpipe is played in a spirited if at times somewhat stumbling fashion, and it ends this Columbia session in a novel and somewhat surprising way. The Stovepipe who emerges from these sessions is a performer of a breadth of tunes, basic in his approach, competent on guitar, a strong but not outstanding harmonica player, but most animated when he's blowing his stovepipe. The tunes are most often loosely arranged, the lyrics brief interruptions of the music or invitations to the dance. The portrait we have thus far, then, is of a fascinating folk musician and repository of traditional tunes of various origins.

It would be three years before Stovepipe got into the studio to record once again—this time at the studios of the Okeh Record Company, and by that time, at least for purposes of recording, the hornpipes were gone and the saints had done marched through. With David Crockett aboard on guitar and occasional vocals, Stovepipe was singing more, and the overall sound, buoyed by Crockett's guitar, was tighter and more forceful.

This next session took place on Monday, April 25, 1927, at which time "Stovepipe No. 1 and David Crockett," as the record label reads, recorded the following songs:

| 80749-A | Court Street Blues | OK 8514 |
| 80750-B | Sundown Blues | OK unissued |

The only issued title from this day, "Court Street Blues," refers to another street in Cincinnati's West End, a street where, Pigmeat Jarrett recalled, Stovepipe played, especially on the corner of Court and Cutter. On this recording Stovepipe plays the stovepipe and sings, but there is only one guitarist, and it is decidedly not Stovepipe who is playing the guitar. It is, presumably, David Crockett, who plays in a hard, finger-picking style that sounds for all the world like an Alabaman such as Barefoot Bill/Ed Bell, suggesting that Crockett had, possibly, Alabama roots. The guitarist was clearly not Lonnie Johnson, who was also in St. Louis recording for Okeh that day just before Stovepipe and Crockett. The performance, regardless, is a strong one, flawless save for the misfortune of a breaking string just before the last instrumental break, though Stovepipe and Crockett both plow on through to the end undeterred.

The lyrics of the song draw on a number of standard traditional blues lines and verses, patched together in a loose manner and held together by the general sense that the singer's blues derive from his inability to understand and deal with his woman, and that he desires to escape the blues:

> Goin away ain't comin back til fall,
> Goin away ain't comin back no more,
> The blues overtake me ain't comin back no more.
>
> Gonna get me a picket off a graveyard fence,
> I'm gonna get me a picket off a graveyard fence,
> Gonna beat you brownskin til you learn good sense.
>
> Hey, what's the matter now?
> Oh, hey, what's the matter now?
> Say you tryin to play quit me honey and you don't know how.
>
> I'm leavin here ain't comin back til fall.
> I'm leavin here ain't comin back til fall.
> If the blues overtake me I ain't comin back at all.
>
> Tell me brownskin what is on your mind?
> Won't you tell me brownskin what is on your mind?
> Reason I ask you brownie you bout to run me blind.

The seeming haphazard progression of the lyrics may in fact reflect the speaker's indecision. He seems to have decided to leave in verse one; by verse two he suggests that he'll try to resolve the situation through violence; however, the third verse finds him attempting to understand what is wrong with his woman; apparently this does not solve his problem and he decides in verse four to leave again; but he ends up questioning his woman again in the final stanza, apparently willing to try again to reconcile through communication. What the lyrics reflect, then, is a troubled lover who is confused about how to handle his difficulties. His vacillation as reflected in the lyrics could be psychologically accurate given his state of mind. As such, these stanzas could be rearranged in a number of different ways and still reflect the speaker's difficulties, and indeed it is likely that Stovepipe, like many folk musicians, did alter and rearrange his songs as it suited him in performance. This version of "Court Street Blues" should be judged a success. Just how successful "Sundown Blues" and the untitled item recorded first the following day—both of which were electrically recorded—were will never be known.

On the next day, Tuesday, April 26, 1927, Stovepipe and Crockett cut four more sides, the first untitled and unissued but the remaining three all issued and among Stovepipe's most interesting recordings:

80754-B	Untitled Item	OK unissued
80758-A	A Woman Gets Tired of the Same Man All the Time	OK 8514
80759-B	A Chicken Can Waltz the Gravy Around	OK 8543
80760-B	Bed Slats	OK 8543

Paul Oliver points out that "A Woman Gets Tired of the Same Man All the Time" had been recorded twice before Stovepipe's version, once in 1923 by vaudeville singer George Williams and once in 1924 by Edna Johnson accompanied by the song's composer Charles Booker,[39] finding that Stovepipe's version compares aurally most closely with the Williams recording, down to the repetition of "I mean" in the song.[40] It is clearly a vaudeville comic blues, and an indicator that Stovepipe the songster was being influenced by the medium of phonograph records to perform popular songs that had been disseminated on shellac. There is only one guitarist on this and the other two recordings from this date, and the guitar is strummed in a fashion closer to the style Stovepipe used at earlier sessions, though the bass work is busier than Stovepipe's. After some stilted stovepipe playing, Stovepipe sings:

I mean I mean my wife I mean here of late,
Ah Ah we don't get along so well.
I mean the older she get I mean the more I do mean
I mean to seem to change her ways.
I mean ah she used to be I mean so kind to me.
I didn't think a wife could be so kind.
If I set down now I see my wife don't pay me no mind.
Ain't it funny how womens can change?
That wife of mine is bout to run me in a strain.
A woman get's tired, I mean real tired, of the same man all the time.
Oh the way my wife been affectin of late
She's bound to make me lose my mind.
When I'm out on my wagon try to sell a little coal
Ah well she's around the corner "who want sweet jelly roll?"
Ah god a woman gets tired, I mean real tired, of the same man
    all the time.

Stovepipe proceeds to sing this verse once again up until the line "Ain't it funny how womens . . . ," then cuts off a bit abruptly. At this point in the song it sounds as if Stovepipe has been notified that his time is running out, since he stops singing in mid-line and switches to a brief stovepipe interlude before ending the song. One of the interesting things about Stovepipe's performance on this song is that he varies the tone of his stovepipe playing in his solo, sounding at first more like a kazoo and then switching to a swooping, juglike sound toward the end of his solo, demonstrating that indeed there is a bit of range to be gotten out of his humble instrument, or perhaps that indeed the stovepipe was used as a resonator for the kazoo.

Stovepipe, however, could not have achieved the range ascribed to him in discographies that is evident on the next song, "A Chicken Can Waltz the Gravy Around." Stovepipe is clearly singing on this song, but the harmonica is playing simultaneously as well, and both the stovepipe and the harmonica play together on the break. Either Crockett is playing the harmonica along with the guitar on this song or there is another musician present. Crockett does not play harmonica on any of his 1930 sides, but he may in fact have been able to pick out the part that is played on this tune. Once again the guitar accompaniment is similar to Stovepipe's earlier playing—perhaps he did play guitar on some of these sides—and the darkey minstrel tune, also found in John Hurt's "Chicken" and Frank Stokes's "Chicken Your Can Roost behind the Moon,"[41] for example, with its popular (with whites) obsession with the chickens theme, is something one might expect to find in Stovepipe's broad repertoire:

My wife she goin to cook breakfast, I walk right to the gate
She set me down to table to chicken on my plate.
I grabbed my knapsack on my shoulder said "Honey you be too late."
In 15 minutes by any man's watch there's chicken on my plate.
Oh chicken oh chicken you can fry 'em nice and brown.
Oh chicken oh chicken you can waltz the gravy around.
Oh chicken oh chicken I don't mean no fault in that.
Fine chickens grow in this town and they wings can't get too fat . . .
Oh when I come to the neighborhood chickens know just what I mean.
Chickens skippin and dodgin No chicken can be seen.
The hen she said to the rooster, "Lord there ain't no use to hide.
Got a sharpshoot gun and it hurts to run
And our wings can't roost too high."

Of course the stereotype of the chicken thief, like the stereotypes of the watermelon stealer, the razor toter, the lazy good-for-nothing, and the sex-crazy buck and wanton temptress, can be a joke to blacks as well as whites—for blacks can laugh about how silly whites are to accept the stereotype, *and* they can laugh about making money by deceiving whites who don't realize that the performers are playing a role.

The recording of "Bed Slats" from this session predates the recording of this same tune by Cincinnati's Bob Coleman in 1929 and King David's Jug Band, which features Stovepipe and David Crockett, in 1930, as well as versions by Clyde McCoy in 1933 and the Memphis Jug Band in 1937, all of which were titled either "Tear It Down" or "Tear It Down, Bed Slats and All."[42] Stovepipe and Crockett's version here is a vocal duet, with David Crockett singing the main lead and Stovepipe singing the responsorial part. Several things tell us this: first, Crockett's voice is a bit lighter than Stovepipe's; second, in verse three of the song the lead vocal and stovepipe are heard simultaneously; third, James Mays identified the lead vocal as being, he thinks, by Crockett. The song also makes the return of the finger-picking style heard on "Court Street Blues" that is unlike Stovepipe's playing style, suggesting that Crockett's style is predominating again on this tune—vocally the song is very loose and freewheeling, giving it the rollicking quality associated with many jug band recordings and appropriate to the wild sentiments and double entendres of the song:

> And I went upstairs about four o'clock,
> I rapped on my door but my door was locked.
> Peeped through the crack and my gal was gone,
> I caught another mule kickin in my stall.

I catch another mule kickin in my stall
Babe, I'm gonna tear it down.

Refrain:
I'm gonna tear it down Bed slats and all (4X)
Catch another mule kickin in my stall
Babe I'm gonna tear it down.

I had a gal and she name was Lise
Everytime you slapped her she would holler police.
She cooked them biscuits she cooked 'em brown,
I think she's a workin when she turned around.

Refrain.

Told my gal the week before last
I had the gait she's a carryin me was most too fast.
I went to the river take my rockin chair
The blues overtake me rock away from here
Catch another mule kickin in my stall
Mama gonna tear it down.

Scat Chorus . . .

The song belongs in the genre that came to be known later as "Hokum," which was popularized by the series of recordings by Tampa Red and Georgia Tom Dorsey in 1928, beginning with the immortal "It's Tight like That,"[43] and although Stovepipe and Crockett do not develop the song lyrically beyond two verses and a refrain, a legacy, possibly, of their nonprofessional street singing aesthetic, the performance is highly successful and infectious, a fitting end to Stovepipe's recording career under his own name. However, this wasn't the last time his stovepipe was heard groaning through a welter of double entendres and finger picking on record.

On Thursday, December 11, 1930, Stovepipe reentered the studio, again for the Okeh label and again in the company of David Crockett, but now the group was dubbed King David's Jug Band, though the songs they recorded were far from psalms:

W404664	What's That Tastes like Gravy	OK8913
W404665	Rising Sun Blues	OK8913
W404666	Sweet Potato Blues	OK8901
W404667	Tear It Down	OK8961
W404668	I Can Deal Worry	OK8901
W404669	Georgia Bo Bo	OK8961

This Atlanta session yielded six electrically recorded songs that featured a larger and more urbane group than on Stovepipe's earlier recordings. In fact, these sides were listed in Brian Rust's *Jazz Records 1897–1942* discography along with the work of a number of other jug bands. Musicians performing here, besides Stovepipe on stovepipe and Crockett on guitar, include a mandolin player and two vocalists. The mandolin player may be a man known as "Dude," who played mandolin with pianist Psycheye Willie and with Bob Coleman's group as well as with Stovepipe. Pigmeat Jarrett praised him: "He was the best mandoline player ever been here! Yes, indeedy, Yeah. There was a lot of mandoline players around, but they couldn't play, not like him. Hm mm! No. *You ain't never* seen a mandoline man take a, put on his leg, this is the neck of it, and play it and make that thing say (sings here). It sang the words, too. Shit. Aw boy he was somethin' else! Blues, blues, strictly blues, 'cause I was playin' the piano."[44] Pigmeat also identifed the mandolin player in the string band picture from the Cincinnati Historical collection (photo taken in Louisville) as this same "Dude."

What is troublesome about the discographical details on this session is that Stovepipe is listed as the main vocalist, and the *only* vocalist, on four cuts, but the vocals do not sound like Stovepipe's. They do sound something like the vocals on the earlier "Tear It Down" recording, which were shared by Crockett and Stovepipe. The vocals on these sides, then, may not be by Stovepipe, but by Crockett or someone else, save the "Georgia Bo Bo" side, which does sound like Stovepipe.

The first song from this session picked up where Stovepipe left off three years earlier, with a hokum style piece that really waltzed the gravy around. The band's version of "What's That Tastes like Gravy?" comes from the same pot as Tampa Red's 1929 "What Is It That Tastes like Gravy?" and Johnny Temple's 1938 "What Is That Smells like Gravy?"[45] but the King David version of this musical question so appealing to the senses of smell and taste is decidedly more rural, with minstrellike lyrics leading to the single line refrain which is much more prominent in other versions of the song:

What's that taste like gravy? Mama says I know you want to know.
S' that taste like gravy when you're sore?
Said kill that chicken and cook him down low,
Said shoot that chicken a sweet jelly roll.
Aw what's that tastes like gravy? Mama said I know you want to know.
I was down in Alabam way down in Dixieland.
Said they caught a possum and they name him Joe and they put him in his barn.
Said they shoot that possum and they cooked him down low,

When the grease come runnin from his Joe Joe Joe.
That tastes like gravy? Mama said I know you want to know.

Well I was born in Alabam way down in Dixieland.
Oh the peoples come for miles around just to hear that (unintelligible)
Well sound so loose, sound so blue,
Sound just like he couldn't blow.
That taste like gravy, Mama says I know you want to know.

Oh skeedle dee dee de leedle beedle de bum,
I said mama said I know you want to know.
Oh skeedle deedle deedle deedle beedle de bum,
I said you don't know my road.
Late night last year when time was tough
I was layin in the coalyard struttin my stuff.
That taste like gravy? Mama said I know you want to know.

It is extremely difficult to understand some of the lyrics in this song. Again, the stovepipe is much in evidence, as it is on all the sides of this date, and never overlaps with the vocal, entering only to blow spirited and swooping instrumental breaks. The scat singing of the final stanza probably stems from the 1928 recording of "Beedle Um Bum" by Tampa Red and Georgia Tom under the *nom du disque* the Hokum Boys.[46] The phrase itself is a "suggestive nonsense phrase, used by low-class Negro women and prostitutes, indicating the female sexual organs,"[47] reinforcing without doubt, if there ever was any, just what the "gravy" is.

"Rising Sun Blues" is another collection of traditional blues verses, sung over brisk boom-chang guitar and intricate mandolin, with booming stovepipe on the breaks. Ivy Smith recorded a song with this title in 1927, accompanied by Cow Cow Davenport and B. T. Wingfield, some three months before she recorded "Cincinnati Southern Blues."[48] However, there is not necessarily a connection between the two recordings, and the "Cincinnati Southern Blues," with its lyrics "She leaves Cincinnati at five o'clock (twice) / You ought to see the fireman gettin his boilers hot," does not necessarily connect Smith with the Cincinnati blues scene, although as a performer on the TOBA circuit she may well have appeared here. Certainly the opening phrase of King David's "Rising Sun Blues" is among the most common in blues:

Wake up this mornin, woke up by the risin sun,
Woke up this mornin, woke up by the risin sun,
I thought about my good gal who done gone along.

I ain't never loved, I hope I never will,(twice)
That lovin proposition sure get a good man killed.

I've twelve little puppies, ten big shaggy hounds,
I have twelve little puppies, ten big shaggy hounds,
Take the whole twenty-two to run my brownskin down.
I ain't never loved, I hope I never will,(twice)
My lovin proposition sure get a good man killed.

Three-quarters of the lyrics from this song are repeated in the next recording that King David did at this session, "Sweet Potato Blues," which is especially notable for its fine singing and ringing, melodic mandolin playing. In addition to the "shaggy hounds" verse, which was recorded earlier by Ishmon Bracey in 1928 in his "Saturday Blues,"[49] and the "lovin proposition" verse, the singer adds two other traditional verses and the marvelous opening verse, with its wonderfully apt imagery:[50]

Ain't no more taters, frost done killed the vine, (twice)
Ain't no more good times with this girl of mine . . .

My brownie caught a passenger, left me a mule to ride, (twice)
When the train pulled out, well, the mule laid down and died.

Ah one thing, baby, I sure can't understand,
There's one thing, baby, I sure can't understand,
She bakes biscuits for her kid man, corn bread for her man.

The predominance of sexual double entendre on this session continues with their version of "Tear It Down," which is a little tighter and slicker (continuing in the hokum vein!) than the 1927 version. The new version contains one similar verse and the same refrain as the 1927 song, as well as some scat singing like that on "Bed Slats":

I had a girl her name was Eve
Every time you hit her she would holler "police."
Cooked them biscuits, cooked em brown,
Started workin when she turned around.
When you catch another mule kickin in your stall,
Gonna tear it down.

Refrain:

Keep tearin it down—bed slats and all, (four times)
When you catch another mule kickin in your stall,
Gonna tear it down.

Miss Ethel, Miss Ethel, you know ain't it a shame?
Just see that monkey whiffin that cocaine.
Went upstairs to ring the bell,
Police in the alley whiffin cocaine.
Well you catch another mule kickin in your stall,
Gonna tear it down.

Refrain

I had a gal and her name was Eve,
Everytime I hit her she would holler police.
Cooked them biscuits cooked 'em brown,
Started workin when she turned around.
When you catch another mule kickin in your stall
Gonna tear it down.

Refrain

Oh ma doodle um a doodle um a doodle um a doodle um
Ma doodle um a doodle um a doodle um a doodle um
Ma doodle um a doodle um a doodle um a doodle um
Ma doodle um a doodle um . . .
When you catch another mule kickin in your stall
Gonna tear it down.

Honestly, the singer on this version sounds different from the singer on the Stovepipe and Crockett version, though when that version is sped up to the key of the later one the vocals sound closer. The 1930 version changes the name of the girl to "Eve" from "Lise" and adds an interesting verse dealing with police involvement with cocaine, a variation of which was included in Luke Jordan's "Cocaine Blues."[51] It is worth noting that for all the humor in a number of these songs, the implicit pervasive presence of drugs, illicit sex, and violence should not be ignored. The casual mention of hitting the woman, Eve or Lise, who would then call the police, portrays a level of violence that would, of course, no longer be tolerated by society, though it was more tolerated at that time, particularly by whites among lower-class blacks who were racistly stereotyped as evidencing such behavior.

Of course, on the reverse side, "I Can Deal Worry" presents a speaker in its second verse who tries to be attentive to the needs of his woman, only to be rebuked for the act of kindness in stanza four:

I'm worried now, Lord, won't be worried long, worried long.
Well, I'm worried now, Lord, won't be worried long.
It take a worried man, Lord, sing a worried song.

Take me, mama, ride me one more time,
Take me, mama, try me one more time,
I don't do better kill myself for tryin.

Just as sure as the birds flies in the sky above (twice)
Well you know, pretty mama, you ain't with the man you love.

Well I looked cooked her breakfast, brought it to her bed, (twice)
Well she taken one bite threw the teacup at my head.

The final tune from the session seems to capture the combination of gaiety and sadness best described by the line "laughin' to keep from cryin' ": "Georgia Bo-Bo" refers to a type of dance, and certainly the rhythm of the music is conducive to that.[52] It is also a veiled reference to sexual activity as well.

> Woman wanna (swing it to its knees?),
> I'm just as blue as any man can be.
> Mama done told me to my face,
> Got another man like to take my place.
>
> Way down yonder where they do the Ko Ko,
> The dance the folks all know,
> Boy the little girls from my home town
> Got to do the shimmy for the muscat wine.
> Go out to the alley sing the blues for me,
> I'm just as blue as any man can be,
> My whole crowd is mighty rough,
> Early in the mornin tryin to strut my stuff.
>
> Laughter in rhythm.

The song is, as Tony Russell pointed out in his review of "Give Me Another Jug," a variant of the "Tip Out Tonight" theme sung by Pink Anderson and Simmie Dooley, and a spirited version at that.[53]

It is, perhaps, fitting, this mask of laughter that closes off Stovepipe's recording career. He was a man of many masks in the studio— the blues singer, the sacred singer, the minstrel singer, the folk singer, the square dance caller, the vaudeville singer, the hokum singer: the songster. And finally we are still not able to tell much of the particular details of Stovepipe's life save for whatever was collected for business purposes by record companies or is recalled by friends who, even at that, remember only bits and pieces, wisps of yesterday's newspaper clinging to burned-out lampposts on West End street corners. Pigmeat Jarrett told me that someone from College Hill recorded something from Stovepipe, but he doesn't remember when, and if it was recorded, it is not likely to turn up. "Yeah, Lord, I miss him," Pigmeat said at the end of an interview.[54] The last time he'd seen Stovepipe was on Rockdale Road in Avondale in the sixties, probably much like James Mays had remembered:[55] his guitar on his shoulder, walking down the streets he'd walked for nearly half a century if not more, with a "Sixth Street Blues," a "Court Street Blues," a "Loveland Blues" for whoever might listen. Yeah, Lord, I miss him.

3

Coles and Colemans

Stovepipe was not, of course, Cincinnati's only blues recording artist. In fact, in the year he first recorded, 1924, another artist may have recorded in Cincinnati. Gennett Records, for whom Stovepipe recorded in Richmond, Indiana, reportedly recorded a small number of masters in Cincinnati, and among these may be the recordings done by "Baby Bonnie," Ernestine Bomburyero.[1] However, this singer is not reported in the yearly city directories, nor is she recalled by any local residents, and her recordings make no specific references to Cincinnati people or landmarks (or people or landmarks of other cities for that matter), so she cannot be connected with Cincinnati in any concrete way. The same is true of Virginia Lee, who recorded one side in Cincinnati for Gennett in 1928. In fact, just because someone recorded in Cincinnati doesn't mean necessarily they were from here. The Thursday, June 12, 1930, recordings of St. Louis artists Walter Davis and Roosevelt Sykes, done at Cincinnati's Sinton Hotel, testify to that fact.[2] And when Cincinnati's next recorded blues artist got to the studios in 1928, it was in Chicago, possibly with Stovepipe on harmonica, certainly with a familiar street on his mind.

It was for the Vocalion label that Kid Cole went into the studio on Sunday, May 28, 1928, to record four sides, all of them issued:

C-1993-	Sixth Street Moan	VO 1186
C-1996-	Hey Hey Mama Blues	VO 1186
C-1997-	Hard Hearted Mama Blues	VO 1187
C-1998-	Miagra Fall Blues [sic]	VO 1187

Company files do not list a name other than Kid Cole for this artist, although comparison with the recordings of Bob Coleman, to be discussed later, suggests that this artist is indeed Bob Coleman, a fact verified by Pigmeat Jarrett. Cole may have been nicknamed "Kid" because of his age—and he certainly sounds relatively young, with his light and bouncy voice on these sides—or because of the designation "kid man," which refers to an inexperienced youth often kept as a lover on the side by a woman who is possibly interested in making her "regular" man jealous or angry. He is not the "Kid Cole" mentioned in Tom Lord's *Clarence Williams* as playing with Williams in 1922[3] since *that* person is likely "Kid Sheik Cola," another New Orleans musician. The first two sides from this session were once included on an LP subtitled *A Selection of Pre-War Memphis Blues Favorites 1928–1939*, with "Hey Hey Mama Blues" given a 1934 recording date, but each of these first two songs make it clear that Cole was a Cincinnatian, "Sixth Street Moan" because of its titular reference to a West End street:

> And it's run here, mama, sit on your daddy's knee (twice)
> Cause I'm sure gonna tell you how you treated me.
>
> And you were drunk last night, mama, baby and the night before,
> Doggone don't you hear me talkin to
> You were drunk last night, pretty mama, and the night before,
> You goin miss your kid man from rappin on your door.
>
> And if it wa'nt for the watchman, mama, the brakeman too, (twice)
> I would grab me a B & O freight, ramble this whole world through.
>
> And I'm goin away, mama, baby cryin it won't be long, Doggone it
>   don't you want to go 'long?
> And I'm goin away, brownskin, honey it won't be long,
> And I swear you gon miss your Kid Cole, baby, baby, when I'm gone.

"Sixth Street Moan" refers to the same street in the titles of two songs by Stovepipe No. 1 from his earlier sessions, and indeed the presence of Sam Jones on this session, playing harmonica on this one side, makes a connection between the two performers and songs, though they are by no means necessarily the same song. Stovepipe's performance unfettered by his guitar playing, is more confident and assured on this side, and the guitar playing, surely Kid Cole's own in light of its similarity to Bob Coleman's on his 1929 side, "Sing Song [*sic*] Blues," is appropriately bright and simple. Vocally, Cole is, as has been said, bright, quavery, and bouncy, and there is a bubbly personality behind the singing and lyrics, a propensity for stretching out lines by tunefully hurrying in phrases or pet names like "mama," "baby," "pretty mama," "brownskin," and "honey" that indicates that there is perhaps a sweet talker and a fast talker at work here, bursting with words that ramble quickly like that Baltimore and Ohio freight set to carry him through this world.

From the twelve-bar AAB structure of "Sixth Street Moan" Cole moves on to a sixteen-bar AAAB tune, "Hey Hey Mama Blues." Stovepipe is gone for the rest of the session, but each of the remaining songs mention Cincinnati:

Don't cry after poor me, sweet mama, when I'm gone,
Don't cry after poor me, Lordy, sweet mama, when I'm gone,
Don't cry after poor me, sweet mama, when I'm gone,
Gonna miss your daddy rollin in your arms.

Oh it's rocks in the mountain and your casket's on the sea,
Oh it's rocks in the mountain, pretty mama, and your casket's on the sea,
Oh it's rocks in the mountain and your casket's on the sea,
I ain't got nobody to love and care for me.

And it's hey, little mama, and it's somethin's goin on wrong,
And it's hey, little mama, pretty mama somethin's goin on wrong.
And it's hey, hey, little mama, and it's somethin's goin on wrong,
I can tell you done quit me by you stayed so long.[4]

And it's when I die lay a deck of cards on my grave (three times)
And it's no more browns in Cincinnati that I crave.

And I'm goin away, pretty mama, cryin it won't be long, (three times)
Get your typewriter, mama, type the (fine?) days I'm gone.

I woke up this mornin with the same thing on my mind,
I woke up this mornin, pretty mama, same thing on my mind,
I woke up this mornin with the same thing on my mind,
Had a heart full of misery, mama, and the screamin and cryin.

And its hmm mm mm and its somethin goin on wrong (three times)
I can tell you gon quit me, baby, but you quit me wrong.

Gonna place my left leg, sweet mama, pon your wall,
Gonna place my left leg, pretty mama, pon your wall,
Gonna place my left leg, and its honey upon your wall,
And you know about that, pretty mama, ain't makin no stall.

Another thing we notice about Cole is his interesting images, which are far from the very general and traditional lyrics of Stovepipe. There are not very many blues songs that mention caskets on the sea, decks of cards on graves, and typewriters within two-and-a-half to three minutes! Cole seems to be making a very conscious effort to be interesting and original, taking traditional opening phrases like "When I die" or "I'm goin' away" or "I woke up this mornin' " and giving them a real twist lyrically. He even takes the same opening line in verses three and seven and completes it differently in each place. Added to his quick and crowded phrasing in this song is another device that, it becomes apparent, is part of his style, and as we look back it was indeed present in "Sixth Street Moan." Cole begins a great number of his lines with "it's," "and it's," and "now it's," as well as with "oh it's" and just plain "and." It's (!) part of his offhand, informal, nervously vivacious delivery that helps keep his songs percolating, and though it is repeated often enough throughout these four recordings to be very much a part of his style, it never becomes tired or bothersome in its repetition because of his energy and his interesting lyrics, like those in the final two verses of "Hard Hearted Mama Blues":

Now it's lovin really really wor-worryin me, Lord, worryin me,
Lovin really wor-worryin me, hmm mm mm mm,
And that good hearted lovin is gonna be the death of me mm
    mm mm mm.
Prison, sure don't wan make it my home, Lord, make it my home,
Prison, sure don't want to make it my home,
I'm a good hearted poor boy just a long way from home.
Tell me cruel hearted mama what's on your hard hearted mind,
    Lord, hard hearted mind?
Tell me cruel hearted mama what's on your hard hearted mind?
Said you keep me in trouble, you worried and bothered all the time.
And I love my baby tell you just how I know, Lord, just how I know.
I love my baby, tell you just how I know.
I would work, rob and steal for her, baby, in the frost and snow.
And its blues woke me up on my telephone, Lord, my telephone,
Blue blues, woke me up on my telephone,
I got a long distance call from my baby, "Daddy, I ain't comin
    back home."
It's two women I'm lovin at the bottom of my heart, Lord, the
    bottom of my heart,
Two women I'm lovin at the bottom of my heart,
That's the one in Cincinnati, the reason why she broke my heart.
Tell me cruel hearted mama what you want your daddy to do,
    Lord, daddy to do?
Tell me cruel hearted mama want your daddy to do?
I'd rather see you murder me, baby, than to leave me too.
And I'm goin away, little baby, cryin it won't be long, Lord, it won't
    be long,
And I'm goin away, little baby, cryin it won't be long,
And get your bible, pretty mama, read the day your daddy's gone.

The incorrectly titled "Miagra Fall Blues," actually "Niagara Fall Blues," is mysteriously titled since the reference is never explained (unless he is simply signifying that the honeymoon is over), but the song is one of Cole's most delightful tunes:

I got the Niagara Fall blues, pretty mama, keep worryin you, Lordy, Lord.
I got the Niagara Fall blues, pretty mama, keep worryin you,
And those Niagara Fall blues, pretty mama, gonna be the death of you.

I walked down my pantry, walked back up my hall, Lordy Lord,
I walked down my pantry, pretty mama, walked back up my hall,
I stuck my head over the transom, another mule was in my stall.

I got the blues so bad that it hurts my tongue to talk, Lordy Lord,
I got the blues so bad it hurts my lovin tongue to talk,
I got the blues so bad that it hurts my baby feet to walk.

Now it's run to your window, heist your shade up high, Lordy Lord,
And it's run to your window, pretty mama, heist your shade up high,
And stick your head out the window to see the worried blues pass by.

I looked down the lonesome road, pretty mama, far as I could see, Lordy Lord,
I looked down the lonesome road, pretty mama, far as I could see,
Another man had my wife and I swear the Nashville Blues had me.

I got the blues in the bottle, got the rattlesnake in my hand, Lordy Lord,
I got the blues in the bottle, got the rattlesnake in my hand,
How can I live in this world, see my baby with another man?

Now it's run here, sweet mama, I'm goin to get you told, Lordy Lord,
And it's run here, sweet mama, I'm certainly goin to get you told,
You ain't the onliest woman in Cincinnati strut your lovin jelly roll.

Now it's listen, pretty mama, what is on your mind? Lordy Lord,
And it's tell me, pretty mama, baby what is on your mind?
And you look like you're worried and bothered, grievin, baby, all the time.

And I woke up this mornin, my pillow slip wringin wet, Lordy Lord,
And I woke up this mornin, my pillow slip was wringin wet,
Telegram from my baby, "Daddy I can't use you yet."

Scat chorus.

Another of the characteristics of Cole's lyrics is that the singer always seems to have difficulty directly communicating with his woman: In "Niagara Fall Blues" he receives a telegram; in "Hard Hearted Mama Blues" it's a telephone call; in "Hey Hey Mama Blues" she is told to type the days he's gone. All, of course, imply either a physical or emotional distance, and it is interesting to note the intervention of the machine into the relationship, making the rejections easier and more convenient. The juxtaposition of references to machines with those to natural images, like that of "rattlesnakes" in "Niagara Fall Blues," provides a fascinating contrast of urban and rural elements. The "rattlesnake" line is of particular interest. The snake as phallic symbol is, of course, common in blues lyrics (and elsewhere), and the rattlesnake in particular as phallic symbol turns up in Charley Patton's "Rattlesnake Blues" and Johnny Temple's "Louise Louise Blues," but Kid Cole's compression of images in this stanza is surely one of the best uses of the image.[5]

The Kid Cole of this 1928 recording is, finally, a fine, interesting, and original artist, an engaging guitarist and attractive singer with a lighthearted edge and an effervescent personality. An instantly recognizable performer, he concentrates on blues songs, mostly twelve-bar AAB compositions, though one is a sixteen-bar AAAB song, but he embellishes them with melodious asides and addresses that set them apart from a mechanical, mundane approach. He is also a blues singer who, like many others, identifies himself with a particular city or location, in this case Cincinnati, and makes no attempt to weed out references to that location in his songs. It is unfortunate that Kid Cole did not record more songs at his 1928 session, but it is evidence that he did so at later sessions, although not under the same name, and not always as the focal point of the performance.

Bob Coleman

Pigmeat Jarrett has verified that Kid Cole and Bob Coleman were the same person, and Patfoot Charlie Collins, leader of a later Cincinnati Jug Band, recalled his name as Bob Cole, not Coleman.[6] The first recordings that the person who called himself Bob Coleman did were sides with a group that called itself the Cincinnati Jug Band, recorded for Paramount in Chicago around January of 1929.

| 21100-2 | Newport Blues | PM 12743 |
| 21101-2 | George Street Stomp | PM 12743 |

Newport is, of course, a reference to Newport, Kentucky, across the river from Cincinnati. Newport was noted for being "wide open" in terms of gambling, vice, and bootlegging, and a place where Cincinnati blues musicians could go to play jobs, including for mobsters and gangsters who frequented Newport night spots.

The song itself is a medium tempo twelve-bar blues, with guitar, harmonica, and either jug or stovepipe. The guitar is in a style close to Kid Cole's, with interspersed bass notes and chords propelling along the rest of the group. More intriguing are the rough country harmonica player, with his reveille-like riffs, and the blasting jug or stovepipe player, who could be Stovepipe. He certainly sounds like Stovepipe as he kicks off "Newport Blues" before the rest of the band follows in, and he can coax a number of sounds out of his instrument. In fact, he makes a sound something like a washboard when he's not blowing notes, prompting discographies to suggest that a second jug player might be involved and that a washboard player is present on the session, though neither is true. Stovepipe was said to have played with a jug band, so it is entirely possible that he was present on these recordings and one of the two that followed, a version of "Tear It Down." The harmonica playing on "Newport Blues" is also similar to the playing on "Sixth Street Moan," which was supposedly by Stovepipe, so if that is the case, then someone else must be playing the jug here. Overall, though, the harmonica seems to have a rougher, more country orientation than Stovepipe's work, though it is not impossible to imagine the man who played "Fisher's Hornpipe" playing "George Street Stomp" as well. However, Stovepipe can't, after all, be everywhere playing everything, especially stovepipe and harmonica simultaneously as on these sides, so other musicians may very well be present. Pigmeat Jarrett mentions that Sam Wright played guitar and "Dude" the mandolin for the band, and James Mays says that Charlie Collins danced with them at their regular spot near Mom's Restaurant at Ninth and Linn, but none of those three is necessarily present on these recordings.

"George Street Stomp" is a notable recording for this work because it was one of the earliest references to Cincinnati in blues songs come across by this author, extending research into that area of town and leading to much of the research and findings presented herein. In the early seventies little was left of George Street. Part had been destroyed by the building of expressways intended to help revitalize the West End area; part had been torn down for downtown parking lots to alleviate parking problems for business customers in the downtown, not West End, area; one block was still occupied by small apartment buildings and a cafe known as "Little Jim's," which housed a jukebox with music by Lightnin' Slim, Slim Harpo, Ray Charles, and B. B. King. It was a far cry from what George Street used to be.

W. P. Dabney described the George Street in days of old:

> In the good old days harlotry played its part here as well as in all young western towns. It is woman's oldest profession, and the only one in which man is the game and to blame. The street of streets, famed wherever Cincinnati is known, was "George Street." Three blocks, East to West, from Central Avenue to Mound, lined on both sides with pretentious houses, neatly, cleanly kept, constituted the principal realm consecrated to the worship of Venus. Red lights above the doors gave it the name of "The

Red Light District," "for red is the flag of health, the banner of love." In later years it became commonly known as "The Tenderloin." The few colored sporting houses existing then were mainly for white men. Many were the colored maids, cooks and laundresses employed in the swell establishments. Strange to say, most of them were respectable, despite the fact that numerous men preferred the maid to the mistress. . . . Prostitution flourished before and after the Civil War. Money was plentiful. White and black women vied with each other for the common game, the white man.[7]

However, with World War I came the order already discussed to shut down the restricted district, and Dabney wrote in 1925 of the effect of that order:

Poor old George Street! Gone were the red lights. Gone were the brightly lettered signs of "Marie," "Lucy," "Kate," "Nellie," "May," etc. Gone was the picturesque darkness. Gone was the quiet of its day, the noise of its night. The weeping white denizens bartered away, gave away, threw away, the furniture for which they had sold their souls. "'Tis an ill wind that blows nobody good." The second-hand dealers were enriched. Negro tenants came and paid double prices to rapacious landlords. The street is now a wreck. The former inhabitants scattered, entered reputable flat buildings, slept by day, and at night through the streets they roamed, "seeking whom they may devour." The Negro women fared better. They wasted no time in tears, being daughters of a race saturated with a philosophy born of centuries of oppression. They flocked into Carlisle Avenue, lower John, and Smith streets.[8]

The music of orchestras of black musicians who entertained in George Street's houses, too, moved out onto the street, and all the area was supposed to have been cleaned up. Residents recall that George was still a place in the twenties and thirties where prostitutes could be found. Millionaire white man William P. Devou still was connected with George Street as a property owner, and he and his colored wife lived in a bare room that "equalled in squalor the worst of his tenements" in the area,[9] and he would have most likely heard the blues performed there: "That was strictly (laughs). Heck, yeah, that was strictly," Pigmeat Jarrett recalled, remembering the blues played on the street there, and James Mays remembered a great deal of playing going on on George as well.[10] As late as 1936 George Street was still prominent enough in the minds of local musicians to be an exhortation to play in a spirited, rough, and rowdy manner, as Walter Coleman on "Mama Let Me Lay It on You" directed his accompanist to "Play it like you did back to George Street," at which point the guitars fairly bounce with enthusiasm. Today the street and the sign posts are gone.

Once the Cincinnati Jug Band recording—"The only country-oriented jug band recording known by a non-southern based group," wrote Henry Vestine[11]—was done, it was time for Bob Coleman to come to the fore for his vocal sides. His first side, a vocal duet, was the piece recorded by Stovepipe and by King David's Jug Band, "Tear It Down," and Paramount ran an advertisement and a photo of Coleman (verified as Coleman by Jarrett and Mays) hyping the "snappy, peppy number with a hot guitar and jug accompaniment and good lyrics" in 1929.[12]

| 21102-1 | Tear It Down | PM 12731 |
| 21108-2 | Cincinnati Underworld Woman | PM 17231 |

Coleman's guitar part is remarkably similar to the guitar part on Stovepipe's "Bed Slats," and the song as a whole bears a far greater resemblance to Stovepipe's than King David's version in terms of music, lyrics, and even the name of the gal, "Lise," which King David changed to "Eve":

Refrain:
I'm gonna tear em down Bed slats and all (4x)
Now if I catch another mule kickin in my stall, mama, gonna tear
    em down.
Now you bake them biscuits nice and brown,
You know about that you got another high brown.
I got a brownskin she's little and low,
She's a toad-low shaker anywhere she go
Now if I catch another mule in my stall, mama, gonna tear em down.

Refrain

Now you drink your whiskey, have your fun,
Run like hell when the police come.

Refrain

I had a girl, her name was Lise,
Everytime you slapped here she would holler police.
Cooked them biscuits, nice and brown.
Thinks she's a workin when she turned around.
If I catch another mule kickin in my stall, mama, gonna tear em down.

Refrain

Told my girl, week before last,
That the gait she was carryin me is most too fast.
I went to the river, take my rockin chair,

If the blues overtake me rock away from here.
Catch another mule kickin in my stall, mama, gonna tear em down.

Refrain

Coleman's additions to the song include the stanza about the police and the stanza that refers to the "toad-low shaker," a popular dance in the 1920s.

This song is not much in the style of the earlier Kid Cole recordings, with a vocal in a lower range and a more agile finger-picking accompaniment. However, the next song, "Cincinnati Underworld Woman," features Cole's characteristic guitar playing, along with a vocal melody that anticipates Kokomo Arnold's "Original Old Kokomo Blues" by five years and Robert Johnson's "Sweet Home Chicago" by seven, thus marking the return of Kid Cole-style vocals *and* lyrics.[13] Bob Eagle has pointed out some of the similiarities between Kid Cole, Bob Coleman, and a number of other performers, as has Tony Russell in two letters to me.[14]

And it's oh, I ain't gonna do it no more, (x2)
The first time I'se at your house, mama, drove me from your door.
And it's rattlesnakes, honey, what makes you crawl so long, (x2)
I ain't had no lovin since my little rattler been gone.

It takes a rock, it takes a rock, mama, rubber ball to roll, (x2)
It takes a Cincinnati underworld woman to satisfy my soul.
And it's, oh, I ain't gon do it no more, (x2)
The last time I'se at your house, mama, made my backbone sore.

And I'm goin to the river take my boat and float, (x2)
And if my underworld mama quit me I'm gonna cut my throat.
And it's, oh, I ain't gon do it no more (x2)
The last time I drank your whiskey, mama, made my belly sore.

In an October 25, 1972, letter, Tony Russell pointed out that the song "is based on the old Texas barrelhouse theme 'whores is funky,' " but Coleman clearly makes the song his own. He also shows very definitely his links to Kid Cole. The similarities with Cole's recordings are evident: besides the nearly identical timbre of the vocal, there are (1) the lines that begin with "and" or "and it's"; (2) the regular use of pet names like "honey" or "mama"; (3) the use of an A line from a stanza twice in the same song that is completed differently in each of the two stanzas—compare Cole's "Hey Hey Mama Blues," with its line "And it's oh, I ain't gon do it no more"; (4) the reference to "rattlesnakes" as a sexual euphemism, as Cole used it in "Niagara Fall Blues," though in Coleman's song it seems to be the female who is the rattler; and (5) the possibility of death if his woman leaves him, as in Cole's "Hard Hearted Mama Blues"—murder in the Cole song, suicide in Coleman's.

If any doubt remains after one listens to and studies these common characteristics—even if some of those characteristics might be common to other blues singers as well—the song that Bob Coleman recorded on Friday, June 7, 1929, in Richmond, Indiana, for Paramount Recording Company should remove it completely.

15167   Sing Song Blues   PM 12791, Her 93014

"Sing Song Blues," actually "Sing Sing Blues" (though there is a kind of sing-songiness to the melody line and performance), is pure Kid Cole, vocals, music, lyrics, and all. The Herwin label released the performance under the *nom du disque* Ben Conway—Coleman had perhaps already conned his way through three sessions under different names and, as we'll see, wasn't done yet. "Sing Sing Blues" is a sixteen-bar AAAB blues, like "Hey Hey Mama Blues," that refers to the famous federal penitentiary that Bessie Smith had already sung about in her 1924 recording "Sing Sing Prison Blues." Coleman was apparently not singing from experience: Gary E. Katsel, Chief of the Inmate Monitoring Section for the U.S. Department of Justice Federal Bureau of Prisons reported that no one named Bob Coleman, Kid Cole, or Walter Coleman, and neither a Bob nor a Walter Coley, had been incarcerated at Sing Sing in 1929 or before.[15] Of course, not all blues songs are autobiographical; Coleman may well have picked Sing Sing because of its notoriety and then fashioned around it a prison blues with a number of traditional elements and lines, once again with his distinctive lyrical idiosyncrasies, that had the ring of truth because a specific prison is named.

> Is you ever been down, mama, you know just how I feel,
> And is you ever been down, little mama, you know just how I feel,
> And is you ever been down, little mama, I swear you know how a
>   prisoner feels,
> I ain't got nobody on the outside to play in the still.[16]
>
> And I laid in prison, my face turned to the wall (x2)
> And I laid in prison with my face turned to the wall,
> Says a no good crow jane woman was the cause of it all.
>
> And it's many old day I dropped my worried head and cried, (x3)
> I did not have no blue blues, mama, just wasn't satisfied.
>
> It's pull on your race horse, and on your derby, too,
> It's pull on your race horse, put on your derby, too,
> It's pull on your race horse, mama, put on your derby, too,
> I ain't got nobody in this wide world to love me, too.

And I looked in the death cell and dropped my worried head and cried,
  (x2)
And I looked in the death cell and I dropped my worried head and cried,
I told the Sing Sing prison boys, "This ain't like being on the outside."
And if it hadn't been for you, little mama, I would not be here (x3)
Drinkin wine, whiskey, mama, and your home brewed beer.

The reference to "blue blues" in stanza three here repeats a phrase sung by Kid Cole in stanza five of "Hard Hearted Mama Blues," indicating yet another connection between the lyrics of the "two" men. The Kid Cole who sang about his woman being drunk in "Sixth Street Moan" and worried about having to make prison his home in "Hard Hearted Mama Blues" now places himself in prison, possibly for bootlegging (stanza one), and now finds himself separated from the alcohol that got him in trouble (last stanza). The singer also blames the woman in the final stanza, suggesting that her love of alcohol has put him in his predicament—possibly his bootlegging activities were meant to supply her, or *she* was bootlegging (her home brewed beer) and he took the rap. Whatever the story, the facts indicate that Coleman was not singing of Sing Sing from personal experience, and that no stretch in Sing Sing kept him from making it back into the studio.

Sweet Papa Tadpole

The music of Bob Coleman and Kid Cole, as has already been pointed out, was sprinkled with references to "mama," "little mama," "pretty mama," and "sweet mama," so it was perhaps inevitable that this "sweet mama" would have a "sweet papa" somewhere, and that this "sweet papa" would in fact be Bob Coleman/Kid Cole. Around July 29 1930, at the Vocalion studios in Chicago, hokum blues stars Tampa Red and possibly his regular partner Georgia Tom Dorsey accompanied a singer who called himself Sweet Papa Tadpole on six recorded sides:

C-5952	Have You Ever Been Worried in Mind—Part 1	VO 1592
C-5953	Have You Ever Been Worried in Mind—Part 2	VO 1592
C-5954-A	You Baby Can't Get Enough	VO 1687
C-5955-A	Keep Your Yes Ma'am Clean	VO 1687
C-5956	Black Spider Blues	VO 1680
C-5957	Weep and Moan When I'm Gone	VO 1680

Tadpole's two-part "Have You Ever Been Worried in Mind," a sixteen-bar AAAB blues like Kid Cole's "Hey Hey Mama Blues" and Bob Coleman's "Sing Sing Blues," features the characteristic light, high-pitched singing we've come to expect from Bob Coleman, though his guitarist is replaced by the smooth and expert slide guitar of Tampa Red, and the lyrics feature Kid Cole/Bob Coleman characteristics as well:

Part 1:
Now is you ever been real weary, partner, lose your mind? (x2)
You ever been real weary and downhearted and, partner, lose your mind?
That's when your huggin woman quit you, I swear it leave you screamin
    and cryin.

You done murdered your poor rider, murdered her in the road, (x2)
You done murdered your poor rider, and murdered the poor girl in the road,
You never miss your pigmeat mama until she's squeezing on your right arm.

And you're motherless and you're fatherless, friendless in this old world,
    too, (x2)
And you're motherless and you're fatherless and you're friendless in this
    old world, too,
A deck of cards and a deck of dice and underworld woman ain't no
    friend to you.

I heard the judge when he sentenced you, the clerk he wrote it down (x2)
I heard the judge when he sentenced you and, poor partner, the clerk
    he wrote it down,
I heard the jury read the verdict that my buddy's Atlanta bound.

I dropped my worried head in my hands, begun to screamin and cryin, (x2)
I dropped my worried head in my hands, partner,and, poor partner, began
    to screamin and cryin
I never missed my buddy until that L & N passed by.

I'm gonna moan this verse, I ain't gonna moan no more,
I'm gonna moan this verse, partner, I ain't gonna moan no more,
I'm gonna moan this verse, partner, and, poor partner, I ain't gonna moan
    no more,
I'm gonna take my buddy from Atlanta some day back to Baltimore.

Part 2:
Now it's what makes a gambler sleep in the mornin fore day? (x2)
I says what makes a gambler, I says, poor boy, sleep every mornin fore day?
It's when the huggin women have quit him and the workin men are spendin
    their pay.

And it's gambler, oh gambler, please take my advice, (x2)
I says gambler, oh gambler, I says, poor boy, please take my advice,

Just get you a hard drinkin woman, settle down, and be a happy man the
    rest of your life.
And it's gambler, oh gambler, what's the matter now? (x2)
I said gambler, oh gambler, I said, poor boy, what's the matter now?
I let him lay in the jailhouse without so much and I'm raggedy, hungry,
    lousy, and out.
You never miss your water til your spring run dry, (x2)
And you never miss your water, I said, gambler, til your spring run dry,
You never miss your baby til you have blacked her eye.
I sing "Lord have mercy, what am I to do?" (x2)
I sing "Lord have mercy," I said, gambler, what am I to do?
I used to have seven hustlin women, now ain't got me one not two.
And it's tell me, rider, what you want me to do?
And it's tell me, rider, what you want poor me to do?
And it's tell me, rider, it's what you want poor me to do?
Said I'd rather see you murder me than talk about leavin me, too.

    The textual evidence that Sweet Papa Tadpole was the same person
as Bob Coleman is pretty strong. In addition to the vocal similarities,
the characteristic "it's" and "and it's" line beginnings are in evidence
here; the habit of hustling many words into a single line is clear
throughout; the reference to the "underworld woman" echoes Bob
Coleman's 1929 "Cincinnati Underworld Woman"; and the last
stanza of part two is very close to the second to the last stanza of Kid
Cole's "Hard Hearted Mama Blues," with its reference to being murdered rather than left. The references to "mama" in various ways are
gone here, replaced by addresses to a "gambler," "partner," and
"poor partner" since the song is addressed to a friend who is being
sent to prison, but Tadpole's method of regularly inserting these references in line after line is the same.
    Of course, the loss of a friend is a natural enough subject for the
blues, but one wonders if the sexual orientation of the persona Sweet
Papa Tadpole is being called into question on this song, with the
longing after the absent friend. The next recorded song, "You Baby
Can't Get Enough," after all, is bizarre in that the male Tadpole sings
in the first person "Your mama can't get enough" and makes regular
references to taking the female part in a sexual liaison:

Oh now it's wind me up daddy like a graphanola, too,
Said we get together daddy I will make your music, too,
Refrain:
Your mama can't get enough, (x2)
It says the reason why I'm wearin it, your little mama can't get enough.

Oh now it's look me over daddy, I'm 7 foot tall,
The movements of my body will make 12 men fall.

Refrain

I'm gonna buy me a brass bed, daddy, shine like the mornin star,
These women get there, daddy, whine like a Cadillac car.

Refrain

Just throw your arms around me, daddy, like the circle round the sun,
Now it's tell your little mama which way you want your raunchin done.

Refrain

I'm gonna love you, daddy, I'm gonna love you down deep,
When I kiss you, daddy, I'm gon put you fast asleep.

Refrain

Now I went to the doctor, daddy, this is what he said,
Got a white livered mama, she needs a brand new iron bed.

Refrain

Now you love me in mornin, daddy, you love me at night,
I got a prescription from the doctor say you should love me midnight.

Refrain

Some me said "a dollar," daddy, I said "no,"
They got twenty dollars, daddy, move your little mama's shawl.

Refrain

In this song, "mama" and "partner" are replaced by "daddy," repeated over and over again as Cole/Coleman did "mama," and it becomes clear that this hokum tune, with archetypal hokum performers Tampa Red and Georgia Tom Dorsey aboard, is meant to be in the line of female impersonator Frankie "Half Pint" Jaxon's homosexual hokum blues. Jaxon had recorded for the same label, Vocalion, with Tampa Red and Georgia Tom, in 1929 before Tadpole.[17] Despite his high, light, and quavery voice, though, Tadpole does not carry off the female impersonation as well as Jaxon does, lacking the general hamminess and possibly the personal commitment to the thrust of the song to carry it off convincingly, though it is a fine vocal performance.

"Keep Your Yes Ma'am Clean" marks a return to heterosexual lyrics with another AB refrain hokum blues, a delightful tune recorded as "Won't You Be Kind" by Luke Jordan in 1929 and as "Won't You Be Kind to Me" by Hattie Hart, also in 1929, though Jordan sang "Keep your back yard clean" and Hart changed that part of the refrain to "Drop down, daddy, and rock away my blues."[18] The song shows Tadpole's strength as a hokum singer, and justifies Vocalion's use of his talents in this vein:

> Now your mama found a jack, it's layin in the grass,
> A bumble bee stung it in the yes ma'am yes.
> Refrain:
> Ah, won't you be kind to me, I'll be kind to thee,
> Only time with me, drinkin wine with me,
> T you be kind to me, it's, mama, keep your yes ma'am clean.
>
> Now it's mama, mama, mama, won't you look at Sis,
> Out in the back yard, mama, doin the yes ma'am twist.
> Refrain:
> Now won't you be kind to me, I'll be kind to thee,
> Only time with me, drinkin wine with me,
> T you be kind to me, it's, mama, keep your yes ma'am clean.
>
> Now I heared the mightly rumblin under the ground,
> Now it must be the devil turnin, throwin his mammy round.
> Refrain (same as stanza 2)
>
> Now the preacher's in the pulpit jumpin up and down,
> Say your mammy's in the basement hollerin' "Pass the liquor round."
> Refrain (same as stanza 2)
>
> Now I'm goin uptown to buy my baby soap and towels,
> That means to take a bath, keep your yes ma'am down.
> Refrain (same as stanza 2)
>
> Now I'm goin away baby, buy you pair bloomers, too,
> That means to wear, mama, to hide your yes ma'am, too.
> Refrain (same as stanza 2)
>
> Now the farmer and the hoe both playing in the grass,
> Now the farmer shook the peephole [?] yes ma'am yes.[19]
> Refrain (same as stanza 2)

The Bob Coleman who emerges from the Tadpole session is less folksy than the man of the Kid Cole session, a bit smoother and more urbane than the man of the Bob Coleman session with the Cincinnati Jug Band, but unmistakably the same person. There are hints in "Have You Ever Been Worried in Mind Pt. 1" that he may have had some familiarity with Georgia since his friend was Atlanta (prison) bound on the L & N (though the L & N did go through Cincinnati, Kentucky, and Tennessee into Georgia), although those lyrics could have come from either Tampa Red or Georgia Tom, both of whom were from Georgia. Whatever the case, the session could be seen as a sign that record company scouts saw in Coleman a man whose talent could possibly be paired with other top drawer talent to come up with substantial record sales, though those sales never materialized. Unfortunately the other titles recorded at this session have not turned up, so the complete portrait of "Tadpole" cannot be painted. However, we can say with some authority that "Tadpole" is very likely Kid Cole/Bob Coleman.

Walter Cole

Though Sweet Papa Tadpole's big sales never materialized, what did materialize was, possibly, Bob Coleman—or someone who sounded an awful lot like him—again. This time the monicker was Walter Cole, the recording company Gennett (Stovepipe's first label), and the recording location Richmond, Indiana, on September 4, 1930. "Walter" recorded four tunes at this session, two of which were issued and all of which bore a striking resemblance to the sound of the Sweet Papa Tadpole incarnation of our man Bob.

16996	Mama Keep Your Yes Ma'am Clean	Ge 7318, Ch 16104
16998	Everybody Got Somebody	Ge 7318, Ch 16104
16999-A	What Makes a Gambler Sleep before Day?	Ge unissued
17001	Ever Been Worried?	Ge unissued

The accompaniment on these sides was possibly by Sam Soward on piano and James Cole on violin, both of whom recorded with groups led by Tommie Bradley and James Cole. However, there is no direct evidence that these men are present on these sides, and in fact neither group recording under the names of Bradley or Cole did any of their recordings until September 30, 1930, although when these groups did reach the studio it was in Richmond, and for the same label as Cole, Gennett.

It is unfortunate that two sides from this session were not issued, particularly since those two unissued sides suggest some strong ties with two songs recorded by Sweet Papa Tadpole: "Ever Been Worried?" could very well be the same song as "Have You Ever Been Worried in Mind Pt. 1" (or Pt. 2!); and "What Makes a Gambler Sleep before Day?" echoes the opening line of the second part of "Have You Ever Been Worried in Mind." It seems much more than coincidence that these two songs, along with the issued "Mama Keep Your Yes Ma'am Clean," a version of Sweet Papa Tadpole's "Keep Your Yes Ma'am Clean" (recorded about two months earlier), account for three of the four songs recorded by this Walter Cole. A comparison of the vocal and lyric idiosyncrasies confirms that the light, high-pitched, quavery voice of Kid Cole/Bob Coleman/Sweet Papa Tadpole is very likely behind these recordings by Walter Cole.

Why the name changes? Possibly there was a fear on Coleman's part that he was breaking a contract—every time he changed recording companies, from Vocalion to Paramount to Vocalion to Gennett, he changed his name. Certainly singers like John Lee Hooker, for example, recorded under various names to allow them to make as much money from as many recording companies as possible, and this may be the case with Coleman. Whatever the reason, "Walter" gives us another interesting version of "Mama Keep Your Yes Ma'am Clean," though only one verse, the second to last, is new:

> Now your mammy's in the backyard takin' up chips,
> Now it's along come a jersey cow shakin up her hip.

Although some of the stanzas are rearranged here, the song is quite clearly the same as the one recorded by Tadpole, down to the "Now," "Oh now," and "Now it's." The new verse adds even more humor to the song, once again in the vein of the dozens, placing the mother in the backyard picking up "cow chips" while a cow switches along ready to "chip in" again.

"Everybody Got Somebody" is a stylized, sixteen-bar ABC refrain blues, very much vaudeville influenced. Coleman had always seemed to be able to slide from folk-sounding to very urbanized, stylized blues, and this one features fewer of his lyric idiosyncrasies, though they are still there:

Everybody is got somebody, ain't got nobody, too,
That is why I love my little girlie, because she goes to school.
And she learns that two and two are four. I swear, sweet mother, that's all she know.
Everybody is got somebody, ain't got nobody, too.
I love my baby, I love my baby, I tell you the reason why,
My little baby, I love my little baby, because she won't lie.
And not because she's big and fat, I ain't gonna pick her to take me back.
Everybody is got somebody, ain't got nobody, too.
Oh, now, the girls don't like me, the girls don't like me because I'm young and wild,

The girls don't like me, the girls don't like me because I'm young
   and wild,
The girls don't like me cause I'm young and wild, I can't help it, girls, I'm
   mother's baby child,
Everybody is got somebody, ain't got nobody, too.

I looked out my window, looked out my window, the sun refused to
   shine, (x2)
I looked out my window, sun refused to shine. I looked at my baby can
   she change her mind,
Everybody is got somebody, ain't got nobody, too.

We notice in this song that the "*Is* you ever been down" of Bob Coleman's "Sing Song Blues" and the "*Is* you ever been real weary" of
Sweet Papa Tadpole's "Have You Ever Been Worried in Mind Pt. 1"
are mirrored in the refrain "Everybody *is* got somebody" of the Walter Cole song. The substitution of "is" for "have" or "has" is not uncommon, of course, in black vernacular English, but when this
characteristic is joined to Walter Cole's other stylistic devices, it becomes another clue in establishing Walter Cole's true identity as Bob
Coleman. Still, many of the "it's," "and it's," and "now" beginnings
disappear here as the text seems to come to Walter more or less composed, perhaps by someone else, causing him to sing in a less individual manner.

This smoothing out of style establishes a possible link with another
singer who recorded on Saturday, June 13, and Monday, June 15,
1931, for Victor in Louisville, Kentucky. Dubbed "Kid Coley," this
singer had the high pitch and quavery voice of Kid Cole, but his
voice was somewhat huskier and older-sounding (more than would
be explained by the three years that separated the two recording
sessions) than Cole's, though this may be due to a more dramatic
theatrical approach to the lyrics, an elaboration of the direction
"Walter Cole" was taking. The first three tunes, from June 13, are
fascinating songs, accompanied by piano and possibly Clifford Hayes
of the Louisville Jug Band, Dixieland Jug Blowers, and Old Southern
Jug Band:

69429-1	Clair and Pearley Blues	Vi 23293, BB B5248, Sr S3331
69430-1	Tricks Ain't Walkin No More	Vi 23293, BB B5248, Sr S3331
69431-	Freight Train Blues	Vi 23369

Paul Oliver suggested that "Clair and Pearley Blues" "might have
been based on the murder in Cincinnati of Pearl Bryan by her lover
Scott Jackson and his accomplice Alonzo Walling in 1896."[20] How-

ever, Coley's song seems to bear little relation to that murder. The story of the two students at the dental college at Court and Central who drugged, murdered, and decapitated the Newcastle, Indiana, girl whose body was found on the farm of John Lock near Fort Thomas made for sensational reading for decades. Even as late as 1966, when James A. Whiteford, a newspaper sketch artist, died, the headline obituary read "J. A. Whiteford Dies; Pearl Bryan Artist," describing his work of seventy years earlier sketching the headless torso of Bryan for the *Cincinnati Post*.[21] Other songs about Pearl Bryan (or Bryant) that have been collected in many areas across the country are seemingly adaptations of a ballad entitled "The Jealous Lover," which itself was based on "The Murder of Betsy Smith."[22] "Clair and Pearley Blues" could be an adaptation of "The Jealous Lover," but certainly the names Clair and Matthew Kelly are not associated in any way with the Pearl Bryan case, and no male accomplice (rather a female co-victim) nor decapitation are described. Coley's is a different story, but not a happier one:

Now come listen, people, while I sing one song, so lonesome and so blue,
Now come listen, people, while I sing one sad song,
Bout two girls I really knowed well and I haven't composed it wrong.

It was on one Friday between midnight and day, so lonesome and so blue,
It was on one Friday between midnight and day,
That Clair and Pearl, Matthew Kelly laid these two girls away.

Now Clair and Pearl lay down to go to sleep in their lonesome bed I mean,
Now Clair and Pearl lay down to go to sleep,
Matthew Kelly walked up, and through their back door did creep.

Pearl, she had a butcher knife some dirty work to do, so lonesome and
    so blue,
Pearl, she had a butcher knife some dirty work to do,
He certainly glad he saw the hatchet, said "I swear I'm gonna fix both
    of you, too."

Finally Matthew Kelly approached them, found the girls still asleep
    in their lonesome bed I mean,
Finally Matthew Kelly approached them, found the girls still asleep,
Matthew buried the hatchet in poor Clair's head deep.

Matthew Kelly walked to the electric chair with his hair combed out in
    a curl, so lonesome and so blue,
Matthew Kelly walked to the electric chair with his hair combined all out
    in a curl,
Try on a brand new suit of clothes, Matthew said, "It will be the last I try
    on in this world."

Now if anybody should happen to ask you who in the world wrote such
    a song, so lonesome and so blue,

Now if anybody should happen to ask you who in the world wrote such
    a sad song,
Tell em it was Kid Coley and he never composed it wrong—and it was no
    lie.

If, in fact, this was based on the Pearl Bryan case, Coley composed
it *very* wrong, so it seems that the insistence in the first and last stanzas that this song is accurate rules out the Bryan case as the source for
this story. All of the narrative details are lacking, unfortunately, for
us to be able to piece together the whole story—what is Matthew
Kelly's relationship with the girls? What do the girls have to do with
each other? Why is one of them sleeping with a butcher knife, and
what is the "dirty work" she has to do? Why does Kelly bury the
hatchet in Clair's head? What happened to Pearley? Of course, it is
not uncommon for a narrative blues ballad to leave gaps in the story
being told, since sometimes the audiences' familiarity with the story
is taken for granted or the spirit of the event or person, like "John
Henry," for example, is more important. But in this song so much is
left out that the listener has difficulty figuring out a relationship to the
characters involved since the situation is so sketchily described, so it
is ultimately a fascinating but unsatisfactory glimpse at a "historical"
event.

Coley does not sound much like Kid Cole in his verbal eccentric-
ities. There are no regular "it's" or "and it's," and only an occasional
"now." Coley does fill up a line of music with words the way Kid
Cole did, and he uses a repeat or tag ending like Cole did, in this case
"so lonesome and so blue," but in truth all of these elements could
have been picked up independently by a different singer. Still, combined with the vocal sound and the similarity of name, a tentative
case can be made that Kid Coley either was or knew Kid Cole/Bob
Coleman.

Songs entitled "Tricks Ain't Walking No More" or "They Ain't
Walkin' No More" had been recorded by Lucille Bogan in 1930
(twice) and in 1931 by Memphis Minnie, but their songs were conventional blues in form and featured lyrics delivered in the first person from the standpoint of a prostitute.[23] Coley's song, more of a
vaudeville or minstrel-type tune with its "silvery moon" and "June-
tune" rhymes (more on that later), is quite different, but very interesting and quite catchy in its own right:

Down Tennessee there lived a gal called Katy Lee,
She run a house on Front Street by the light of the silvery moon.
Now the hustler called around one day,

He approached her in a nice decent way,
He said,"Now Katy, ain't you got no dough today?"
You could hear Katy Lee say,
So she yells like this, from her lips Katy Lee did hiss:
Refrain:
"Tricks ain't walkin no more, tricks ain't walkin no more.
I been up ever since the rise of the sun,
Thirty went by I ain't even caught a one.
The landlord's singin the blues, the gals ain't sellin no more booze."
She says, "They come around every night with that same old stuff
     about
Tricks ain't walkin no more," I say,
"Tricks ain't walkin no more . . . "

Now, next night in June Katy Lee hummed a lovin boy tune
Now the plain clothes men knocked at Katy's front door
She heard them come, but tricks ain't walkin no more.
Now they knocked. Katy come to the door with a plea.
She said, "Now listen, officers, won't you all please listen to me?
Time they done got hard, don't you see. Whyn't you have a little pity
     on me?"
So the time she yelled out loud, everybody heard Katy Lee in a crowd.
Refrain:
She said, "Tricks ain't walkin no more, tricks ain't walkin a bit more.
I been up ever since the rise of the sun,
Thirty went by and I even caught a one.
Tricks standin on one corner and the police standin on the other.
Said if you can't get the tricks bring the police's mother. Bring somethin."
Cause they come around every night with that same old stuff about
"Tricks ain't walkin no more," I say,
"Tricks ain't walkin no more."

The song was recorded, of course, during the Depression, when the
number of prostitute customers or "tricks" dwindled due to lack of
money. It is interesting that Coley places this scene in Tennessee,
since Kid Cole mentioned having the Nashville blues in "Niagara Fall
Blues," again a very tenuous but possible connection between the
two. More interesting is the house that Katy Lee (also the name of a
Mississippi riverboat) ran: when Coley sings "She ran a house on
Front Street by the light of the silvery moon," he may be playing on
the presence of a bar, the Silver Moon Cafe, at 91 Front Street in Cincinnati. Earlier the Silver Moon had been Pickett's:

"Pickett's Saloon" was known from Pittsburgh to New Orleans, and
when Chicago was but an infant, Pickett was a celebrity, the King of the
Levee, 91 Front Street! Ye Gods, what memories rise before old residents

and visiting aristocrats who in the days sought the slums for recreation! That region finally became knows as "Rat Row," and then followed the metamorphosis of Pickett's place of pleasure into the "Silver Moon," its leading resort for residence and joy of all sorts. The inhabitants, white and black, made a beaten path to "Bucktown," and many were the daily pilgrimages to and fro, of hankerchief-headed, short-skirted, calico-dressed women, and "overalled" men, in various stages of inebriety. . . . "Rat Row" was in its decadence. "The Silver Moon" and other places of lowly pleasure went down financially as well as physically, for the frequent floods devastated the buildings, and temporarily drove to high ground, the human rats that infested them.[24]

Wendell P. Dabney's description of the final demise of the Silver Moon Cafe in 1925 makes it clear that it was a well-known house on Front Street and renders it entirely possible that Coley's song alludes to this Cincinnati establishment. Of course, since the Silver Moon Cafe was so famous, the fact that Coley referred to it does not necessarily connect him with Cincinnati any more than his singing about Tennessee places him there, either; but it is intriguing in light of all the other evidence that Coley exhibits yet another possible connection to Cincinnati and the Cole/Coleman recordings.

From the Katy Lee-riverboat connection Coley moved on in his next recording to another mode of transportation in "Freight Train Blues":

Me and my baby had a fallin out, I jumped up and leave but I didn't have
  no railroad fare, (x2)
Now the lonesome burg that I stopped in, I didn't know no one there.

So I knocked on a lonesome door, it was between midnight and day,
I knocked on a lonesome door, it was between midnight and day,
I heard a kind hearted voice drive my kind voice away.

Now the door it was locked, partner, and they had the window pinned,
Now the door it was locked, partner, and the window pinned,
She said, "I can't catch your voice, papa, and you can't get in."

So then I hung my worried head and I slowly walked away,
Hung my worried head and I slowly walked away,
Cryin "Never mind, mama, I'll get even with you someday."

Then I went back to the station asked the conductor please let me ride
  his train,
I cried, "Hey, Mr. Conductor, please let a poor boy ride your train,"
He looked at me sad and lonely, said "I'd do it in a minute, but I
  don't know your name."

Then I went around to the brakeman, begged him to let me ride
  the blinds,

I said, "Oh, Mr. Brakeman, let a poor boy ride your blinds,"
He shook his head sad and lonely, said "I'd do it but you know this
    train ain't mine."
Then I slowly hung my head and I walked down the railroad track,
Once more I hung my head, slowly walked down the railroad track,
This time I waited for the next freight train, ah, let me come back,
    mmm, mmm.

The connections with Cole/Coleman in this song include the word-filled lines, the references to "partner" as in Tadpole's "Have You Ever Been Worried in Mind Pt. 1," the use of "-hearted" as in Kid Cole's "Hard Hearted Mama Blues," and the humming also found in Kid Cole's "Hey Hey Mama Blues" and "Hard Hearted Mama Blues," though admittedly those characteristics might be found in many other blues songs. The song features some strong traditional elements—phrases like "between midnight and day" and "then I slowly hung my head" and the verses addressing the conductor and brakeman—but with enough of Coley's distinctive approach to make it more than a run-of-the-mill blues recording, a good example of how much style can enhance the traditional subject matter and make it even more attractive. It was a good ending to a successful day of recording—an interesting blues ballad, an intriguing vaudeville blues, and a traditional twelve-bar blues from a performer very capable of carrying off all three in an engaging manner.

Taking Sunday, presumably, as a day of rest, Coley was back in the Louisville Studio on Monday, June 15, 1931, for one more recording, his last under that name:

69442   War Dream Blues   Vi 23369

With "War Dream Blues" Coley got back to the twelve-bar AAB blues, the first three stanzas especially packed with words and sung Cole/Coleman style:

I'm goin away, I'm goin away, and your cryin won't help you none,
    Lawd, Lawd,
I'm goin away, oh honey, and your cryin won't help you none, Oh Lord,
Count the many thin hours you done your lovin lovin daddy wrong,
    Oh Lawdy, Lawd Lawd.
This world have made a change, it was a change, made a change since
    19-4, I mean,
It was a change, oh, honey, it's made a change since 19-4, I mean.
That many boys who done went to France never did get back to
    their homes no more, Oh Lawdy, Lawdy me.

Now it ain't but one thing, ain't one thing that I thought would be the
    death of poor me, Lawd, Lawd,
T'ain't but one thing, oh, honey, one thing I thought would be the
    death of me,
That's when Uncle Sam took all the beer and liquor shipped it way
    cross the deep blue sea, Ah, Lawdy, Lawdy, Lawd.

Now nobody knows the trouble that I see,
Nobody knows the trouble that I see,
My achin heart full of misery.

Eagle rock me, mama, please turn your lights down low,
Eagle rock me, honey, please turn your light down low,
And if you go away I know I can't rock no more.

Now then you rock me, honey, please don't squeeze me too tight,
When you rock me, mama, please don't squeeze me too tight,
Aw, if you give me plenty slack, I fix you up just right—fix you up
    just right.

We see in Coley's lyrics the "lordy, lord" line endings that we saw in
Kid Cole's "Niagara Fall Blues," Cole's interchangeable use of
"honey" and "mama," the (admittedly common) "goin away" phrase
used by Cole in "Sixth Street Moan," the use of "lovin" as an adjec-
tive (lovin daddy) similar to Cole's "lovin tongue" in "Niagara Fall
Blues," and the use, three times, of "Now" to begin lines in the song.
Coley's "War Dream" seems to be as disconnected as dreams can often be, wandering from infidelity to death and separation, lack of alcohol, and sexual intercourse, though the general direction of the
song seems to proceed from the state of being separated to the desire
to be reunited, which is either imagined (dreamed) or experienced in
the last two stanzas. The "war," it seems, consists of the battle of the
sexes, the battle over alcohol, and the battles that left the men dead
overseas in France, all of which fade as the dream of sexual pleasure
takes hold—the pleasure principle, as it were, displaces the demands
of society as the focus of the song.

Finally, it seems much harder to make a case that Walter Cole and
Kid Coley are in fact the same person as Kid Cole/Bob Coleman,
though I have tried to make such a case here. Walter Cole, in fact,
seems least like the "other" performers, though it might be argued
that Walter Cole and Kid Coley, at least, are the same person. There
are no contemporary accounts from Cincinnati residents placing either a Walter Cole or a Kid Coley in Cincinnati, but from the evidence already presented, and the evidence to come, I would place
"them" as either Bob Coleman or a cohort, possibly a brother, who
influenced or was influenced by him.

Nearly five years passed before a Cincinnati musician hit the studios again as a featured performer. This time it was Saturday, February 8, 1936, in Chicago. The recording company was different—Decca—but the name of the performer had a familiar ring: Walter Coleman! Walter accompanied his vocals with his own guitar, backed by another unidentified guitarist, and the two of them performed in a bouncing, power-charged Piedmont blues style that helped rank their duets among the best in recorded blues, aided by Walter's light voice and bright personality and at times fascinating lyrics. Walter recorded four songs that day, two with references to Cincinnati:

90609-A	I'm Going to Cincinnati	De 7168
90610-A	Greyhound Blues (Tell Me Driver How Long's That Greyhound Bus Been Gone?)	De 7168
90611-A	Mama Let Me Lay It on You	De Unissued Yazoo L1040 (LP)
90612-B	Smack That Thing	De 7157

Dixon and Godrich suggest that the Decca files indicate that it is possible that Walter Coleman is the same man as Walter Cole,[25] and Cincinnati city directory records support that possibility. The 1932–34 directories list a Walter Cole living at 614 Smith Street (West End), the first year as a laborer, the last two as a musician. In 1935 Walter Cole is listed as a janitor living at that address, and in 1936–37 Charlie Collins, perhaps the man who danced with the Cincinnati Jug Band, lived at that address. In 1940, 1942, and 1945 Walter, listed as Walter Coleman in 1940, lived at 552, 550, and 551 George Street respectively, with other people at the same residences, and even a wife, Rosa L. Cole, in 1942. That wife is not listed with him in 1945. A death certificate subsequently found for a Walter Coleman who died in 1946, when Walter disappeared from the city directories, lists a man who is separated and blind. His last listed occupation from 1945 was a musician, and his residence, 739 Carlisle, is a few houses down from the one-time residence of a Robert Coleman at 747 Carlisle. In fact, in 1935 a Robert Coleman was listed as living at the same address, 614 Smith, as Walter Cole(man). Blues researcher Dave Moore wrote me in 1978 that he was confident on aural evidence that Walter Cole and Walter Coleman were indeed the same person.[26] There may, then, have been two separate people who recorded under the variety of Cole/Coley/Coleman/Tadpole names, and, if there were, the difficulties in sorting them out are very real. A comparison of the lyrics and sound of Walter Coleman with the recordings done under the other names does not make possible any definitive conclusions, but it does provide some interesting clues to the Coleman mystery.

"I'm Going to Cincinnati" is undoubtedly the most fascinating of all Cincinnati blues recordings for Cincinnati history buffs; it can also rank as a bona fide classic of recorded blues. The playing of the guitarists is fully integrated and exciting, the music positively springing from the grooves in the instrumental passages with a verve that is contagious. Walter Coleman's vocal is light and high pitched, with less of a vibrato than Kid Cole and the others and less of a dramatic staginess than Walter Cole or Kid Coley. Five years, of course, have gone by, and halfway through the thirties the era of the vaudeville blues singers is even further away—Bessie Smith had made her last appearance in the studio in 1933, Ma Rainey in 1928, and both would be dead within three years—and in the meantime the recordings of professional stage singers were being replaced by semi- or nonprofessional blues singers either transported to major recording centers or, since 1927, recorded in the field.

Of course, the Depression brought hard times to the record industry, particularly during the years 1931–34,[27] which very likely accounted for the lack of Cincinnati Cole/Colemans in the studio between 1932 and 1935, and by the time Walter Coleman got to Chicago in 1936, he was probably ready to give the engineers whatever they wanted, as Cole/Coleman always had. The new style was brasher, more self-assured, with strong Piedmont influences that suggest that the other guitarist, who may be playing lead to Walter's bass string work, brought a great deal to the new, updated sound coming from Cincinnati:

> Now I'm goin to Cincinnati, I'm goin to spread the news,
> The fanfoot in Chicago sure don't wear no shoes.
> Refrain:
> Because I'm goin to Cincinnati, the times is good,
> I'm goin to Cincinnati where they eat fried food,
> And I'm goin to Cincinnati, boys, where the bottle is good.
>
> Now when you come to Cincinnati don't get too full,
> You're liable to meet the cop that they call Stargel Bull.
> Refrain
>
> Now when you come to Cincinnati stop on Sixth and Main,
> That's where the good hustlin women get the good cocaine.
> Refrain

Now when you come to Cincinnati stop at Hoghead Joe,
Where you get your turnip greens and your good hog jowls.
Refrain

Now, I'm goin uptown, buy my baby soap and towels,
To wash under her arms and keep her right odor down.
Refrain

Now the meanest man that I ever saw
A judge in Cincinnati called Judge Shaw [?].
Refrain

I got a bone in my throat, I can't hardly swallow,
There's a place in Cincinnati called Locklander Hollow.
Refrain

Of all the issued or discovered cuts by Walter Coleman, four of the six take this twelve-bar AB refrain form—and the other two are versions of an eight-bar blues with a recurring eight-bar refrain. This was a common enough form, one used by Sweet Papa Tadpole on two songs, "You Baby Can't Get Enough" and "Keep Your Yes Ma'am Clean," and on Walter Cole's version of the latter as well. More characteristic of the various Cole/Coleman recordings is Walter Coleman's use of "now" to begin six of seven of his sung verses. That is a device seen in recordings by Kid Cole, Kid Coley, Walter Cole ("Mama Keep Your Yes Ma'am Clean" uses the word just as frequently), and Sweet Papa Tadpole. Another link with Tadpole is his use of a verse very similar to the one that is verse five in Coleman's tune and verse five of Tadpole's own version of "Keep Your Yes Ma'am Clean":

Now I'm goin uptown to buy my baby soap and towels,
That means to take a bath, keep your yes ma'am down.

Interestingly, when "Walter Cole" recorded the song two months after "Tadpole," this verse was absent, replaced by the verse about the mama in the back yard taking up chips. Whatever the reason, the lyric helps even more to link up the recordings from the three dates and suggest at least an association.

Walter Coleman's lyrics are fascinating in themselves, though, with the various references to Cincinnati people and places following the brief swipe, in stanza one, at the fanfoot women in Chicago, the location of the recording session. Fanfoot women is a slang term referring to "loose" women—prostitutes. Coleman seems to be mocking the rural ways of Chicago hookers, who are going barefoot rather than adapting to the big city ways. The references to food and drink in the refrain are taken up a bit later in the song, though the reference in stanza two to "getting full" is possibly a reference to getting drunk as well.

The "Stargel Bull" of stanza two is a reference to a man also known as "Police Stargel" or Willard R. Stargel, Sr., a Cincinnati policeman for twenty-three years who later entered the construction business with the Kirchner Brothers in 1949.[28] James Mays recalled that Stargel was a cousin of his, and a tough but fair policeman, an opinion corroborated by Pigmeat Jarrett and others. Stargel's son Willard added that the nickname "Bull" stemmed from his father's reputation as a bully in his younger days, though resident Cleveland Green affirms that Stargel was not a bully as a policeman. He did, though, mean business: if a crowd of boys assembled on the corner and looked like they might be up to no good, Stargel would simply tap his nightstick on the curb and tell the boys he'd be back in fifteen minutes in order to disperse the crowd; if he had to arrest someone, he didn't even have to use handcuffs, he'd just tell the offenders to go on down the station and turn themselves in. Having spent all of his life in the Sixth Street area, he knew the people and they knew him as a tough and honest cop to be respected. Stargel's sometime partner "Police Toney," John B. Toney, had more a reputation among residents for toughness and club wielding. Known as the "Black Chief" in the West End, he killed two men in the line of duty (both had drawn on him) and assisted in solving numerous major crimes in the area. A Cincinnati patrolman for nearly twenty-three years, he retired in 1948 from District Seven, Walnut Hills, and died in 1978.[29]

On the other side of the law is the procurement of cocaine by prostitutes in stanza three. The reference to "hustlin women" parallels similar references by Kid Coley in "Tricks Ain't Walkin No More" and Sweet Papa Tadpole in "Have You Ever Been Worried in Mind Pt. 1," and the location, which is named as either 610 Main or Sixth and Main, is interesting. The occupant of the northeast corner of Sixth and Main in 1936 was the Dow Drug Company, while 610 Main was the Frisco Lines/St. Louis/San Francisco Railroad Company traffic department. Lockland resident Robert Bates said he doubted that the reference was to the drug company, stating rather that a number of cheap hotels in the general area of Sixth and Main were more likely the places where cocaine connections were made.[30]

When Pigmeat heard this lyric he identified it as a lyric characteristic of "Black Jack," not of Coleman, and he went on to insist that the words were Black Jack's: "Now that's Black Jack's. Black Jack's. Black Jack was the only man played them kind of blues. Yeah. And if anybody ever got it, they learned it from him. And the 'Dirty Dozens' and all of that. Now he got the 'Dirty Dozens' from me. *Then* you could sing it because you played it where they went for it."[31] His real name, according to Joe Duskin, who used to "follow" him, was Jack Johnson, and he was probably born around 1905. Pianist-organist Jon Thomas recalled his long fingers and his presence at weekend rent parties: "Yeah, that guy played the piano, and, baby, he used all them things! He looked like that and I looked and I said 'How the hell he do that?' And I couldn't get it! I don't think that's what he did for a living, but he could play the piano. Course, I never see—I was too young then to follow up. I couldn't have got off my street anyways, I was twelve or thirteen. And he'd come in and play that thing and I'd just look at him. Awh, that guy was so good."[32] At about 5'7", 120 pounds, he was not a big man, but his reputation as a piano player and creator of lyrics of the rough underworld set him apart in the minds of people who still remember him.

Hoghead Joe's was, according to James Mays, at Sixth and Plum, though Pigmeat Jarrett recalled it being at several locations, among them between Sixth and George, on Carlisle, and at the Cincinnati Post Square. Wherever it was at the time, you could get all you could eat—more—for fifteen cents to a quarter, and the food, Pigmeat added, was great. Another resident told a different, and unreliable, story about Hoghead Joe's changing locations every time the rent was due. The same resident recalled, upon hearing the reference to "fried food" in the refrain to the song, a different restaurant in the West End served the best fried food. That is, the hamburgers tasted great until about an hour after they were eaten, at which point the eater got sick! "Funny this was," he confided, deadpan, "bad as the rat problem was in the West End—you know it was bad down there, I never saw one rat in that man's store, and this man's hamburgers had the best crust on it. It wasn't hamburger, and I know he must've been using them rats. And I always went back, though, cause his hamburgers tasted so good."[33] Where they eat fried food, indeed!

The title of Cincinnati's meanest man, according to Walter Coleman in stanza six, goes to a Cincinnati judge whose name sounds like "Shaw" or "Landshaw." Pigmeat Jarrett agreed: "Shaw. Yeah, Judge Shaw. You damn right he was a tough judge! Yeah, he was a tough judge. Yeah, shit—workhouse bound! Yeah, yeah, shit. Now, now, he was tough, but a good prosecutor . . . yeah, pretty rough man." Unfortunately, the records of judges who served during the 1930s do not offer up a Judge Shaw or Landshaw for us to pin the blue ribbon on, and neither do recollections of veteran Judge Gilbert Bettman.[34] At one point it seemed as if Walter M. Shohl may have been a candidate for Coleman's "honor," but Shohl was a Court of Appeals judge only from 1918 to 1921 and thereafter a member of the law firm of Dinsmore and Shohl. By the time Coleman recorded his song, Shohl would have been off the bench for fifteen years. Shohl did remain active publicly: he was vice chairman of the University of Cincinnati Board of Directors, president of the Cincinnati Bar Association, and president of the Ohio Board of Bar Examiners, and he had a room dedicated to him in 1967 at the U.C. College of Law. But unless he had passed out such harsh sentences—or a harsh sentence to Coleman himself—that he maintained a tough reputation over a decade later, it is not likely that he is the judge named in the song. And there is, in fact, no evidence that he was harsh in his trying or sentencing. Unfortunately, then, this judge seems to be more or less untraceable. Perhaps it was a nickname—Judge Pshaw!—expressing disgust or contempt for the judge. Pigmeat gives no indication that it was. Ultimately, the charge must be dismissed for lack of evidence.

Coleman's reference to "Locklander Hollow" in the last stanza is actually an allusion to Lockland, which was "incorporated in 1865, and rated a city in 1930." Settled permanently in 1827 when the Miami and Erie Canal was opened, Lockland took on an industrial importance because of its location, taking its name from the canal locks. The industries attracted and employed many blacks, but "the grubby shacks set up for the mill hands" were eyesores that remained until around 1940, when an airplane engines plant scheduled to be located in Lockland precipitated development and renovation in the city.[35] A January 9, 1935, article in the *Cincinnati Times Star* entitled "Lockland" described in patronizing and racist terms the black residents of the city:

Lockland is an interesting little place, if one is interested in the actions and reactions, the waves and wavelets, the currents and eddies, the boilings and broilings, the loves and hates, the means and laughter that constantly take place among these whimsical colored folk that God has made my own—or vice versa. In Lockland proper, that is, West Lockand, or Old Greenwood, although it is the center of a considerable Negro population scattered up, and a bit down the valley, there are only eight small town blocks of Negroes. Within those eight blocks the gamut of Negro life, as lived in America, is run. Here, cheek by jowl, or in close juxtaposition, as we higher mathematicians term it, live the saint and sinner, the hard-boiled guy and the ambitious youth, the bullet-headed Negro into whose mind no light will ever seep—and the keen-minded kid whose brain is like unto that of a German Jew! Lockland has a Loop, just like

Chicago—down Walnut to Locust, north to Maple, east to North Wayne, and south back to Walnut. Within this loop and on its fringe, enough material to supply a Balzac or a Hugo, goes continually on—"Lockland Triangle."[36]

Another article from the *Times Star* of December 28, 1938, was headlined with the claims by resident Herman Lyon that conditions in Lockland were intolerable: it reported that Lyon asserted that "Gaming [was] 'Again Rampant in Lockland,' " charging that "small children were permitted to play slot machines and that bookmakers operated unmolested."[37] The charges were repeated in the October 26, 1942, *Times Star*,[38] though they were refuted by the Lockland police chief in the same paper two days later.[39] Pigmeat Jarrett asserts, however, that Lockland was "in bloom" in the thirties, with plenty of stills and speakeasies, the owners of which actually competed against each other for the entertainment that could be provided by the best local musicians. Locations of such activity included, according to Jarrett, the "Farm House," "John Tyson's" [sic], and "McLemore's" [sic] from the early twenties on.[40] However, Coleman's reference to "Locklander Hollow" is a mystery to Jarrett, who never heard Lockland or any location in Lockland ever called by that name. It is therefore likely that Coleman invented that designation to rhyme with "swallow" and complete his suggestion that that area was wide open in terms of illegal alcohol activity—if Prohibition (1920–33) had indeed put a blockage in his throat, preventing him from drinking alcohol, Lockland would help remove that barrier. Coleman's song certainly provides a fascinating view of the "underworld" of the area, naming people and places forgotten or incompletely portrayed in the "official" histories of Cincinnati, so his song has, in addition to its great musical value, a historical value as well.

Coleman's next recording, "Greyhound Blues," refers not to the dog but to buses run by the Greyhound Company, whose many connections with both large and small towns helped make it the largest intercity transit system in the world. Like the train and the boat, both of which are relatively common in blues lyrics (particularly the train), the Greyhound bus was a natural for blues songs dealing with the departure of a lover or friend, and Coleman's song also makes use of a refrain line that probably borrows from the line "How long has that evenin train been gone" recorded and made famous by Leroy Carr in 1928.[41]

Now, my baby woke this mornin, the same thing on her mind,
She grabbed an awful Greyhound, then she went a-flyin.

Refrain:
Won't you tell me driver, and it's tell me driver,
And it's tell me driver how long's that Greyhound bus been gone?

Yes, she pull like a Greyhound, it turned around the bend,
It takes the good Lord tell my baby be back again.

Refrain

Now I feel like poppin a machine gun in my baby's face,
I'll let some lonesome graveyard be her resting place.

Refrain

Throw your arms around me, mama, like circle round the sun,
You tell your little daddy which way you want your lovin done.

Refrain

I'm motherless, fatherless, friendless in the world, too,
Those card and deck of dice underworld women ain't no friend to you.

Refrain

Now the driver toot his whistle, Roosevelt blowed his horn,[42]
Since the good gin and whiskey come in they stole my woman and gone.

Refrain

Once again we see the associations with the Cole/Coleman constellation: "and it's" in every refrain, "now" in three stanzas, and the occasionally crowded lines; the reference to "circle round the sun," an admittedly common lyric, also in Tadpole's "You Baby Can't Get Enough"; and the references to "deck of dice" also in Tadpole's "Have You Ever Been Worried in Mind Pt. 1" and "underworld women" from the same song and Bob Coleman's "Cincinnati Underworld Woman." Also notable is Coleman's replacement of the conventional "feel like slappin a pistol in your face" with a popping machine gun—more violent, more overkill (real overkill), made even more startling by the offhand, lighthearted delivery. The lyrics again mirror the wavering of the left-behind lover who in one stanza envisions murdering his woman, in the next talks about serving her well in terms of her sexual needs. And although the singer states optimistically that they should "play it til she come back" in the instrumental break, ultimately alcohol and the Greyhound seem to have won out as the separation ends up permanent.

"Mama Let Me Lay It on You" is the first recorded version of the song better known through Blind Boy Fuller's April 28, 1936, version and Georgia White's May 11, 1936, recording (credited to Coleman on the label, and also recorded for Decca), and familiar also as having the same tune as the song "Mama Don't You Tear My Clothes."

Another song, "Can I Do It for You," which featured the same melody, was recorded by Kansas Joe and Memphis Minnie six years earlier, in 1930, and "Sheik Johnson" recorded a "Baby Let Me Lay It on You" for Decca on March 27, 1936.[43] Though Coleman's version is not as well known, it is clearly superior to Fuller's 1936 recording and the 1938 sequel Fuller recorded, the smooth vocal and agile guitars perfectly matched to the feel of the song. Just whose song it was, if authorship is discernible, is anybody's guess, and how Fuller ended up recording it in New York City two and a half years after Coleman recorded it in Chicago is as well. Certainly, as has been said, Walter Coleman would sound at home in the Southeast as an instrumentalist, and it is possible that he spent some time there, though surely his ties as demonstrated by his recordings are strongly with Cincinnati. The fact that he is not remembered by residents here argues either for residence outside the city with occasional visits or a *nom du disque*, unknown to residents in Cincinnati, that hides Bob Coleman. The song is the only eight-bar blues recorded by Cincinnati blues artists in the twenties and thirties, and its references to "mama," "baby," and "now it's" certainly has its ties to the other Cole/Coleman recordings:

> Refrain:
> Mama, let me lay it on you, (twice)
> I'd give anything in this whole round world,
> Mama, let me lay it on you.

On the thunderously exciting out chorus comes the immortal "Aw, play it like you did back to George Street!" and "Aw, stomp that thing!" that make for a rollicking close to the song, one which finds Walter signing *about* a "kid man" and also singing *as* one (as Kid Cole did). The lyrics of Blind Boy Fuller's version, except for the refrain, are totally different, and the vocal not as melodic as Coleman's. Georgia White's version has identical lyrics adapted to a female vocalist, obviously since the lyrics are credited to Coleman. Most interesting is the fact that Fuller's "Mama, Let Me Lay It on You No. 2" from 1938 features a vocal melody much closer to the melody in the Coleman and White versions, suggesting that perhaps Fuller had heard the other versions, either recorded or in performance by some artists, and adopted that line. Of course, Fuller may have changed the vocal melody on his 1936 version in the interest of being more distinctive and then fallen back on the better-known melody in his second version. The lyrics are again different from Coleman's in Fuller's second version, save for one verse about a "diamond ring," which is also present in a simplified form in the Kansas Joe/Memphis Minnie recording. Whatever the ultimate source, Coleman does give his everything in this song, leaving the listeners not "cold in hand" but with a hot piece of shellac to keep them company.

Coleman's next recording, "Smack That Thing," refers, like Roosevelt Sykes's 1929 reworking of "Pinetop's Boogie Woogie" titled "Boot That Thing," to sexually suggestive body movements described more mundanely in Papa Charlie Jackson's hit recording of 1925, "Shake That Thing." Bob Eagle has pointed out that Barrelhouse Frankie (Frances Wallace) recorded an "I Had to Smack That Thing" for Paramount in 1930, and that the two songs may be related.[44] This Coleman recording has features that link him in some way to each of the other pseudonymous performers in the Cincinnati Coleman cluster, along with one more reference to the mysterious Cincinnati underworld scene:

Now, wake up this mornin, girl, feelin sad,
You know I want somethin that I ain't never had.
Refrain:
You want to smack that thing, (twice)
You want to smack that thing, mama, I ain't got a thing to give away.

I went to my gal's house the other day, and I didn't go to stay,
I got to smackin that thing and I stayed all day.
Refrain

Now it's roll down your window shades and close up your blinds,
To keep your next door neighbors from hearin you whine.
Refrain

I got a brass bed, mama, shine like the mornin star,
When I rock you in it gonna bounce you like a Cadillac car.
Refrain

Run here, sweet mama, I'm gonna get you told,
You ain't the onliest woman in the world strut your jelly roll.
Refrain

The first time I met you standin in my back door,
I told you standin like that tricks ain't walkin no more.
Refrain

Now the girls don't like me cause I'm young and wild,
I can't help it, girls, I'm my mama's baby child.
Refrain

Now you green cabin girls, you needn't flirt,
You got fly specks on your underskirt.
Refrain

Here, again, are the line beginnings "now" and "now it's" present in songs by Kid Cole, Kid Coley, Walter Cole, and Sweet Papa Tadpole, along with the references to "mama" and "sweet mama" also present in many recordings by those artists. More substantial are Coleman's fourth stanza, a variation of stanza three of Tadpole's "You Baby Can't Get Enough"; Coleman's fifth stanza, a version of stanza seven of Kid Cole's "Niagara Fall Blues"; his repetition in stanza six of the "tricks ain't walkin no more" line used by Kid Coley; and stanza seven's use of the words from stanza three of Walter Cole's "Everybody Got Somebody." Surely these are more than passing coincidences: they are clear ties among the "performers" that support the argument that they may very well, in fact, be the same person. Another point of interest in this song is Coleman's final verse, with its "green cabin girls." Pigmeat Jarrett explained the reference:

> Yeah, well, that's just like section, section housing, see. See, Coal City used to be in bloom, across the railroad tracks . . . that's way down on River Road. Coal City. You go cross the railroad tracks. Where all of that was section houses. Houses was over there, you understand what I mean? And that's where they go. All-night functions. Railroad men and things would be there. You know, come there, you understand . . . that's where they went to have good times at . . . yeah, I played there. Hell, yeah, me and Peg. . . . Pimp houses, but they was real houses . . . just like the railroad men, they wives and things they stayed in them houses and all them guys worked on the railroad.[45]

The musicians who played at the green cabins were paid by pimps, and at times those musicians were drawn from the many who arrived in town riding the rods or stowed away in boxcars. The Green Cabin girls were prostitutes who worked the traveling transients and railroad workers who stopped off or stopped over in town. When Coleman sings of the fly excrement on their undergarments, he seems to be suggesting that everyone knows who they are, what they're for, and, presumably, what they're "worth." It may be a joke, but one can't imagine it going over too well with the "girls" themselves, although the comment does smack of a kind of familiarity with the green cabin girls that indicates that Coleman may have, indeed, worked there (at least). The song was a fine completion to a highly successful session aesthetically, and successful enough for Decca to have Coleman back in the studio again soon.

Soon was Wednesday, June 3, 1936, in Decca's Chicago studios, this time with pianist Jesse James and an unknown jug player accompanying Coleman's vocal and guitar. For some mystifying reason the earlier version of "Mama Let Me Lay It on You" remained unissued, but this session started out with a rough and ready version of the tune that was issued as the other side of "Smack That Thing." Two other unissued titles were also recorded at this session:

90611-C	Mama Let Me Lay It on You	De 7157
90764-	Mama Don't You Think I Know	De unissued
90765-	Carry Your Good Stuff Home	De unissued

Coleman's new version of "Mama" features some old lyrics, some new ones, and references to a Cadillac 8 and V-8 Ford that anticipate Fuller's references to a Ford machine in his 1938 version. This version by Coleman is sung in a higher key, and the vocal itself sounds closer in timbre and vibrato to Kid Cole! The instrumental passages belong to the raucous piano of Jesse James, but Walter's vocals and lyrics, references to George Street and all, carry the song:

Refrain:
Mama, let me lay it on you, (twice)
Give everything in this whole round world,
Mama, let me lay it on you.

I'm gonna buy you a Cadillac eight, just, baby, get your business straight,
I'd give everything in this whole round world,
Mama, let me lay it on you.

Refrain

And I'm goin upstairs to turn my lamp down low,
And if your bed breaks down,
See me streakin on the floor.

Refrain

I'm gonna buy you V-8 Ford, I'm gonna drive it to your door,
I'd give everything in this whole round world,
Mama, let me lay it on you.

Refrain

Mama pull off your dress, put on your nightgown,
I got a funny feelin, mama, in my sack,
Baby, won't you pile it down.

Refrain

I've got a brand new brass bed, shine like the mornin star,
Any time I rock the George Street women,
I'm a rock you like a Cadillac car.

Refrain: Now it's etc.

Coleman's last verse before the refrain appeared in his previous recording of "Smack That Thing" and in Tadpole's "You Baby Can't

Get Enough," minus the reference to George Street women included here. "Carry Your Good Stuff Home," which is available even though it was, like "Mama Don't You Think I Know," unissued, starts off where "Mama Let Me Lay It on You" ended—in bed:

> Now, you comin in my house, mama, want to go to bed and stay up all night,
> Said somethin bout that good stuff, you want to fuss and fight.
> Refrain:
> Carry your good stuff home, just carry your good stuff home,
> Just carry your good stuff home, mama, you don't want me to have it all night long.
>
> I ain't gon put no gun on you, mama, no razor, too,
> You don't want me to have that good stuff, carry it back home, too.
> Refrain
>
> Now I'm goin away, little mama, cryin it won't be long,
> I'm sorry, mama, I can't carry that good stuff along.
> Refrain
>
> Now I've got a brownskin, boys, she's seven feet tall,
> The movements of her hips'll make the president crawl.
> Refrain
>
> Now you can shoot your dice, mama, you can shake, rattle, and roll,
> She's got somethin good, boys, make you leave the wife and your home.
> Refrain

The reference in the second to last verse about hip movements making the president crawl is outrageous fun, although FDR, and Eleanor for that matter, probably would not have gotten too much of a kick out of it. Certainly this is one of the earliest recorded references to the phrase "shake, rattle, and roll," though it was preceded by Kansas Joe's 1931 recording "Shake Mattie" with Memphis Minnie in the studio on second guitar.[46]

Once again we see lyric ties to other Cole/Coleman performers: The "going away / won't be long" line used by Kid Cole and Kid Coley; the seven-foot-tall woman of Sweet Papa Tadpole's "You Baby Can't Get Enough"; the dice and gambling so prominent in various underworld references by Kid Cole, Kid Coley, Bob Coleman, and Sweet Papa Tadpole; the use of "now" and "it's"—again the pattern of connections is maintained, from the 1928 recordings of Kid Cole to the 1936 recordings of Walter Coleman. These were the last recordings by Cole/Coleman, a very strong ending to a varied career from which some conclusions can be drawn.

First, Kid Cole and Bob Coleman are definitely the same singer. Not only have they been identified by people who knew them but a comparison of Cole's recordings with Bob's "Sing Sing Blues" presents irrefutable aural evidence. Walter Cole is the least like the other performers in terms of his lyrics, but he too sounds similar enough to be the same person as Bob Coleman. Sweet Papa Tadpole and Walter Coleman seem pretty surely to be the same performer as well, and Kid Coley and Kid Cole also demonstrate a closeness in style and lyrics. It seems that all of these singers were the same person, Bob Coleman, or two people, brothers perhaps, whose stylistic similarities sometimes made them nearly indistinguishable from each other on record. If, indeed, there were two different performers—and there were not likely more than that—then it would be a good guess to venture that Kid Cole and Bob Coleman were the same person, and that the recordings done by Walter Cole, Sweet Papa Tadpole, Kid Coley, and Walter Coleman were all done by a different person. The city directory information that places both a Bob and a Walter Coleman living at the same West End address, 614 Smith, in 1935, suggests that there indeed were two performers, two very fine performers, who may have been related, were certainly acquainted, and who acquitted themselves and the city of Cincinnati very well in their trips into the recording studios, playing it like they did back to George Street.

The pairing of Coleman with pianist Jesse James was not a chance collaboration in the studio, nor were James's recordings with Coleman the only ones he did. In fact, Jesse James's four recorded sides, issued under his own name, or in one case, as "Hooker Joe," were recorded just before he accompanied Walter Coleman, all at the Decca Studio in Chicago on Wednesday, June 3, 1936:

90760-	Sweet Patuni	De unissued; Post 439
90761-A	Southern Casey Jones	De 7213; VoE V1037
90762-A	Lonesome Day Blues	De 7213; VoE 1037
90763-	Highway 61	De unissued

It isn't known whether Jesse James was his real name or not. It was the only name that Pigmeat Jarrett knew him by, but Pigmeat does not know the real names of many of his old musical acquaintances. Taking the name of the legendary outlaw immortalized by "Billy Gashade" in the Jesse James ballad would have been a wonderful public relations ploy, and certainly the pianist was a rough-and-ready-key pounder who went at his work with both barrels. Although Karl Gert zur Heide collected some information that James lived in Memphis in the postwar years and worked and even broadcast out of Little Rock, Arkansas,[47] Jarrett insisted that James, a "good fellow," stayed in Cincinnati on Fourth Street, moving to Kentucky around 1955.[48] In later years, James had trouble sitting, much less playing, because of bad hemorrhoids, but he could still play the last time Pigmeat saw him, over thirty years ago:

> Jesse James. Me and him run together for a pretty good while . . . like I played here, he played there. Now they get me up there next, on this Friday, I'll be up there and he'd be down here. Now Saturday, he would be down here and I'd be up there. They would change around like that, you know. In different places. And at McLemore's and in the Farm House, that was up—this was in Lockland. This is up in the Farm House and down to John Tyson's, that's where the still was at. You understand what I mean, make the moonshine, where you got all the moonshine at, you know. If I tell you this, you won't believe it, but (they) clean the slop jars so, so if the law run in, they ain't gonna fuck with the slop jar. Cause they'd think it's, you know. But it's moonshine.[49]

Such was the milieu of Jesse James, again the whorehouse, gambling, and bootlegging establishments that could often be the milieu of the blues in the urban environment. But out of it James brought, as did so many other blues singers, performances of great beauty and value, though sometimes almost repulsively beautiful. "Sweet Patuni":

> Ah, wake up, mama, wake up and don't sleep so sound,
> Give me what you promised me before you laid down.
> I could get my tuni, only thing I love.
> Make you weep like a willow, sling snot like a turtledove.
>
> I got a gal and the kid lives out on the hill,
> She got good tuni and serves anyone she may will.
> She got good tuni, I'm a fool about my yam, yam, yam.
> Get my yam, yam, yam, goin back down Alabam.
>
> Now come in here baby, and sit down on my lap,
> Sit one side, I forgot to tell you I had the
> Clap your hands together, Charlie, Charlie, where you been so long?
> I been down in Tennessee and I couldn't stay there very long.
>
> I got a job in the freight house tryin to learn how to truck,
> A box fell on me this mornin and like to bust my
> Nut house for crazy folks, folks got sense don't go there,
> All the friends I had done shook hands and left there.
>
> I got a gal and the kid playin deef and dumb,
> Her movement in her hip'll make a dead man
> Come on out my window, don't knock on my door.
> And I done told you two or three times, don't want you no more.

Now run in here baby, cause I done got kinda sick,
Ain't nothin ailin in my stomach, is something wrong with my
Dixie Dam was a camp in Georgia, you can't stay there very long,
All the friends I had done shook hands and gone.

Now here's a verse I don't want a soul to miss,
I been takin charity groceries got to go outside and
Shet your mouth, boy, four of us can't talk at once,
And I done told you two or three times I don't want me no junk.

James delivers this song with the verve and spirit of a barrelhouse pianist, shouting, growling, exhorting to his audience in a most raucous fashion. His juxtaposition of "weep like a willow" and "sling snot like a turtledove" is startling and memorable, as is the way he balances flamboyantly and roughly on the censorship rope, hollering at his audience so that no one misses his next near-vulgarity, and smiling, pleased at his cleverness. A great deal of his personality leaps from these grooves, and we can imagine that we are not far away from getting our whore house blues straight.

James followed up "Sweet Patuni" with a stomping version of the Casey Jones ballad, "Southern Casey Jones." Based on the life and death of Irishman John Luther Jones of Cayce (hence Casey), Kentucky, an engineer on the Illinois Central (I.C.), James's version echoes faintly the original version by Negro engine wiper Wallis Saunders, which was itself based on a song entitled "Jimmie Jones," and veers more in the direction of the popular ragtime ballad penned by T. L. Sibert and Eddie Newton, though James hurtles like a runaway train through lyrics that would have scandalized the widow Jones, already grieving that her "Casey" had wrecked his "Cannonball Express" into a freight train at a double curve at Vaughan, Mississippi. The whistle of No. 382 would now be silent, but people like Furry Lewis, who recorded the ballad in 1927 and 1928,[50] and Jesse James, in addition to a number of white country singers, would sing on. It seems almost ludicrous to say, but this is how "Jesse James" sang "Casey Jones":

I heard the people say Casey Jones can't run,
Ahma tell you what the poor boy done:
Left Cincinnati bout half past nine,
Got to Newport News before dinner time.
Fore dinner time, fore dinner time,
Got to Newport News fore dinnertime.

Now Casey Jones said before he died
He'd fix the road so a bum could ride,
And if he ride he had to ride the rod,

Risk his heart in the hand of God.
Hand of God, in the hand of God.
Had to risk his heart in the hand of God.

Now, the little girl said, "Mama, is that a fact,
Papa got killed on the I.C. track?"
"Yas, yas, honey, but hold your breath,
Get that money from your daddy's death.
From your daddy's death, from your daddy's death.
You'll get money from your daddy's death.
Lawd, your daddy's death, from your daddy's death,
You'll get money from your daddy's death."

When the news reach town Casey Jones was dead,
Women went home and outted out in red,
Slippin and slidin all across the streets,
With the loose Mother Hubbards in their stockin feet.
Stockin feet, stockin feet,
Loose Mother Hubbard in their stockin feet.

Now Casey Jones went from place to place,
Another train hit his train right in the face.
Peoples got off but Casey Jones stayed on,
Natural born eastman but he's dead and done.
Dead and gone, he's dead and gone.
He's a natural born eastman but he's dead and gone.

Here come the biggest boy comin right from school,
Hollerin and cryin like a daggone fool.
"Look here, mama, is our papa dead?
Woman's goin on and outted out in red.
Real good shoes and their evenin gown,
Following papa to the buryin ground.
To the buryin ground, to the buryin ground,
Followin papa down to the buryin ground."

"Now tell the truth, mama," he say, "is that a fact,
Papa got killed on the I.C. track?"
"Quit cryin, boy, and don't do that,
You got another daddy on the same damn track,
On the same track, on the same track,
Said you got another daddy on the same track."

The final verse apparently stems from the vaudeville version, which
was supposedly slanderous since Jones's wife was totally faithful to
him. Alan Lomax in *Folk Song U.S.A.* reports stanzas very similar to
stanzas three, four, and six in James's song,[51] so James's version was
not original, but it was delivered in his individual style, forceful and
convincing, as if James himself had known Casey Jones. That is due

in part to James's reporting of dialogue, his profanity at one point, and his reference to Cincinnati in stanza one. Unfortunately, the Illinois Central did not run from Cincinnati to Newport News—the Chesapeake and Ohio did—so his attempt to personalize the story actually falsifies it in terms of the historical narrative. However, it does supply a slight suggestion that James was familiar with Cincinnati.

James's recording of "Lonesome Day Blues" suggests that he was familiar with at least one of the three versions of "Stop and Listen" recorded by the Mississippi Sheiks in 1930 and 1932, which in turn drew their inspiration from Tommy Johnson's "Big Road Blues," recorded in 1928.[52] Of course, James doesn't have the delicate falsetto that Tommy Johnson has, but the sound of his rough-hewn voice rasping that falsetto leap is a thing of beauty in its own right, and when he exhorts us to "stop and listen" and asks, as Ma Rainey did in her 1928 recording of "Hear Me Talking to You," whether he's being heard, one does indeed stop and listen:

> Now today's been a long lonesome day, you hear me talkin to you,
>   did you hear what I say?
> Lawd, today has been a long old lonesome day.
> And now my rider, eee, eee, Lawd, will be the same old way.
>
> I been to the nation, round the territory, you hear me talkin to you?
>   Got to reap what you sow.
> I been all through the nation and round the territory,
> But I ain't found no heaven on earth, Lawd, nowhere I go.
>
> I'm goin to the big house and I don't even care, Don't you
>   hear me talkin to you? I'm scoldin to my dear,
> I'm goin in the mornin and I don't even care.
> I might get four or five years, Lawd, I might get the chair.
>
> Ow, stop and listen, see what tomorrow bring, you hear me talkin
>   to you? Start to playin,
> You better stop now and listen and see what tomorrow bring.
> It might bring you sunshine, Lawd, and it may bring rain.
>
> Some got six months, some got a solid year, you hear me talkin
>   to you, buddy, what made you stop by here?
> Some of em got six months, pardners, and some got a solid year,
> But I believe, my pardner, Lawd, got lifetime here.

James's first verse is very similar to the opening verse of the Sheiks' 1930 "Stop and Listen," but his "stop and listen" verse four is not the same. James's reference to having been to the "Nation" alludes to the "Indian Nation, which became part of the state of Oklahoma in 1907" and included pockets of black Indians,[53] and if the song is taken to be autobiographical, which it is not necessarily, then we can assume that James was both widely traveled and as rough and rugged as his voice and piano sound, facing the "big house" and "the chair" as he does. In fact, Paul Oliver reported that James "was reputedly on parole from prison when he made his four titles."[54] However, the song is a pastiche of traditional and well-known lyrics from blues hits combined in James's inimitable style, so this may just be James singing as a "mythical bluesman" rather than singing as himself.

James's final recording, "Highway 61," makes another tentative tie between James and Memphis since the song was "a blues standard performed by virtually all Memphis musicians of the period."[55] Of course, Memphis singers were not the only people familiar with Highway 61, which ran from New Orleans through Memphis to St. Paul, but Memphians Jack Kelly's and Will Batts's versions from 1933 are justly prized, and Jack Kelly's first version, his first recording, was his biggest seller.[56] Jesse James's first verse is virtually the same as the first verse of Kelly's, which was copied by Batts. All of James's other verses are different, though, and they reveal the extent of his wanderlust:

> I'm a leave here in the mornin out on highway 61, (x2)
> And if I catch my woman, Lawd, won't we have fun.
>
> I have heard people talkin, say the Greyhound bus can't run, (x2)
> If you don't believe it meet me in the mornin out on highway 61.
>
> I'm gwine leave you, baby, on highway 61, (x2)
> So you can stick your head out the window and look at the Greyound
>   bus run.
>
> I've got an angel in heaven, square St. Peter up for me,
> Angel in heaven, square St. Peter up for me,
> Say if you don't catch her on highway 61, Jesse, take God to tell
>   where she could be.
>
> I had me a girl, "What make you like 61 so?"
> My friends all have asked me, "What make you like 61 so?"
> I say I like it cause it's on the highway, and it rolls by my baby's door.

On this last cut before Walter Coleman took over the vocal chores, James is joined by the jug player present on the Coleman sides, and the two combine to create a blues that is not as supercharged as the previous three recordings, though James has not inched one iota toward the Perry Como school of vocal delivery. Lyrically, James indulges in a bit of outrageousness: the idea of getting an angel to work a deal with St. Peter in one's best interest is surely the creation of a metaphysical hustler. Perhaps that is a good way to characterize

James: part hustle, part humor, part hubris, a straight shooter, a seventh son of a seventh son born with—well, a unique personality, a powerful singer and player and, very unfortunately, an under-recorded artist.

These are the recorded artists who were associated with the Cincinnati blues scene in the twenties and thirties.[57] Although none were major blues stars in terms of record sales or influence on other blues performers, Stovepipe is of great interest historically and musically, and Cole/Coleman and Jesse James recorded a number of songs worthy of being called blues classics—in fact, "Southern Casey Jones" was reissued on an LP entitled *Country Blues Classics Vol. 1*. But these recorded artists represent only a small number of the blues artists who performed in Cincinnati during that period. The others we will never hear, for the most part, but we can hear about them from the people who knew them and played with them, and we can still hear the stories of people like Pigmeat Jarrett, who began playing in the second decade of this century but never recorded until the seventies, and James Mays, another performer from the early days, who has not yet recorded but whose performances have entertained generations of listeners. The blues of the twenties still have a few of their original players left, so they are not gone yet. But we must hear from those players soon, before they've been here and gone.

4

Pigmeat Jarrett

I had been researching the history of the blues in Cincinnati for several years by the time I first met Pigmeat Jarrett, but only in my spare time off from school, and though "George Street Stomp" on the original LP *That Jug Band Sound* (OJL 19) had led me down to what remained of George Street and my brief contact with Patfoot Charlie Collins, I hadn't been able to dig up much else save for a few references from Cincinnati city directories. But since Collins had told me that he walked to the West End every day to see his friends, and since they weren't all right there on George Street, it seemed logical for me to head on down a few blocks past the opulence of Cincinnati City Hall to the squalor of the West End to see what, if anything, any of the people, ranging in age from babies to octogenarians, who hung out on the street corners, at pool halls and pony kegs, or at makeshift shelters or portable barbecue stands on the street, knew of the blues musicians of the past. Out front of a pool hall near Central and David, several black men in their forties told me, "Oh, you want Pigmeat. He's way back there. He knew all of those guys back there." They directed me to a small shack on David Street about the size of a one-car garage, set right up to the sidewalk where you could rap on the door as you walked past.

The person who rattled open the door the cold winter day I knocked was about 5'4", maybe 100 pounds, dressed in an old suit and wearing a hat, even though he was inside. In fact, I haven't seen Pigmeat when he wasn't wearing a hat more than once, and *then* he was very upset that someone had removed it from his head. When I asked about blues in the twenties, Pigmeat responded, with terse replies, suspicious, I suppose, of my interest; and though he invited me in, he remained elusive in his replies and in a sense has always been protective of his past and privacy, although my latest interviews with him have been much more successful. Inside it was very hot, maybe 80 degrees, doubtless due to an overworked stove-heater in the middle of the room, and very crowded with items like radios, record players, and televisions that needed repairing and various suits and shirts hanging from shelves and whatever else could accommodate a hanger.

What he gave me that day was names, names of many blues players who had been here, and one other offhand remark: he used to play. Piano. Since I was working at WAIF radio, a community access radio station located in the Black Walnut Hills section of Cincinnati on which I had a weekly radio show at the time, I had access to a piano, and I suggested we get together and get him to a piano. He agreed to meet me on Saturday for that purpose, but because of previous field experience, I didn't really expect him to show up just like that. It was nothing about Pigmeat in particular that made me feel that way, you understand, but countless difficulties with all sorts of informants that made me the cynic. I was delighted to be wrong this time when Pigmeat answered his door that Saturday ready to go and we headed for Victory Parkway and the Alms Hotel to put Pigmeat in front of a piano for the first time, he said, in about twenty years. One of the great things about WAIF was its flexibility and the unselfishness of its staff. That morning Smokey Joe Bakan was doing his show, a kind of potpourri of music and talk, when Pigmeat and I arrived and went down into WAIF's outer studio, separated by a wall and one pane of glass from the control room, so that the noise from the studio could vaguely be heard there. Pigmeat walked up to the piano in his own unhurried fashion, a seeming mixture of modesty, boredom, unassuming pride, and weariness that undercuts any expectations you might have about a quality performance, tested a few notes from one end of the keyboard to another by tapping them with a mechanical karate chop motion, shook his head sadly, and proceeded to transform the worn-out piano, and his life, with his playing. Joe Bakan heard it, and he looked at me, and I at him, and he rushed to get patch cords and microphones and stands to put this man on the air immediately. Of course, the audience couldn't see his bouncing, rolling, flamboyant playing style, and we weren't miking his stomping feet, which he uses in such a marvelous percussive way, but many people would be able to see him from that point on, in the City Artists' Program, or at Arnold's, or Cory's, or Bogart's, or some festival; and they could hear him at least as he played and sang those lines "I advise all you young men please don't be no fool like me." He is, of course, nobody's fool.

Once on the way to a job in Pennsylvania while he was asleep, I talked with guitarist Phil Buscema about some songs that we were going to play that night and Phil made like he was going to remove that hat, Pigmeat as still as a statue. But once Phil's hand got near—not *on*, mind you—the hat, Pigmeat's eye shot open and he warned, "You don't mess with my hat, now," and then resumed his pose, aware of everything that was going on around him while keeping us off guard with his act. He slept, I think, for the rest of the trip.

James Jarrett, Jr., was born around 1899 in Cordele, Georgia, in Crisp County, where U.S. 280 crosses I-75, south of Macon. His father, James Jarrett, Sr., was "geech," that is "geechee," which refers specifically to "blacks from the Ogeechie River country in Georgia, the southern part of South Carolina, and the adjoining sea islands"[1] where there are residents who even today can still speak Gullah, "an old mixture of native African and possibly nineteenth-century English."[2] Pigmeat still speaks the dialect today on occasion, proudly, as if it implies membership in a very exclusive club, which perhaps it does, to put the more "educated" about him in their places. James Sr. and his wife Ollie Jarrett, along with their three-year-old son, moved to a mining camp in Rockhouse, Kentucky, where his father worked as a miner for five or six years.

At that point the family (Pigmeat was one of fourteen children) moved to Cincinnati, setting up residence, according to Pigmeat, on Carpenter Street in the East End. City directories, however, show James M. and Ollie H. Jarrett living at a house at 4795 Morse Street, which was east of Eastern Avenue, from 1916 through 1920. Pigmeat recalls walking from his East End residence downtown to the Harriet Beecher Stowe School, which he says was on McFarland Street but was actually at West Fifth Street, and slightly later at 635 West Seventh, at Seventh and Cutter. Pigmeat remembers clearly his principal, the first black female public school principal in Cincinnati, Jennie D. Porter, and a teacher, Miss Drayton, who allowed him to play the piano at school. The teacher was almost certainly Lillian Drayton, who W. P. Dabney listed as a teacher at Stowe,[3] and who, along with his mother, was instrumental in getting Pigmeat started at the piano:

That's where I learned how to play. I'se stayin after school, cleanin off the blackboard, take up the pencils, and while she would be gettin dressed to go home, she would let me bang on the piano. That was my teacher. Her name was Miss Drayton. I'd be playin on the piano, I'd done heard the band play, play the march, and I'd learn how to play the march. Yeah. And then from then on every evenin, she'd let me clean up things, play the piano. And then when I come outta school, no more school, my mom, she

had a great big old, one of them great big old baby grands—well, they'se
better than these they got now. I'd pick on it, but I couldn't play it, nothin
like that. Cause she always played church songs, me mom did, see. Me
mom could play a little. Church songs. Things like that. And if I be tryin
to play the blues she—what I done heard, you know—she'd run me out
of it! Yeah, so, when I got up about seventeen years old, I run away from
home.[4]

It is an old story, the parental prohibition against playing the blues,
one heard time and time again from blues performers over the years,
and Pigmeat's solution found him going not only to another residence
but another state. A white man named Tony took Pigmeat to his residence on Fourth Street in Newport, Kentucky, and there kept him
and fed him for several years with the consent of Pigmeat's parents.
Up to that time Pigmeat had heard some blues music on the victrola
at various functions and box suppers, but he heard much more of it
in the speakeasies in Southgate Alley, where the bootleg liquor flowed
and the dice would shake, rattle, and roll continually. However, the
area was not rough, according to Pigmeat—no fighting, cussing, or
snatching pocketbooks, and the law would just sit drunks up along-
side the wall on the sidewalks rather than run them into jail. In addition, the food was cheap, so Pigmeat found himself in a milieu he
enjoyed, hearing more blues, and learning how to play them. Ultimately, Pigmeat moved to Southgate Alley, just below the police station, and remained there until a family tragedy brought him back
across the river to permanent Cincinnati residence.

That tragedy was the death of his father, at this time working for
the Union Gas and Electric Co., who choked and strangled on a meal
of cornbread and buttermilk and, in Pigmeat's words, "bust his
heartstring." Pigmeat doesn't remember exactly when this was, but
James M. Jarrett disappears from the city directories in 1921, as does
Ollie, who appears again in 1930 and in 1933–34, listed as the
widow of James and as living in the West End at 421 Clinton. At any
rate, Pigmeat was back in Cincinnati, and with several years of blues
playing under his belt, he was ready to join a thriving blues scene.

One of the qualities of which Pigmeat is most proud is his originality, his striving to express his own emotion and personality in his
music. Others he had heard play, but what he wanted to hear from
himself was himself: he had heard the rest, now he wanted to hear
Pigmeat's best:

I started to make it up myself. I said, "Well, shoot, if they can do that, I
can do better n that." Than I would try to play somethin different from

them, different. . . . So I started to playin, makin up somethin myself. Well, I know if they can do that, I can do that. Well, now my sister was pretty good on the writin. Yeah, my sister, she read music, you understand? And she tried to show me how to read and do that. And "No, I can beat that hustle! Hm. Mm. I can beat that." In here and in here [points to heart and head]. See, the way I play, I play somethin that I can feel myself like if I wanted to play somethin about you or something like that, it come to me, it just come to me. Just like you there, like you done wrote it, and I'm readin it, you know what I mean, it just come to me. I couldn't read a note ifn one or twenty of em was in front of me. But I bet I can play just what you play, you understand? I like to play some of my own, you know. Now, I hear your tune, some tune like that, I can play it. But I don't play it. I make my own tune and see how it sound. "Now that don't sound like he played it. Believe I'll play it this way. Sounds alright to me!" And then when I go to the function, I play it and see do anybody holler and get up and try to dance, you know. They wasn't doin no walkin, no how, the house be like that, you know? They'd holler and they be slippin them pennies and dimes and nickels, man, that was money, that was good money! Oh, man, sometimes I'd have pockets full! I'd have pockets full! And that made me feel that much better, then I got so I commenced to singin better and better. Well, I had a pretty good voice. Singin ALL night long! Shit. Man, sometimes I'd have twenty-thirty dollars, and man that was heaps of money. *Boy*, that was heaps of money! Bought me a little old suit, with the straps on [laughs], with the straps [laughs]. Them damn button shoes [laughs]. You know, with the [laughs] on it. Them was so tight, but they pretty, you know [laughs].

Clearly Pigmeat, and other performers, put a premium on originality, and there was a great deal of friendly competition among piano players. One of the best was Psycheye Willie, a tall, dark brownskin pianist with gaps in his teeth, a fine singer who stomped his feet when he played the piano—something Pigmeat picked up and incorporated into his own performances.[5] The technique gives a percussive restlessness to Pigmeat's sound, the stomping and sliding simulating not only stick and brush work on a drum head but also a lot of leather and concrete wear on a shoe bottom. Pigmeat said of Psycheye, "But boy, that man could sing and stomp," and he described an encounter in a Cincinnati speakeasy with Psycheye: "He told me, he said, 'Come on. Rest me up.' If there were five piano players there, all of em got a chance to play. You know what I mean. Cause they wanted to hear em, you know. And I started to playin! Well, I played the boogie woogie for a while, then I said, 'Now, everybody playing that.' But I played it a little different, see. Yeah, he brought out the boogie woogie. Nobody but Psycheye. Psycheye Willie, that's his name.

Psycheye Willie . . . but Pinetop Smith didn't bring *that* out. Psycheye Willie! He was the onliest man ever to bring that out." Little else is remembered about Psycheye; he never recorded, and only pianist Big Joe Duskin of other interviewees remembered him, as a man who ran the kids away when they clustered around him. And though it is unlikely that he brought out the boogie woogie as Pigmeat claims—the music had previously been known by such names as "fast western" and "the rocks," and had been recorded by artists like Jimmy Blythe as early as 1924[6]—he will always be remembered by Pigmeat as the man who brought out the boogie woogie in Cincinnati.

Pigmeat also recalled that not only was musical talent necessary but showmanship as well. In the speakeasies and later in the clubs, and especially in the days when vaudeville was playing on Central Avenue between Fourth and Fifth, flamboyance was the order, and Pigmeat filled it: "See, I used to could do tricks, too, see. Yeah, I used to be playin the piano. . . . I didn't have no mike—didn't know what a damn mike was! [Laughs] . . . This is the piano here, and I used to be pretty active. I used to do tricks anyhow. And I would get up on the piano, they'd keep in time because of my feet, and then I'd be sayin, I'd be sayin . . ." At this point Pigmeat stood up and began performing with a bouncing walk and a puckish slyness.

> Whatcha gonna do when your rent come around?
> Nobody to pay but mm mm.
> Then I'd say:
> No more money can you pay.
> So that throwed you and me to be put outdoors.
> Ain't that a mm mm mm?

You understand, put some in. But you could say the real words. You understand what I mean, because this is in the club, you understand what I mean? See? But you see, the way I played the Dirty Dozens, I changed it because you can read between the lines . . . and I used to could dance, too, don't let nobody jive you. Yes indeedy. Used to walk on my hands. Shit. I got a kick out of that.

And so, we can imagine, did Pigmeat's audiences. "I wasn't nothin but a clown," Pigmeat added, and with his band, including Sam, Buster on drums, and Raymond on sax (Pigmeat doesn't remember their last names), he was free to clown as much as he wanted.

Some of the places he played didn't sound like joints to clown around in—too much, anyway—but names can be deceiving: "We played down the Bucket of Blood—that was down on Freeman. Yeah, shit . . . Aw, now, they just called it that . . . that's where they had all that, well they mostly, that's where they had all that, well, that pork rind was goin good. Pork rind, home brew, and all that shit." Somehow, pork rind wasn't what you would expect Pigmeat to be leading up to in his discussion. The name "Bucket of Blood," of course, wasn't original: many joints had the name and it turns up regularly in toasts that deal with "bad" men. Big Joe Duskin suggested that it got its name when a man got punched in the face and bled a great deal all over his clothes; James Mays added, "Too many nonsense people went in there. I seen two guys cut each other to death. That's why they called it 'The Bucket of Blood.'"[7] There was another place called the Bloody Bucket out on Camargo Pike in Madisonville, another place where many black musicians played a great deal. It is likely that both took their names from black folklore rather than from some earned reputation, though they may have earned that reputation after the fact.

Another local musician that Pigmeat recalled was Baby Ruth, a man whose ability and reputation rivaled Stovepipe's. Baby Ruth, too, was a one-man band, and a fine guitarist and harmonica player. Pigmeat recalled playing with him and Sam Wright:

> Baby Ruth . . . Hell, he was, by hell he was a *guitar* player! Yeah, he played with me. Yeah, we played, we played up the Cotton Club. Then we played on Sixth Street. Then we played Mom's. She moved up on Sixth Street . . . Sixth and John. Boy that was a helluva place. . . . [Baby Ruth] went to, he went to, he went down there in, he went to Georgia, and he tried to get me to come down there . . . last time I heard he was doin good. That's been a many moons ago, now. That's been a long time. Now he could play a guitar. And Sam Wright. Them old timers, them was the best blues made around. Yeah, shit. Talk about make that guitar talk, heh, they'd *make* em talk! Yeah . . . sometimes you'd see em use bottlenecks, you know. You understand what I mean. Yeah.

We remember George Herman Ruth and the candy bar now, but unfortunately the musician, unrecorded, is a fading memory, like guitarist Sam Wright, mandolinist Dude, pianist C. Bailey, and sentimental pianist Lonzo.

However, there were other performers who played the local scene from time to time in the twenties and thirties who were better known, though not commonly associated with Cincinnati blues. Pigmeat remembered Leroy Carr playing in Cincinnati, at Babe Baker's place on Sixth and Mound across from the Cotton Club's location. Carr's partner, Scrapper Blackwell, recalled vividly "Leroy and himself sitting in the show window of a music store faking a performance of one of their latest hits, mouthing the lyrics, while a loudspeaker blared the recording to all who passed by or stood gaping through the glass."[8] And then again, there was Carr's "George Street Blues," recorded August 16, 1934, which included two verses referring to Cincinnati locations:[9]

> You take me to Seventh, I'll make Fifth all by myself,
> If you take me to Seventh, I'll make Fifth all by myself,
> And when I get to Fifth and Plum, she better not have nobody else.

> When it's on Fifth and Vine, baby, take me while you can, (twice)
> When I get down Georgia line, baby, please just be my friend.

Robert Bates also recalled seeing Carr in speakeasies in the thirties, but Pigmeat claimed he played only for Babe Baker, and he explained why: "He played for Babe, Babe Baker. . . . He was runnin this place for gangsters, you understand. What you call a dago, you know. See, them was colored people, you know, friends. Dago. Yeah. They stuck with us, the colored people, you understand. If you was all right. But if you got out of place, they called the hit man for your ass. [Laughs]. That's right. I'm tellin you the true fact. That's all I ever worked for . . . they had a nice club. Well, you know, they started a beer garden and then they had the dance, right in back of where I played. Isn't that somethin?" According to Pigmeat, gangsters were the rule in the West End, and rule they did:

> Man, shit, this place used to be full of gangsters. I mean, you know what I mean. Hell, they run all the business, you know. But they put you, you know, they mark you, you understand what I mean. God damn. If you wanted to get—if I wanted to get rid of you, I put the mark on you. On the car. You couldn't see it. . . . Man, them gangsters was something else. . . . Then them guys would begin to get rough. They had some colored guys round here, boy, come from up in Chicago, and started somethin down there. They don't fuck around down there no more. . . . Yeah, all up by the reservoir and things, shit. Yeah, they go so rough down there, shit, they said "We ain't gonna get in the hornet's nest again." Cause that was a hornet's nest down here. Yes indeedy. Yeah, John, like you have Central Avenue, back down as far as you go. You didn't come down there less you was alright, you know.

However, just as Pigmeat insisted that things were not as tough and violent then as they are now on the streets, he found that the gangsters caused little trouble for musicians as well: "Aw, yeah, a musician didn't have no trouble. No kind of trouble. He had backin' everywhere. Yeah, shit. Yeah, you say somethin to me wrong or somethin like that, shit, they wouldn't say nothin to you, now, God damn, boy, but when you hit, when you hit that alley, though, when you hit them streets, in the alley you goin! They gon carry you to the alley and beat your God damn brains. Beat your damn brains out, that's right. Yeah. Catch you upside the wall or somethin." Other residents recall in later years the presence of gangsters in Cincinnati who kept somewhat of a hold on the black music scene, but it is still today not a subject discussed very readily or specifically. Suffice it to say that there were reputed gangsters here in Cincinnati whose presence was felt the same way that the presence of reputed gangsters in other cities was felt, with a mixture of violent authority but often kindheartedness and even admiration for the musicians who provided the entertainment in establishments that housed or fronted for illegal activities.

If Leroy Carr spent his time at Babe Baker's, another visitor, Fats Waller, got around a great deal more. Robert Bates saw Fats in some speakeasies; Joe Duskin shined his shoes on Clinton Street; and Pigmeat Jarrett remembers him before he hit big:

Aw, shit, yeah. I knew Fats. Me and Fats was all right. Shit. Down on Cutter and Court. Been a long time. That's been many moons, man. . . . Twenties, yeah, shit. . . . They played in the speakeasy and then, later on when they opened up the beer garden, again, you know, with the jugs that had the big kegs, you know—course, you got the wine settin up on the bar, draw the wine from that, you know. Yeah, he played all up there in Sixth Street, with them big . . . [laughs]. Boy, he sure had some lips on him. . . . Man, he clowned, hell, yeah, boy, he clowned [imitates smacking lips]. Boy he tickled me. Yeah. But you woulda never thought he'd a made it, though. Aah, shit . . . first he started off he wasn't doin shit cause he was playin up there at Pickett's, up there next to where I was playin at . . . on Sixth Street. Now, see, Pickett's had one of them, well, they had stoves and things, you know, and like you got an old stove, gettin them stoves and—wood stove, coal stove, you know. Painted, they had that whatchamacallit, paint there make that stove look just like brand new. Yeah. That was a drawin card, you was playin in there, see. Yeah, well, that drew people tention, you know.[10]

Pigmeat's memory of Fats Waller's fame is a bit faulty. There is no record of Waller being in Cincinnati before he arrived here to play for WLW radio in 1932. By that time Waller had been recording under his own name for ten years, on piano and pipe organ, had recorded two vocal sides in 1931, and had collaborated in the shows *Keep Shufflin'* and *Hot Chocolates*. By that time he had published over sixty songs, including "Squeeze Me," "Ain't Misbehavin'," "Honeysuckle Rose," "What Did I Do to Be So Black and Blue," and "I'm Crazy 'bout My Baby," so Waller was hardly an unknown. However, his successful popular/vocal career was ahead of him, and his radio exposure on WLW and in New York "doubtless increased his fame and popularity, and must have influenced executives at the Victor Talking Machine Company in their decision to offer Waller a contract, which gave them the exclusive right to record him."[11]

In the autumn of 1932 Waller's new manager Phil Ponce booked Waller for "Fats Waller's Rhythm Club," a series of shows on WLW radio, and on the late-night show "Moon River," which "consisted entirely of classics, light classics and ballads."[12] Cincinnati Conservatory of Music student Kay C. Thompson recalled Waller's mugging at her through the studio window the first time she met him,[13] and a pianist and singer from Xenia, Ohio, Una Mae Carlisle, recalled a similar experience.[14] The one-shot appearance that grew into a two-year engagement was a real boost to Waller's career, offering him the chance to perform his jazz on piano and classical selections on the organ, and to appear in a skitlike format that allowed Waller to play a deacon who listened to a member of his flock confess to being "infected by jazz" and who ultimately succumbed himself—to use his humor.[15]

Waller's son Maurice recalled that the family moved into a "little white house near the Cincinnati airport," where he knew he was far from Harlem when he "first saw those trolley cars equipped with cowcatchers,"[16] and the two years in Cincinnati were full of ups and downs for Fats. Waller did have some annoying habits, though, including his "habit of tossing empty gin bottles into the organ loft,"[17] and Cincinnati columnist Mary Wood reported that Fats was fired by Powel Crosley when he heard Waller "desecrating the organ dedicated to his mother by playing jazz on it,"[18] although Ed Kirkeby reports that it was a misunderstanding with Ponce that ended the engagement.[19] Regardless, Waller brought his brand of jazz and occasional blues to Cincinnati and was, according to Pigmeat, a regular in the speakeasies.

Of course, Waller was more of a jazz player than a blues player— and Cincinnati had quite a few jazz players here, too, including trumpeter Bill Coleman, who lived here from 1909 to 1927, cornetist Wild Bill Davison, who performed with Roland Potter's Peerless Players, pianist Charles Alexander, tenor saxist Edgar "Spider" Courance, guitarist Richard "Hacksaw" Harney, and many others[20]—but he could play the blues where he wanted to, and surely he did at some point during his Cincinnati tenure, poised at the piano near that painted stove at Pickett's generating his own Fats Waller brand of heat and quenching what has been described as his prodigious gin thirst. He was, one suspects, a welcome addition to the scene.

Other musicians Pigmeat recalled were "Little Joe," a small, brownskin man who "blowed his mouth like a horn." Little Joe followed Leroy Carr into Babe Baker's and was, according to Pigmeat, the first black man in Cincinnati broadcast over the radio. Pigmeat also remembered Black Boy Shine (whose real name was Harold Holiday), who played "down there on Fifth Street." Cleveland Green, too, recalled Black Boy Shine, as well as Leroy and Buddy Carr, Waller, and Peg Leg Bates playing the Midnight Rambles frequently.[21] Black Boy Shine recorded in 1935–37 in Fort Worth, Dallas, and San Antonio, in a style associated with Texas blues piano, but it seems that he did spend enough time in Cincinnati at some point to leave an impression on local residents. Inevitably others were around in Cincinnati in the twenties and thirties, playing their blues in the joints and speakeasies, or playing spirituals, like the blind "genius" Roosevelt Lee recalled hearing here in the thirties.[22] But as time passed and the music changed, larger clubs began to predominate, and although musicians continued to play on the streets, the jug band and speakeasy era began to draw to a close. Larger bands, often with horn sections, took over at spots like the Cotton Club at Sixth and Mound—Pigmeat had a larger band himself including Sam, Buster on drums and Raymond on sax.

The Cotton Club was the most important club in Cincinnati in terms of booking and promoting black entertainers. The club was housed in the Hotel Sterling on Sixth and Mound, which had originally been the ornate Carlisle House, then a residence hotel, then temporary headquarters for a Jewish congregation, and even a hospital. But when the neighborhood became increasingly black, the hotel became a hotel for blacks as well. Hotel manager Nathan Michelson, a white man, turned the Grand Ballroom into the Cotton Club after an unsuccessful stab at making a skating rink profitable and, Prohibition notwithstanding, the club was a great success. After Michelson died, hotel owner William H. Menke leased the ballroom to Harry Ferguson, whose widow took over when he died in 1947, and the club lasted into the late fifties. Finally, it was bought by the city in 1960 and leveled in 1962. But the club is remembered for its class acts and great talent, especially when Lee Rainey, who subleased from Ferguson and booked acts, presided. And it was known for its famous visitors: Joe Louis, Mae West, Ezzard Charles (owner of the Coliseum at Seventh and Mound), Pearl Bailey, and many others frequented Cincinnati's only integrated nightclub of the time, and they helped make the club the attraction that it was for its patrons.[23]

"The Cotton Club was the biggest thing going, then," Pigmeat Jarrett told me, and Big Joe Duskin recalled it as a beautiful ballroom packed with the best and most exciting musicians in town.[24] You could meet famous out-of-towners there, like Joe did, or Lonnie Bennett, who recalled sneaking in when he was underage; or you could make local connection like Big Ed Thompson did when he met H-Bomb Ferguson there. To Philip Paul it was a mecca, exciting, always a calibre show, and it was important to have such a showplace for the best black talent, there in the neighborhood, where people could see not only Lonnie Johnson, Tiny Bradshaw, Illinois Jacquet, Earl Bostic, Hank Ballard, Duke Ellington, and Count Basie but locals like Pigmeat, Big Ed Thompson, Nelson Burton, and others on the same stage.[25] Like its Harlem namesake, it was a drawing card and galvanizer, an important night spot for blues and jazz performers, and an important part of Cincinnati history.

As musical styles changed, it became more difficult for the old-timers to get jobs playing in local clubs unless their styles changed as well. Eventually, Pigmeat quit playing in the forties. During the fifties he did plumbing and electrical work, and later odd jobs around a funeral home on the corner of David Street.

Pigmeat's comeback was remarkable in that even though he hadn't played piano in some thirty years, it all came back to him very quickly, and his talent was recognized with grants from the City Artist's Program, which sent him traveling to schools and senior citizen centers to play his music, engagements at places like the John Henry Folk Festival and at night spots around the United States and in Canada, and a recording contract from June Appal records. It was on one of WAIF's Blues Cruises that I was approached about producing a recording session for Pigmeat to be released on the June Appal label. The session went remarkably well considering the circumstances. It was recorded at Watson Recital Hall at the University of Cincinnati College Conservatory of Music, a place where Pigmeat had never been before, on a piano he had never played before. Because portable equipment was brought to the city to do the recording and time was tight, the session started at 7 A.M. on July 18, 1979—awfully early in the morning to garner good music from most performers, much less a seventy-five-year-old man. Still, Pigmeat, his skills honed by engagements on WAIF radio's Blues Cruises on the river and appearances at local bars Arnold's and Coco's,[26] persevered and overcame the adverse conditions, buoyed by the fact that the June Appal Company paid him—and very well—in advance for his efforts.

It did take some getting used to, though, this recording business. Pigmeat's performing aesthetic was that of the barrelhouse performer, whose task it was to set up and sustain a rhythm for the dancers, continuing indefinitely—as long as the dancers could hold out and remain interested. At that rate Pigmeat's LP would have contained two songs, maybe, and not sustained the interest of the record buyer listening to the music in the privacy of the home. After several long takes, though, and some coaching about how to construct and pace the song for a three to four minute recording, Pigmeat picked up the recording knack and worked well.

Partially because of the request of Pigmeat and June Appal, and partially to add diversity to the LP, guitar by Ed Thompson and harmonica by myself were added on three tunes each. For one thing, Pigmeat's style was not as driving as it used to be, and it was felt that some accompaniment would add impetus to the songs. In addition, Pigmeat performs in three keys—not bad for a blues pianist, really— and the use of harmonica in two positions and guitar was meant to help vary the sound of the recordings as much as possible without violating Pigmeat's music. Ed Thompson, then playing with Albert Washington, was one of the if not *the* only non–B. B. King blues stylist in town, and was judged most likely to maintain the flavor of Pigmeat's music while still updating it a bit from its twenties roots. I had been playing with Pigmeat at WAIF, on Blues Cruises aboard the Johnston Party Boat "Chaperone," and at Arnold's and Miss Kitty's for some time. Still, the instrumentation was a bit of a change from what Pigmeat had been used to for much of his career, though he had in fact performed with bands that featured rhythm sections and horns. The LP, then, represents not so much Pigmeat as he actually plays—he *never* plays songs as short as the LP cuts—but as he was asked to present his talent in a different medium. Whether such interference with the creative artist represents undue meddling or not is, of course, open to question, but ultimately a greater range of Pigmeat's talent is displayed in the limited parameters of the LP disc as a result of the practice.

What still comes through is Pigmeat's approach. He performed in the studio as he does in the club—like he's on the street, or on the front stoop, in the West End among his friends. He sings of storms ("Thundering and Lightning") and stresses ("Don't You Feel Bad"), yelling at friends that pass by (spending almost the entirety of "Hey Joe" shouting just that, exactly as if he expects an answer), hamming it up, especially on his hilarious version of the "Dirty Dozens," a verbal game that consists of a contest of insults involving one's relatives that was probably first recorded by the Scrap Iron Jazz Band in Paris around 1918, though it was much better known on record through the three versions recorded by Speckled Red in 1929 and 1930.[27] Also of interest is Pigmeat's version of "Mr. Freddie," which Pigmeat claims his own. However, it is clearly related to J. H. Shayne's 1924 version with Priscilla Stewart and to Jimmy Blythe's 1926 version as well, though Pigmeat does add his own touches.[28] And Pigmeat's "Walking Blues," complete with miked shoe steps, is a swinging romp over the gin-stained sawdust floors of haze-filled back room gambling joints.

Reviewers responded variously to the LP. Fred Dellar of *New Musical Express* called it "practically a piano blues lesson," and A. Coats rated it "excellent," calling it "a joyous reflection on life." Gary M. Pitkin went one step further and wrote that the album "belongs in all blues and Americana collections." But Chris Lunn criticized the production and sound quality, finding the harmonica and guitar "unnecessary," though he had only praise for Pigmeat's contributions. Leonard Duckett, however, found the harp to be "down and dirty" and Thompson's guitar to be "very effective, giving depth to the music and reinforcing the piano voice."[29] Finally, the LP seems to reflect Pigmeat's weaknesses and strengths: he is not the most agile improviser, nor does he have a barreling barrelhouse bass—his right hand is not lightning and his left hand doesn't thunder—but his sparse, subtle, insinuating playing can sneak up under the arches of your loafers and set them to work, and the quavery vibrato from the back of his throat can switch from delicate to piercing, from pianissimo to darn near fortissimo, with great unexpectancy. Pigmeat was justly proud of these recordings, as he was of the two cuts, "Pigmeat's Name" and "Freddy," another version of "Mr. Freddie," that he recorded for the TEME (Traditional Ethnic Music and the Elderly) project designed and produced by Malcolm Dalglish and Grey Larsen in 1978 and 1979 and released on the June Appal LP *Snow on the Roof, Fire in the Furnace.* Those recordings, his continued performances, and the efforts of people like his friend Carolyn Clark helped Pigmeat land a place at the 1992 Chicago Blues Festival, as well as a "Pigmeat Jarrett Day" in Cincinnati on June 19, 1992, at which time he performed at the main Public Library for a crowd on hand and the local cable video cameras.

Recently Pigmeat celebrated a birthday, somewhere around his ninety-third, at Cory's, a local nightclub in Clifton, where he holds down the piano stool on Monday nights, and a number of his friends showed up to wish him well. He has made a great many friends outside of the West End in the past few years, white friends, friends he wouldn't have made if he hadn't returned to music. He always remembers wistfully his experience at the Winnepeg Folk Festival in Canada, when 15,000 fans howled and cheered their approval of his playing. Once he told me about it, suddenly getting very quiet and as sad as I'd ever seen him. He shook his head regretfully: "If all this had happened just thirty years ago, forty years ago. Back then I could play, there were things I could do. If it had happened then, it would have been great. But it's happening now."[30] Pigmeat needn't worry. He has seen a great many things: the death of his friends and fellow musicians, the death of his wife Margaret and his friend Loreatha, the deterioration of the West End, even a hernia operation in 1991, at which time blues musicians from around the city demonstrated their love for him by performing at a benefit at Cory's. He has also seen his rebirth as a musician and the resurrection of a piano style that will last as long as musicians continue to return to that fountain of youth known as the blues. Pigmeat's signature: "My name is Big Time Black, Muck the Muck Man, Chief of Black Diamond, some call him lucky, but he gone again, better known as E. D., Walso, Steno, jive for short. This is old Pigmeat, y all. Thank y all."[31]

5

James Mays

Doris Van Owen was my senior high Sunday school teacher at Oakley United Methodist Church. She was also a grade school teacher, sweet, proper, kind. One Sunday during class she told me she knew the nicest black man who was a janitor at her school who played harmonica for the kids, sometimes in the halls, sometimes in classes. She knew I would be interested, being a harmonica player myself and being interested in black music as well. The man I finally met in the neat, well-kept home in Walnut Hills near DeSales Corner proved to be a first-rate harmonica soloist in a style reminiscent of the gentle lower-register work of Jazz Gillum, with the control and tone of a sedate Deford Bailey, but with a real country blues feel to the comping chords he played in between his single-note runs. He performed songs like "Boots and Shoes," "You Better Mind," and "Tuxedo Junction" with an ease and grace that stems from a well-spent life of dignity, honor, hard work, and faith in God. Soft-spoken, with a friendly and loving smile, he called me Stevie, and still does, the first person to do so since my Aunt Leah Rae called me that many years ago. It feels good.

The pleasure Mr. Mays took from playing for the children at Parham School was a joy to behold. He loved to play for them, they loved to hear him, and his warm beautiful tone and stately vibrato on his church songs matched that love note for note. This was clearly not the wild liver, the hard drinker, the womanizer, the unrepentant bluesman of legend. This was a man who took his hardships with patience, lived his life with perseverance, and put forth his emotions in both sacred and secular song with a gentle, burr clover voice that was a distillation of the aged and mellow sweetness of black music. On July 22, 1979, when he appeared on a show on Cincinnati's Channel 48 entitled "Cincinnati Blues" along with myself, Joe Duskin, Pigmeat Jarrett, and Albert Washington and the Astros, he made no

flamboyant finger rolls, made no long introductions to his songs, in-
dulged in no histrionics. He played, he finished, he played again—
calmly, evenly, as if he is grateful that he can play. And, in fact, he is.
This talent he feels he has gotten from God is, in performance, his gift
to God and the world, and whether he plays blues or religious music,
he knows he brings some happiness into the world. That is, he
knows, godly. "Oh, I can play," he says matter of factly, without a
hint of boast or swagger, but as if it gives him a great deal of con-
tentment. I'd imagine it would.

James Mays was born on September 18, 1912, in Crawfordsville,
Georgia, remaining there until age five. However, by the time he left
Crawfordsville, he had already met the primary influence on his harmonica playing style and was, in fact, already a harp player. It was his
uncle, Myron Stewart, who first put the harmonica in his mind and
his hands, at age four:

> He came from work one day. And I asked him, I say, "Uncle Myron," I
> say, "Will you buy me one of them harps?" I'll never forget that. "Yeah,
> baby, I'll buy you one." And I said, "When?" I said, "Will you buy me
> one today?" He said, "Naw, I can't get you nary a one today." And I said,
> "Why?" He said, "Well," he say, "your uncle ain't gonna have enough
> money today." And I said, "Well, how much do they cost?" He said, "A
> quarter." I say, "A quarter!" I was four years old. I say "A quarter?" I say,
> "Well, that's not a whole lot of money, is it, Uncle Myron?" "Naw! Naw,
> baby, that ain't much money. . . ." I heard him play. Well, he could play
> good. He could play "Lost John," "John Henry," uh, he could play, uh—
> oh, he could play several kind of blues. One was the "Tuxedo Junction."
> And you know I heard him play, I said, "Uncle Myron?" I said, "Won't
> you buy me one of those harps?" And I said, "Well, when you gonna get
> it?" He said, "Next Saturday." I said, "You really gonna get me one?"
> "Yeah, I'll get you one." And he did.[1]

When his uncle got home with the harmonica that Saturday, he
wasn't quite prepared for the progress that little James would make
playing it:

> He gave me the harp and I asked him to play. I asked him to play the song
> he played "from yesterday, Uncle Myron." So he played. He played . . .
> yeah, he played "Jelly Roll Blues." That's what he played . . . he just
> played by hisself. He would play in the church. They would ask him to
> play church songs in the church, he told me so. . . . He said "Here your
> harp, baby." I run there, I said, "Thanks, Uncle Myron." I wasn't tall
> enough, I grabbed him around his legs and I hugged him. He picked me
> up, said, "Well, you welcome." And he said, "Now, what you gon do
> with this?" I said, "Well, I'm gon play it." You know, just like that. "You

gon play it!" I said, "Yes, sir I'm gon play this harp." He said, "Aw, you ain't gon play!" I said, "Yes sir, I'm gon play this harp, Uncle Myron."

So, the next Saturday when he came in from work, I say, "Uncle Myron!" I said, "You wanna hear somthin?" "Wanna hear what?" I say, "You wanna hear that piece you played for me?" He said, "Yeah, can you play it?" I say, "Sure!" I went over there and I stood between his legs, I'se standin between his legs, and he picked me up and sit me in his lap. My mother, she came out, my mother twin sister, she came out, and my grandfather, he came out, and my grandmama, she come out, my Aunt Clara, she came out, one of my aunts, they all standin there. . . . My Aunt Clara, she said "Look at that baby!" That's what she said, she said "Look at that baby playin the harp like that!" She said, "You learn him to play like this?" Uncle Myron said, "I ain't learned him nothin! He asked me to buy him a harp and I bought the harp for him. Just bought the harp last Saturday and gave it to him. And he asked me to play a piece for him. Played the same piece he heard me playin and I played it. So now he's playin it." They got excited.

The sight of a four-year-old child playing "Jelly Roll Blues" on the harmonica must have been something to see, but it was not something that Crawfordsville would see for long. When Mays was almost five his family moved to Atlanta, where they stayed through a year and a half of his schooling and then, without Mays seeing or hearing any Atlanta blues performers that he can recall, they moved to Cincinnati near Fifth and Mill, described by Mays as where the Butternut Bakery is located now, which is 747 West Fifth. Mill Street ran from the Ohio River north to 721 West Fifth Street—from Front Street to Fifth Street—and between Fourth and Fifth on Mill Street was the Barnes Alley described earlier, where a "hard" game of dice resulted in the death of a man. Mays was not quite seven years old when he moved to Cincinnati, but he remembers vividly seeing the musicians on the streets: "Oh, yeah, on the streets you could see a whole lot of different guys. You could see guys with harp in they hand, harp in they mouths; some of the guys couldn't play, they thought they was playin, you know. That's the way it was. . . . Sometimes just right in the streets cause the police hardly ever bothered em. On Linn Street was one special place. That's where this guy named Charlie Red, that's where I run into, met Charlie Red there."

Guitarist Charlie Red was later remembered by Mays as the same person as Charlie Collins, the "Dancin Charlie" of a later version of the Cincinnati Jug Band that played from 1933–34 through the fifties—without Bob Coleman. When I met Charlie Collins in 1971 at Little Jim's, a hole-in-the-wall bar located on the last remaining occupied block of George Street, Collins listed the personnel of his jug band: Charlie Collins (guitar), Johnny Johnson (washboard), Taylor Moore (bass violin), and Tom Pickett (violin), all of whom were remembered as jug band members by James Mays. Collins made no mention of any jug or harmonica, but did state that Bob Cole (*not* Coleman) was a kind of manager/booking agent. Interestingly, he did claim to have recorded, but not "George Street Stomp"; rather, he said the band recorded "Louisville Stomp" and one other side. A "Louisville Stomp" was recorded by the Dixieland Jug Blowers in Chicago in 1926, but this was a clearly a different group. There is always the possibility that the record company changed the titles of the songs and that "Louisville Stomp" could be the Cincinnati Jug Band's "Newport Blues" or "George Street Stomp." Under those circumstances, Collins would have been slightly mixed up on his date of 1933–34 for the formation of his band.

At any rate, other residents besides Mays recalled the jug band: "They sure used to raise sand up and down the street here. Somebody always had em busy playin parties in Kentucky and around."[2] As a dancer, Collins was unequaled, stealing the show from many an itinerant musician in from the South on the latest freight and collecting a stack of dollars: "Charlie was always clownin and when he danced nobody noticed what they was singin; they just throwed dollars—they sure made some money, just off me." Another man claimed, in roughly the same words seventeen years apart, "Charlie'd kick his foot so high you'd think a pistol'd go off." Pianist Big Joe Duskin remembered seeing a man, probably Collins, who put tar and bottle caps on his feet to simulate tap dancing, drawing large and enthusiastic crowds in the forties.[3] However, by the fifties the band had disbanded, and in 1971 Collins was an elusive and suspicious shadow. He spoke sparingly and suspiciously, and the last time I saw him he stated, "I'm the only one left from the band, all the others have gone," as he looked nervously to the door of Little Jim's.[4] Seconds later he was gone, and I never saw him again, though he did pick up a copy of the "George Street Blues" article that I left for him behind the bar at Little Jim's. He died around 1979, and Charlie Red, Patfoot Charlie, who walked from Walnut Hills to the West End every morning of his twilight years, and walked back in the afternoon, even though he was in his seventies, visits his George Street stomping grounds no more.

More importantly for Mays, he met guitarist Amos Johnson, and when Mays got older to where his parents would let him off his street, the two of them hooked up to form a duo, playing on the streets, where police would "stand up and look at you play, if you playin good" rather than run you off, and at box suppers.

The people was there, mostly they was there to buy fish, buy fish and drink, see. And, see, where we played at practically all the time peoples bootlegged, they sold bootleg, you know, sold whiskey, they bootleg whiskey. See. And never did have no problems. No problem. Well, there was one, I think it was one time me and Amos. Yeah, I know . . . it was down on Ninth Street somewhere. . . . Anyway, there was a guy—some woman, she just kept comin over where I was. Me and Amos sittin side by side, she kept comin over there and she said she wanted me to play another piece for her: "I likes to hear you play that harp." And I said, "Sure," I said, "I don't mind playin—" She named something or other and me and Amos played the piece. So then her boyfriend—I guess it was her boyfriend cause they was young, I guess it was him, I guess that was her boyfriend cause I don't think they was married, you know—but anyway, he come over there, snatched her away from there one time, and me and Amos was so close, and Amos, when he snatched her away, he snatched a pocket knife out. Amos did. Yeah, he was very touchy, you know. He didn't want nobody to mess with me. So he snatched his—I never will forget that. He snatched his pocket knife out and he told me, he said "Lets us go in here." He said, "See the house lady. See if she want us to play anything else cause we ain't gonna be in here long cause," he said, "this guy," he said, "he don't want his woman to talk over here and ask you to play."

Happily, there were no further difficulties at the box supper, and Mays and Johnson lived to play other functions, jobs that were more lucrative than the job selling papers that Mays had had, even though he was quite a hustler on his job. At the box suppers in the thirties, Mays and Johnson would make ten dollars a piece for three hours' work, performing songs like "Stormy Weather," "Careless Love," and a piece they "really got down on," the "M and O Blues." They seem to have rarely played originals, and I have only rarely heard Mays sing lyrics he composed himself. Their partnership was lucrative enough that they stayed together regularly for ten years, during which time Mays worked at a bakery in the daytime. In addition, Mays knew another harmonica player in the thirties, Willie B. Williams from Atlanta, but Williams stayed only about one year and he never played with Mays and Johnson.

Ultimately the two drifted apart and Mays left the bakery to work for the Cincinnati Board of Education, first as a custodian at Heberle School on Dayton and Freeman for twenty-five years, and then at Parham Elementary School for "six years, three weeks, three days." All the time he played his harp for the kids at school. Also during this time he performed on Harris Rosedale's radio and television talent shows, winning each time he was on and taking home the prize of a gold watch for his rendition of the "Mama Blues," which imitated the crying of a baby.[5]

Finally, though, the father of four with two jobs stopped playing functions in the sixties, limiting his playing to school, church, and home. Although he went to Harriet Beecher Stowe school, he sometimes sings "Ain't got no education cause I didn't go to school / but when it comes to lovin I'm a lovin fool," but one senses that, in a different way, he is right about that second part. He does love—the church, the kids, the blues. "I know the blues will pass," he says, "will pass quite fast." And he means get over, not fade away. Watching him take a pocket knife to his Hohners, cleaning them with the skill, posture, and seriousness of a micro surgeon, one can see that a dignified craftsman is at work, one who has had no trouble finding a place for the blues in his religious universe. "Jelly roll, jelly roll, ain't so hard to find," he sings, then smacks his harp against his hand and admonishes, "You better mind, you better mind, you got to give an account at the judgment, you better mind." Then he looks up and asks, "How you like that, Stevie?"

I like it just fine.

6

Big Joe Duskin

Now a blues "veteran" of some two or three years, I fully expected to find at best a mediocre imitation of pop-boogie piano when I first went to meet Big Joe Duskin at his house on Ryland Avenue in Bond Hill. Even after coming across Albert Washington, and even after my Walnut Hills High School friend Sandy Suskind, himself a fine reed player and guitarist, told me about how good Big Joe was, I still didn't expect much as I entered the comfortably furnished basement of a middle-class home through the open garage door. But once he played! I had a 78 of "Boogie Woogie Prayer" by Pete Johnson, Albert Ammons, and Meade Lux Lewis, plus several LPs of their material and recordings by Roosevelt Sykes as well, but I had never expected to hear anything like that *live;* and I had played along with those recordings, particularly that 78 since it lent my playing more authenticity (!), but I never expected to play Sonny Boy Williamson to the pianistics of a contemporary Blind John Davis. "Hey, Steve!" Joe yelled for the first of countless times over the years as I joined in while he played. He was, from the first time I met him, boisterously friendly and familiar, as he is with almost everyone he meets, speaking like a bosom friend or admiring fan rather than the object of admiration. He hadn't played out for years, he told me, though clearly the piano in his basement was getting a boogie woogie workout quite often, but now he seemed interested in playing for everyone. With his ability, his personality, and his colorful language—a bothersome person was a "no good dirty bat"; in his own hilarious and good-natured way he would talk about how he would "whup the cowboy shit out of that no good dirty bat, Steve"—he was a natural, though it wasn't immediately apparent to club owners.

A club owner from Mahogany Hall in Mount Adams—a predominantly white and "hip" hilltop community noted for its laid-back and quirky atmosphere in the seventies—called me on my job at

Zayre's department store on Colerain Avenue to ask if I could play there the following weekend with my band. When I suggested that I could do the job with a boogie woogie piano player—a great one— the owner hesitated, and it took some time to convince him that we ought to let Joe do the job for one night. One night, of course, led to a longtime engagement, as many as four nights a week of hauling electric piano and amps up Mount Adams's hills, of playing five and one-half hours and then heading downtown for White Castle cheese-burgers at 3 A.M., dreaming of European tours like those described in *Blues Unlimited Magazine,* so far away from Big Joe's beginnings.

Joseph L. Duskin was born in Birmingham, Alabama, elaborating: "over in Cottageville out from Tuxedo Junction. That was the name of the place I was born by a midwife the second month, the tenth day, and the twenty-first year, February the tenth, the twenty-first year."[1] It was a large family that Perry N. Boyd Duskin and Hattie Fuller Duskin were attempting to raise in the South where the Klan had re-cently been revitalized, in 1915, and where the political influence of the Klan was at its height in the early twenties. So the children, John, Elliot, Joe, Mary Magdalene, Alfred, Louis, Sharon, Virginia, and Matt, all shared a past blighted with the ugliness of racism. Joe was between six and seven years old when his family left Alabama, but he remembered the presence of the not so invisible "Invisible Empire":

Now, Steve, I remember back during the days, back during the Klan when they was movin. I didn't understand it, but I knew what they did and all that by hearin the old people what they talked about. And they told us any time we go in the presence of whites or whatever say "Yassur" and "No sir." Well, then we was brought up in that manner. Not only them but blacks as well, see. And I remember my cousin, Handy Fuller, he went into a store, broke in it, Steve, it was a white grocery, and he broke in the store and he stole a sack of potatoes and a loaf of bread and a chicken. And he put a note in the cash register and he said "Mr. Kramer, I know you gon find this note and I'm Handy Fuller. I broke in your store because my kids was hungry and that and I got this to feed it and I'll go to work and I'll put this back." Well, the Klu Klux Klan come and got him out of the house that night, Steve. And when they did, I'm looking at em. I saw they hoods but I couldn't understand, I thought they was ghosts, and the way I'm crying and all that, and one of em kicked me right back in the hind parts back there. I ain't never had nothin hurt me so bad in my life when this guy kicked me like that. Well, I crawled right out of the way and got into bed and I seen em when they put this rope around his neck. They says, "We gonna hang you. You'll never break in another store around here. Specially a white man's store." So they took him out, Steve, and I crawled out the back and went round through the tall weeds and I brushed em away where I could see it. And I seen em when they put him on this mule, they had his hands tied behind him. They put this big rope on his neck and said "Hit that horse on his ass as hard as you can so he can drop right from him and break that black bastard's neck." Now this is what they said. I'm tellin you what they said. Okay, when the horse, they hit the horse real hard with a whip, he runned out, my uncle—cousin—fell, and when he fell I heard his neck snap like that, see. They said "Leave the bastard stay there and let somebody come get him." They said "Now, let's do better n this. Get that mule and tie him back and drag his ass right back in front of his people and drop his black ass and leave him stay there." So that's what they did. . . . So finally I come cryin and come round the back way and told my Aunt Judy, I said "They brought cousin Handy's body and they laid it out in the drive." And she went out and she grabbed him up, Steve, because they didn't know it, they just dragged the boy there in the road. And she was huggin and crying and said "Awh, Lord, my son!" Oh, and she was just so pitiful about it and we all cried and all of that, so they buried him and that was that.

That was that! Joe narrated, matter-of-factly, a chilling commentary on the commonplace nature of Klan treachery. It wasn't Joe's only brush with the Klan in Alabama, nor was it the only one that ended in death:

There was a Doctor C. J. Hawkins that was deliverin babies and that. And this white party—I don't know whether it was J. B. Todd, I don't know who that was—called for him cause they couldn't get another doctor, he's closest one. And when they called for him my dad and them told me that Dr. Hawkins say he was goin up there to deliver the baby and said "Now, here's the message that they give on the phone. They said if I don't deliver that baby, and if I do deliver the baby and it was the baby's dead or come out dead and if he dies when he come out, then they gonna hang me." So he told my dad then, they said "Well don't go up there, Doc, let em get . . ." He say "I can't. I done swore to do this, I've got to go." So he went on up, Steve, in his little wagon and his horse and buggy, and he got out, they told me. And the old man and them say they watched him when he went in the house. Say when it was about seven, eight or nine or ten hours he didn't come back out, then they start to wonder. They had those old phones, you'd ring em like this at the time, you know. So they decide to go to the sheriff and see if the sheriff'd go up there cause his horse and buggy was still up there tied. And he went up there and they says, the sheriff knew his name was Stony Brooks. He knew my dad real bad, and he said, "Mr. Duskin," he says, "the old Doc is hung back behind the house back there." He says, "Come on go up and you can get the mule and bring him back down with his wagon and his body." And that's what they did.

Even at such a young age Joe was old enough to be familiar with piano-playing blues performers, familiar enough to run off and hear them at old shacks in the foreboding Alabama night, but even those memories are colored by the Klan:

I used to go through the swamps, Steve, and when I'd hear a piano play—especially at night—I'm gone! I didn't care if it was crocodiles, snakes, or whatever, I'm gone over there. That's how music enthusiastic, that stuck with me. I went over there, and I was pretty muddy from walkin—and wonder alligator hadn't got a hold. And I come on over and maybe I stepped on some of em, I don't know, getting across like bricks and that. So when I got on over, I crawled in the window and got behind the piano, an old piano was, didn't have many notes on it, and they was tryin to do the best they could by playin and they had a guy with a guitar—they didn't have but two or three strings on it. They made some music, I could hear it, but it sound good, some of the notes they was playin. So when they got ready to go, somebody heard me snorin back there and they opened the piano back, say "Hey look! Here's a kid back there." Said, "Ain't that old man Duskin's boy?" So my uncle Bob said "Lord have mercy! The old man kill that boy if he caught him out this time of night." So they shook me and woke me up. He say "How'd you get over here?" And I told him, so he spanked me, "You get killed comin through those swamps, boy!" So he put me in a wagon on the back and my old man was hollerin, you could hear him.: "Joe, Oh Joe!" He kept hollerin and goin on. So my Uncle Bob say, "When I stop this wagon, you jump off and run under that porch as fast as you can." So it was dark you couldn't see, and I jumped off and stopped the wagon and I run under the porch. My Uncle Bob say, "Come here, Perry!" He come there, said "That boy layin under there sleep." Said, "Why don't you put that boy to bed?" "Oh, that dirty bear hugger"—that's what he'd call us. He got me up and I wasn't sleep at all. I act like I was asleep, put me in bed, went on like that. And so he told me never to go through those swamps like that; he said they infested with too many bad snakes, water moccasins, and whatever, you know. And I caught myself tryin to go out—to make a long story short, Steve, to go out one mornin time to go through the woods to play that old piano. And I saw the alligators with they mouth open. Well, I didn't go cross the creek, so I started to go cross the other way and I saw the grass movin and there was one in the grass. And then this one leaped over and caught the other one and they went to fightin and rollin and rolled in the water. I got by em and when I went by I saw a man with a rope round his neck, Steve, snakes comin out of his eyes and ears and mouth, and I stood there cryin like mad cause I didn't know and the man wouldn't answer, you know. And I saw this rope and I remembered my uncle like that. And then finally my uncle Bob was comin through with his horse and whip and buggy, you know, and he heard me cryin. So when he come over he come over and had his wife. They said, "Awh, Lord, that's Dawson somebody!" Said, "They finally hung that boy and he didn't do nothin to nobody!" So they finally got his body and run the snakes away and carried it and buried it and that's the last I run out through that a way. Now that's how I got very enthusiastic over the blues and that, Steve.

Walking through alligator swamps and snake pits to hear and play the blues sounds almost like the exploits of a toast hero, and indeed perhaps it was a heroic effort to brave the dangers and create the music that was imbued by them. Joe claims to have met famed blues pianist Roosevelt Sykes and Sykes's mentor Red Eye Jesse Bell in Alabama while he was still a child, but surely it would not have been a deep or lasting personal relationship, though Joe has retained his interest in Sykes's music over the years. Eventually the Duskin family packed up and moved from Alabama to Cincinnati, which has remained Joe's permanent home, and Joe settled down to perfect his boogie woogie and blues piano style.

Joe first practiced on the piano of a neighbor, Millie Jenkins, and when his family moved from the West End's Hopkins Street to, finally, 1503 Gorman Street, Joe took to visiting his uncle, who allowed him to visit whenever he wanted. Eventually, the Duskins got a piano of their own at their house. Joe, with the music of Jesse and Willie James, Psycheye Willie, Black Jack, Leroy Carr, who Joe claims to have heard at the Graystone inside Music Hall (called the Topper Ballroom for events patronized by whites), and Fats Waller going on around him, began to pick up the fundamentals of blues piano. Visits by Washboard Sam, Rosetta Tharpe, Marie Knight, and, Joe says, Gary Davis also sparked his interest, and he remembered meeting Tharpe, Marie Knight, and Sam Price at a Holiness Church on Seventh Street: "They'd get in the horse and wagon and go up and down the street and like that until the police would tell them they can't do it, they got to get a permit to do it." And although it seemed not a bit incongruous to Joe at the time to be playing both hymns and blues, it did indeed seem that way to Perry Duskin. The now familiar story of the parent's admonition against playing the blues is a story he tells as well, and a story that features a father who was more strict about playing the devil's music than the minister was:

Ah, you know, when my dad got here to Cincinnati, never did want me to play the devil's music, and I used to be down on old piano on Hopkins Street, God, he'd bust my tail because I'd be just monkeyin, didn't know what I was doin. When I finally got to church, you know, where we used to go where I could play, when you'd go, I'd go to start playin. And so he come in one Sunday and he heard me playin the piano and said to me, he said, "If I catch you playin the devil's music again, I'm gonna take that bull whip and I'm gonna beat you almost to death with it." He said, "I don't want you playin no devil's music in this house." Say, "This is a house of prayer." Well, my old man was, I kinda thought he'd jump outta his tree sometime when he get like that. So we finally moved from there to Hopkins Street up above, and then Betts Street, then Wade Street, and then we'd move on Central Avenue, Poplar Street, all different places til we got over on Gorman Street. That's where the old man got a little piano and brought it in. And he told me, says "Don't never play no devil's music on it!" So I could play church songs, too. So he had a minister and his wife come by. That time you could get pop a nickel apiece. You know, bit bottle of pop. And he told—the old couple come in and set down—and he said, "My son gonna entertain you." And he says, "I'll go get some pop and refreshments, cookies and stuff." Then while he was gone I played so many church songs, the old man asked me, say "Can you play anything other than church songs, son?" I said, "Yessir, I can." And he says, "Well, play some of it." I was beatin out some boogie-woogie when the old man come. God dog! The old man threw me down and started beatin me so bad with that bull whip. He stopped and they said, "Duskin! Wait a minute!" He said, "He didn't do that on his own, we asked him if he could play anything else, and he said yeah." "HE SHOULD A TOLD YOU THAT I DON'T LOW THAT IN HERE!" And you know he chased those two old people out and they never did come back to the house no more.

That didn't, however, stop Joe's father from continuing to send young Joe to church to play the piano for services. But one Sunday when Joe didn't go to church was particularly memorable, making Joe wish that he was "Nearer, My God, to Thee":

So when I got home the old man was gettin ready to go to church one Sunday and I was laying in bed. He says "What's matter, you ain't goin to church this mornin, boy? All the rest of em goin." I says, "Dad, you walks there and I gotta walk with you twelve miles to church." I said, "I'm sick. I can't go. I can't. I'm sorry. I just can't do it." He says—well, he'd walk to church, he wouldn't catch no bus, man, we had to walk with him to church. Gettin up at seven o'clock in the mornin and get there around nine thirty, we'd be so tired. So he finally said, "If you're—I'll leave here—YOU DON'T GET ON THAT PIANO AND PLAY NO DEVIL'S MUSIC." I said, "O.K., dad." I was layin in the bed. So some of the kids seen him when he was gone, but he never took his umbrella, he'd forgotten it. He never would leave that umbrella, I don't care if it was shinin, sleet, or whatever. And they said, "Hey, your dad's gone." I said, "He is?" They said, "Yeah, let's play some boogie-woogie." I said, "Stand out that window and watch if he should come back. Then let me know so I can swing in on a church song." So the old man come round the corner, and they couldn't let me know because of all em started runnin. And I just beat it out, Steve, he standin there lookin in the window like this. And when I turnt round! In the same, bout "Be not dismayed whate'er." And when I got to the place where I said, "God will take care of you"—"I'm comin in there and take care of you right now," he said. Steve, that old man beat me so bad, Lord, man, I was prayin for him to kill me, man. He was beatin me so bad with that bull whip. And he actually brought blood out of it, out of my back and all that. Mom come in, she says, "Aw, Lord, what you be"—she had went to the market, see—she said, "Lord, Duskin, you'd beat this boy and he bust his back on the skin was blee-din," man, and all that.

Later when the police stopped Joe and wanted to punish the person who had whipped him "like a damn hog," Joe went back and told his father: "I said, 'Dad!' I said, 'You know the police stop me a while ago and they asked me about this whippin that's on my back and all that.' He said 'I WISH TO GOD THEY WOULD COME IN HERE AND TRY TO TELL ME HOW TO USE MY . . .' Then I wouldn't say nothin. I just went away. I wouldn't say nothin cause I know how the old man was. I says, 'I don't want him to get killed or nothin like that or hurt no-body neither one.' So that's what, I never did reveal that, but that's what actually happened, Steve."

Eventually Joe went to his father and told him that he was going to play the devil's music, that he loved it and that he *had* to do it. His father exacted just one promise, a small one, but one that terminated Joe's blues trills and tremolos for the next sixteen years:

He says, "Why don't you make a vow with me that you won't touch the devil's music til I'm dead in the grave?" He was 89, Steve. And I figured, "Well, he can't be around much longer now." And I figure, I said, "God, Uncle Handy died and he's not 80 years old yet, and the old man is 89." So I figured, "Well, 90 would be the most for him anyway." So, Steve, I'd go to church every Sunday, *playin* that music, like to run me nuts! So when the old man got over a hundred years old I went to mom and I said, "Mom! God, look at dad!" I said, "You member the time he was talkin; he—I can't play the piano til he's in the grave." She says, "Well, I don't know. He's not sick or nothin." He'll walk from here to Dayton, Ohio, and walk back. He wouldn't take a bus, Steve. And, God, when he come round a hundred and one I just forgot it. I just threw up both hands. I said, "God, I won't never do that no more." I went into the Army and come out—three years and nine months come out—but when I come out the old man was a hundred and four years old. And I said, "Pop, you still here?" I said, "You done lost one leg, I see." Me and him got to talkin; and he says, "Yeah. HAVE YOU PLAYED ANY OF THAT DEVIL'S MUSIC SINCE YOU BEEN AWAY?"[2]

It was foremost on Perry Duskin's mind, and it stayed there until he died at the age of 105, at the exact time he prophesied, twelve o'clock noon, in the arms of a son that loved him.

It seems, though, that during the period before his father died Joe did learn a bit about boogie woogie firsthand. Somewhere around the age of eighteen, probably a few years later, Joe met white pianist Freddy Slack, who accompanied Big Joe Turner and T-Bone Walker on some sides in 1941 and 1942, and who had his own orchestra, which recorded some sides with T-Bone as well. Slack was an early influence:

> Then when "Down the Road Apiece" come out, this is when the music started jumpin. You start gettin into the boogie woogie. And that's when I started learnin, learning how to play that, from Freddy Slack. . . . I tell you what, Shug Lumps's daddy was a kind of help on the train. And he'd always get one of us take us up with him and bring us back. So he asked me if I wanted to go up with him, I told him "Yeah." So he's goin to Salt Lake City. He stopped off and had his girlfriend, they went down to this great big concert hall. That's the first time I heard Freddy Slack. And when I heard it I left them and went round to the back and got in the back on the stage and all and I met him. And I said, "Mr. Slack!" I said, "I love that boogie woogie you play. I wish to God I knew how you handled that bass." He looked at me and he says, "Well, come in here a minute." I went in and his hands was like that, Steve. Great big hands. And when he set down and started to play that I watched how he did it. But I didn't know how to read no music. I just watched. And then I had to do it one single finger. I couldn't put them together. And I kept hearin that and I'd slow that record down. And I got with a teacher, told me, say "he's usin triads, like one, two, and, you know, like that." And that's how I learned that bass. And when I learned that bass, then I started to puttin the two notes to it and dropped it down. So then I got so I could play just like Freddy Slack note for note, see.[3]

Joe was also seeing a great many musicians in the clubs—Art Tatum at the Graystone, and, in Louisville, where Joe stayed for five years, Nat King Cole and his trio and Slim Gaillard at the Brown Derby. He even sat in, either briefly or on breaks, with the Sweethearts of Rhythm, Basie, Ellington, Tiny Bradshaw, J. B. Townshend, and Snookum Russell, who, Joe claims, had a young Willie Dixon on bass.

Joe's big thrill was meeting members of the famed Boogie Woogie Trio, the masters of the boogie woogie. Joe still plays Meade Lux Lewis's "Honky Tonk Train Blues," first recorded in 1927, note for note, though he only met Lewis briefly, while Joe was in the army and in New York.[4] Joe also recalled working as a driver for Charles J. Johnson, who had a church on Flint Street in the West End, whose business took the two of them to New Jersey, where a collection of Pete Johnson and Albert Ammons sheet music under Joe's arm at a local music store prompted a small concert violinist to strike up a conversation with Joe and ultimately introduce him to boogie woogie king Albert Ammons. The violinist made the introduction:

He said, "Do you ever pray?" I said, "Well, most of the time, when I think about it." "If you prayed, your prayers would be answered. Here he comes now." He was kind of a little guy, had a kind of cute walk about him comin down. . . . And I told this lie, I said, "You know, I drove all the way up here to New Jersey to see you, Mr. Ammons." I said, "I've heard of your son, that blows saxophone, but I wanted to meet the champion of the ivories." He laughed, he said, "Oh, ho, ho, come on." He said, "You just pullin my ———", I said, "No, I'm not doing that." And he says, "Come on now, I'm going down to a little joint now." He says, "I play down here every day," and he says, "you can hear me play." But got down there and, Steve, if you'd see that guy's fingers! First song he played was "Boogie Woogie Dream!" The first thing he played. And Steve! God, to watch that man, his fingers the way he'd do. Aw, man! His fingers was a little bit thicker than mine, and the way he'd do that he set there like this here [imitates facial expressions captured in the film short "Boogie Woogie Dream"] . . . and, Steve, after seein that guy playin that stuff like that I didn't leave there. And when it was almost time for Johnson to go to church he had to get a cab, man. I just couldn't make it.

And although Joe said subsequently that he did not meet Pete Johnson while he was in the army, he recounted a different story in 1973: "And I met Pete Johnson. Onliest time I ever remember playing with Pete Johnson, me and Jessie Wise—he was a boogie woogie piano player—we used to play double boogie woogie solos, and we was playing a USO show where Pete Johnson was playin. And that's the only time I had a chance to play with him. And he about left me in the dust, man! I was so nervous, you know, playing with a big guy like that. And he told me, 'You'll make a good piano player one of these days.' "[5] The influence of these pianists showed when, Joe claims, he went in to cut his first twelve-inch record at Wurlitzer on the sixth, seventh, or eighth floor, at the age, he says, of nineteen:

And I put, I'll tell you what I put on there. I put "Blue Lou in C Sharp Minor," I put "Down the Road Apiece," "Honky Tonk Train," "Yancey Special," and I had a nice number of stuff down and I loaned that record out to one woman by the name of Nancy . . . [forgets last name] and she took that record and I never seen it no more, Steve. And that was a masterpiece of mine. . . . I cut that when I was nineteen years old. That's when I started to gettin a lot of things goin out and playin for different places. And I'd play for the police balls and . . . I was real good at that time, Steve. I could play anything you wanted to hear. I don't care what it was, I could do it. I was somethin like Errol Garner.[6]

With such a talent and breadth, Joe was quite a hit, both with the USO while in the service, and in clubs sitting in with or meeting Jimmy Yancey, Fats Domino, Arnett Cobb, and others, or playing with his own orchestra. Of course, like any bandleader, Joe had some trouble with sidemen, but his own two-fisted style helped him overcome that: one night when Joe's band didn't show for a party Joe was doing, Joe performed himself, and reaped the benefits: "The place was so packed and the piano was dropped below pitch. And I sat there and played that thing, and they said, 'Boy, you don't need nothin else!' And I made about two hundred something dollars that night. And I brought all that change in, pennies, nickels, dimes, quarters, silver dollars, fives, tens, twenties, and they just loaded me down when I got ready to go out. My wife said, 'I knew you said you was goin out to play, but I didn't think you get this much money playing the piano.' She thought I robbed a bank! She wouldn't touch the money!"[7] Eventually, though, remembering his father's "request" and finding his music not as much in demand as it had been, along with the demands of working as a mailhandler for the post office from 1945 through 1979, Joe left the music business, though he did keep a piano to play to amuse and satisfy himself. When I met Joe in the basement of his Bond Hill home on Ryland Avenue in 1971, he was obviously a great player who enjoyed the music he performed so well, but he had no intention of playing in public again—that is, until I heard him and encouraged him to "come back": "If it hadn't been for you," he told me, "I never woulda played no piano no more. I was done with it."

Fortunately, Joe *did* come back, though some club owners were skeptical. Until they heard him. First came the year of playing up to four nights a week at Mahogany Hall in Cincinnati's Mount Adams. This attracted the attention of *Cincinnati Enquirer* columnist Bob Brumfield, who wrote a column describing the music as "a treat for sore ears"[8] and Joe found himself in demand, playing with myself, Phil Buscema, or Dave Heil on guitar, Rico on trumpet, or duets with Tom Johns or Tom Dooley, and a host of other musicians at places like Dollar Bill's in Clifton for the university crowd, Chapter 13 in Mount Adams, at Edwards' Manufacturing in downtown Cincinnati in a band with Albert Washington in the late seventies, and at Clifton's rock concert hall Bogart's, opening for B. B. King, Muddy Waters, Sonny Terry and Brownie McGhee, and others.

Joe's career was also boosted by appearances on WAIF radio's "Blue Jungle" radio show, where he met Ben Sandmel, who produced Joe's Arhoolie LP, and on three of WAIF's Blues Cruises in the seventies. Joe always preferred to play the 88s, but eventually he switched to playing the electric piano in the clubs because of the demand for electric blues and to compete with the amplified instruments that accompanied him.

Joe was well known for trying to please his audience as best he could: he would try to play *any* request (between the two of us we could cover the blues requests, and *eventually* Joe learned songs like "Last Date" and "Green Green Grass of Home" because, for some reason, people would request those songs from a blues and boogie woogie band), and he was notorious for letting *anybody* sit in. Joe was obviously trying to encourage young people by allowing them to sit in, but the endless parade of musicians varying in ability sometimes made seeing Joe in a club a bit frustrating, particularly since most people were really there to hear Joe, would have been happy to hear Joe by himself, and weren't satisfied to watch Joe chord away behind occasional novice musicians. Still, Joe was the most popular bluesman with white audiences in Cincinnati, first choice to open for visiting blues bands at Bogart's or at Coco's, where the two of us opened for Robert Lockwood on January 22, 1984. And the Mr. Clean of the blues playing his bleachless boogie woogie in 1986 at "Sudsy Malone's" laundromat/bar—an idea that didn't necessarily wash very well with Joe.[9]

He also had his brushes with local TV on the Nick Clooney variety show, and on July 6, 1982, on Robin Wood's "Cincinnati Alive" cable TV show, both shows that Joe and I did together. Additionally we appeared together on Bob Shreve's late night movie TV program on June 30, 1979. Joe was getting a lot of local attention.

But by this time, of course, Joe had begun to travel far beyond the boundaries of Cincinnati. Articles in *Blues Unlimited Magazine* in 1973 and *Living Blues* in 1974 prompted inquiries from boogie woogie enthusiasts in West Germany and Holland, and soon Joe was playing his music in many other countries: in one postcard from October 1988, Joe wrote "I've been to Netherlands, Amsterdam, Holland, Norway, Sweden, Belgium, Spain, Italy," and he could add to the list France, Canada, and England.[10] Joe wasn't quite prepared for the reception he got in Europe—to sellout crowds. "They go to concerts like hockey games," he told me, "and they love the blues and boogie woogie." In Europe he got the chance to meet musicians like Junior Wells, Buddy Guy, Lowell Fulson, Professor Longhair, James

Booker, Eddie Clearwater, Lloyd Glenn, Memphis Slim, Willie Mabon, and many, many others, and the tours have provided him with experiences he'll always cherish, though traveling 150–200 miles per hour on the autobahn, he says, was not one of them.

More recently, Joe has been to England, playing to large sellout crowds. A six-week European tour in 1987 included about twenty British dates, during which time Joe was thrilled to play on London's Trafalgar Square, though he passed up a chance to play before Parliament:

> But some how or nother, they'll get you, you gotta strip naked, Steve, they look under your toenails and everything. And they said, "Duskin, they gonna keep you there for about four hours and they gonna ask you all kinds of questions and look in your ear and everything. Yeah, they gonna screw . . ." I said, "Aw, Lord, I don't wanna play there if I got to go through all that crap." I just forgot that. That's what you gotta do when you go over there to Queens to play for any of them over there, Dukes or whatever. They'll keep you in there for about four-five hours lookin in your eyes, your mouth, your nose, they look up your rectum, in your penis and everything. I just told em "Naw, I ain't goin through all that just to play no music." But they pay you some good pounds. But I said, "If I got to stay in there for four hours, hell, I won't be able to sit down and play when I get out of there, you know."

While in England, though, Joe was "strongly featured in the boogie documentary recently televised by ITV's "South Bank Show," which also had contributions by Paul Oliver and Frances Smith and archive footage of past boogie woogie masters."[11] Additionally, Joe recorded several accompaniments to British blues guitarist Dave Peabody on Peabody's Waterfront LP *Americana,* and then Peabody returned the favor by accompanying Joe on Joe's 1988 Special Delivery LP.

All of Joe's out-of-town bookings haven't been in Europe, however. One of the most memorable was the 1979 San Francisco Blues Festival at which Joe performed. Denis Lewis described his performance: "A new name to me was Big Joe Duskin, but after his performance it's a name I won't forget. He is quite simply a brilliant boogie woogie pianist. Opening his set with a rocking version of 'Down the Road Apiece,' he went on to play such boogie woogie classics as 'Boogie Woogie Prayer' and a superlative rendering of Meade Lux Lewis's 'Honky Tonk Train.' A listen to his first Arhoolie album ('Cincinnati Stomp') will give a pretty clear indication of his piano playing ability, not to mention his powerful singing voice."[12] One selection by Joe recorded at this festival was released on an anthology on the Solid Smoke label.

Joe was at the festival to promote the release of his Arhoolie LP, *Cincinnati Stomp*, in 1978. Joe had recorded previously: the "lost" LP recorded at Wurlitzer was first, then a 45 recorded at Shad O'Shea's Counterpart Studios, with myself on harmonica and Larry Goshorn on guitar, featuring "Frenzy" (actually "Boogie Woogie Prayer") and "Betty and Dupree" that turned up once on a jukebox at Dollar Bill's, though I've never seen a copy of it anywhere else. Joe's Arhoolie LP, then, was the first to give him wide recognition and, after some initial problems (the LP was slated to come out on Delmark but was switched to Arhoolie after Joe recorded an LP's worth of material for Bluebeat), the LP came out to good press. *Blues Unlimited*'s Bruce Bastin called it "A very solid production which can be recommended wholeheartedly to anyone with a smattering of interest in *good* boogie woogie," asserting that "Duskin is no mere copyist" and that "the title track is a stormer, showing he can hang in there with the best."[13]

Of the twelve cuts, four feature a very effective band including Truck Parham and S. P. Leary accompaniments, recorded in Chicago. The other eight are Joe alone, all recorded at the Fifth Floor Recording Studios in Cincinnati in February and August 1977. Fifth Floor was run by Rich Goldman, who had sat in on guitar with Joe a number of times. Honestly, the LP is not Joe at his best. His singing seems at times uncertain and hesitant, due, says Joe, to the fact that they recorded the piano and vocals at separate times rather than together. Still, it is a very fine traditional blues LP and debut recording.

Joe has done other recordings, both with the Black Cat Bone Band and solo for Bluebeat, but nothing was released because of contractual problems, though Joe says that the Black Cat Bone session, which was supposed to have been a rehearsal session, has been released. Finally, Joe's second LP was released ten years after his first, to somewhat mixed reviews. John Rockwood of *Living Blues* raved that the LP "is an album filled with rocking, boogie woogie piano, and a horn section that just doesn't let up";[14] in *Blues Unlimited*, however, Dave Williams hears a lack of confidence in Joe's vocals that detracts from what is otherwise a "very enjoyable record" with a strong horn section but stylistically inappropriate guitar from Peabody.[15] Still, the LP has been selling well behind Joe's touring in England, and a recent appearance at the 1989 New Orleans Jazz and Heritage Festival has only served to enhance the reputation of Cincinnati's boogie woogie master. In 1991 the Wolf label released an LP of duets with a drummer recorded in 1982 that once again demonstrates his true mastery of the idiom.

Now divorced and remarried, Joe spends a great deal of time touring, not playing as much in Cincinnati as he used to, and the city is
poorer for that. But when he is in the clubs, you are promised great
music, wonderful stories, and heartfelt, though not always progressive, philosophy. On Women's Lib, for example:

I figure the man should be the boss, Steve. There should not be no woman
boss, period. Now not that he should come up to her and try to make her
do something, but he should have enough love, and she should have
enough sense in her heart to do what the man tell her to do, long as it's
done in a nice, legitimate way. Not because of the Woman's Lib where she
think, "Well, who is he to tell me what to do?" I believe if a man is married and a woman is married, there shouldn't be no fifty-fifty basis. And
I should put this in here, Steve, to kind of regulate some people's mind,
because a lot of people out there are not infidels, they know something
about the Bible, too. God told Eve. He said, "Thy desire shall be until thy
husband, and *he shall rule over thee.*" So that's my teaching that I've been
taught from my youth up. It's not because of my parents but it was because of what God said. That's what gets this world in a great turmoil like
it is, and that's what makes these guys write these sad blueses, and all
these blues about these women and all that because they actually experienced this kind of stuff.[16]

From the bars to the schools (for Tom John's music classes at
Anderson and at Seven Hills School) to the concerts to the festivals to
his basement, Joe's music expresses his exuberant personality, expresses it in such a way that you love him no matter how vehemently
you might disagree with him, because somehow he makes it important to you that he likes you. Whether it's his encouragement, his musical ability, or his ability to sometimes make you feel like what
you're saying is the wisest or most important thing in the world, it is
a gift he has that transcends problems you might have with him.

In 1988 Joe sent me a postcard from London: "If it had not been
for you I'd have never gotten this far." Of course, the truth is, if it
hadn't been for Joe himself he'd never have gotten this far, and I sus-
pect that if it hadn't been for Joe, I never would have gotten this far,
either. "Steve, I'd never forget you," he continued, and the words
touched me beyond words, except to echo his:

Joe, I'd never forget you.

7

King Records

Contemporary testimony suggests that those blues singers who were playing in Cincinnati in the twenties and thirties continued to play in the forties, fifties, and sixties—and, performers like Jarrett, Mays, and Duskin are performing still today. But increasingly as musical styles and tastes changed and amplification became more prevalent, the street musicians and speakeasy performers were eclipsed by the high-powered and more urbane blues and rhythm and blues artists who began to emerge from places like Kansas City, New York, Chicago, Houston, and Los Angeles in the late thirties and early forties. So while in the background, on the streets, you could still hear Stovepipe's old style blues, increasingly the clubs, the radios, the record stores, and the print media were pushing a more "up to date" sound that often showed musically that it knew Stovepipe was there, but let him know that they would not waltz the gravy around but jitterbug it. But the new blues "stars" in Cincinnati did not develop some aspect of the blues that had gone before in Cincinnati. The popular blues styles that predominated around the country took hold here, and it was once again the major individual talents and personalities, and not some overall unique sound, that characterized the post–World War II blues scene in Cincinnati.

The *Cincinnati Times Star* of November 1, 1944, carried a small item tucked away on page five, column three, concerning a new business venture about to be launched in Cincinnati. Printed under the headline "Phonograph Records to Be Made Here," the story outlined an ambitious start for a company that would later become the number one independent rhythm and blues label in the country:

> A new industry for Cincinnati was revealed in the formation of the King Record Company to manufacture phonograph records. Sidney [sic] Nathan, 1108 William Howard Taft Road, senior partner and majority

owner of the new enterprise here, stated that a factory site already has been leased for five years at 1540 Brewster Avenue, Evanston. Machinery and equipment is being installed in the area of 9,000 square feet and production is expected to be underway in about 30 days, it was stated.

"At the outset," Nathan said, "we will use only hillbilly music and vocal numbers and the first release will consist of six numbers. We intend to later produce records of 'hot jazz' and sepia music. All recordings will be original numbers and made by our company." A staff of writers has been secured and such stars of the hill-billy field as the Delmore Brothers, Grandpa Jones, and Bill and Evalina have been signed, according to Nathan. He explained that the necessary materials consisting principally of shellac and clay were obtainable, being non-essential to the war effort.

About 70 persons will be employed when the plant begins operations and an initial output of 10,000 records a day is expected by Nathan. A sales office will be maintained at the Evanston plant, also at 1531 Central Avenue, according to present plans.[1]

The big plans were partially the result of the chutzpah of one man, Sydney Nathan, who sat the helm of King Records, with a hearty crew to support him, and made it one of the most important country *and* rhythm and blues labels of all time.

Actually, the record business was somewhat of any iffy proposition at this point. For one thing, the shellac used in making 78 rpm records was scarce because the supply from the Far East was cut off by the war, so nonmilitary use of shellac was limited by the War Production Board. For another, American Federation of Musicians boss James C. Petrillo called a musicians' strike on August 1, 1942, to try to force the record companies to establish a fund for unemployed musicians who, he felt, were adversely affected by the presence of jukeboxes and radio stations that lessened the need for live music. There were also machinery shortages and rationing that affected the industry as well. On the other hand, independent record companies benefited from the refusal of the major labels like Victor, Decca, and Columbia to cooperate with the unions, and there was a small explosion of independent record companies after October 1943. Peter Grendysa outlined the independents' advantage with the union over the holdouts of the major labels: "If you had a small record company that you just started out at that time, hey, you would go down, you would sign an agreement with the union, agree with what they wanted. You could record. Whereas Decca and RCA Victor and Columbia were sitting with their arms folded saying 'We shall not yield to these demands,' a lot of small record companies said, 'Hey, we'll yield. What the heck. . . . Let's start producing records.' "[2] And produce they did, especially in the non-pop fields of country and blues, which the major labels let slide in favor of pop artists with more immediate and guaranteed sales. Jon Fox catalogued a number of the many labels that sprung up: in New York—Beacon, Savoy, De-luxe, Keynote, Manor, Apollo, National, and Atlantic; on the West Coast—Capitol, Aladdin, Modern, Specialty, Imperial, Four Star, Gilt-Edge, Black and White, and Exclusive; also Mercury, Miracle, and Chess in Chicago; Peacock and Gold Star in Houston; Bullet and Rich-R-Tone in Tennessee; and, of course, King in Cincinnati.[3] These labels recorded some of the most significant performers in country and blues music, which is to say in postwar music, in the last five de-cades, and they eagerly and tremendously filled the gap left by the majors who, even though they had capitulated by 1944, had given over an important market to small independent labels on the thresh-old of changing not only the music industry but the musical taste of America, even the world, through the efforts of people like Sydney Nathan.

Sydney (according to him the "y" instead of an "i" predicted his ability to make money) Nathan was born to Frieda and Nathaniel Nathan on April 27, 1904, in Cincinnati.[4] The baby boy was born with asthma and poor eyesight, both of which dogged him for the rest of his life. At age five he was given a set of trap drums by an uncle and set about learning to play, and he reputedly later learned to play the piano from a local black musician as well. Syd was enthusiastic about the drums and put effort into his playing, as he did into his school-work, though that was made particularly difficult by his poor vision: "What I learned, I learned by memory. . . . I couldn't even see the blackboard."[5] Eventually, poor grades in high school, particularly in Latin, caused Nathan to drop out of high school as a freshman and take a number of jobs, all the while continuing to play his drums. Over the years Nathan worked in a pawn shop, jewelry sales, a park concession, a shooting gallery, bucking rivets, as a bus boy in a men's club, and even in wrestling promotion. Syd went to Arizona at age eighteen to try to alleviate his asthma, but soon he was back in Cincinnati, working with his father in real estate and wrestling promotion.

In 1932, Syd got a job with Max Frank at Frank's radio on Vine Street and a bit later he got a job as a rod man with the county in the Engineering Department. In 1938 Syd had a scrape with the law when, as a shooting gallery operator, Syd was charged with obtaining money under false pretenses when he refused to pay on a card that allegedly had the heart imprint shot off it.[6] Syd reportedly produced a magnifying glass and claimed he saw part of the heart still there. A gallery employee told the shooter that he had a winner, but Syd refused to pay, so the warrant was issued. However, on September 9, the two charges were dismissed, though he was fined $50 on two other affadavits related to his games of chance.[7]

In 1939, for a number of reasons, Nathan moved to Florida where his brother, David A. Nathan, was beginning medical practice. There Nathan set up a photo finishing business out of which nothing developed and, nearly broke, he returned home to Cincinnati to open a record shop at 1351 Central Avenue for $30 a month rent. He stocked mostly black music until the former boss Max Frank sold Syd his stock of several thousand records, 85 percent of them hillbilly music, which brought some new customers into Syd's store: "They were wandering into Syd's store, those tall, gaunt-faced folks with the lonesome sound of the mountains in their talk. For the war was the real thing, and the Cincinnati factory smokestacks were beckoning with plumes of smoke, signalling the hill folk to come up from Kentucky and Tennessee, and over from West Virginia. There was money in the big city."[8] The work and money attracted both blacks and whites to Cincinnati, and Syd was ready not only to sell them records but also to record them himself. Actually, Syd already knew how lucrative the selling business could be, when, in 1938, at Syd's new record shop in the 200 block of West Fifth Street, he parlayed a six-dollar loan into a big profit:

> Six bucks meant more to me in 1938 than $1600 now. One night I saw the fellow at Beverly Hills with a gorgeous babe. I figured he would be in the next day with my six bucks. He didn't show. For three weeks in a row I saw him at Beverly with the same babe. Finally on the dance floor, I grabbed his shoulder, told him that if he could afford Beverly, he certainly could repay me. He turned red, blue and green, told me he didn't have it. The next day he offered me 300 hillbilly, Western and race records, old ones from his juke boxes, at 2 cents a platter. He figured I could sell enough of them for ten cents each to get back my six bucks. I took him up.
>
> The first afternoon I made $18. Naturally, I wondered how long this could go on. I bought more old records from juke box operators. Some I sold for a dime, some 15, 20 and 25 cents.[9]

When Syd went to Florida he sold that record shop to his brother Sol Halper, but now he had a new shop and even more evidence that this was indeed a lucrative business. Fifty-thousand-watt WLW radio's "Boone County Jamboree"/"Midwestern Hayride" familiarized Syd even more with the hillbilly music that looked so promising, and helped him make contacts with musicians like Merle Travis, Grandpa Jones, the Sheppard Brothers, Chet Atkins, the Delmore Brothers, and Hank Penny. It is also likely that the programming on WCKY, featuring Nelson King, Lonnie Glosson, Marty Roberts, Wayne Raney, and Jimmy Lagsden with a wild mix of country music and corny commericals, caught Syd's ear as well. Syd was ready to move into the field of recording and, in November 1943, announced the release of his first two records on King. Both were hillbilly songs, recorded in his shop on Central Avenue and cut in Dayton, Ohio. Syd knew that the disc quality was poor, so he searched for a record pressing plant, which he found in Louisville. The plant had been set up in conjunction with the American Printing House for the Blind, and it was there he learned, with the help of George W. Weitlauf, that side of the record business, returning then to Cincinnati to make his own record pressing plant a reality.

In August 1944, King Records was incorporated. The partnership consisted of Syd Nathan, Dorothy Halper, Doris Nathan, wife of Syd's brother the doctor, Bernice Steinberg, a cousin, Lawrence Sick, and Howard Kessel, also a relative of Syd's. The original partnership was formed with less than $25,000, with the aid of attorney Louis Rubenstein. From his experience in the record business, Nathan realized that the major labels were expending their materials and efforts more on their classical recordings. So with his record store know-how, financial backing, and some good old-fashioned library research, Nathan decided to start King from there.

And start from there he did, though he was almost stopped even before he got started. First, they needed a building, and that they found at 1540 Brewster, formerly Fries and Fries, Inc., extract manufacturers, located next door to the Avondale Ice Company at 1538 Brewster in Avondale. However, there were restrictions on the plating department for the building, so Syd sent for George Weitlauf from the American Printing House for the Blind, a draftsman, to come to Cincinnati and draw up some plans for the building. When St. Francis Tool of Indiana sent faulty presses to Cincinnati for the building, Nathan went to Airhart Foundry and built the plant from scratch. In the meantime, King had received the machinery for the plant but had never paid for it when, lo and behold, that machine company went bankrupt, charged with making things for people without the priority needed during wartime. King still needed someone to handle the mechanized end of the operation, so they called in John Wolfe, who had been working for Ditto Printing Company, to make the machinery they needed but could not buy.

That hurdle passed, they next ran into other problems: not only did the building need a bigger boiler but the company needed, and lacked, priorities from the War Production Board. However, with the help of some friends they eventually bought the materials they needed, the carpenters completed their job, and the plant was ready for production.

The *Cincinnati Post* of October 8, 1946, reported that two corporations were now replacing the record company:

Formation of two new corporations as successors to the King Record Co., 1540 Brewster Avenue, was announced Tuesday.

A. E. Slapin, one of the incorporators, said the New King Record Corp. will continue to manufacture records at the Brewster avenue plant, while the Royal Distributing Co. will handle distribution of the records.

King produces King hill-billy records and Queen jazz records, turning out about 100,000 a week from 100 master recordings. In addition to Mr. Slapin, incorporators are Samuel A. Rubenstein, with offices in the Keith Theatre Building, and Howard Kessel.[10]

It was Howard Kessel who became Royal Plastics Co. president, the man who had been there with Syd from the beginning, counseling business decisions and fiscal responsibilities when the heat of Syd's excitement might have led him to snap decisions or deals not in the best interest of the company. And Kessel remained through the years to continue giving his help and support to, and making his living from, the business.

However, Syd was having other problems, too: he was declared totally blind, and took a gamble on an operation that could have caused him to lose his sight. That gamble paid off, as did his gamble on building King Records.

Build it they did, and they got underway quickly. After some more hillbilly releases, Syd set up a subsidiary label, Queen Records, for black artists' releases, called race records. The first release on Queen was done by a Cleveland, Ohio, native born in 1919, Benjamin Jackson, affectionately known as "Bull Moose" because, as many people have suggested, he looked like a bull moose. Jackson had been discovered by bandleader Lucky Millinder in 1943, and had recorded with Big Sid Catlett in 1945 and with Millinder for Decca between 1945 and 1947.[11] Millinder, under contract to Decca, was unable to record for King, but A&R man Henry Glover, a former trumpeter for Millinder, was able to get Jackson and members of Millinder's band in the studio to cover Joe Liggins's "Honey Dripper," and Jackson followed that up with six other releases for Queen, including songs like "Embraceable You" and "Cleveland Ohio Blues," and sessions for King through the mid-fifties. Jackson's million-selling hit "I Love You, Yes I Do," coauthored by "Sally Nix" (a Nathan pseudonym like the name Lois Mann), caused some problems for King because the song had already been presented to another publishing company, forcing King to pay punitive damages to Decca Records.

Despite the problems, Jackson continued to record and be a big seller for King: the "blue" blues "Big Ten Inch Record" and "Nosey Joe" have become R&B favorites, and Jackson and his Buffalo Bearcats proved to be valuable artists for King Records. Jackson died of cancer in Cleveland, Ohio, on July 31, 1989, after a comeback that took him from his job as a cafeteria worker at Howard University back onto the stage and into the recording studio for some much-deserved recognition as an R&B pioneer.

In 1947 Queen also acquired twenty masters from J. Mayo Williams's Southern label out of New York, the masters for the 20th Century and Southern/Harlem labels, and some titles recorded for Gotham by Earl Bostic. In addition, King recorded quite a bit of gospel during this time by the Wings over Jordan Choir, the Swan Silvertone Singers, and the Harmoneers, as well as others, but eventually the label was put to rest on August 21, 1947, with Queen 4174. Queen had featured sides by Brother John Sellers, Slim Gaillard, Walter Brown, and Johnny Temple, among others, and had served its purpose. Syd was now ready to jump into the R&B field wholeheartedly, and a separate label for his newly signed black stars Ivory Joe Hunter, Wynonie Harris, and Lonnie Johnson was unnecessary.[12] And besides, "Tomorrow Night" by Johnson and "I Love You Yes I Do" by Jackson would finish first and second on the Billboard top ten race chart for 1948, giving King two bona fide hits and a vast amount of name recognition. Truly, blues and R&B would help the label.

But the move away from "separate but equal" record labels was significant in another sense: King Records had, they felt, a commitment to smashing Jim Crow. The *Cincinnati Post* reported on King's practices in 1949:

> Two years ago they told Ben Siegel, of the King Record Co., 1540 Brewster Avenue, that it couldn't be done.
>   "Cincinnati is a border town," said the skeptics, "you can't get Negroes and white people to work together. It's too close to the south."
>   But Mr. Siegel didn't believe them. He told Sidney [sic] Nathan and Howard Kassel [sic], officers of the company, that he'd be King's personal manager only if they'd let him run his department as he saw fit. They backed his policies.

The skeptics were wrong. King hires 400 employees, and the non-discrimination policies have needed no "backing." Here's the way things stand today: The musical director, assistant office manager, foreman of the mill room, set up man on the production line, assistant promotion director, legal secretary, a dozen stenographers and 20 percent of the factory workers are Negroes.

There is a Chinese bookkeeping machine operator and a Japanese comptometer operator.

All groups have joined on summer picnics, Christmas parties and baseball games. The plant sponsors a Negro and white team in a city industrial league. "We pay for ability," says Mr. Siegel, "and ability has no color, no race and no religion. Our hiring policy and our promotion system are based only on the question of the individual's capacity to fill a given job."[13]

The article goes on to relate how King asked on applications whether people would have difficulties working with people of other races or religions, but didn't allow answers there to influence hiring policies: in fact, Siegel felt that people who did not want to work with someone of another race would sometimes change their minds when they were actually put in such a situation. King did have, indeed, a fairly progressive policy in this area at the time. Of course, suggesting that there were no problems is very likely an overstatement—some studio musicians have told me that they had been slighted or insulted on at least one occasion in the studio, and some felt that they were paid less than the white session men—but overall King seems to have made some effort to practice an equal employment and promotion policy.

Syd was also ahead of his time in his policy concerning the blending of country and rhythm and blues songs and styles, before Ivory Joe Hunter and Ray Charles created hits from the blend, and before Sam Phillips put his Memphis Sun label on the map. Henry Glover, A&R man and later vice president of King Records, discussed their practice:

Sam Phillips has received great recognition because he did the novel thing of recording R&B with white country boys. He deserves credit, considering that Elvis Presley, Jerry Lee Lewis, Roy Orbison, Carl Perkins, and Johnny Cash all emerged from the Sun label. But the fact is that King Records was covering R&B with country singers almost from the beginning of my work with Syd Nathan. We had a duo called the York Brothers who recorded many of the day's R&B hits back in '47–'48. They sounded something like the Everly Brothers, whom they probably influenced. We were more successful doing the reverse—covering C&W hits with R&B singers. In '49, as you already know, Bull Moose Jackson's hit "Why Don't You Haul Off and Love Me" was a cover of a Wayne Raney country hit. And Wynonie Harris' "Bloodshot Eyes"—on R&B charts in '51—was originally a Hank Penny country record. I'll confess that we didn't think we were doing anything remarkable. It's just that we had both types of artists, and when a song happened in one field, Syd Nathan wanted it moved into the other.[14]

There was, obviously, a strong profit motive behind the move, as Glover realized: "You see, it was a matter of Cincinnati's population. You couldn't sell Wynonie Harris to country folk, and black folk weren't buying Hank Penny. But black folk might buy Wynonie Harris doing a country tune. And since Syd published most of the tunes we recorded, he was also augmenting his publishing income and building important copyrights. He was a smart businessman and didn't miss a trick."[15] Syd's motives, then, were not altruistic, but they were smart business, and they did effect a positive change:

> These ideas that he came up with were looked upon as sorta strange at the time, but, by doing this, he sorta made explicit what was always sort of tacitly assumed, and that was the interplay between black and white music. . . . Nathan simply brought it into the studio when he had people like Henry Glover working on white records. The Delmore Brothers, for example had Henry Glover in the studio when they created "Blues Stay Away from Me." They listened back and forth a lot, and I think all Nathan did was to recognize a fact: Hey, these two musics are swapping juices, and why pretend they're not. . . . He in many ways was a remarkably open minded man. He perceived this wonderful notion of American music as not being segregated into different styles of music, but one big cross-ethnic whole. But he did that not because of . . . altruistic motives, he did that because it was a way to make money.[16]

One might say, another great American trait. And if King helped bring blacks and whites together in the studio and closed the gap in the record-buying public, the company may have also helped effect social change through improved race relations resulting from the power of the music to bring people together. Ralph Bass, who had worked for Black and White Records, run Federal for King in the fifties, and later joined Chess Records, saw the social benefits:

> I'll tell you the major contribution. Without getting up on the soap box, without having marches, we brought black and whites together with music. I remember in Atlanta, Georgia, when "The Twist" came out. Hank Ballard was the featured act at this big club and they were lined . . . the whites were lined up, they were lined up, blacks and whites together, all down Auburn Avenue, to try to get into this club. The police came, man, and they said, "We'll have a riot. Let 'em alone. Let 'em go." So here, whites and blacks together. We gave them a common denominator, a

common love. We appealed to the one emotion that the law couldn't do a damn thing about, their common love of music. And so, I think, through King and other labels, this was the great contribution: to break the shit down . . . especially in the Deep South. Break it down.[17]

One of Syd's smartest moves was hiring a black executive, Henry Glover, for A&R work with King. Glover stated that he was "perhaps the second black man to ever have an executive position with an independent record company in the United States,"[18] following the lead of Paramount's J. Mayo Williams, and Glover was certainly a highly successful producer of both rhythm and blues and country acts. Glover was born in Hot Springs, Arkansas, and attended college at Alabama A&M, graduating in 1943 and continuing his graduate work at Wayne University in 1943 and 1944, quitting eight credit hours short of his masters degree, but gaining valuable experience while there by writing arrangements for Jimmy Lunceford. An education major who wished to teach music, Glover studied trumpet with the man who taught W. C. Handy, and later went with Buddy Johnson, Tiny Bradshaw, Willie Bryant, and Lucky Millinder.[19] It was with Millinder that Glover came to Cincinnati, and to King: "I came through Cincinnati with the Millinder Orchestra and Syd Nathan came to see Millinder and I about making some records. Millinder couldn't do anything himself because he had to live up to the terms of his agreement with Decca. He did let Bull Moose Jackson, Panama Francis, Sam "The Man" Taylor record, and later the saxophonist by the name of Bernie Peacock. . . . [I] was the arranger and first trumpet player with the orchestra."[20] They cut a number of sides in the early days at a studio in downtown Cincinnati built by Earl Herzog, until Syd's temper got him asked to take his business elsewhere, at which point Syd built his own studio. Glover was an employee in the early forties:

> My duties at King in the early days were general. I did quite a few things. Syd was a very brave man. He was in the midst of building equipment. He and I designed the original echo chamber and it was at King that one of the very first was used. We duplicated the system in our early mixing set-up at the King Studio and it's still existing. My duties were not inhibited only to the blues and R&B. I did many of the country and veteran artists like Moon Mullican. I did all of Moon's early recordings, and Grandpa Jones. I recorded Cowboy Copas and the York Brothers. The Everly Brothers copied their style. Let's see, Boyd Bennett was one of the original rock groups . . . we had a thing that Moon and I wrote together called "I'll Sail My Ship Alone at Today's Funeral"; a country standard, it's in our catalog.[21]

Coming in on the ground floor of the company and working along as it was built up, Glover had an ideal chance to learn the business inside out, and he approached the opportunity with intelligence and verve:

> As I said, I worked with Syd on many projects in the early days of the record company. Naturally, putting together a pressing, printing, studio distribution complex, there were many things that you could do and you at the same time learn. I moved to Cincinnati in 1949, and stayed until 1950 in order to learn the basics of the recording setup; a rare opportunity not only for a black man but also for a white. I was taught the basic fundamentals of the business of music and the studio mechanics and such. So, as I said, it wasn't a matter of my experience with Syd or with the company which is being tied down to the musical end. I've received great knowledge of the business and as well as the complicated copyright situation, licensing and publishing, which I'm still at. Fortunately, I had a fairly decent education and I protected all of my songs with copyrights and I own 50% of every song this company has ever recorded by any artist. I recorded and wrote for a company called J & C, and in their catalog are big hits like "Fever," "Twist," and "Drown in My Own Tears."[22]

Glover might also add that he wrote or cowrote such songs as "Pot Likker" (Todd Rhodes), "I'm Waiting Just for You" (Millinder), "Rock Love," and "Honky Tonk." His swing band background helped King become "a major purveyor of big band rhythm and blues,"[23] but Glover was clearly an outstanding utility man and a most valuable player for King. Session man Ray Felder recalls Glover's work in the studio, sometimes smoothing over Syd Nathan's rough and rowdy ways:

> Syd Nathan was a beautiful guy. He was kind of rough on the artists sometimes, you know. Because Syd was the kind of guy that knew what he wanted. At the time he knew what was sellin. Because he knew what was sellin the records that he produced. And there was a certain tune that didn't have that certain flavor that he had, he knew what he wanted. He would say, "Hey, like I want it like boom de boom be boom de bop de bop," you know. Not musically, but it was just something he was trying to explain, you know, to clarify. But then he had A&R men like Henry Glover, and those guys they knew just about what was going on.[24]

Bassist Ed Conley described Nathan in very dramatic terms: "Screaming, turning red, big cigar struck up in his mouth, you'd think he was getting ready, you know, to go into conniptions or heart attack, he would get so excited, you know, about things. And he just wanted things a certain way and that was it."[25] But even more than

his calming influence, it was because of Glover's musical expertise—
an expertise Syd lacked—that Glover had charge in the studio. Finally, though, the multitalented Glover made important—essential—
contributions to the King Record legacy and the legacy of R&B:
"Henry Glover was a multiple talent—arranger, songwriter, record
producer. As a songwriter he ranks with the leading creators of R&B
material, though he little likes the R&B handle. . . . Glover's biggest,
if not his best, song is 'Drown in My Own Tears,' a 1952 best-seller
for Sonny Thompson, with a vocal by Lulu Reed. Thompson's was
another of the swinging blues bands nurtured by Glover. Glover's
lachrymose ballad became a standard in 1956 when Ray Charles
made the definitive version."[26]

Years later when I met him at King Record Studios on Brewster
Avenue, when he was vice president of Starday-King Records, the
gracious and patient Glover was in the middle of a hectic time, looking over some masters and preparing to return to New York. He
rushed in, finishing off his lunch, remarking that he'd been "running
late for the past five years."[27] His busy-ness certainly helped make
the business what it was. Glover died on April 7, 1991, of a heart attack at the age of sixty-nine.

Ralph Bass was another successful producer for Syd's stable of labels. He was born Ralph Basso in New York City to an Italian father
and a German mother on May 1, 1911. After an injury to his hand
put an end to his hopes for a career as a violinist, Bass became a disc
jockey and later literally bluffed his way into being a record producer
for the Black and White label, whose head thought Bass looked like
he knew what he was doing, even though he didn't. Beginning in
1944, Bass produced such artists as T-Bone Walker, Lena Horne, Jack
McVea, Charlie Parker, and even Jan Garber, joining up finally with
Herman Lubinsky and Savoy Records in 1948 as West Coast R&B
man. During this three-year tenure with Savoy he recorded artists like
Sonny Terry and Brownie McGhee, The Robins, Johnny Otis and Little Esther, and Linda Hopkins. In 1951 he moved from Savoy to King
to take charge of the Federal subsidiary, created expressly for him[28]
after he had been contacted by advance man Jack Pearl and wooed by
Nathan:

Well, after a few weeks, Jack Pearl got hold of me, told me Syd Nathan
was in town, and asked me to talk with him. Money was running short.
I got a written contract and became one of the first record producers to
have a production deal. It wasn't much—a half a cent a record—but it
was unheard-of in those days. And a publishing firm, Armo, of my own.
They established a new label for me, which I called Federal. I produced

the Dominoes, the Midnighters, the Five Royales, James Brown, Ike Turner, Etta James, Johnny Otis, Little Esther. Those were some of the acts I brought to the label.[29]

Bass might have also added such names as Smokey Hogg, Preston Love, Pete Lewis, Little Willie Littlefield, John Lee, Henry Hill, Jimmy Witherspoon, and Johnny "Guitar" Watson to the impressive list of artists he produced for Federal during his tenure for the label, which lasted until 1958. In 1958 Bass left for the Chess/Checker/Argo/Cadet group, leaving behind an illustrious group of artists and recordings that justified Nathan's faith in him. Two years later bandleader-vibist Johnny Otis, the "Hand Jive" man whose R&B revues at the Barrelhouse in Watts and touring across the country were legendary, became the West Coast A&R man for King. There were, of course, other A&R men and producers for Nathan, but none matched the successes of Glover and Bass, not even respected musician and producer Gene Redd. Glover and Bass brought the music the knowledgeable and sympathetic direction it needed to take hold, and to take King to the top.

But, of course, without talented performers the classic records could not have been made, wherever they came from—and Glover and Bass were responsible for finding the talent, too—the top artists who recorded for King in the blues and R&B field are among the national treasures of American music.

One was Roy Brown, whom King actually "inherited" through a deal with Deluxe Records. Brown, a singer from New Orleans, who joined the Linden, New Jersey-based Deluxe label in 1947, came to King after Jules and Dave Braun, who owned Deluxe, severed their relationship with King and joined forces with Fred Mendelsohn to form Regal Records. The move prompted both the Braun brothers and King to sue for breach of contract, the Brauns claiming lack of promotion, Nathan claiming mismanagement, but King ended up with all previously released titles, including titles by Annie Laurie, Paul Gayten, Billy Eckstine, and Benny Carter and, most importantly, the contract of Roy Brown.[30] Born September 10, 1925, Brown sang in church choirs and gospel quartets as a young man, but by 1945 he was winning prizes singing pop and blues songs in amateur shows. After recording two sides for Gold Star in Houston in 1947, Brown joined up with Deluxe later that same year and recorded his most famous tune in July of that year, "Good Rockin' Tonight," a tune later covered and made a bigger hit (because of better distribution) for the King label by Wynonie Harris and recorded for Sun by Elvis Presley.

Brown recorded in various locations like New Orleans, Dallas, Miami, and Cincinnati for Deluxe from 1947 to 1951, and from 1952 to 1955 his recordings were released on the King label. In 1955 he left the label, to return for just two further sessions in 1959. Brown's records, though, were very good for King's business, and established him as a top R&B artist with a distinctive style, as Henry Glover recognized:

> Roy Brown, however, did come up with very big records. Like many artists that had a series of things in those days he sang songs about "Fanny," "Fanny Mae." Many songs now refer to "Fannie Mae." I think this particular origin of the name is in black folklore. They always refer to the hind parts as the "fanny." It was a sort of tongue-in-cheek description of a woman and perhaps how she looked; her shape or something. He constantly sang songs about "I want my Fanny Brown" and different things. Roy also had a very big boogie record called "Boogie at Midnight," that I wrote with him. . . . I will say that if Roy had been a guitarist, he would be as popular today as B. B. King, because in those days Roy was bigger than B. B. King and people said that B. B. sounded like Roy Brown.[31]

Brown's switch from Ink Spots and Frank Sinatra songs proved very beneficial to him, indeed, so he decided to stay with the blues after his success with "Good Rockin' Tonight": "So sure enough I started to sing the blues and would you believe this, my first sixteen releases, *the first sixteen releases* made the Top Four in Rhythm and Blues. In 1949 I had four tunes in the Top Ten simultaneously, I was very happy about that. 'Long about Midnight' was a hit, 'Rainy Weather Blues' was a hit, 'Rockin' at Midnight' was a follow-up to 'Good Rockin'' that was a hit. 'Please Don't Go' was just a fair record. 'Boogie at Midnight' was one of my biggest records, it went to the white kids for the first time, the first time I sold to the whites."[32]

By 1950, although Brown was riding high with hits, he was not reaping the monetary rewards of his artistry, and he considered his move to King records from Deluxe his "downfall"[33] because he had no say about who had his contract and he felt he was being cheated on his royalties. Later, when he complained, he was blackballed for a time, but his reputation still carried him for club dates. And, of course, he still had that powerful, expressive, high-pitched falsetto voice that made songs like "Hard Luck Blues," with its "Rocks on my pillow, cold ground is my bed" lyrics, "Laughing but Crying," with its perfectly insane, almost surreal laughter, and "Butcher Pete" artistic successes. Any song with a chorus like

He's hackin', he's whackin' he's smackin' (3X)
He just hack, smack, choppin' that meat

has to be a candidate for the list of most bizarre songs of all time, particularly when it's a double entendre song dealing with sexuality!

Brown switched to the Imperial label, recording for them between 1956 and 1958, before returning to King for two final sessions in 1959. However, these sessions were very rock-and-roll oriented and, though Brown was in fine form, these are not his best records. His association with King over, Brown moved to a number of different labels, including Home of the Blues, Bluesway, and Mercury, and a triumphant appearance with Johnny Otis at the 1970 Monterey Jazz Festival and to more frequent dates once he decided to get back in the business after so many disappointments.

Wynonie Harris was already a star when Roy Brown, who had offered "Good Rockin' Tonight" to Harris for recording, had his first big hit. The native of Omaha, Nebraska, was born August 24, 1915, and worked during his younger years as a dancer, drummer, and co-median with the nicknames "Sugarcane" or "Peppermint Cane" and "The Mississippi Mockingbird." Harris settled in Los Angeles, work-ing as featured vocalist for Lucky Millinder's band, recording his first big hit, "Who Threw the Whiskey in the Well," for Decca but leaving before Millinder went with King and made Bull Moose Jackson a star.[34] By the time Harris joined King in 1947, he had recorded for Aladdin, Apollo, Hamp-Tone, and Bullet, accompanied by the likes of Johnny Otis, Illinois Jacquet, and Arnett Cobb, and even singing vocal duets with Big Joe Turner. Actually, the duets were appropriate, since Turner was the father of the huge-voiced shouting style that be-came atomic-powered with the vocal cords of Harris. Roy Brown, who did his own friendly "Battles of the Blues" with Roy Milton, re-called how Harris would treat Turner when they appeared on the same stage: "Now you talk about conceited, I thought I was con-ceited but this guy! He did it in a joking way, he was billed as 'Mr. Blues,' he was! He and Joe Turner would be on the same stage, he'd make Joe Turner look like a fool. He'd walk up to him and say, 'What you gonna sing, fat boy?' Joe Turner couldn't read or write and Wynonie would say, 'Sign this autograph!' "[35] It is not a flattering portrait of Harris, particularly in light of saxist Preston Love's asser-tion that when Harris first saw Turner he "went crazy over the big blues shouter" whom he later idolized and "tried to imitate and emulate."[36] Calling Harris an "unbelievable, unlikely man," Love ex-plained his affection for Harris: "He was known for being a profane and raucous individual, but he was a very warm man. The cursing and vulgarism, the sex thing and all that, was a façade he put forth. But he'd give you his right arm, he'd give you the shirt off [*sic*] his back. He did. I could get anything I wanted from him. No matter how many times I borrowed money from him, he wouldn't accept it back because he was making more money than I was in the band."

There was, of course, a great deal of sexuality in Harris's records, and his own sex appeal was responsible for at least part of his success. King was, after all, known for having more than its share of "smutty" records, among them Bull Moose Jackson's "Big 10 Inch Record" and "Nosey Joe," Roy Brown's Fanny Brown records, and Wynonie's "I Like My Baby's Pudding," "Lovin Machine" and "Keep on Churnin (Till the Butter Comes)." King continued to capitalize on this "blue blues" market, even releasing an entire LP entitled *Risky Blues*. The fact was, sex sold, as it did in any other business, and Harris had the looks and presence to sell it hard. King session drummer, Philip Paul, who recorded with Harris in 1954, recalled a wild Harris: "Oh, yeah. But he was fun to record with. He had an exciting, driving way of singing the blues, you know, it made you feel good, you know. So we put up with it. Sometimes we would have to wait for him, you know, to come over to the studio. But he'd come in there and we'd get a tape right away. He was a natural. It was like performing in a club when he recorded. Great! Oh yeah, he's handsome, a handsome guy. I guess that's why he had so many problems, you know. Cause the women liked him, see."[37] With a voice loud enough to break your eardrums but desperate enough to break your heart, and physical gyrations that left little doubt as to what the "rock" in "Rock Mr. Blues" referred to, Harris made flamboyant sexuality his trademark, and it was a flamboyance—at least partially a front, if Preston Love is right—that carried over into other areas as well, like into a friendly feud with Roy Brown. Henry Glover explains: "They had sort of a friendly feud going with each other because they were both popular at the same time. I do recall in Columbus, Ohio, or some place, they jumped up on each others' Cadillacs and banged the hoods off. The two of them, at the time, were making enough money to buy new ones the next day."[38]

Harris had a string of hits for King, including two country western songs, Louis Innis's "Good Morning Judge" and Hank Penny's "Bloodshot Eyes," done up R&B style. His "Grandma Plays the Numbers" was a comic blues which apparently evoked a decidedly noncomic reaction—threats of watery graves if King continued to market the recording. Sex, booze, gambling, that was Wynonie

Harris's forte, and the flashy dressing, flamboyant, fast-talking, Cadillac-driving tomcat with the explosive voice turned the subjects into celebrations during his 1947–54 stint with King. He left for Atco and then returned briefly in 1957 for two unsuccessful sessions before switching to Roulette in 1961 and to Chess in 1964. By 1967 he could no longer sing, and at a benefit in 1969 his throat cancer tortured him so badly that he could hardly laugh. On June 14, 1969, at the age of fifty-six, Wynonie Harris died, his end—like the final song he recorded for King—a "Tale of Woe." His voice gone, sick and weak, nearly forgotten, even after some belated recognition from a show at the Apollo in 1967, Mr. Blues was coming to town no more, unless it was riding on a turntable, not a big Cadillac. His own number had come up but, we should remember, he left the winnings with us.

The big R&B and jazz-blues recorded by Brown and Harris was, as has been said, part of the legacy of Henry Glover, who brought Lucky Millinder to King for some memorable work from the band of the leader who had toured Europe in 1933 and directed the Blue Rhythm Band in 1934, appeared regularly at the Savoy, and recorded for Decca with vocalists including Rosetta Tharpe, Trevor Brown, and Wynonie Harris. There were other orchestras, like that of Todd Rhodes out of Detroit, whose drippingly bluesy Ellingtonian "Blues for the Red Boy" hit the R&B charts in 1948, followed up by "Pot Likker" in 1949. The best of the somewhat larger R&B combos was led by Youngstown, Ohio, native Myron Carlton "Tiny" Bradshaw.

Bradshaw was born to father Pearl Bradshaw and Lillian Boggs on September 21, 1907. He majored in psychology at Wilberforce University with the intention of becoming a doctor, but he turned his attention to the psychology of stomping rhythm and blues in his days with King. Becoming interested in music at around age fourteen, he had learned drums from his father and began playing with combos, forming his own orchestra in 1933 and outfitting them in "plum-colored jackets, black bowties and two-tone shoes."[39] Bradshaw began recording with Decca in 1934, as a kind of " 'Super' Cab Calloway,"[40] and recorded later for several labels, including Savoy, before joining King in 1949 with a smaller outfit of all-out house-rocking R&B screamers. By 1950 his hepped-up "Well Oh Well" was a best seller, and in 1952 he hit with "Soft," which became his theme song (one ad billed him as "Mr. Soft"—no sex symbol, he!). Part of Bradshaw's success came from his bandleading ability, but he was also a fine band pianist and soloist and a forceful vocalist. He cut a string of riff blues that are memorable, including "Breakin' Up the House," "Walk That Mess," and "The Train Kept a Rollin," often

featuring the blasting and rasping tenors of Rufus Gore, Red Pry-
sock, and Sil Austin. Philip Paul, who was asked to join Bradshaw's
band when Bradshaw heard him at the Savoy, joined the band at Cincinnati's Cotton Club in around 1951 and stayed with him for nine
years. It was a tough outfit: "We knew we had to work hard. Like we
would play an hour set; he didn't restrict us. We was basically a blues
band, but we had, at times we had some guys in the band that were
very good jazz players. Sonny Stitt played with us. Johnny Griffin
played with us. Al Sears played with us. We had all kinds of musicians out of Duke's band playing with us. So when they came in the
band, even if it was for one night or two nights, they really had to
work. Noble Watts, Sil Austin—oh God, we wore out tenor players.
But Red was the backbone; he could really handle it."

Listening to the recordings done for King between 1949 and 1958,
it is easy to imagine that the tenor players might need an oxygen machine in the club. Another sax player who could "handle it" was Rufus Gore, Jr., born on February 7, 1928. Gore grew up in Cincinnati
and lived here with his father, Rufus, mother, Pearl, and drumming
brother Edison (born November 4, 1929) for some time at 824 York
Street. Sax player Ray Felder, who played many King sessions himself,
recalled him: "Him and I both played with Bradshaw. And he played
on some of the sessions with King's and I did, too. As a matter of fact,
we'd play them together. As a matter of fact, we played that 'Fever'
with Willie John together. Yeah. 'Mailman Sack,' 'Soft.' A lot of good
tunes. Yeah. He could blow. He had a great big sound." Philip Paul
remembered him as an outstanding player:

> He was a little eccentric. He took things a little further than the average
> guy, but he played better than the average guy, so everyone accepted his
> little quirks, just to have him play with them. He had a beautiful tone. He
> was very inventive. But he was moody. Very moody. He was my room-
> mate quite often on the road, and I just looked after him. I had to kind of
> take care of him . . . it would kind of affect his playing sometime, but we
> knew he had the talent to really incite a crowd. In fact, he played this
> channel on "Soft." You know, that bop a bop a da da, da da da da da. He
> played that. . . . Oh, he could really play a ballad. He had a big sound.
> Beautiful player.

Singer-pianist Jon Thomas recalls that Gore left for New Orleans in
the late fifties,[41] and Edison Gore's son Art, who plays drums with
various outfits in Cincinnati, reports that Rufus and Edison are both
deceased, Edison in 1976 and Rufus in 1981.

Bradshaw did not survive the advent of rock and roll and faded
from the limelight in the mid-fifties, though he did cut one final

session for King in Cincinnati—with Ray Felder, Jon Thomas, Philip Paul, and outstanding bassist Clarence Mack, whom Felder said could "make that bass talk"—in 1958. According to his death certificate, Bradshaw had problems with diabetes, and heart and kidney problems that dated back to 1952 and 1953, but the cause of death is listed as "cerebral accident." He is buried in Cincinnati at Union Baptist Cemetery. His gravestone says simply Myron "Tiny" Bradshaw, 1908–1958—disagreeing, by the way, with the date of birth of 1907 listed on his death certificate—but the name Tiny Bradshaw really says a great deal.

Another top King R&B artist who emerged from black big bands to become a groundbreaking star was Earl Bostic, born in Tulsa, Oklahoma, on April 25, 1913. At one time a grammar school teacher, Bostic gave up teaching for the clarinet but later left the hard life of the road musician for a time to hone his musical skills at Xavier University of New Orleans. By the thirties the clarinet specialist had worked with such musicians as Cab Calloway, Cousin Joe, Hot Lips Page, and Fate Marable, joining with Lionel Hampton's big band in 1943 and arranging for Calloway, Paul Whiteman, and Louis Prima as well. Above all, though, Bostic was an awesome alto player with a *big,* rasping sound that served notice that the authority was on the scene. At jam sessions in New York, Bostic was known for blowing other musicians off the bandstand with his powerful playing. In 1952, John Coltrane played with Bostic: "I went with Earl Bostic who I consider a very gifted musician. He showed me a lot of things on my horn. He has fabulous technical facilities on his instrument and knows many a trick."[42] That seems to be pretty much the commentary on Bostic. Ray Felder gigged with Bostic, with Gene Redd and Pinkie Williams also in the band, and he recalled the experience fondly, but with a bit of frustration as well:

> Yeah, I was on the road with Bostic about a year . . . well, Earl was—he wanted everything, you know. He was demanding, but not too demanding. He was always very friendly, you know. And he would call everybody, instead of saying, "Hey, pardner," he would say, "Hey pardno," you know. "Hey, pardno, what you know pardno." But the only thing about Bostic, Bostic could play. He could play, man. And the people liked when he played, but the musicians, man, they would really catch it because they never got a chance to play. That is why I—I'm surprised I stayed with him as long as I did, but the thing of the deal was it was a lot of experience for me. And it was a lot of exposure, too, because I met a lot of musicians. But actually we did a lot of singing then. You know, he would play the saxophone and we would get harmony. Like "aaah," you know, and all

that stuff. Man, and this was, these things can become pretty repetitious when you're doing this every night. . . . People walk up to you and say, "Hey, man, when are you gonna play your horn?" You know, and you say, "Oh, man, you know" and you try to shunt it away. He never did let anybody else play. It was always Bostic. Even, you know, you would think if you played nightclubs, you know, give the guys a chance to stretch out, but it was never like that. At the time he had these hits, man, and the people wanted to hear those hits. But only way the guys got a chance to play, man, we'd be in town on location and just go and find a jam session somewhere and have a ball, you know . . . he was more in the mechanical way of, the technician way of playing. Knew his instrument well, you know. And, but I was more in the good funky blues type saxophone playing at that time.

A listen to a song like his rendition of "Bugle Call Rag" affirms Bostic's superb technical facility and displays the rasping and wide vibrato that at times borders on anticipating the work of Albert Ayler but is firmly in the tradition of the honking and screaming R&B sax players of the forties and fifties from Illinois Jacquet on. Bostic's early King recordings are generally considered his best, being harder R&B performances, including his fine "845 Stomp." But from his first recordings in 1945 on, Bostic could be counted on for solid professional performances, spirited if sometimes predictable. Trouble was, someone discovered mainstream pop for Bostic, and he made an endless succession of R&B Muzak versions of songs like "Blue Moon," "September Song," "Arrividerci Roma," and other songs that sold well but detract from his reputation as a top R&B star. Still, songs like his number one hit "Flamingo" and top ten hit "Sleep" reveal a marvelously talented performer who brought R&B virtuosity and the pop mentality closer together. What more could Syd Nathan ask for? Bostic died of a heart attack on October 28, 1965. "Always a gentleman, stayed in his tux," H-Bomb Ferguson said of him.[43] I'd have to imagine, though, that he loosened the collar.

Another of King's big R&B combo leaders with roots in the swing bands provided them with their biggest hit. William Ballard Doggett, born in Philadelphia on February 16, 1916, switched from trumpet to piano at age nine and later went on to work with the Ink Spots, Louis Jordan, Lionel Hampton, and Lucky Millinder. Doggett began to work as an arranger-pianist for Millinder, including arranging Millinder's 1940 hit "Trouble in Mind," which quickly brought him other opportunities and allowed him to expand his abilities: "In short order he worked and/or supplied arrangements for the likes of Jimmy Mundy, the Savoy Sultans, Erskine Hawkins, the Ink Spots,

Lionel Hampton, Louis Jordan, and Ella Fitzgerald. He also played on many of these artists' biggest hits. Most importantly, by now Doggett had finally honed to perfection his dynamic concepts of arrangements. He now had a sure fired [*sic*] ability to squeeze the most out of a song. This strength was to ensure his continued success as tastes and styles changed throughout the 1940s and 50s."[44]

After taking up the organ upon seeing the success of his friend Wild Bill Davis, Doggett recorded backup on "Smooth Sailing," "Rough Riding" and "Air Mail Special" for Ella Fitzgerald, and his career was on its own special delivery route. Ray Felder, who liked playing with Doggett because he had "swinging, fresh charts," stayed on the road with Doggett from the days before Doggett's big 1956 hit "Honky Tonk" until 1962. The "Cincinnati Flash," as Doggett called him, recalled the session for "Honky Tonk": "We were in the studio and we were kind of jamming like, you know. The thing came about . . . we were just messing around, man, it was a hit. We hadn't even planned on recording the song. And just started jamming and playing. Here it is." The record skyrocketed, selling over four million discs and bringing Doggett's combo—Doggett did not even play a solo on the record—including Clifford Scott on sax and Billy Butler on guitar—into great demand. Doggett was never the flashiest or best keyboard man in the business—indeed sax and guitar handled most of the solos on his myriad of instrumentals that followed "Honky Tonk"—but he was able to arrange songs with just the right balance of various instruments and create an attractive sound. Although he never again matched the success of "Honky Tonk," songs like "Slow Walk," "Hold It," and "Rainbow Riot" were respectable follow-ups. "Honky Tonk" is still being played in clubs and on radio stations all over the country, and Doggett, though unfortunately remembered primarily for his greatest hit, is still remembered by multitudes of fans and, I would imagine, by King Record execs who recall the time when one of the biggest sellers of 1950s R&B was an offhand addendum to an incomplete recording session.

Of course, King had its share of female R&B singers in the late forties and early fifties. One was Jackson, Tennessee's Mabel Smith, born in 1920 and discovered by Dave Clark singing at the Rock Temple, Church of God in Christ in 1935. Later she joined Christine Chatman's Orchestra, recording for Decca in 1944 and King in 1947 as Big Maybelle. Maybelle stayed in Cincinnati for some time: on Carlisle and on Fifth Street according to Pigmeat Jarrett; on Beale Street in Lincoln Heights according to Lonnie Bennett; at Court and Baymiller according to Roosevelt Lee; and on Findlay and Freeman according to Vince Morton.[45] They all remember her playing places like the Cotton Club, the Ebony Club, the Sportsman's, and the Club Alibi, and being a real crowd pleaser with that huge voice, the biggest since Bessie Smith growled her last blues. Ray Felder recalled that she "was a lot of fun . . . well, you know, she'd kid around with the guys, and the way she would sing then, was almost the way she would talk, you know, sincere, and she had a muscular voice." Fred Mendelsohn, who later took her to Okeh, first saw her in Cincinnati: "Ernie Waits, a DJ in Cincinnati, told me about her. She was playing at a gambling club, I think it was the Club Alibi, in Covington, Kentucky, just across the river. In those days it was wide open, they gambled with silver dollars, not with chips on paper money—completely segregated, of course—and Maybelle would walk around the stage, and one of the songs she would sing was 'Don't you wish your gal had great big legs like mine?' And she'd lift up her dress, and the guys or ladies sitting at ringside would put silver dollars in her stockings."[46] Maybelle later went on to have more success with Okeh ("Gabbin' Blues" in 1953) and Savoy ("Candy" in 1956), but a drug habit reduced her to a pitiful state, and she died in Cleveland on January 23, 1972. Peter Guralnik reports that Fred Mendelsohn heard that her last words were "Thank God."[47]

Ralph Bass was also able to coax from Savoy to his Federal subsidiary young Esther Mae Jones, a Galveston, Texas, native born December 23, 1935. She had won a talent contest at Johnny Otis's Barrelhouse Club in Watts at the age of thirteen (although she was too young to get in!) and began recording as Little Esther Phillips with Otis for Modern and Savoy, hitting with three of the top ten R&B hits of 1950: "Double Crossing Blues," "Cupid's Boogie," and "Mistrusting Blues."[48] When Bass left Savoy for King, he brought Esther with him, and between 1951 and 1953 she recorded thirty-two tracks, mostly in Los Angeles, though her first and last sessions were in Cincinnati and her second was in New York. Phillips recorded some great sides for Federal, including the rocking "Looking for a Man" with Lady Dee on piano and Pete Lewis on guitar and the slow moaning "I'm a Bad, Bad Girl." She sang "I like my man like my whiskey—aged and mellow" on "Aged and Mellow Blues," hinting that alcohol had perhaps already entered her life, and indeed alcohol and drugs precipitated a later downfall. Still, she was producing solid material for King, including a storming, all-out "Mainliner" with the Robins and "The Storm," which reputedly used a flushing toilet for sound effects. Her last King session, with Rufus Gore on sax and Hank Marr on piano, produced two good tunes, "Cherry Wine" with a full, jazzy sax solo, and a growling rendition of Lieber and Stoller's "Hound Dog." Phillips left Federal and went on to Decca, Savoy, Warwick, Atlantic, and Kuda, having success with "Release Me" in 1962 and with a version of idol Dinah Washington's "What a Difference a Day Made"—a disco version which Phillips deplored. Triumphant appearances at Monterey, on the "Tonight Show," and Don Kirschner's "Rock Concert" (and at Cincinnati's Viking Lounge in 1974) revived her career, but she died prematurely, at the age of forty-eight, on August 7, 1984, leaving a strong recorded legacy, particularly on Savoy and Federal.

While King was appealing to a younger generation with their jazz-blues and R&B stars, they weren't ignoring more blues-oriented singers either. One of the best was Alonzo "Lonnie" Johnson, surely one of the greatest and most influential bluesmen of all time. Born February 8, 1889, in New Orleans, Johnson was a multi-instrumentalist (guitar, piano, violin, harmonium, kazoo) and singer whose recording career stretched from 1925 with Charlie Creath to the soundtrack of the film *Blues like Showers of Rain* in 1970. In between those years he established his smooth vocal delivery and nimble guitar work as pinnacles of blues recording for Okeh, Columbia, Decca, Bluebird, Disc, Aladdin, King, Parade/Paradise/Rama, Prestige-Bluesville, Storyville, and Spivey. He also had an exceptional career as an accompanist, backing jazzers like Ellington, Armstrong (with a beautiful solo on "Hotter than That"), and the Chocolate Dandies (sensitive playing on "Paducah") and blues singers like Victoria Spivey, Clara Smith, and Texas Alexander, not to mention some of the most breathtaking jazz recordings ever made in duet with white guitarist Eddie Lang. Johnson had been a "star" a couple of times before he got to King, recording for them from 1947 to 1952, most of the sessions in Cincinnati. His "Confused" made the R&B charts in 1949, but it was "Tomorrow Night" that gave him his biggest chart hit, a ballad of the type Johnson always liked to sing. During his tenure with King, Johnson recorded accompanied only by his guitar ("Backwater Blues" and "Careless Love"), with small piano/bass groups similar to his Bluebird recordings ("Jelly Roll Baker," a reprise of an earlier hit), jump tunes with drums ("Nothin' Clickin' Chicken"), and with stomping big bands ("I'm Guilty"), demonstrating a power and versatility matched by few blues performers. He even recorded two Delmore Brothers tunes, doing a fine job on "Trouble Ain't Nothing but the Blues" and "Blues Stay Away from Me." His electrified guitar emphasized even more that his guitar playing was a clear forerunner to the B. B. King style, a fact King readily acknowledges.

The label for Stovepipe No. 1's "Lonesome John" on Columbia provides us with his real name, Sam Jones. Photo by Per Mathews.

Label photo of Walter Coleman's "I'm Going to Cincinnati," a classic blues performance that provided a wealth of leads to the Cincinnati blues scene. Photo by Per Mathews.

The first release under the name of Bob Coleman touts the powers of the "Cincinnati Underworld Woman," backed with "Tear It Down," also recorded by King David's Jug Band. Photos by Per Mathews.

David Street in Cincinnati's West End, where Pigmeat Jarrett lived at the time he was located and made his performing comeback. Photo by Steve Tracy.

James Mays at his home in Walnut Hills. Photo by Steve Tracy.

Big Joe Duskin.
Photo by Steve Tracy.

Release by blues great
Roosevelt Sykes on the
mysterious Cincinnati label.
Photo by William L. Taylor
and Steve Tracy.

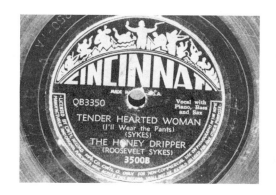

Sign from King Record Studios on Brewster Avenue, c. 1971. Photo by Ed Tracy.

Sign for James Brown's section of King Record Studios, c. 1971. Photo by Ed Tracy.

Former King A&R man, then vice president, Henry Glover. Photo by Ed Tracy.

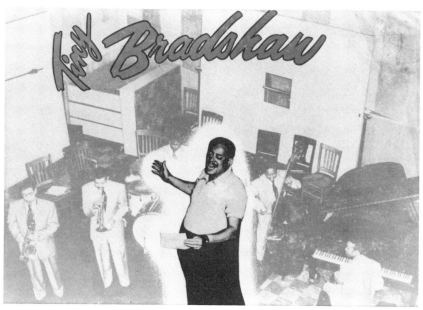

Myron "Tiny" Bradshaw superimposed over a shot of King Recording Studios, from the cover of a Bradshaw LP on King. Courtesy of Dudley Radcliff. Photo of LP cover by William L. Taylor and Steve Tracy.

The only known action shot of King sideman/saxophone master Rufus Gore, whose playing enlivened many King recording sessions. Photo courtesy of Art Gore.

Freddy King influenced a whole legion of blues and rock guitarists with the series of monumental instrumental and vocal recordings he did for King in the sixties. This shot is from the cover of *Freddy King Gives You a Bonanza of Instrumentals.* Photo of LP cover by William L. Taylor and Steve Tracy.

One of King's best blues women, fine singer Lula Reed, who was vocalist on the premier recording of blues standard "Drown in My Own Tears" by her husband Sonny Thompson. Courtesy of Dudley Radcliff. Photo of LP cover by William L. Taylor and Steve Tracy.

H-Bomb Ferguson and one of his many wigs. Photo by William R. Ferris.

Flyer announcing one of H-Bomb's comeback appearances at a local college hangout, Collage. Courtesy of Michael Riley. Photo by William L. Taylor and Steve Tracy.

Publicity still of Jon Thomas.
Courtesy of Jon Thomas.

Boots Johnson at home in 1988.
Photo by Steve Tracy.

Albert Washington and the Astros at Walnut Hills High School, 1972. L to R: James Darks, drums; Walter Cash, bass; Big Ed Thompson, guitar; Albert Washington, guitar. Photo by Ed Tracy.

Lonnie Bennett on keyboards with Albert Washington and Big Ed Thompson, guitars. Photo courtesy of Lonnie Bennett.

The last version of Albert Washington's band before health problems curtailed his performing activities. Back L to R: Debbie Washington, Albert Washington, Roosevelt Lee. Kneeling: Landy Shores and Bobby Goode. Courtesy of Albert Washington.

Rare single on the Boyd label features backing by Cincinnati's "Blues Bees." Courtesy of Dudley Radcliff. Photo by William L. Taylor and Steve Tracy.

Publicity still of Steve Tracy and the Crawling Kingsnakes. L to R: Richard Berry, Dudley Radcliff, Steve Tracy, Phil Buscema, Hudson Rivers III. Photo by Cathy Tracy.

Local Mount Adams folk/blues/ jazz night spot "The Blind Lemon" handed out souvenir matchboxes, recalling Blind Lemon Jefferson's classic recording "Match Box Blues." Photo by William L. Taylor and Steve Tracy.

Johnson lived in Cincinnati from at least 1949 to 1955; he is listed as living with his wife Kay at 828 Rockdale Road, near Rockdale and Reading, during those years, employed as a musician. Roosevelt Lee recalled seeing him at the 33 Club in Newport with Kid Malone and Ray Felder in the band. Felder recorded with Johnson in 1951, and did a few dates with him:

> Well, I played with Lonnie Johnson over the river, and I knew him as a musician. . . . It wasn't a personal thing that we really knew each other. But he knew me as being a musician with his group and he recognized that and he'd speak and rap and talk and have a few drinks over the river and everything. . . . If I'm not mistaken, I think sometime he'd put his guitar on his back and then play it. I believe. . . . He was a well-liked entertainer and he would mingle with the people a lot. He would always—during intermission, he was always around people laughing and talking, and very, you know, joyful, you know, very jolly. He wasn't what you call a guy that really belts out the blues. It was like a natural thing. It was tellin a story, man, you know. The women and guys would really dig it because the lyrics was really about life.

Ultimately Johnson left King—there were some legal problems, apparently—and worked as a custodian at the Ben Franklin Hotel in Philadelphia until the "Blues Revival" got him back in the business and took him to Europe. He settled in Toronto in 1965–66 and died of a stroke in 1970. His was a remarkable career, and if his King recordings present in some ways a streamlined Johnson who doesn't match his earlier instrumental fireworks, they still present a great performer *capable* of matching them and bringing a smooth blues sensibility and seasoned ability to the label.

Ivory Joe Hunter was another smooth-voiced blues singer who recorded for King. The Kirbyville, Texas, native, born in 1914, first recorded on July 11, 1933, for (probably) John Lomax of the Library of Congress, but later formed his own combo in Texas in the thirties, counting such players as Arnett Cobb and Illinois Jacquet among his band members. After recordings for Ivory and Pacific, Hunter joined King in 1947 and produced eight hits for them, including the beautiful "I Quit My Pretty Mama," with its sensitive piano solo, and the country ballad "Jealous Heart" before leaving for MGM and the big hits of his career—"I Almost Lost My Mind," "I Need You So," and for Atlantic "Since I Met You Baby."[49] Hunter did a number of recordings after his tremendous Atlantic success, mixing uniquely rhythm and blues, country, and pop sounds into an individual style, and he made an appearance at Monterey that brought him two LP dates, but he would never again reach the same success he had found earlier, though he was honored by the Grand Ol' Opry for his contributions to country music. He died November 8, 1974, an important contributor to blues, soul, country western, and pop history.

If the singing of Johnson and Hunter was refined, another King artist, Clarksdale, Mississippi's John Lee Hooker, sang with an earthy feeling that was chillingly stark. Born August 22, 1917, Hooker was one of eleven children of two Delta sharecroppers. He sang spirituals in church at an early age, later picking up some guitar from his stepfather William Moore and working with such blues artists as Robert Nighthawk in the early 1930s. He found (and finds) no problem in mixing the two, as he told me in an interview:

> It ain't no devil. The blues not no devil music. . . . I don't believe in the devil music, I don't believe in heaven and hell. I believe in doing good deeds to be pleasin people, you making people happy with your songs and your music. I think you brought a blessing to the whole world . . . people got their own ideas what they wanna do. And some people believe in that. Some people believe in the devil and the hell and stuff like that. I do a lot of good things. I'm a good person. I'm a very easy goin person, and I help a lot of people, and I love people, but I don't believe in that devil and hell and heaven. You know, I think you heaven is what you make it. Your hell is what you make it.[50]

"Ain't no heaven, ain't no burnin hell," goes the old blues, "when I die can't nobody tell"—so believes John Lee Hooker, who casually mixed performances of both sacred and secular music in Mississippi and, after leaving there, in Cincinnati, where he lived in the 1930s: "Oh, yeah, I stayed there about three years. But I didn't get no break there and I left there. I was in Cincinnati when I was around eighteen, maybe somewhere like that. I wasn't doin anything. I really didn't come known until I got in Detroit. You know, it's a lot of people that admired me in these places where I would play at in other cities, like Cincinnati, but I didn't get a break until I got into Detroit. Then there was a record company there [Cincinnati] called King Records, but they never did get to hear me [at that time]. I was just beginning to kind of get into it."[51]

While in the area Hooker worked with gospel groups like the Big Six, the Delta Big Four, and the Fairfield Four, but he also played blues around the area as well.[52] There were no famous blues singers here then, he told me, but he had certainly "heard of the jug band" and made quite a few friends while he was here, playing around in smaller places and gaining experience in music while he worked in the daytime at the Phillips Pump and Tank Co., which was located at 904 Evans Street near Walnut Hills. Eventually, Hooker left Cincinnati for Detroit, where he gigged around and finally recorded, for

Modern Records in 1948, beginning a remarkably profuse recording career that has placed his hypnotic sound on many, many labels: Regent, Savoy, United Artists, Green Bottle, Specialty, Prize, Sensation, Acorn, Chance, JVB, Fortune, Gone, Staff, Gotham, Kent, Chess, Atco, Vee Jay, Stax, and, of course, King, Federal, Deluxe, Audio Lab, and Rockin' among them. Most of his recordings for King labels—sessions in 1948, 1949, and 1950—were cut in Detroit, but there were two 1953 sessions probably done in Cincinnati. Hooker remembers doing sessions here at Brewster Avenue with "Big Syd," and the sides were issued on Deluxe, Chart, or Rockin', and later on Atco and Atlantic LPs after they were purchased by Atlantic from Henry Stone. The sides recorded for King labels are among the very best of Hooker's career, including the low-down, moaning "Nightmare Blues" and "Moaning Blues" and, from his Cincinnati sessions, "Real Real Gone" and "Blue Monday."

Henry Glover told me about his work with Hooker:

> John Lee Hooker, with whom I had the pleasure of recording—conducting recording sessions, was very unique. He was extemporaneous in his creativity; he wrote songs as he played and his foot was his rhythm, and I believe that my amplifying of my recording—I put the microphone on his left foot to pick up the sound of his patting his foot as he played—had a lot to do with the influence of this four beat that they use today. Of course with him trying to compose a song, play the guitar and pat his foot all at the same time, it wasn't always the best rhythm you ever heard, but at least he would try his best to do it. My early experience of recording him, I used a 4 x 8, 3/4 inch plywood board on the floor. He sat by that and put a microphone on the sound of his foot.[53]

Hooker was recording for whoever he could at the time—for King under the name John Lee Booker (a real fooler!), Texas Slim, or John Lee Cooker(!). But a Hooker by any other name is just as sweet, and the Hooker cuts from the King catalogue are among the label's most distinguished low-down blues although, Hooker stated to me, "They never did release that stuff til I got famous." Hooker, of course, went on to a long and illustrious career in the blues and folk revivals, playing festivals in this country and around the world, appearing on television and in films, and even doing a soundtrack for the Democratic National Committee TV commercial in 1964. In the seventies, Hooker came to Cincinnati's Xavier University touring with Canned Heat behind their recently released joint album, but the concert featured more Heat boogie than Hooker blues. As of 1990 he is still going strong with his dark, mesmerizing voice and insistent and earthy guitar playing, one of the miracles of the blues—witness the national success of his LP *The Healer,* which was even featured on MTV. The recording, though, doesn't come close to the power of his King label output, and his more recent, superstar oriented LPs only demonstrate the magic of his crowning achievement at King.

There were other country blues artists who turned up on King as well. One was Country Paul, real name Edward P. Harris, not the country artist Paul Howard, a singer-guitarist born in Leasburg, North Carolina, on August 22, 1923. Harris recorded eight sides for King in 1951 and 1952 in New York City, where Glover found him, though he had recorded for Acorn, Savoy, and Sharp in the two years previous to his King sessions. Glover remembers him as "a very sickly young man at the time" who was "in his early twenties" when the recordings were done.[54] "In a couple of years he passed," Glover added correctly, since Harris died on October 22, 1953.[55] His earlier Savoy recordings showed the influence of Blind Boy Fuller and Lightnin' Hopkins, but the Hopkins influence came much more to the fore on his King sessions. But whether he recorded as Carolina Slim, Jammin Jim, Country Paul, or Lazy Slim Jim, he was an interesting artist whose recorded output, and rare Sharp LP, is certainly worthy of attention. Even better was Ralph Willis, born in Alabama in 1910 and transplanted to North Carolina during the thirties. There he met a number of North Carolina bluesmen like Brownie McGhee and Blind Boy Fuller, and though "Bama" did not join in the street groups who performed for money in the area, he did get a recording career underway in 1944, recording for Regis, Signature, 20th Century, Jubilee, Prestige, King, and Savoy. His best sides were firmly in the North Carolina or southeast blues style, including a wonderful version of Luke Jordan's "Church Bell Blues," a boogieing "Amen Blues," and the sensitive "Blues Blues Blues." Of his Savoy sides, "Goin to Virginia" with the immortal lines "Tell me girl what in the world would you eat / Make your breath smell like your feet" was best, and his King sides, cut in 1953, were his last. With Brownie McGhee and Sonny Terry aboard, he cut five slow blues and boogies in a forceful style that exhibited less of his intricate guitar work than his earlier sessions, though Sonny Terry does some of his finest playing on "Why'd You Do It?" Willis was seemingly well situated to take part in the folk-blues revival as a friend of Sonny and Brownie, who were both in the thick of it, but his death in 1957 robbed him of that chance and left only some wonderful recordings to remind us of what we almost missed.

Sonny Boy Williamson imitator Robert Henry also visited the King studios in March of 1953, cutting four sides that imitate the tongue-twisted vocal style and distinctive harmonica of Williamson rather well. Glover mentioned the session:

> Robert Henry was a kid from Dayton, who wandered into the office one day and made an audition for me. He was, he had to be unique for me to even think of recording him. He played the piano, the guitar, and the mouthharp and sang all at the same time. . . . One song that he had in particular, that I liked very much because it related to me, my knowledge of the old traditional, what we called country-folk blues, it sounded so authentic that, that was my reason for recording him. I think the title of it was "Something Is Goin' Wrong with My Lovin' Machine." Some of his lyrics and expressions were so typical of the old authentic blues singers that down through the South years ago you'd see walking the street playing for a nickel or dime . . . sometimes they'd dance also.[56]

The Henry recording to which Glover referred was a reworking of Williamson's 1940 "My Little Machine," and "Early in the Morning" was a Williamson tune as well. The session, of course, was not a commercial success, but King was at the time in the habit of recording many things that came down the pike and so, thankfully, Henry made four recordings before dropping back into obscurity. It has been suggested that he had some connection with Detroit because of his inclusion on an LP entitled *Detroit Ghetto Blues* (Nighthawk LP104), but Glover placed him in Dayton.

Much better known is William Thomas Dupree, better known as Champion Jack Dupree because of his experience as a professional boxer. Born on the Fourth of July, 1910, in New Orleans and raised in the same Colored Waifs Home for Boys that housed Louis Armstrong, Dupree learned piano and traveled around playing with Drive Em Down, Papa Celestin, and Kid Rena, finally reaching the recording studios in New York in 1944. Through the years he recorded for a multitude of labels—Asch, Joe Davis, Solo, Continental, Alert, Apollo, Derby, Harlem, Red Robin, Groove, Vik, and Atlantic, to name a few—and under a number of names—Brother Blues, Big Tom Collins, Blind Boy Johnson, Meathead Johnson, Willie Jordan, Lightnin' Jr., in addition to Champion Jack Dupree. His earlier recordings especially show the influence of blues performers like Leroy Carr, Peetie Wheatstraw, and Walter Davis, but by the time of his first recording for King, cut in New York in 1951, he was certainly his own man. His "Heart Breaking Woman" is a powerful performance with strong guitar from Brownie McGhee, another influence. He was back with King in 1953 in New York, but his style had mellowed from his first session, and Dupree was pushing a more laid-back blues approach, sometimes with a tongue-tied delivery that was greatly comic, and with top notch sidemen like the great guitarist Mickey Baker and George Smith on harmonica. Dupree's "Tongue Tied Blues" was a big record for him, as was his 1955 cover of Willie Dixon's Checker Record of "Walking the Blues," cut in Cincinnati, according to Henry Glover "one of the very first basic, hard country blues things that went into the pop market, if not the first."[57] But nearly all of Dupree's King recordings were exceptional for his humor and delivery, stellar accompaniment like the bottleneck guitar on "Failing Health Blues" (a thinly disguised "Goin Down Slow") or harmonica on "Sharp Harp." Dupree went on to record many sessions, perhaps even too many, and to TV, film, concert tours, and exhibitions of his paintings, but little of his recorded work matches his King output of 1951–55. He is, quite simply, an original and engaging entertainer whose talents came to fruition especially during his King days.

Many other blues and R&B artists cut for King, including the "famous" Eddie Vinson, Gatemouth Moore, Memphis Slim, Jimmy Witherspoon, Ike Turner, Earl Hooker, and Earl King—and the not-so-famous, Cal Green, for example, who was guitarist for the Midnighters for a time in the late 1950s and cut a fine rock and roll flavored single for Federal, "The Big Push"/"Green's Blues," which featured marvelous guitar solos and strong sax. Chicago singer Lee Williams made a good version of Ike Turner's "I'm Tore Up." "River Boat Dock"/"In the Morning" by Washboard Bill provided an opportunity for the sax man, King Curtis, to wail some of his best work, supported by ace session guitarist Mickey Baker. And the lesser-known but wonderful vocalists Annisteen Allen, Marie Henderson, and Annie Laurie proved themselves worthy of a great deal more attention than they got.

But there were also two blues "Kings" who made some of their finest recordings for the King stable of labels as well: Albert and Freddy. Albert was born in Indianola, Mississippi, on April 25, 1923, and he made his recording debut for Parrot in 1953. From 1959 until 1962 he cut some sides for Bobbin in St. Louis, which turned up on King later, and in 1963 he recorded at King in Cincinnati. Sides like "Let's Have a Natural Ball," "Don't Throw Your Love on Me So Strong," and "Dyna Flow" are classic string-wrenching blues from King featuring tight bands, solid arrangements, and a confident and assured singer and guitarist at the top of his form. Three years after his last King session, Albert began his classic series of Stax recordings that helped establish him as one of the blues greats and brought him to a new audience with the release of his Live Wire-Blues Power LP cut at the Fillmore. King continued to tour and do the big festivals as well as club dates, garnering the respect he deserves for his oft-imitated style. His appearance at Bogart's in the early 1980s found him still in top form, with a tight, professional band to support his powerhouse playing. Unfortunately, he died in 1993.

The other King is Freddy, whose recordings for King Records, all done in Cincinnati between 1960 and 1966, are among the remarkable treasures of electric blues guitar. The Gilmer, Texas, native was born on September 30, 1934, a country boy who left for Chicago in 1950, with a Harmony guitar in his hand and a willingness to develop his guitar style by borrowing from Chicago bluesmen Eddie Taylor, Jimmy Rogers, and Robert Lockwood.[58] King gained experience playing in the clubs in Chicago, getting his first electric guitar and eventually recording for the El-Bee label in 1956 with "instructor" Robert Lockwood also on the session. Freddy attempted for some time to hook up with Chess Records, who rejected him because he "sounded too much like B. B. King"[59] but later Syl Johnson introduced Freddy to Sonny Thompson at Federal, and Freddy was on his way.

His first work at Federal was on a session with Lexington, Mississippi bluesman Otis "Smokey" Smothers, a guitarist who had worked with Howlin Wolf's band in Chicago. Seemingly much enamored of the Jimmy Reed sound, Smothers nonetheless recorded some strong material at his first King session, due in no small part to Freddy King's contributions on guitar. The next day Freddy returned to the studio and launched a brilliant career and a string of hits. Three of the six cuts that he recorded that day—"See See Baby," "Have You Ever Loved a Woman" and "Hideaway"—became hits, and the products of his next session, "Lonesome Whistle Blues" and "I'm Tore Down," also hit the charts. After "San-Ho-Zay" and "Christmas Tears" also charted, King could boast six R&B top ten hits.[60] One of the great things about Freddy's recordings was their crackling vivacity and verve, attributed by Philip Paul, session drummer, to Freddy's manner in the studio: "It was like playin in a club with him, you know. He'd just say, 'O.K. 1, 2, 3 4, let's go' and you'd just follow him. And every session was like that. So it was enjoyable. . . . We'd work until we'd get the right sound, but he didn't want to continually do takes. He wanted that spontaneous feeling, and you could hear it in all his recordings. I always enjoyed recording with him. . . . He'd come in and say, 'I want to play this,' he'd play it for you, and that's all you'd need."

Indeed. With top notch musicians like Paul, Bill Willis, Fred Jordan, Sonny Thompson, and Gene Redd, Freddy created some of the best blues vocal and instrumental recordings of the sixties. It has been suggested that too many instrumentals were recorded behind the success of "Hideaway" and "San-Ho-Zay," but all one needs to do is just listen. What other blues instrumentalist can carry off the number of instrumentals that Freddy did? Who else could develop Chicago blues style guitar riffs into such funky and brilliant songs as "Manhole" or "Nickelplated," or the tender and beautiful "Sad Nite Owl," the laid-back "Cloud Sailin'," or the driving, pounding "Texas Oil." And name more than a handful of performances equal to his amazing reading of western swing man Herb Remington's "Remington Ride," most assuredly one of the true triumphs of electric guitar playing, the kind of demonstration that makes you proud to be a human being because you can be categorized as a member of the group that produced *that*. Then there are the experiments, the bossa nova blues that Freddy endured, and the pop-blues. Even to these he brings an expertise that raises them above the ordinary. His duets with Lula Reed, the "Drown in My Own Tears" woman who was married to Sonny Thompson, were interesting, too, but finally it was Freddy's blues that made the real grade. Unfortunately, apparently DJ troubles for King Records prevented Freddy from having hits after 1961, even though his output was of the highest caliber, and eventually he went on to other labels like Cotillion, Atlantic, and, in his rock phase, Shelter and RSO. He died in Dallas, Texas, on December 28, 1976, of hepatitis and other complications, finally recognized as a distinctive, powerful blues performer, an influence to many, but finally most important because of the legacy he left on King labels.

King Records, of course, had vocal group recordings as a mainstay of their catalog as well. The Dominoes, featuring Juilliard graduate Billy Ward and lead singer Clyde McPhatter (later with the Drifters), gave King a number of big hits, including "Have Mercy Baby," "The Bells," and "Sixty Minute Man." The latter, sung by bass singer Bill Brown, was the top R&B record of 1951. Hank Ballard and the Midnighters provided more hits: "Sexy Ways," "Work with Me Annie" and (the inevitable outcome song) "Annie Had a Baby," "Teardrops on Your Letter," "Finger Poppin' Time," "The Twist," and others. Chubby Checker covered the latter, but Ray Felder, who was on the original session, remembered: "Matter of fact, we did—we were the ones that put out 'The Twist.' We did 'The Twist' and Hank Ballard put it on an album. And this is where it got hidden. Chubby Checker came along. Matter of fact, the saxophone player took my—baritone sax player, I believe—played my solo almost note for note." With Checker copying Ballard and the saxophone player copying Felder, the record started a national craze. Drummer Philip Paul, also on the

"Twist" session, fondly recalled recording with Ballard: "He was a great guy to record with. Yeah. . . . It was an all-day affair, like. It was like a party, you know? Nothing was constructed. They was partyin. They said, 'O.K., let's do another one,' you know. It was relaxed. It was enjoyable. That's the kind of guy he is. He should still be on top, really." The Platters, Otis Williams and the Charms, Patti Labelle and the Bluebelles, the Checkers, the Swallows, the Five Royales—all appeared at one time or another on a King label.

But King's most successful singer, "the artist of all artists," as Glover called him, was John Davenport—Little Willie John.[61] Johnny Otis discovered him in Detroit and took the seventeen-year-old to Syd Nathan, and from there it was hit time. "All around the World," "Need Your Love So Bad," "Talk to Me, Talk to Me," and his biggest hit, his No. 1 hit in 1956, "Fever." Henry Glover expressed great admiration for his talent, but acknowledges his difficult nature as well: "He was a really, truly great singer. I would say that blues came so natural to him that he was just a master at that and no one living during that day could touch him. He had some of the greatest blues gymnastics and voice gyration that you could ever dream of a person having. He was a typical rhythm and blues artist, egotistical, he of course became involved in drinking and some of the other vices that go along with the business. It seems as though some of these artists are the ones that perform better. The very nice artists don't make it. Willie John was a headache."[62] But he was the kind of headache you would suffer. Bassist Ed Conley echoed the sentiment: "The only other person that I could say was as wild as [Wynonie Harris] would be Little Willie John. And he was pretty wild. He was a spoiled little brat. That's the truth of it. But he could sing! He had the flair . . . the guy was good, but he was a spoiled brat, temperamental, and they put up with him."[63]

Glover may not have known the problems that walked into his office at 5 o'clock one afternoon when he first met John, but he knew enough to get John and musicians in the studio in New York within three hours to record his first hit, a cover of a Titus Turner song, "All around the World." And in the studio? Ray Felder: "Oh, yeah, he was very professional. Young guy, man. He died at a young age but he was very professional. Oh, he was really talented! And the people loved him. . . . He could have went a long ways. Real talented. And I used to like the stuff he did. And I used to like recording with him. And he was kind of a witty guy, you know. He would get along with the guys and have them laughing. It would make the guys' day, you know."

Later John was involved in a street brawl murder in 1961 and served some time, dying of pneumonia in prison in 1968 and bringing to a premature end the promising career of a great R&B artist, second only to Soul Brother No. 1 James Brown as top solo artist for King Records. Brown paid his own tribute with the LP *Thinking about Little Willie John and a Few Nice Things* (King 1038), the tribute of a new king to an old one.

One thread that ties the blues, jazz-blues, R&B, and vocal group material together is the studio musicians. Often the same musicians would be present not only on those sessions but on country and whatever other sessions as well. Their top notch abilities helped produce recordings of lasting value for King as well.

Ray Felder was born in Cincinnati's West End, and got involved in music after he had heard it at clubs like the Cotton Club. He played in his high school band, as well as in a marching band and in the 17th Special Services all-black jazz band in Germany while he was in the service, at which point he got involved in music theory and harmony. Upon his return to Cincinnati he played at various clubs—J. K.'s in the West End; Babe Baker's; the Cabana Lounge; Screw Andrews's 333; Sportman's Club; the Alibi; the Play Bowl—with people like Curtis Peagler, Woody Evans, Snooky Gibson, and Kid Malone. In the early fifties Felder joined Jay McShann's band on the road, recording with him in Kansas City, possibly on a label owned by McShann. Felder had the opportunity to play the Jazz at the Philharmonic with Flip Phillips, Illinois Jacquet, and, just out of Ellington's band and sitting in in Kansas City, the great Ben Webster.

Felder did his first recordings with a man who was born and raised around Seventh and John in Cincinnati's West End. Pinnochio James played around the Cincinnati area at places like the Club Alibi and the Sportsman's Club, but later left with Lionel Hampton and finally wound up doing an Okeh recording session with Felder, bassist Ed Conley, and pianist Herman Smith—all three of whom also worked as sidemen at King—in New York City on October 23, 1952. One of the sides James recorded, "333 Jump," may in fact have reference to the local 333 Club, which he may have played and certainly would have known. Felder described James an an Eddie Vinson-type singer who didn't do much recording while with Hampton—only two sides. But for Ray it was another session, more experience in the studio. Influenced by players like Arnett Cobb, Louis Jordan, Sonny Stitt, Gene Ammons, Dexter Gordon, Charlie Parker, and John Coltrane, Felder developed a strong, blues-rooted style, playing tenor, alto, and flute, that was ideally suited for King-style R&B, as Syd Nathan and Sonny

Thompson recognized. Thompson heard him play some gigs in Cincinnati and invited him to join with King, starting a long association that found Felder backing such artists as Little Willie John, Wynonie Harris, Lonnie Johnson, Hank Ballard, Earl Bostic, Lula Reed, Sonny Thompson, Freddy King, and Amos Milburn and Charles Brown, as well as with the Sugar Canes, a group he led. Ray stopped doing sessions for King after Syd Nathan died, but he continued to play and record—with Jack McDuff, Wild Bill Davis, Bill Jennings, Groove Holmes, and with his own band.

Drummer Philip Paul was born in New York City on August 11, 1925. His father was from the Virgin Islands, his mother from St. Thomas, and his father and uncle had a family band that played calypso and influenced him to take up the drums at age nine. After private lessons and high school band, Paul went to the Manhattan School of Music. While in New York, Paul played with Milt Larkin, recorded for Decca with Buddy Johnson, and cut some sides with Basie sidemen accompanying Jimmy Rushing. While he was playing at the Savoy, Tiny Bradshaw heard him and six months later he joined Bradshaw at Cincinnati's Cotton Club, remaining with Bradshaw for around nine years. Through Bradshaw Paul got hooked up with King, and countless sessions followed: Bradshaw, Wynonie, Bull Moose Jackson, Bill Jennings, Titus Turner, Hank Ballard, Hank Marr, Tab Smith, Gene Redd, Smokey Smothers, and, of course, Freddy King—and that's just the blues and R&B sessions. Additionally, Paul recalls the 1960 Christmas LP session with Charles Brown, which also featured Redd, Bill Willis on bass, Fred Jordan and Ed Thompson on guitars, and Amos Milburn as well. Paul also cut with Grandpa Jones, Bonnie Lou, Cowboy Copas, Hawkshaw Hawkins, and "a group from Argentina" (at 2:30 in the morning!), testifying to his great versatility as a musician. Paul got out of music full-time about eight years ago, settling for good in Cincinnati and working with Woody Evans, at the Ebony fashion shows, and free-lancing, and is known as an always solid, always dependable, multidimensional drummer.

Bassist Ed Conley was born in Covington, Kentucky, in 1928, and attended a segregated school called Lincoln-Grant. As a youngster he studied piano for four years with the principal's wife, played snare drum in the school band, and was finally switched by his band teacher over to the bass. In addition, he studied at one point at Artie Matthews's Cosmopolitan School on Ninth Street, impressed by Matthews's dynamic, no-nonsense style. During the forties he began listening to black big bands—Basie, Ellington, Erskine Hawkins,

King Kolax. After his military service, he attended Howard University in Washington, D.C., buying a bass with his mustering-out pay. Back in Cincinnati, Conley began playing cocktail bar pop tunes with Frank Payne at a place in Avondale called Toddy's Bar and Grill, and then at the 19th Hole on Rockdale. Later, when they went into the Downbeat Club, a black club in Walnut Hills, they had to change their repertoire to suit the tastes of the black patrons, and from there they went to the 333 Club, where they were the house band and backed up Lonnie Johnson. For three or four years he studied with a Cincinnati Symphony Orchestra bassist, Joseph Van Ryck; later, while he was working at the Cotton Club with Slide Hampton, Bill Doggett heard him and asked him to make a session with him. That was the beginning of Conley's work at King, which encompassed not only blues and R&B but country western sessions with Bonnie Lou and some work with Ruby Wright as well. Conley characterizes himself musically as "available and reliable," not a highly ambitious musician: "I didn't have the kind of drive and will that some of the guys came up with." The advent of the electric Fender bass and the proficiency of Bill Willis, who worked in the plant at King, on that instrument, spelled the end of his work at King, but not before Bill Doggett, Lonnie Johnson, Little Willie John, Earl Bostic, Roy Brown, Hank Ballard, John Puckett, and others had benefited from his expertise on the bass.

There were, of course, other regular studio musicians: saxist Rufus Gore and his brother, drummer Edison Gore, whose son Art is now a respected local drummer; guitarist Clifford "Wig" Bush, who played on Jon Thomas's "Rib Tips"; vibist and guitarist John Faire; pianist Woody Evans; bassist Clarence Mack, who was with Bradshaw and according to Ray Felder "made that bass talk"; drummer Calvin "Eagle Eye" Shields; and guitarist Fred Jordan, who helped enliven Freddy King's records so much and is recalled by Philip Paul as "very talented. Very inventive. They would call him to come through with a fill or something to ignite the record, and he would do that."

Musicians like these are the unsung heroes of King Records, who did enliven countless sessions with their musical expertise for a flat rate, no royalties. What do they think of the work at King? Philip Paul:

> Well, like I would get a call *the same morning*. You know, maybe 7 or 7:30 A.M. Can you get over here in a half hour? O.K. I'd get up and walk over there. And, uh, maybe the artist wouldn't be there. But maybe who-

ever the A&R man was may have, would have a little riff or something in his head. He'd say, "It goes like this" or something, you know? And we'd wait until the artist arrived and the artist would sing. Maybe they couldn't keep four bars together. But we'd work until we put something together. If it took all day. . . . Yeah, with the little head sets. And they used all kinds of recording devices. But basically they never came, very seldom did they come in with charts for everybody and say play this, play this, play that. It was always—Syd Nathan wanted you to do something fresh all the time. I don't care if you recorded three albums a day, he always wanted something different. He didn't want the same beat on every tune. And you would have to sit there and come up with something. Because he would be in the booth hollering at you, you know. I look back on that and it was very insulting at the time, but it was a lesson also, because he provided musicians an opportunity to record under those conditions and see what recording was really about.

Paul recalls playing kettle drums, wood blocks, even a suitcase in place of a bass drum, to get the "right" sound. Paul reemphasizes: "You had to be creative. I keep repeating this because that was a requisite for being on the staff over there." Horn man Felder recalled more charts at sessions, but he, too, remembered the effects: "Sometime we did a lot of hand clappin. That was the guys in the band. Sometime it would be something where, hey, man, it might be an old washboard or somethin or rubbing some sticks together or anything. It's the kind of sound that maybe Syd—'Hey, I can hear that certain sound in there. Try this.' And we would do it. Or somebody there would do it. Might even be a spectator. Conley also found the sessions interesting, but he probably enjoyed them a bit less on account of the famed Nathan temper: "At any session Syd Nathan was there and you could count on him to interrupt, disrupt the recording session because it didn't meet his approval or what he considered to be the right way to do it or the right sound. He was a very bombastic, energetic, hard-driving type of guy. And he had an idea about things and, you know, funny, really, but let's face it, he made a success out of it, so I couldn't argue with that." And indeed it is difficult to argue with Nathan's success. Though there were some misguided musical experiments, many others also testified to the intelligence, strength, and shrewdness it took to build King.

King, of course, was not left untouched by the concerns with payola that erupted in the late fifties. The front page of the November 20, 1959, *Cincinnati Enquirer* reported that King, along with Coral, Capp, Roulette, Dot, Imperial, Cadence, Liberty, and Gone Records, was subpoenaed by New York District Attorney Frank Hogan.[64] The same day the *Cincinnati Post* reported that Nathan said that "his firm has paid off disc jockeys all over the country and that he has the checks to prove it."[65] The article continued:

"It is a dirty rotten mess," said Nathan, "and it has been getting worse in the last five years."

Nathan said his company made regular monthly payments to disc jockeys for about a year in 1957–58. "In that period," he said, "King spent $1800 a month on 'payola to disc jockeys'." Nathan said he still pays one disc jockey in Chicago $25 a month.

"But mostly we quit it; and I'll tell you why," he said. "Our statistics showed that we didn't get our records played any more often whether we paid or not."

By March 4, 1960, King was accused of making payments to disc jockeys by the FTC—odd because Nathan had admitted it in print four months earlier!—and the October 18, 1960, *Post Times-Star* reported that the "Local Firm Bows to FTC on Payola": "The Hit Record Distributing Company of 3414 Colerain Avenue and president Isadore Nathan were forbidden to pay concealed payola. The consent order was agreed to, although agreeing to abide by the order did not constitute any admission of guilt." Also named in the consent order were Starday Records and Publishing Co., Inc. and Starday International Sales Co., Inc. of Madison, Tennessee, whose records King was to print and who would later buy out King in the mid-sixties.[66] It was a difficult time, but King came through it and continued putting out fine records, although there were decreasing numbers of the old rhythm and blues and blues hits and more from the emerging superstar talent James Brown, who gave the firm the hit records it needed in the sixties to keep it alive.

When Syd Nathan died on March 5, 1968, in Miami Beach—his home six months of the year (he spent the other six at 6325 Elmview Place in Bond Hill)—he left behind a company that had been deteriorating for some time, and would eventually be sold a number of times. The first sale was reported in the October 22, 1968 *Cincinnati Post:*

King Records Inc., Cincinnati-based country and western recording firm, is being sold to Starday Recording and Publishing Co., Inc. of Madison, Tenn., also a major country and western producer.

Purchase is being made from the estate of Sydney Nathan, King founder.

The deal will merge two closely allied record firms. Starday is headed by Don Pierce, long-time friend of Nathan's, and Hal Neely, former vice president and general manager of King, now executive vice president of Starday.

Neely will become president of King after sale negotiations are completed.[67]

King was bought by Starday, whose records King had and would continue to press, only to be resold to Lin Broadcasting the next month. That sale was reported in the November 14, 1968, *Post:*

> Lin Broadcasting Corp. plans to acquire Starday Records and Cincinnati-based King records for about $5 million . . .
> A Lin spokesman says both King and Starday will be operated as subsidiaries under the present management of Don Pierce, Starday president, and Hal Neely, former vice president and general manager of King and now executive vice president of Starday.
> Lin Broadcasting is a diversified Nashville, Tenn. firm with interests in radio and television stations, a telephone answering service, art galleries, and training and educational programs.[68]

By 1973 *Blues Unlimited* was reporting that a power struggle among the bosses at King—Neely, Freddy Bienstock, and Lieber and Stoller—had resulted in Neely being voted out of office: "a skeleton staff are keeping the non-hit-for-nine-months premises open."[69] Gusto finally acquired the King material, and, throughout it all, reissues of classic King blues, R&B, and country have come forth, though often the same material was reissued over and over again. More recently, "Sing" records has been issuing old King LPs with original covers, putting into print King material that has been hard to get for years, and recordings also continue to be issued on the King, Official, and Mr. R&B/Route 66 labels, the latter with excellent presentation full of great notes and fine photos.

Nathan's wife Zella, his son Nathanial, and an adopted daughter, Mrs. Beverly Cook, all survived him and saw him buried at Judah Touro Cemetery in Price Hill. King continued, of course, especially with reissue after reissue of old material, but there was also a time when they took sledgehammers and axes to thousands of records behind the warehouse on Brewster. Now people are recognizing more and more the great contributions of Syd Nathan, King Records, and its staff and artists to American music: "They was one of the best labels in the world for cuttin records at that time," guitarist Big Ed Thompson told me. "And you can hear today, you can take and play one of King's records right now, and compare it to any record, in any record company, and you can hear that *mmmph.* . . . It's beautiful."[70] Cincinnati—and the world—were lucky to have had it.

Another label that was based in Cincinnati in the mid-forties is as obscure as King Records is famous. The Cincinnati label, according to the record labels licensed by Cincinnati Record Manufacturing

Co., seems to have leased material from other labels; so far as is
known, none of the material issued on the label was recorded here,
though in fact not much is known. Researcher Galen Gart told me
in a telephone interview that *Billboard* magazines from the relevant
period made no mention of the label at all.[71] We do know that
the label issued recordings by the following artists: Joe Williams with
the Three Chocolates, Inez Washington and the Four Kings of
Rhythm, Roosevelt Sykes, Lem Johnson, and Brother John Sellers.
Williams, born Joseph Goreed in Pigmeat Jarrett's hometown of
Cordele, Georgia, on December 12, 1918, later went on to fame with
Count Basie and as a solo artist. His Cincinnati label recording,
"Round the Clock Blues Pts. 1 and 2," was issued as Cincinnati 2300
(MXQB3345), featuring a purple label with silver lettering. The
Washington release, Cincinnati 2301, "New That Ain't Right"/
"Soldier Man Blues" (MX512/513) featured a red label with silver
lettering. Roosevelt Sykes's Cincinnati release, "I Wonder"/"Tender
Hearted Woman" was reissued as Cincinnati 3500 (MX QB3349/
QB3350) with a black label with silver lettering. Lem Johnson's "Es-
skay Blues"/"It's A Good Deal" was Cincinnati 3501 (MX N501-
N503). No information is available on Brother John Sellers's record.
The records by Sellers and Johnson were recorded in New York
City—indeed, Johnson had recorded for Decca in New York City in
1940 and 1942—and the Williams record was probably recorded
there, too, but Sykes cut his in Chicago, suggesting that the small label may have been leasing material. Both Sellers and Johnson recorded for J. Mayo Williams's Southern label and for King Records
as well, but no connection between Cincinnati and Southern or King
has been established. Additionally, Sykes's recording of "Tender
Hearted Woman" on Cincinnati 3500 also appeared on Black and
White 100, suggesting a connection between those labels. Paul
Reiner, who took over Black and White around 1946, was a distrib-
utor from Cleveland, Ohio, so he had connections with the state but
not, so far as is known, the city. A search of city directories and telephone books from the 1940s and 1950s turns up no references to a
Cincinnati Record Manufacturing Company, so for now the mystery
of the name of the record label remains just that—a mystery.

There would, of course, be other small labels in Cincinnati that released blues records, some excellent ones, but none of the labels,
sometimes one-shot deals or producers of just a handful of records,
match the output of the industry giant built by Syd Nathan, Howard
Kessel, and their partners. Still, the small label had its function, and
it aided artists like H-Bomb Ferguson and Albert Washington in cre-

ating and building a following for their own brand of blues. VLM, Finch, Big Bang, L and W, and many others will all be discussed in a later chapter, but they should be mentioned here as partaking of the kind of artistic spirit that took King to the top.

8

H-Bomb Ferguson

Another man who recorded at King at one point in his career is one of the wild men of rhythm and blues. Local musicans report on his unorthodox playing style: one night at a club where he was playing, he found some carpenter's tools that had been left behind by some workman doing repairs and promptly began pounding and sawing his way through rocking piano R&B. The story may or may not be true—I don't think I'll lend him a piano—but listening to his wild patter and uninhibited style, seeing his pet boa constrictor and many colored wigs, one senses that the unexpected can be expected. The obvious spiritual cousin is Screamin' Jay Hawkins, a real screamer if you've ever heard one, whose coffin antics and bizarre recordings are legendary. But when *this* man sings, it *is* like an H-bomb.

H-Bomb Ferguson was born Bob Ferguson in Charleston, South Carolina, in 1930 or 1931 (he is not sure which). His father was a Black Indian minister who shared many other religious people's concerns about the secular nature of the blues, the devil's music, and the Reverend Ferguson, a trombonist himself, sent young Bobby to music school to learn church music with a stern order not to play the blues. The young boy liked the blues, though: "Whenever he would catch me playin the piano, playin the boogie woogie, he hit me across my hand with a stick. Told me, 'That's bad,' you know, 'That's the devil.' I said, 'One of these days I'm gonna play what I wanna play. . . .' Cause I really loved the blues. I wanted to play it—always did."[1] But the music caused a great deal of difficulty with his father for H-Bomb, who these days recalls a difficult domestic life for him and his mother as he grew up, prompting a resentment he carried to his father's funeral: "Man, I think about things my momma went through, my father—he was a minister—and I tell anybody, he was alright, after I got older. He wasn't shit. He whipped your fuckin ass, and get up in church, and everybody say, 'Reverend Ferguson.' When he died, I came when they was puttin him in the grave. I meant to be late. What got me was he could get up in church and talk so nice and come home and kick your *ass*, buddy. I swear, I won't lie on it."[2]

His father's religious hypocrisy in such matters likely drove the boy even further away from the church and toward the blues. What better way, after all, to turn the twenty-five-cent-an-hour piano lessons for which his father was paying into rebellion? But, then, he had to endure the piano teacher's rule, too: "She used to take her old sharp ruler and hit me across the hand. 'D! D! D! D!' She'd made you stay on one note for like twenty minutes. She'd walk all around, go in the house, come back out. She said, 'You hit C. I said D!' Crack! 'D! D! D! D! You learn that, then you get to the next one.' Crazy! But later on, it paid off. I appreciate it. But at the time, I really didn't want it. I was like 10, nine, 10 or 11."[3] When his mother tried to convince him that he should listen to his father's edicts on blues, Ferguson decided he'd had enough and moved in with his sister, learning even more about playing the blues from a friend of his brother-in-law.

During this time it was the great blues singers Big Joe Turner, Jimmy Rushing, and T-Bone Walker that inspired him, especially the gymnastics of Walker, who did the splits and played guitar behind his head, showing Ferguson the value of a wild stage show, as Wynonie Harris and Tiny Bradshaw did later. At seventeen, Ferguson started as a serious musician, he told me, forming a band in North Carolina that caught the notice of a touring Jack "The Bear" Parker, who asked him to go on tour. The money wasn't good, Ferguson said, on the one-nighters, but they'd record in New York. Ferguson told researcher Barry Lee Pearson that it was Cat Anderson's band that encountered him at age sixteen and later returned for the young man, who dropped out of eleventh grade and left.[4] Whichever the case, against the will of his father but with the blessing of his mother, he left—"I threw my stuff in a little plastic suitcase and I was gone"—as Bobby Ferguson but soon became, thanks to manager Chet Patterson, the "Cobra Kid": "He said, 'See, when you came out, you was so damn skinny, but you got a big ass mouth. So you strike people, you catch them off guard. See, when you walk on the stage, Bob, I'm gonna tell you, people think you gonna sing low because of your size. And when you open your mouth, the god damn building falls out. So you strike people like a snake.' "[5]

Now, New York City is a bit different from Charlotte, North Carolina, entertainmentwise, and Ferguson soon found out the pecking order: "I thought for a while," he told me, "when I first got to New York City I was real good. Til a guy comes up there behind you, a guest star, and make you feel like two cents. So I know I had to get my act together." When you're third billed, he found out, you get to sing only two songs or so between the appearances of the main attractions. This situation disappointed and frustrated him, but also gave him some much-needed experience and exposure.

One of his best supporters and advisers in New York City was comedian Nipsey Russell, who then worked as MC and DJ at a club called the Baby Grand. Russell encouraged Ferguson to move around to different clubs, to avoid settling in and becoming stagnant at one place. He also advised H-Bomb on his singing, which at that time was a pretty close imitation of King recording star Wynonie Harris.

> I admired him. I really did. Cause when I was singin at that particular time, Nipsey, he said, "Why don't you vary your tone a little bit, because you sound a little like Wynonie," and he was already out there on King Records. I said, "What could I do?" He said, "Vary your voice a little bit, and maybe you'll make it, cause people'll think you're copyin him." "Oh," I said, "Now, I just like him. And I sing on this kick." Well, he told me to try and vary it and get away from him because you don't need two Wynonie Harrises. So I tried. Then I came up with this act, and I tried to change around.

Russell, too, took him to the people at Derby Records at 125th and 8th Avenue in New York, where he made his first recordings around March 1951 with Jack "The Bear" Parker's orchestra:

D-726	My Baby Was a Winehead Woman	Derby 759
D-727	Hard Lovin Woman	———
	I'm Gone, I'm Gone	Derby 769
	Jumpin' and Shoutin'	———

The label filed for bankruptcy, however, and Ferguson made only twenty-five dollars for his efforts. Ferguson then moved to the Atlas Record Company, recording with Charlie Singleton's orchestra, with Big John Greer on tenor sax and Lou Donaldson on baritone sax, sometime between 1950 and 1952:

I Love My Baby	Atlas 001
Rock, H-Bomb Rock	Atlas 1250
Gone with the Wind	Atlas 002
Blow Mr. Singleton	———
On My Way	Atlas 005
Good Time Gal	———

December of 1951 found him back in the studio with Parker, and, according to Ferguson, James Moody, for a session for Prestige

Records, all but two sides of which went unissued:

275	I'll Get You Baby	Unissued
276	Feel Like I Do	Prestige 918
277	Money Mad Woman	Unissued
278	My Love	Prestige 918
279	Whiskey Head Gal	Unissued
280	Little Girl Blues	Unissued
281	My Number's Up	Unissued
282	I'm Wise Baby	Unissued
283	Paradiddle Joe	Unissued
284	Jumpin' at Jack's	Unissued

It was, again, Nipsey Russell who put Ferguson in touch with Lee Magid, who was to produce some of Ferguson's best work, for Savoy, on December 12, 1951, and January 10, 1952. Ferguson told me that Chet Harris named him H-Bomb, but he told Pearson that it was Magid. Since his name appeared on records as "H-Bomb Ferguson" before the Savoy sessions with Magid, his contention that it was Harris may be correct. Whoever it was, he reproduced the conversation:

> And he said, "You know, to be a small guy"—and that was really big—"you got a lotta mouth, when you sing. Sound like you go to pieces." He said, "That 'Bobby Ferguson' ain't gonna work in show business." I said, "What's wrong with that?" He said, "It don't go with what you're doin. You got to have somethin that stands out because you are awful loud." I said, "Well, what kind of name should I use?" He said, "I tell you what." You know that H-bomb was out at the time. He said, "You heard of the H-bomb?" I said, "Yeah, that's what they drop on people." He said, "That's what I'm gonna call you." I said, "Naw, naw, I don't want to be a bomb." He said, "No. It fits you—We gonna leave your last name—But I'm gonna take 'Bobby' out of there. Call you H-Bomb Ferguson." I said, "That don't sound human." He said, "You're not."

Bobby Robinson, on the other hand, says he was "hung up" on being called H-Bomb—he had to have a nickname.[6] Whatever the case, the name stuck, and Ferguson's first four Savoy sides, recorded with Julius Watkins on trombone, Pinky Williams on alto sax, Purvis Henson on tenor sax, Kelly Owens on piano, Leon Spann on bass, and Parker on drums, are dynamic, Wynonie Harris-inspired, explosive blues.

HBF4131-1	Slowly Goin' Crazy	Savoy 830, SJL 2244
HBF4132	Preachin' the Blues	Savoy 848, SJL 2244
HBF4133	Sundown Blues	Savoy SJL 2244
HBF4134	Good Lovin'	Savoy 830, SJL 2244

With H-Bomb's Harris-type vocals and appearances in New York, it was inevitable that the two would run into each other, and they did, at the Apollo:

He was playin at a bar in Harlem. And I was at the Apollo Theatre. You know, they had the show up there for one week. So after the show, I went back in the dressing room and he was standin there. And he said, "Hello Wynonie Harris, Jr." I said, "What?" He said, "You know me? I'm Wynonie." And he had a guy with him—"This is Wynonie Harris. You the one that try to sound like him." He said, "Oh, that's all right. You been helpin me cause I tell everybody when I'm travelin that you my son," they ask about me. You know he was old enough at the time. I said, "Oh, the pleasure's all mine." He said, "Why you wanna try to act like me?" I said, "No, I don't. I like the way you sound. I don't wanna be like you." And we went out that night and got drunk.

Savoy liked him enough to have him back for a second session on January 10, 1952, with Pinky Williams and Parker back as well, adding Leon Comegeys on trombone, Count Hastings on tenor sax, Jimmy Neely on piano, and Laverne Barker on bass, for seven more sides:

SHBF4143 Give It Up	Savoy 865, SJL 2244
SHBF4144 Big City Blues	Savoy 836, SJL 2244
SHBF4145 My Brown Frame Baby	Savoy SJL 2244
SHBF4146 New Way Blues	Savoy SJL 1176
SHBF4147 Bookie's Blues	Savoy 836, SJL 2244
SHBF4148 Life is Hard	Savoy SJL 1176
SHBF4149 Hot Kisses	Savoy SJL 1176

Six months later he cut two sides with Varetta Dillard, on July 18, 1952:

SHBF4211 Tortured Love	Savoy 865
SHBF4212 Work for My Baby	Savoy SJL 1176

That was the last of H-Bomb's work for Savoy, unfortunately. They were hard-driving sides with H-Bomb's thunderous vocals and insistent delivery solidly backed by a top notch band with fine arrangements. But by 1952 H-Bomb was on the road, doing one-nighters with a man who remains his friend to this day, B. B. King.

On that first tour of forty-one one-nighters, booked by Universal Attractions, B. B. was promoting "Three O'Clock in the Morning" and H-Bomb and Tiny Bradshaw's band shared the bill as they toured the South promoting their music. But it was the South, remember, and the living wasn't easy:

Macon, Georgia; North Carolina; Wheeling, West Virginia; the restroom in the restaurant—*back door*. We did. We would play a dance, most of them be in a barn, big old barn; the band would play, when you get through, get somethin to eat, you go to the back door, you get your sandwich and go. They had the colored and the white sign, and you couldn't come in the front door. But here's what got me—the dance would be mixed, but you couldn't go over there to eat with them. They would go to the front, I would have to go round to the back to get ours. Most of the time we would get it to go. We used two station wagons. We would get the sandwiches, jump in the wagon, and eat it on the way.

H-Bomb remembers the hard times, sharing a hotel room, and a bed, with B. B., eating sardines and crackers and drinking Dr. Pepper when they had any money left from their ten to twelve bucks a night pay, but sometimes suffering the "miss meal cramps." There was also the time that their rented station wagon caught on fire at four o'clock in the morning about forty miles outside of Anniston, Alabama:

> It burned up. The sheriff came by, said, "What happened to you guys?" I said, "Well, this is B. B. King and I'm H-Bomb and we just did a show in Anniston, Alabama . . . that was about two-three hours ago, and the wagon caught on fire. We're tryin to get to the next town to get us a ride." He said, "Well, you guys get on in here, cause I don't want you hangin around here. You might fool with some of these white women." I said, "No sir, nothin like that, as soon as we get through, we're leavin. We're just trying to get another car to go to the next town," which was Mobile, that's 186 miles from there. So he took us to this little town, we called the bookin agent.

The dance halls roped off to separate whites and blacks, the poor facilities (if there were any at all), the poor pay, the racial insults, he encountered it all on the road. "I went along with everybody else," he laughed, "otherwise I might not be here today." But he has fond memories of the musicians and fans, and of the kindness and generosity of B. B., who gave Ferguson $150 to help him get home when he was stranded after a job with an unpaid hotel bill in Memphis, Tennessee.[7]

B. B. King biographer Charles Sawyer paints a somewhat different picture of H-Bomb in his depiction of the shrewd King's attempts to endear himself to the Bradshaw band and thus receive as much support from them on stage as possible: "On the same bill with B. B. was another new face, a singer named 'H-Bomb' Ferguson, whose only talent seemed to be his ability to sound very much like the widely known and much liked singer Wynonie Harris. What H-Bomb lacked in original talent, he made up for in unbridled conceit. Seeing him made B. B. realize that his own insecurity was an asset in this situation and he feared the worst for H-Bomb, who might receive his comeuppance at the hands of Bradshaw's musicians, eager to put him in his place. . . . H-Bomb lived up to his name—if not his image of himself."[8] It is not a very charitable view of H-Bomb, who certainly did sound like Harris but has proved that he has other musical as well as storytelling talents as well; the "conceit" is at least partially rooted in the wild *image* he tries to project, the stage persona he has taken on to help promote himself. One would not say that he is as original or talented as B. B. King, but then how many people are?

Ferguson next recorded two sides for Specialty at WGST radio studio in Atlanta on March 30, 1953, accompanied by Jesse James Jones on sax, Eddie Lee Foster on sax or trumpet, Cleveland Lyons on piano, Wesley Jackson on guitar, George A. Miller on bass, and Woodi Harper on drums. These sides were slated for release on Specialty 465, but they were not issued at the time, appearing finally on a Specialty CD release in 1992/1993:

You Made Me Baby	Specialty unissued
She's Been Gone	

Seven months later Ferguson was in New York to record two titles for the Sunset label on October 26. The session featured, in addition to Charlie Singleton and another unknown tenor sax player, jazz great Lou Donaldson on alto, Teddy Cromwell on bass, and John Marvell on drums:

Nanny Miss Fanny	Sunset 107
Evernight	

All the while H-Bomb was still working, taking Mel Walker's place with Johnny Otis for a while, singing with Little Esther. His final New York session was with Andy Kirk's orchestra on March 31, 1954, where he recorded one side, which was released with a flip by Mel Moore:

Hole in the Wall Tonight	Decca 29167, MCA 2-4105

Eventually H-Bomb turned up in Cincinnati at—where else?—the Cotton Club, where Big Ed Thompson remembered first meeting him: "He came into town hoofin; he didn't like nobody to know it, though. He came into town dancin on a tap dancin club or somethin like that. He don't like nobody to know that. He came here. So we always kid each other about hoofin. And we just say, you know, he's a hoofer. I mean a tap dancer. So he come to town with a show and they ended up down there and stayin for a while in Cincinnati. Here he met this girlfriend of his behind the bar. Boots. And they got it cooked up and got to goin steady and they finally married each other. And so H-Bomb made his home here."

When he came to town, Ed said, he still sounded like Wynonie Harris, but he was trying to do his own material, and before long, H-Bomb was hooked up with John Finch and cut his first record in Cincinnati in 1957. The record featured Ferguson on vocal and piano, Big Ed on guitar, Billy Malone on tenor, Benny Reynolds on alto, and probably Roy Copeland on bass and Cecil Cooper on drums, according to Thompson:

| She Don't Want Me | Finch 354 |
| My Baby Left Me | ———— |

H-Bomb's next record was cut north of Oxford, Ohio, near Miami University for the Big Bang label, a relatively new label run by William D. "Bang" Meyer, who has a store in a bar on Route 27. Ed Thompson says that the same band from the Finch recording did the Big Bang session, which took about forty-five minutes to complete.

| Spaghetti and Meatballs | Big Bang 103 |
| Sackie Sak | ———— |

By this time H-Bomb was sounding much less like Wynonie and was much more firmly in the New Orleans-feel rock and roll field behind, say, Fats Domino and Little Richard, mixing their piano work and playing he'd heard by a man called "Hick" in New York into his own approach. He discussed the "change" with me: "That was when I decided to do a little changing over. You know, because the fad in the music business was goin the other way. What I did, originally what I was doin on Savoy was rhythm and blues. . . . Savoy didn't want that rock piano sound in the rhythm and blues. So I would stand up and sing and they would have a piano player there. . . . So [later] they went into the rock bag. So I was told to get into the rock bag."

H-Bomb claims to have played in a New Orleans style *before* his Savoy sessions, suggesting that he was really playing rock and roll *before* it officially came out. Regardless, he was recording again, switching from Big Bang to ARC in 1958:

| Little Tiger | ARC 9001 |
| Cryin' over You | ———— |

Then he switched back to Big Bang for a 1959 session, again north of Oxford, Ohio, for one final Big Bang single:

| Rain Rain Rain | Big Bang 105 |
| Boogie Down | ————— |

Personnel for this session is not known, but Big Ed Thompson was not on it, for some reason, though he was on Ferguson's next session, which took him back to the big labels:

So after that I went over to King Records. That's that Federal label, James Brown got me on that.

He said, "H-Bomb, quit wasting your time, man, you ain't doing nothing." That was right after that *Spaghetti and Meatball* on the Big Bang label, red and white.

He said, well, he was talking directly, they had owed him so much money they gave him a piece of the company. That's when James Brown was hot.

He said, "Man, I'm gonna get you on King label."

I said, "What?"

"Man," he said, "You're wasting your time with all these little bullshit companies. And meet me over there tomorrow at 2:00, I'll talk to Syd Nathan and get you a session."

What that turned out then I was cutting something that came out on Federal label he did that but I got paid. I got $3,000 off that one album. I didn't know they'd beat me for the rest but I got a lot of work behind it. I was working seven nights a week.[9]

The session, which produced six sides, was cut in November 1960. Although it is often listed as being recorded in Baltimore, Big Ed Thompson, who was on the session, claims that it was cut on Brewster at King Records with Henry Glover presiding. In addition to H-Bomb's vocals and piano and Big Ed's guitar, the record also featured Thomas Badgett on tenor. With Sonny Thompson and Gene Redd encouraging H-Bomb's rock and roll tendencies, H-Bomb cut loose with some more powerful and rocking sides, especially the driving "Midnight Ramblin' Tonight," and all of the session was issued on either Federal or Audio Lab (a King budget label) or both:

F1350-2	Mary Little Mary	Federal 12441
		Audio Lab 1567
		—————
F1351-1	I'm So Lonely	
F1352	The Mess Around	Audio Lab 1567
F1353-2	I'm Crying Boo Hoo Hoo	Federal 12339
		Audio Lab 1567
F1354	Lady Queen	Audio Lab 1567
F1355-2	Midnight Ramblin Tonight	Federal 12339,
		Audio Lab 1567

Unfortunately, H-Bomb, unfamiliar with the business of royalty arrangements, unknowingly sold his rights to his King material, as he had done with Savoy, losing any opportunity he had to make any more than $3,000, if, indeed, any more was forthcoming. H-Bomb continued to play around Cincinnati at various clubs, using his wild stage act and strong vocals to keep him working, and he claims to have done some recording at Chess Records in the sixties with the same band from the King recordings, including possibly a side called "The Lost Lover." Eventually, though, he got out of the business when the lack of adequate pay and the touring grind got too hard. He worked for some time for city waste collection and played the occasional gig, until an interview with me on WAIF radio and a spot at Bogart's for a WAIF fund-raiser prompted local music enthusiast and WAIF DJ Michael Riley, along with Tebbe Farrell, to work on rejuvenating his career. Since then he has recorded two singles for the local Radiation label:

vcl/piano

Lonesome Avenue	Radiation 001
I Ain't Gonna Run	Radiation 002

vcl/piano with Big Ed Thompson, guitar; Russell Givens, bass; Kevin Wilburn, drums; Thomas Badgett, tenor sax

Shake and Bake	Radiation 001
Heart in My Hand	Radiation 002

He has also taken to wearing different colored wigs, influenced by Flip Wilson and Rick James, *and* added Boo Boo, his pet boa constrictor, to his outrageous act, until it died recently. Appearances in concert with George Thorogood and in Thorogood's "Hand Jive" video (taped at Cory's), his own video, and appearances at various festivals and clubs like the Senate, Collage, Cory's, and Bogart's (in Clifton and Walnut Hills) have enhanced his reputation even more. He even made it to Holland with Big Ed and the All Stars on November 19, 1988, for "Blues Estaffette '88," where he got rave reviews: "At first it seemed we had been invaded by a fugitive from an Amsterdam transsexual nightclub but it turned out to be H-Bomb Ferguson in tight fitting red flared trousers and a shoulder-length pink wig. He sat down at the piano, informed the audience that H.B. really stood for 'Hot Boy' and then proceeded to tear the house down. He and the band had the place in uproar with a succession of pounding Esquerita-esque rockers and an emotional rendition of 'My Heart Is in Your Hands.' "[10]

Another single recorded for the Finch label under the name "H. Bomb Ferguson and the Bluesmen" appeared in 1989:

Medicine Man   Finch V-23811 M
I Had a Dream   ———

H-Bomb's next effort, an LP, came out in 1990. His career, particularly in light of his success in Holland and his signing with the Earwig label in 1993, appears to be looking up again, and his brash and ebullient personality is once again a familiar sight (and sound) around Cincinnati. In fact, Ferguson has even shot a video, though not state of the art by any means, that manages to capture something of his resurgent energy.

"That's life," he smiled comfortably, referring to the ups and downs of his career. "I just shout em everywhere I can."

9

Albert Washington

I was in a dark blue station wagon with a push-button gearshift, automatic, on Madison Road in Oakley in 1969. After I pulled into the parking lot of the apartment house at 4404 Brazee Street, where I lived with my parents, I pushed the park button in the upper left corner of the dash, but left the engine, racing a little bit harder now that I was in park, running, listening to the radio. We remember things— where were you when JFK was shot, or Bobby, or King? What were you doing when you got the news? But this wasn't the end of someone's life, it was the beginning, and as I sat there parked my life perceptibly picked up speed as I raced toward an ever-accelerating involvement with the blues. On the radio was not Kennedy but Washington, not a president, though a number of his records were released on the President label in England; a first in his own way: my first knowledge of a blues performer in the city of Cincinnati. I can't lie, I don't remember the exact date or time of day, but I remember vividly waiting for the end of the song to find out its title and the name of the performer. After all, this was WSAI—Top 40 radio—hardly the place one expected to hear a blues song. The song: "Turn on the Bright Lights." The artist: Albert Washington. And, to use the vernacular of the time, he turned me on to the blues in Cincinnati.

Seconds later I was through our door and on the telephone to WSAI, getting the name of the record label, Fraternity, and just as quickly hunting down that number in the white pages. I got through, surprisingly, to Harry Carlson, who owned the label, and one week later I was in his office, listening to professionally recorded live music—never released, by the way, though it sounded great—performed by Albert Washington at Vet's Inn. It was something of a stretcher, I suppose, to tell Carlson that I wanted to interview Mr. Washington for *Blues Unlimited* magazine, since I had never written for them before, but that was what I *intended,* and in fact my article did appear in that magazine, welcomed with much sympathetic encouragement for a sixteen-year-old would-be blues journalist by one of bluesdom's best friends and champions, Mike Leadbitter. When Albert arrived about one half hour after I did, dressed all in black with a waist-length black jacket and wearing a process wig, he was quiet, serious, and extremely surprised at the interest of a young white boy in his blues. But it wasn't a distrustful surprise or a self-protective quiet; it was the reserve of a humble man, one perhaps who doesn't really realize how much he can move people with his performances, a Cincinnati legend, really, who still plays small bars for fans who've followed him from club to club for thirty years. One of his own song titles says it best: "I'm the Man." He *is* the man, quietly going about making great blues, devoutly committed to his family, his religion, and his art.

Albert Washington was born on August 17, 1939, in Rome, Georgia, the fifth child of Jerry and Helen Washington, and the second boy. Although there were no other musicians in Albert's family, he recalls clearly that music was a big part of his Baptist church upbringing, even before the time of his baptism at age nine: "At first I didn't go for the blues. At first I was nothin but gospel. Yeah, cause I really loved the gospel, you know."[1] Still, Albert couldn't help but hear the blues in Georgia—"That's when *really* the blues was played back in them days," he states positively—both on 78s and "them old roll pianos." His favorite blues artist in those days was the frequently salacious Blind Boy Fuller, whose songs like "What's That Smells Like Fish" and "Get Your Yas Yas Out" sit somewhat uneasily beside some of Albert's other favorites of the time: the Golden Gate Quartet (first recorded 1937), the Dixie Hummingbirds (1939), the Pilgrim Travellers, and the Angelic Gospel Singers. However, Fuller was not only a singer of suggestive blues but a spirited, popular, and influential singer and guitarist who is a major contributor to the blues tradition, and though Albert is not stylistically similar to Fuller in any way, he recalls Fuller's spirit and virtuosity and attempts to inject that depth of feeling for the blues into his own music.

When Albert was around ten years old his family moved to the Cincinnati area, at first on Second Street in Newport, Kentucky. Albert's father worked in construction until, when Albert was fourteen or fifteen, a tragic accident ended Jerry Washington's life and sent Albert to Cincinnati:

> My daddy used to work for C. Y. Thompson Construction. And they always told him bout sittin up on them pipes, up on the truck, them big old

pipes. So he was sittin up on them pipes, the pipes rolled off, and he rolled down. He tried to get under the truck but he didn't get his leg under there quick enough. One of them big pipes smashed his leg off. So, we lost him. He lived a while, then he musta took some kinda fit because he died after that. And my mother, she begin to wonder. And that's how come she brought me to Cincinnati. Thought maybe it was better about jobs. More money or what.

The father's death also obviously influenced the already devout Helen Washington to be more concerned about the spiritual life of her family and she encouraged Albert in his gospel singing, which he loved and still loves. But he would also sneak into various clubs in Newport and Cincinnati to hear blues and R&B:

The first artist I loved really so well was B. B. King. So I started. Him and Sam Cooke, see. B. B. King and Sam Cooke, that's who I was always walkin around the street singing some of their songs, you know, yeah. When I was too young Sam Cooke used to come to the Sportsman Club over in Newport. Yeah, I think it was either the Sportsman or either the Copa Club. And I used to sneak in there, you know. We sneak in the back door, as little boys, I used to love him sing . . . then Charles Brown and Amos Milburn. We used to sneak under there and lay behind the organ, listen to them play the blues. Good, too! Them was the days.

Big Maybelle, Stepin Fechit, Cab Calloway, Aretha Franklin—Albert was a "backdoor guest" for shows featuring artists of this stature, but the kids weren't always welcome at the clubs. Albert recalled a run-in with Screw Andrews: "I was kinda scared of that guy. He started to shoot us one night. Yeah! Bout three or four of us young boys done sneaked in there and messin with them slot machines, you know. We was gonna win us some money. He lined us up like, I guess it's to scare us, sayin 'I'm gonna shoot all the three of y'all tonight.' Boy I was scared then. . . . I didn't go back in there no more."

Helen Washington's admonition to her son to "stay in the church" came to fruition musically when Albert joined up with the Religious Gospelaires. There has been some confusion about Albert's presence on their recordings because they also had a lead vocalist named Robert Washington, and the group itself, formed in 1954, was based in Dayton, not Cincinnati. Albert himself reports that he was with the Gospelaires "out of Lincoln Heights." He explains: "Well, I'm gonna tell you now, the group out of Dayton and this group, they were the mix of the group. See, part of the group be with these in Lincoln Height half the time and part of em be with them in Dayton. So they just use who they think was more powerful when they get ready to do the big thing, you know."

Albert recalls them getting "a lot of albums out," including for the Peacock label, and he himself recorded with them around 1959 or 1960, singing lead on some songs, including "Too Close to Turn Around," and playing guitar, with two songs being released on an LP entitled *Heaven Is My Goal.* Washington remembers particularly Paul Arnold as a lead singer, along with another lead singer, Ross Ford, as two members of the group, although the personnel was ever-changing. In Robert Laughton and Cedric Hayes's unpublished manuscript "Post-War Gospel Records Discography," Paul Arnold is listed as lead singer for the group, though Ford is not.[2] Neither is Albert listed as a group member, and the song "Too Close to Turn Around" does not appear.

Next Albert formed a group with his cousin Mamie P. Dixon singing lead: "Then I got me a little group called the Washington Singers, and they sound like the Staple Singers. We patterned after them. Went all down in Georgia, Mississippi. . . . Yeah, we recorded a couple of things with them. . . . Well, we never did get with no big label, just with a little label we had. Name of the little label we had was 'Fly High,' I believe." The group recorded two songs around 1964 or 1965, "Somewhere down the Line" and "The Downward Road Is Crowded," but the group did not stay together long. Besides that, Albert was already rehearsing blues and R&B material, as well as working for Simon and Fischer Automotives, where he worked for sixteen years. Something had to give:

> I think where the blues come in at, the blues come in when you need more. Yeah, I had worked at Simon and Fischer for about sixteen years. I got laid off and that's when I went into trouble there bout gettin another job. So I picked that old guitar up. Well, at first I wasn't intendin to go out into the nightclubs, cause my mother always told me, "Stay in the church." So after she died, I met Mr. Joe McPherson. He say, "I don't know why you layin around here sufferin, man, as good as you can play the guitar." He say, "Come on out here. I got a little place I think you can start workin at makin some money. So he take me out to Vet's Inn on Eastern Avenue. We started out about ten dollars a night a man. Worked ourselves on up. Been goin ever since. That was 1962.

McPherson had come upon Albert the blues singer almost by accident: he lived down the street from him and happened to hear Albert and bassist Willie B. "Sonny" Watt rehearsing B. B. King and Sam Cooke tunes. What with their rehearsing every day, it was inevitable that someone would hear them. Luckily, McPherson was a man who knew the blues—he had booked the Blues Bees, Leroy "Sugarfoot" Bonner and Robert "Cherokee" Singleton, at his Vet's Inn in the fifties to much success, particularly when sidemen Dan on bass and Jose began to rock behind Sugarfoot's guitar and Singleton's vocals—and he knew that Albert had what it took to draw a crowd.

Albert still found himself at this point straddling the gospel and blues fields, and although it didn't bother him, there were, as there always are, people ready to gossip:

> Well, after I got into the club I was still in gospel for a long time til people just got to talkin so much, you know, bout playin in the club and playin in the church, and they made a real big thing out of it. So I just stayed on the blues field cause I would have the income there. I had two little boys, had to raise them, and so, I think the blues come from a need more. Cause I had said to myself I wasn't never gonna sing no blues or go in a night-club. I used to walk by them things and when I get to where a club was on that side of the street, I'd cross over on the other side. But now, see, I been makin a livin doin this for so many years I just feel like it's another job, that's all.

And although Albert remembered his mother's request, and her feeling that playing the blues in a club was a sin, the needs of his wife and children were pressing, and the blues helped him get over: "But she don't know how it helped me since she's been gone. I done raised three families. I'm on the third one now."

So the blues were financially helpful for Albert, and they weren't the sinful music, necessarily, that other people tried to tell him they were. Actions, he feels, speak much louder than words:

> Well, I went through the Bible pretty well. I never seen nothin in there what's in it about no blues. They don't even mention the blues in the Bible. It mention the filthy song, and if you sing a song that's not worth listenin to in the public, now that could be a sin. See, it's accordin to the words that you put into a song. See, I know they got some songs, "Get up, get up off your seat and jam, G.D." Cussin. Well, I believe that's against the religion. But as long as you treat people right, I think most things about livin right is about treatin somebody right. Don't mistreat nobody. Cause just as sure as you hurt somebody's feelin you is gonna be hurt somewhere down the road somewhere. So I believe if you do that, the Lord gon take care of you anyway.

Those things that Albert learned and practiced as a gospel singer naturally carried over into his blues singing, not just technical capabilities, but also a spiritual and emotional drive. He told Bill Cummerow "I try to keep that gospel feeling in everything I do,"[3] and indeed it is present in all of his performances; how much he has to try to keep in there is another question: "In a lot of my blues songs, a lot of my records I got out, you can hear me say, 'Lord have mercy!' In a lot of them I do at the club now. The reason I say that cause I can feel somethin. When there's some song that I be singin I can feel the fire from the Holy Ghost in me. A lot of people say, 'How do you do that singin the blues?' I don't know. It just in me. And I feel it, you hear me say, 'Lord Have Mercy.' In a lot of my records, a lot of my songs right now. I can't help that." Actually, Albert didn't need to "help that": he wasn't the first to cross over the gospel style into the blues or pop field, and the gospel soul helped give his music the soaring, spiritual edge that at times approaches an unearthly beauty.

One can find such an edge on Albert's first blues recording, done for John Finch in 1962, as Albert Washington and His Kings:

M-5036	You Gonna Miss Me	Finch 10990, VLM 334
		Bluestown 703
M-5037	Ramble	———

With Sonny Watt on bass, Tim Pleasant on drums, and Big Ed Thompson on guitar backing Albert's own vocals and guitar, Albert created a classic minor-key blues, with ominous bass, a unison guitar riff with a cutting tone that sharply contrasts to the bass, insistent chording, and above all some of Albert's best upper register moaning, at times almost field holler-like in intensity as he sings "You never miss your water til your well run dry." It is a vocal that mounts toward heaven, but it comes from hell, the wailing hell of the blues, and the song is a match for the best Cobra vocal work of Magic Sam and Otis Rush, whose own minor-key blues are considered classics as well. The flip, "Ramble," was an original and distinctive blues, a strange, busy tune with rooted blues lyrics and integrated guitar work. The song has a nervous energy that almost embodies the insistently itchy, rambling mind, and features strong picking from Albert's longtime friend and guitarist Big Ed Thompson. The record did not make Albert a great deal of money—none, in fact, when it was reissued, unbeknownst to Albert, on the Bluestown label out of Boston—but it did establish him as a talented blues performer.

Albert's manager at that time, Wade Hill, next moved Albert over to the VLM label for his next record release. VLM stands for Vince L. Morton, the owner of the label, who got into the business after he met John Finch, a co-worker at General Electrical from 1955 on. Morton met Albert in 1963 at Mom's Tavern on McMillan and followed him to the Vet's Inn to hear Albert's music. At that time, of course, Albert was under contract to Finch, but since the two knew each other and worked together, the idea of collaborating on a single by Albert seemed natural as well. Morton had recorded one previous single at the 950 Morris Avenue studio, a single by the Blues Bees that came out on Finch, but Albert's single sold well at the time and continues to sell today: "Each record I put out paid for itself. It didn't pay me a lot of money. Now that 'I Haven't Got a Friend' that's Albert—I made money off that. And it still sells. I get calls for that now."[4] The calls came from Canada, Japan, and all around the United States—not for large quantities, but considering the record is twenty-five years old and on a small label, its staying power is astonishing. It was 1964 when Albert, backed by the same band that recorded his first blues record, cut one of his most enduring sides, one that still gets requests in the clubs from the large and loyal following that has stayed with Albert since he first started the blues—a crowd estimated by Albert to number about 550 in 1972, and a group that has not diminished in numbers from that time.[5]

| W-299 | I Haven't Got a Friend | VLM 1099 |
| W-300 | So Tired | VLM 1100 |

Kicking off with a lowdown, almost Lightnin Hopkins-style lick, "I Haven't Got a Friend" features heartfelt vocals and some fine traditional lyrics:

Sometime I wonder, "What kind of city did I drift in?" (Twice)
You know I been here a long time, I haven't even got a friend.

"I got a lot of so-called friends" he shouts as an aside, punctuating his words with guitar breaks and a solo in the B. B. King mould over a restless walking bass and strong second guitar from Big Ed. The flip, "So Tired," is an attractive, almost Earl Hookerish instrumental with more Hopkins/B. B. licks blended together over a medium tempo backing, an interesting side, but the topside, according to Albert, really took off and became a national hit. Unfortunately, Watt and Drummond did not want to leave their day jobs to tour, and so Albert did not capitalize fully on the single's success. He recalled canceling out on a job in Cleveland: "Lady come down here at Vet's Inn and want to shoot me. Yeah. She come down there and she said, 'Yeah, I done spent all my money, bought them tickets, had to turn em back in.' Say, 'Cause of what you do I have to [Albert laughs], bad as I hate to do it I have to shoot you.'" Luckily Albert didn't get shot, though he has seen a number of shootings and cuttings in the clubs during his nights as a performer, but it is a recurring motif in Albert's career, that of the singer insufficiently able to capitalize on his success in a major way. For whatever reason—fear of losing a regular local job

for the more iffy recompense of tours, unreliable musicans, or whatever—Albert has been at the brink of strong financial success, as he
was with "I Haven't Got a Friend," but he hasn't achieved the financial rewards he deserves.

So while Albert did some limited touring behind that record, he
also continued to play small clubs like Vet's Inn, Mom's, Satan's Den,
and the Soul Lounge, and plan for his next record. This one came
about when local DJ Shad O'Shea and Ray Allen came to Mom's on
McMillan and hooked him up with Harry Carlson and Fraternity
Records, housed on the third floor at 413 Race Street. Carlson had
done a session with a white newcomer, an amazing guitar virtuoso
named Lonnie Mack, in the summer of 1963, resulting in hits with
"Wham" and "Memphis," and Mack would join Albert on a session
later. But Albert's first Fraternity session, produced by Ray Allen
around 1965 or 1966, featured a studio band put together at Louisville's Sanborn Recording Company.

ZTS B128026	Doggin Me Around	Fraternity 982
		President 137, LP 1008
ZTS B128027	A Woman Is a Funny Thing	————
	These Arms of Mine	Fraternity 1002
		President 182, LP 1008
	I'm the Man	————
	Tellin All Your Friends	Fraternity 991
	Rome, Georgia	————
	Woman Love	Fraternity 1010
		President 227
	Bring It on Up	————

None of these cuts were actually blues recordings, but there is
some fine soul/rhythm and blues here, including the wonderful eight-
bar ballad "Doggin Me Around." With fine guitar riffs, trumpets,
saxes, and harmony vocals, and a Wilson Pickettish feel, the song is
a strong forerunner to Albert's later "Love Is a Wonderful Thing,"
and Albert to this day still receives small royalty checks from places
like Jerusalem and Brazil (!) for this record. The flip kicks off with an
almost Everly Brothers feel, but there is little doubt that Sam Cooke
inspired "A Woman Is a Funny Thing," a tuneful pop-soul side with
a celeste break that discusses a woman who "get in your hair like an
old boll weevil." The other artistic success of the session was "I'm the
Man," another song popular in the clubs years later, where the bass
man would churn out an extended vamp at the end of the song while
Albert worked out on guitar and vocals—something he would use to
greater success later on "Loosen These Pains and Let Me Go." Fi-

nally, Albert says he cut two more sides for Fraternity at this time, "Jealous Woman" and "You Got to Pay Your Dues," but copies of those recordings have not turned up.

Albert's next session, though, took place in 1969 at the Jewel Studios of Rusty York, of "Sugaree" fame. This time Carlson was producing, and with some musicians from the Dapps, a band that also recorded with James Brown, Lonnie Mack on guitar, Tim Drummond on bass, Denny Rice on piano, Ron Grayson on organ, Rusty York on harmonica, and an unknown drummer, Albert produced the artistically successful and popular "Turn on the Bright Lights": "Carlson the one that wrote that. He say him and his wife was in the kitchen cookin, and said his wife told him to turn off the light, you know, when he come out the kitchen, and he thought about that song then, 'Turn on the Bright Light.' "

Although Albert, of course, had a regular band working in the club, Carlson used studio musicians and Mack, though Albert had never met them:

> Well, that's the first time I ever met him, yeah. I been hearing that "Memphis" for a *long* time, and that's the first time I ever met him. But, *man,* that's a guitar player! Don't let nobody tell you he ain't. Cause he's a *guitar* player! This man had a amp bout as big as a book, readin book, that's how big it was, but it was fatter, you know. That's what he played through. I said, "You'll never make it with that little amp," he say, "Watch me." Ah, he was playin so strong when we got ready to cut the session, you know, cut the record out, he was still leanin up against the wall, *gone!* So Rusty say, "Let him go head, he's havin his fun, let him go head. So we can run him on the tape by his self. He can play."

And play he did! The session produced six sides:

Turn on the Bright Lights	Fraternity 1016
	President 242
Lonely Mountain (Prod. by Tony Fullman and Levi Norman)	———
Hold Me Baby	Fraternity 1021
I'm Gonna Pour Me a Drink	———
Having a Good Time	Fraternity 1029
	M in the Street 2111
He's Got the Whole World in His Hands	(Replaced by "Crazy Legs" on 2111)

"Bright Lights" was the highlight. It reached number seventeen on WSAI radio, a local white pop radio station, and was a hit also in San Francisco, according to Albert, and other locations around the country. In *Blues Unlimited*, Ian Cull called attention to the record's "uptight, screaming, high pitched, schizophrenic guitar breaks,"[6] and Keef Hartley found the record "a very nice blues with a really dirty guitar sound."[7] Albert again set out touring across the country with this record and "I'm Gonna Pour Me a Drink," a "Bright Lights" sound alike, but again the really big break didn't happen. The other songs from the session were not blues. "Lonely Mountain" is socially conscious and personal at the same time, with a stylistic nod to Sam Cooke and, perhaps, Arthur Conley's "Sweet Soul Music." Albert sings "I climbed that lonely mountain where the sky begins," and describes what he sees in his anthem to self-reliance:

> I looked down and what did I see?
> A lot of troubled people just like me.
> I see a sick society and I know it don't have to be.

"Hold Me Baby" is pretty successful funk, with an Aretha-style opening giving way to JB, with Ramsey Lewis-style piano, churning bass and horns, and a more controlled Mack on guitar. A chunky, funky dance tune.

The Fraternity sides turned up in the United Kingdom on President records in the seventies, though somehow Albert did not know they had been released there. When I showed him reviews he just shook his head—he was glad they were out, but some royalties would have helped, too. Truthfully, legal financial arrangements with Fraternity may have been stipulated that Albert was not entitled to any royalties from overseas releases—it is impossible to say, and it wouldn't have been the first time an artist sold his music outright and did not benefit from later royalties. But the record did bring him some fame in England, and from an unlikely place, it seemed—Japan! " 'Turn on the Bright Lights' played in Japan for five years. Five years. We had about six of the Japanese come over here to the Vet's Inn one night. They said, 'We came to see the man that made the "Bright Light," yeah.' " Later, a version of the song was recorded by Jerry Garcia on a solo LP, but his version didn't match Albert's for beauty or intensity.

In 1970 Albert's manager Harry Carlson signed Albert to a contract with Starday-King Records, and Albert is listed in the King discography as recording at the studios on Brewster Avenue on May 19 and October 16, 1970. Unfortunately, the discography is incomplete and inaccurate for Albert's work for Starday-King, from the misspelling of Harry Carlson's name (as Cartson) to the listing of all titles as unissued and the inclusion of titles not recorded at Starday-King. A number of titles are recognizable as earlier Fraternity issues, like "I'm the Man," "These Arms of Mine," "Woman Love," "Lonely Mountain," "Hold Me Baby," "I'm Gonna Pour Me a Drink," and "A Woman Is a Funny Thing," while "Doggin Me Down" is likely "Doggin Me Around," "Everything Gonna Be All Right" possibly "One More Chance," and "Higher" possibly "Bring It on Up." Albert does recall doing a couple of sessions at Starday-King during the same month or so. Four singles resulted from the sessions:

SL1955	Loosen These Pains	Jewel 822
	and Let Me Go	PLP 727/728 (Japan)
SL1956	Go On and Help Yourself	———
SL2172	Love Is a Wonderful Thing	Jewel 836
SL2173	I Wanna Know How You Feel	———
SL2207	Betty Jane	Jewel 837
SL2208	If You Need Me	———
K13787	Ain't It a Shame	Deluxe 45-135
K13788	Somewhere down the Line	———

The sessions included Albert on vocal and guitar, backed by Andy Johnson or Lonnie Mack on guitar, Hal Byrd and Scooter on horns, Hubert Herb on piano, Lonnie Bennett or Jimmy Thompson on organ, Walter Cash on bass, and Cornelius Roberts on drums, along with stray trumpet added here and there. Though the songs were not all blues, these are again some of Albert's strongest and most popular tunes. "Loosen These Pains" is an archetypal mid-tempo groove tune that just rocked the clubs with its infectious beat, punctuating horns, funky groove bass, and gospel-type blues piano playing underneath Albert's proclamation "Baby, I'm tired of being dogged around / If you don't want me, honey, put me down." The song should have been a gigantic hit, one that would have pushed the beautiful "B" side to the spotlight as well: "Go On and Help Yourself." The moving gospel-blues piano intro leads into one of Albert's most emotional, soaring vocals backed by an uncluttered combination of guitar, bass, organ, drums, and moaning horns. The lyrics are heartfelt, bedrock blues:

> You said you gonna leave me woman,
> Well, go on and help yourself (twice).
> Cause one day, one day I know you gonna leave me,
> And I'll be so glad, so glad I have someone else.
>
> When I first met you baby, ev'ry, ev'ry,
> ev'ry thing was alright (twice).
> You used to hold me in the mornin,
> I know you used to love me every night.

The piano break neatly balances blues and gospel with jazz phrasing while Albert talks fervently about finding someone else. The song is a real triumph. Mike Leadbitter of *Blues Unlimited* wrote that Albert was "in good form . . . but production is poor,"[8] but really it is hard to imagine the song being any better than it is.

Jewel 836 brings us one of Albert's prettiest songs, "Love Is a Wonderful Thing," which worked a bit better in the clubs without the busy horns, and the Sam Cooke-inspired "I Wanna Know How You Feel," again with over-busy horns. Jewel 837 presents a strong version of Wilson Pickett's blues ballad "If You Need Me" with strong vocal pyrotechnics and insistent pleading from Albert. The flip, "Betty Jane," boasts a Latin rhythm with bongos and congas, a nice guitar riff, and vocals by Andy Johnson with Albert. It is a churning cut, percussive and full of gospelly piano, with funky lyrics about the woman who is

> 38 in the hips, 18 in the waist,
> She's a good lookin woman with a baby face.

Jacques Demetre rightly heard a Staples Singers influence in the cut, and praised the pianist for his "superb" accompaniment, but Mike Leadbitter's review directed blues fans to look elsewhere, though he called this a good record for soul fans.[9] But his best is on the release on Deluxe, a King subsidiary, where Albert hits another peak for blues fans. Roy Brown had recorded the song, A&R man and vice president of King Henry Glover's composition, previously, but his smooth ballad rendering pales before Albert's version of "Aint It a Shame." Led by Lonnie Mack's restrained guitar and underpinned by a rock-steady bass, Albert preaches in smooth and soaring tones while one of the most tastefully used female choruses—Gigi and the Charmaines—echoes and underlines Albert's pleading. And the marvellous vamp out! Leadbitter called it "typical intense Albert," but that kind of intensity is really atypical.[10] The flip side is psychedelic funk with tasty guitar and something that sounds like an echoing flute, female chorus, and chording piano and "you never miss your water" in the lyrics—not of blues interest, really, but strong for its genre.

Rusty York had been involved in the production of a number of these songs for Albert, and some of the songs recorded at Starday-King came out on Jewel Records. Also at this time, however Albert went back into the Jewel Studios, recording with the same band at Starday-King, for a release on the Rye label:

111238A	Case of the Blues	Rye 954
111239B	One More Chance	——

Both songs were brass heavy, "Case" an interesting variation on twelve-bar blues with a boogaloo beat, "Chance" gospelly with a trumpet solo, both a bit overproduced but featuring strong contributions from Albert.

Albert had, of course, always had white friends and fans in the music business, but his records normally sold to blacks and it was mainly blacks who went to see him in the clubs. However, with profiles in *Blues Unlimited* in 1971 and *Living Blues* in 1972 this began to change a bit, particularly in regard to his overseas record sales. In the clubs it was still primarily black crowds who came to see Albert at the Vet's Inn, his regular night spot and what Albert called a real blues club. After I had heard Albert's "Turn on the Bright Lights" and interviewed him for *Blues Unlimited*, I began going to see Albert at the Vet's—a small, funky bar with a pool table and jukebox in the front room and live music in the crowded back room, with Albert on a two-foot-high platform stage churning out his blues. Sometimes people would sit in. Singer and dancer "Caldonia" Reynolds, who claimed that Louis Jordan wrote "Caldonia" about her, first shook her butt in my face at the Vet's—all in fun, of course, since Caldonia would always find some shy innocent to embarrass in front of the roaring crowd.

Caldonia was born in Lexington, Kentucky, and she toured with Tiny Bradshaw, playing places like the Apollo and becoming acquainted with performers like Duke Ellington, Butterbeans and Susie, James Brown, and B. B. King. She settled down and performed in Cincinnati mostly during her later years, often with Albert at the Vet's and at Peebles Corner, but also at other clubs and at benefits. In 1976 she told Ed Bedinghaus that she had lost her mother and brother and separated from her husband, but had fairly recently danced at the Playboy Club and the Blue Angel (the latter as a go-go girl!),[11] and she lasted another eight years, until 1984, when she was stricken at a friend's house and pronounced dead at University Hospital on May 3, 1984, at the age of sixty-three. I can remember playing a show with Cal at the Workhouse at Christmas, the great pleasure the men got from her performances and virtuosity, but it was those performances at the Vet's I'll remember best. I eulogized her in 1984: "Caldonia was a *truly great* dancer—lithe, resilient, always funky and spirited whether she was tap dancing, floor walking, or shaking on bar counters and table tops. The last time I saw her was at a B. B. King concert. King recognized her from the stage and invited her to dance as he sang 'Caldonia.' Most of the people in the crowd got up on their feet and strained to see her strut, hand on hip, and flex her butt and leg muscles in the faces of the nearest males. Cal didn't hold back. I'll bet she strutted her way through the Pearly Gates."[12]

"Connie" would also sit in. Connie was a female impersonator who danced in an exotic costume with a flaming torch that she placed in her mouth and ran up and down her arms and legs, setting them afire. One night, she had to put a man in his place:

> One night Big Ed Thompson had just finished picking saxophonist Jimmy Forrest's "Night Train" on his guitar and swung into "Caravan," and Connie was doing her dance, stealing fire from the scratched end of a kitchen match, sweeping the fire up and down her arms and legs with a torch, balancing the flame on the tip of her rigid tongue extending from her upturned head, when a man roared out over his beer breath that Connie wouldn't burn because she could never get hot. Connie spit out the fire at his scuffling Florsheims and stamped it out with her bare foot, pulled the electricity on the band's instruments and said with a saucy thrust of her hips, "Honey, I'm more man than you'll ever be, and more woman than you'll ever get."[13]

Of course, many other musical guests sat in, too, like Guitar Red and the tremendous baritone sax player Virgil Schooler, but Albert was really the show, and at the Vet's he was unbeatable, and the crowd was his.

I was one of the white people who went to see Albert at the clubs during this time (he reciprocated by coming to Walnut Hills High School in 1972 to play), and I was surprised that he not only invited me to sit in with him at the Vet's and later asked me to play regularly but also that he invited me to play on a recording session at Jewel in 1972. With Johnny Dollar on piano, Ed Thompson on guitar, Walter Cash on bass, and Cornelius Roberts on drums, we cut two sides:

| L and W 491 15A | So Good | L and W (No number) |
| L and W 491 15B | Before the Sun Goes Down | L and W (No number) |

The "L and W" of the label stands for Lee and Washington, the Lee referring to Roosevelt Lee, who was Albert's manager at that time and served in that capacity off and on for some years. Lee was born on Clark Street in Cincinnati's West End on August 15, 1930, and in his post-teen days he listened to out-of-town blues stars at the Cotton Club, Sportsman's Club, 936 Club, and many other places, eventually forming his own band, Roosevelt Lee and the Roulettes, in the fifties, playing blues, rock, pop, and country western. Around 1951 Lee recorded for Carl Burkhardt at Rite Records, 3930 Spring Grove Avenue, for the Hilltop label, including the sides "Hey Little Girl I Got Eyes for You" and "Boogiein the Blues," singing and playing horn. "Hey Little Girl," which also featured John Godfrey on vocal and piano, Joseph Ellison on alto sax, Oscar Crumlin on bass, and Lloyd Charlton on drums, was sold to Leonard Chess and became a minor hit, behind which the group toured all over the country for Universal Attractions. Lee recorded a single with Kid King, "Lazy Pete"/"I'm So Sad," for Excello's Ernie Young at WLAC Studios in 1954. Three years later he cut "Come Little Girl"/"Don't Leave Me Baby" for Justin Huber of Huber Musical Enterprises on Blue Rock Road in Blue Ash, using the same band that played on the Hilltop recording. He claims they also cut sides for Decca, including "Yes You Do," "Cougar [sic] Baby," "Hey Boy," and "Thoughts on Dreams." Eventually, though, Lee phased out of performing for managing and promoting, working especially with Albert in promoting and, in this case, getting Albert's single out on their joint label. "So Good" is a rollicking blues, another twelve-bar variation with strong piano from Dollar and vocals and guitar from Albert and, I'm afraid, only a passable harmonica solo. Still, it is a driving side, full and blasting out of the grooves. The flip is a latin-tinged soul tune with congas and no harmonica, and of little blues interest.

Also in 1972, Albert cut a pair of sides at Rite Recording studios for his M in the Street label, with wonderful piano and organ from Johnny Dollar, bass by Sonny Watt, James Darks on drums, and Ed Thompson on rhythm guitar all laying down a funky rhythm for Albert's vocals and guitar on "Ninety Nine Pair Shoes" and ballad backing for "What a Beautiful Day":

Ninety Nine Pair Shoes	M in the Street 553-20
What a Beautiful Day	———

There is a party atmosphere to the song, the band members jiving it up at the opening of the song, and Albert providing a commentary just as rollicking as the piano in between traditional lines like "I'm gonna leave here runnin; walkin just ain't fast enough" and "just because I'm a stranger, girl, don't you dog me around." You could wear out "ninety-nine pair shoes" tapping your feet to this one. "What a Beautiful Day" is a slow ballad with some sweet falsetto passages and almost country touches in the piano, but with a surprising lyric: "What a beautiful day in my life since you went away." The tender delivery of such a rather caustic lyric is unexpected, but finally effective, and Albert proved with this record that he'd lost neither his humorous nor pretty side.

Not that there wasn't some friction in the studio, between Sonny Watt and Johnny Dollar, friction that could have upset the festive atmosphere:

> My bass player back in them days . . . you know, he didn't go to church or nothin. So the piano player, Johnny Dollar, Christian-hearted guy. So he was out to Rite's cuttin that record bout "What a Beautiful Day"/ "Ninety Nine Pair Shoes," and Johnny was gonna put the organ on that first. But Sonny started to messin with him. Something he mentioned to Sonny about God. And Sonny, the bass player holler and told him, "I don't wanna hear nothin about God. I don't believe in that." So that just got on his nerves, you know? He say, "I can't record any more tonight." I could understand his point, you know? *Now,* so the bass player trying to be a preacher, now he comes over to the Sha-Rah, "When you gon get out of here?"
>
> I say, "I ain't."

Luckily, problems were overcome, and the record was an aesthetic success.

Next out was Albert's first recording on his own Preston label:

God Is Good to Me	Preston 902014
God Hear My Prayer	———

The music for both sides was cut at his earlier King Records session featuring Lonnie Mack, Denny Rice, and Bo Dollar and the Coins on a version of "Love Is a Wonderful Thing." In 1972 Albert went into his bedroom at 847 Dayton Street and preached/ recited/sang the words to "God Is Good to Me" and "God Hear My Prayer," creating two new songs for a projected LP, *Eternal Life,* which was never released. There is quite a bit of righteous fervor in Albert's recitations, particularly of the Lord's Prayer, but the lyrics to "God Is Good to Me" are perhaps a bit too repetitious to be effective. However, the recording did demonstrate that the religious side of Albert was ever-present and ready to emerge.

But at this point Roosevelt Lee brought about a development that put Albert potentially on the brink of his biggest success of his carrer: a contract for an LP on the Eastbound label. The recordings were originally slated to be done in Cincinnati at Shad O'Shea's Counterpart Studios, reuniting Albert with the man who had earlier helped put him and Fraternity together, but eventually they were done at

TMI studios in Memphis, with Bernie Mendelsohn producing, Pea-Shooter arranging, and horns by the famed Memphis Horns. Albert recorded two other songs besides the ones included on the LP: Elton John's "Daniel" and Jimmy Hughes's "Steal Away," but these two songs were left off the LP in favor of the remaining ten tunes:

2892	No Matter What the Cost May Be	Eastbound EB 9007
		Chess PLP-6024
2893	Feel the Need	_____
2894	My Mother's Prayer	_____
2895	Mischievous	_____
2896	If I Lose Your Love	_____
2897	I Can't Stand It No More	_____
2898	Do You Really Love Me	_____
2971	You're Messing Up My Mind	_____
2972	Wings of a Dove	_____
2994	Sad and Lonely	_____

Down Home Music gave the LP high praise: "Southern soul recorded in Memphis. Excellent arrangements and tough sounding band featurings [sic] The Memphis Horns. If you enjoy funky seventies soul then don't pass this up! A couple of nice blues cuts too. Could be a classic."[14]

And indeed the LP is a classic! Though Albert was at first thrown off a bit by the arrangements, he adapted quickly. The LP is a mixture of James Brown funk grooves ("You're Messing Up My Mind"); pretty ballads ("My Mother's Prayer," in a Joe Tex-type mould, and "Do You Really Love Me," nodding perhaps to Sam Cooke); blues hybrids (the churning "No Matter What the Cost May Be," with an interesting mix of fast music and slow-paced vocals, and the hauntingly beautiful and bluesy "If I Lose Your Love"); a remake of "Loosen These Pains" entitled "I Can't Stand It No More"; and Albert's masterpiece, "Wings of a Dove." The King discography lists a title, "I Let Nothing Separate Me," as being recorded at Starday-King, and if it was—Albert doesn't recall it—it was likely a forerunner to "Wings of a Dove." Albert originally wrote and performed the song as an eight-bar blues, but it was changed to a twelve-bar blues in the studio. Taken at a tough, pounding, slow pace at times, and a smooth and slow one at others, the changes in dynamics and tension are perfectly timed, and Albert's sweet and soaring gospel tones deliver the pretty and tender gospel-tinged lyrics, with a marvelous mixture of sacred and secular elements, with incredible power:

If I had wings like a beautiful dove, Oh, I'd fly away.
I'd let nothin separate me, nothin, nothin, separate me from that little
  girl of mine.
Oh, I'd let nothin separate me from that little girl of mine.

If I had a river I had a river to cross
Lord if I had a mountain, a mountain to climb
Oh, oh no baby, I'd let nothin separate me from that little girl of mine.
No, I'd let nothin nothin nothin separate me from that little girl of mine.

I'm gonna search every town no matter how hard it may be.
Oh I'm gonna find my baby and bring her home to me.
Nothin, nothin separate me from that little girl of mine.
No I'd let nothin nothin nothin separate me from that little girl of mine.

Albert really *feels* this, and shows it, and the understated piano and
incredibly tight and pushing rhythm section give him plenty of bedrock blues support. Wow! The guitarist takes his time, with no show-
boating, just pretty preaching with the occasional hard-edged run.
After the solo, Albert pulls out all stops to positively raise the hairs
on the back of your neck (and arms and legs and whatever). Someone
yells "Whoo!" at the end of the song, and one imagines that emotions had been brought to an exquisite fever pitch in the studio. This
is a classic blues, certainly one of the best recorded in the sixties and
seventies, and a true representation of what heights Albert can
achieve in the blues field. Special mention should be made of the female choruses on the record which, like the chorus on "Ain't It a
Shame" earlier, are very tastefully and appropriately done, models,
really, of how much they can add to a blues song if done correctly.
Unfortunately, the LP didn't sell as well as it should have, and though
Albert did some touring, again not even this pushed him into his
rightful place as a blues and soul star. Albert did get a large van out
of the deal with Eastbound, emblazoned with Albert Washington and
the Astros (changed from the Kings after the time of his Fraternity
recordings), which he still drives, a reminder of his closest brush with
the big time. The LP subsequently came out in Japan—the Japanese
seem to have had an enduring interest in Albert's music—but he received no royalties. He even had to buy copies of the Japanese release.

Albert was not much in the studios for the next few years. He was
slated to do the Nick Clooney television show with me in the early
seventies, but developed some throat problems and was replaced by
Joe Duskin. He did continue to come to the WAIF studios for special
marathon fund raisers during those days, and appeared with me on a
TV show entitled "MCM78" in 1978, singing "Albert's Blues" and
backing me on "Mean Old Frisco." Also during this time Albert re-

corded a song in the attic recording studios of local blues fan/har-
monica player Frank Lynch, again with me on harmonica, entitled
"Someday Darling," a version of Little Johnny Taylor's "You're
Gonna Need Another Favor," which was never released. From
Lynch's attic we proceeded to Albert's basement in his new house
on Ravenna in Madisonville, this time cutting a single on the Preston
label:

> I Walk a Long Ways   Preston 912046-3269
> Going Down to the Graveyard   ———

The topside was sung by Albert, accompanied by his own piano,
keyboard by his wife Debbie, my harmonica, and Albert's over-
dubbed drums and lead guitar. Albert was singing in a lower key than
usual, so his falsetto is not much in evidence here, but he overcomes
that and the limitations of relentless overdubbing on a home tape machine to come up with a nice side. I sang the flip, an original composition featuring my harmonica, guitar by Phil Buscema, piano by
Lonnie Bennett, bass by Hudson Rivers, Tom Storer on drums, and
Albert on lead guitar at the end of the song. Although the single was
hampered by marginal sound, it did sell out 1,000 copies, and it gave
Albert something to push as he played in clubs like Gus's Place, a bar
he mentioned in another unreleased recording from this period, a version of Sam Cooke's "Having a Party." Again, this was recorded in
Albert's basement, with Albert on vocal, piano, guitar, and drums,
Debbie Washington on bass, and myself on harmonica. This was not
Albert's most prolific period in the studios, this period after his LP,
but he continued to play regularly, four or five nights a week, with his
wife on bass, Ed Thompson or Landy Shores on guitar, Bob Goodman (Bobby Goody) or Ben Irvin on drums, at Gus's or the Sha-Rah,
paying the rent and playing the blues, soul, and rock and roll. The
Sha-Rah, Albert's regular gig at the time, has been owned by Charles
and Phyllis James for three decades, and the North Avondale club on
Reading Road has hosted acts like Bobby Bland, Rufus Thomas, and
Etta James.[15] It became Albert's job to keep it packed, and he did,
with many of the people who first saw him at the Vet's Inn years ago.
    After the period of recording in his basement, Albert once again
got back into a regular studio in 1985—Rusty York's Jewel Studios—
this time reaching back into his early days of blues listening to record
a version of Blind Lemon Jefferson's "Matchbox Blues," though he
doesn't remember Jefferson's version: "It wasn't like that, though. It
sound kinda draggy-like. But it was way back. I was a little boy. I
was around six or seven." Albert was playing mostly piano now in

the clubs—since he needed to sit down as he played because of his diabetes, he said—and he played it in the studio, too, with Debbie Washington on keyboard bass, Phil Buscema on guitar, myself on harmonica, and Bob Goodman on drums.

| Matchbox | Jewel 8415 |
| Nobody Knows What Tomorrow May Bring | ——— |

Bez Turner mentioned in his review that the songs were cleanly recorded, and found the B side "Nobody Knows" to be "well played and sung," while Mark Harris called it a "pleasant enough" 45 of "wholesome blues,"[16] but again with a push from WNOP, where I was then doing a radio show and had Albert over to talk about the record, and strong pushing from Albert, the record sold fairly well locally, keeping Albert's name in front of the record-buying public.

Albert's latest record release was cut at Group Effort Studios in Kentucky, and is being promoted by his manager Roosevelt Lee, who also produced the session:

| Taste of Chicago | Westworld 708033XA |
| Fat Rat | Westworld 708033XB |

The name of the band is now the "R&B 4 Leaf Clovers," but it is still Albert's group that he uses in the club—Debbie, Landy, and Bobby—who accompany his vocals, keyboards, and guitar, through the discoized James Brown workout on the A side, and the reworking of Little Son Joe's "Black Rat Swing" on the flip. Unfortunately, Albert has been sidetracked by problems with high blood pressure, diabetes, and cataracts in the last couple of years, resulting in hospitalization for a period of time, but he still managed to record a song (in his kitchen!) that was released on a Jewel label Christmas CD, and began what could be a strong comeback with the recording of a CD release for Bob Devere at Iris Records in New York. On October 10, 1992, Albert was the guest of honor at the First Annual Greater Cincinnati Blues Festival, coming out of retirement to wow the crowd there with three new songs.

But Albert sees the blues today as being different from the way it used to be:

The blues now is more, try to be more prettier. They don't really get down in the deep blues, they try to mix it with a little bit of, you know, the professional stuff. Yeah. The kind of singin like maybe Al Green used to do. See, now some people call *them* blues, but as far as I'm concerned it wasn't no blues. Wasn't no *really* blues he made but "Love and Happiness," and that wasn't really *deep,* down in the blues. . . . See, I like Little

Milton, B. B. King, Albert Collins, Albert King, I like all them the way they do the blues. Them's the kind of blues I really like. . . . See, now the way they sing blues then, them is blues. To me it is blues. But the rest of them is a tetch of the blues.

And as he looks back over his life and his efforts to survive and make his music, he sees the battle between good and evil that has taken place, and the trouble that misguided religious fanatics have tried to cause him. He answers them with unswerving faith and determination:

Lord has been good to me since I been in nightclubs. So if it was a sin—a lot of people come in and tell me, "You know, the devil can be good to you." I say, "It ain't no devil. Only time the devil come alive is when you start arguin and raisin sand and fightin and going on. Then *you* brings him up. Other words, the wages of sin is death. He been dead, he sinned. He been dead. If you don't bring him up he just lay there. He won't, he won't be nothin! But you go to start arguin in here, he'll come up, and he keep gettin bigger and bigger til he make you hit somebody. He'll get into you. He'll get in your arms and things and control you and there's where the trouble start, he'll make you shoot or cut somebody." I said, "But if you leave him alone, he gon leave you alone. But God is always gon be by our side. We know is a God. Cause the trees keep growin, the fruit keep growin. Who doin that? Hmm! Kids keep gettin born. Who gin em life? Now we know the devil don't—what you see the devil doin? He don't do nothin til you do it. . . ." So I keep tellin people "ain't no Satan. You got to build him up." The same as you start layin some bricks and buildin up, you start arguin or raisin sand, or livin wrong. Mistreatin somebody. You buildin him up. He's gettin closer and closer to you then. Then he gets so close he's in. After you build up he get so close til God'll move away. . . . Don't matter what kind of disease is out there, he can't get you if you close to God. He ain't gonna come in God's arms and snatch you out. Heart attack, sugar—I got sugar, high blood. But everybody ask me why I'm not on insulin. It don't get that bad! It don't get that bad. But just as quick as I move away from God, it'll kill me. It'll kill me.

He believes it sincerely, and wishes just as sincerely to maintain his closeness with his God, and his music. In 1990 his problems with diabetes intensified to the point where he gave up playing regularly in clubs, particularly since it had become more difficult to keep a decent, responsible performing band together. A number of visits to the hospital culminated in an operation to remove cataracts from both of his eyes. He found himself recuperating around the same time his old playing partner, Big Ed Thompson, was recovering from a slight stroke, in October and November of 1991. But Albert, of course, has no plans to give up playing and singing the music he loves so much, and he responds with the indomitable spirit of African-American music:

But I'm dependin to live a hundred and thirty. That's what I'm dependin on. Yeah, and still singin!

10

The Blues Scene—
the Fifties to Today

Two musicians who have spent some time in Albert Washington's bands but also continued to work outside and after their tenure with him are among the best blues instrumentalists currently working in the city: Big Ed Thompson and Lonnie Bennett. Guitarist Thompson was born in Bethlehem, Georgia, on January 22, 1934. He was not, he says, very musical as a child. Although he recalls his mama playing on grandpa's pump organ, he confined his musical activity to blowing whistles made out of hickory sticks, playing the comb, and sneaking off to listen to rhythm and blues in the evening on a radio station out of Covington, Georgia. Slightly later he began listening to WCKY in Georgia, especially the Grand Ol' Opry, where Dave Macon, Minnie Pearl, Roy Acuff, and Sam McGee stood out, though Grandpa Jones was his favorite "because he had some fire in his pickin."[1] Nails, a board, and chicken wire soon were fashioned into Ed's first "guitar," and he began trying to make some chords on his makeshift instrument.

At the age of twelve or thirteen Ed came to Cincinnati and got a twelve-string guitar for eight dollars at a Lockland pawn shop. He made it into a six-stringer, tuned to "Vastapool"—that is, open tuning—ordered a book by harmonica player Wayne Raney of WCKY, and began learning chords for the hillbilly music he was interested in playing. However, once he heard some blues on the radio via the Ernie Waits and Babe Baker shows on WZIP, Ed was hooked on the blues. Although he didn't admire any singers in particular, Ed was inspired by instrumentalists: "It looked like I just liked the horn. I just liked the spirit of Illinois Jacquet, or somebody would play 'Flying Home,' or just be rockin and rollin. You know, just really up tempo, loud, and a lot of fire. That's the kind of licks I like as a musician."

Ed's first band was the "Gospeliers" of Lincoln Heights. At age fifteen or sixteen he began playing R&B with a band that included Ricky Williams and Billy Malone, and he played with a jazz band at Wayne High School as well. In fact, Ed was playing acoustic guitar until his teacher, Mr. Ted Turner, told him to go electric and wrote out the chords to such songs as "Misty," "Lover Man," "Perdido," "A Train," and "Body and Soul." Ed credits Mr. Turner with helping him a great deal technically, but found that the blues was a totally different field that required more "fire" than the jazz music did.

By age eighteen Thompson got his first good big gig, in Hamilton at "Big Brother's" with his R&B band, which had been playing and winning trophies while making two to three dollars a man on Saturdays. With Steve Reese on piano, Billy Malone on sax, Ed on guitar, and Ricky Williams on drums, the Swinging Rocks were born. Later they were called Harold and the Swingin Rocks, and sometimes included Lonnie Bennett on keyboards. Ed also spent some time with the Rocketeers and the Drivers, and during his time with these bands he recorded, he claims, with the Swinging Rocks (on the VLM label) and another single, "Satellite Rock" for Estel Lee's Este Records; played on the bill with Ellington, Basie, and Tab Smith at the Cotton Club; at the Regal and State theaters (five shows a day!); and once on the bill with blues great Big Joe Turner.

Next Ed hooked up with saxophonist Lynn Hope, who was born in Lincoln Heights and who played here in the early sixties. Hope played R&B sax instrumentals in a bluesy/jazzy style, and had recorded for Aladdin records throughout the fifties. The members of his band were mostly family members and, as devout Moslems, were often seen performing wearing turbans. By the time Ed joined in 1960, the hits, like "Tenderly" and "Song of the Wanderer" and "Morocco," were past, but it was still a hot band that was a good draw. The Drifters, the Coasters, the Shirelles, and B. B. King all benefited from Big Ed's musical presence at this time as well, and he recorded at Victor and ABC Paramount during the early sixties, too. Also during this time Ed got into the King Records studio to cut some sides with the Drivers and to do the Christmas LP with Charles Brown, as well as record some sessions with Sonny Thompson as A&R Man. Eventually, Ed left Hope and joined up with Jon Thomas, whom he met when the Drivers opened up for Thomas at a club. While on the road Ed cut some sides with Thomas for ABC Paramount, including "Flip, Flop and Fly" and "Boss Hoss," and he stayed with Thomas until New Year's 1963. At that point he formed Big Ed Thompson and the All Stars, playing the Magic Moment, the

Wein Bar on Gilbert Avenue, the Queue Lounge on Dana Avenue, and the Playboy Club. Eventually he began playing some jobs and recording with Albert Washington, and after they became a hit at the Vet's Inn, Ed stayed on with Albert for years, becoming an integral part of Albert's sound and providing guitar fireworks in his distinctive style on instrumental songs like "Honky Tonk," "Hand Clappin'," and "Red Top."

After many years with Albert, save for a short time when Andy Johnson replaced him on guitar, Ed left to re-form his All Stars and perform with H-Bomb Ferguson from 1983 to 1987. At that point he split with Ferguson and led his All Stars around the city to become one of the most popular blues bands in town, featuring his own singing and remarkable guitar. The All Stars also played at such events as the Cuyahoga State Park Arts Festival and the National Folk Festival in Hilson, Ohio. However, Ed's career was interrupted when he suffered an aneurysm and two strokes. The blues community responded with three benefits, one each at Cory's, Burbank's, and Flanagan's Landing, an outpouring of love that speaks volumes for Ed's reputation as a blues player and human being. He died on April 22, 1993.

Ed's guitar work betrayed his interests in hillbilly music in his almost bluegrass flat picking style that was wonderfully adapted to the blues, and in horn players as he combined jazz horn lines with well-placed sliding techniques to simulate a horn sound. As a blues guitarist Ed was one of the few players around who did not come off at some point as a B. B. imitator, due no doubt to the absence for the most part of string-stretching in his playing, but his playing proved that you don't have to stretch a string to play the blues on guitar. This quiet, unassuming man with a quick sense of humor never showboated never overplayed—he just casually waited his turn and played the blues, Ed Thompson-style, often smiling, cracking up, really, if he felt the crowd acknowledged too much what he was doing in his solos, or if, say, Caldonia had gotten up to do her racy act, or Connie was doing her female impersonation fire dance. He was a good-natured, good-timing, wonderful musican whose music deserves to be heard much more than it has.

Pianist/organist Lonnie Bennett was born in Brundage, Alabama, on July 17, 1937. He came to Cincinnati at an early age, living first at Valleyview (where GE now stands) and then to Lincoln Heights. His first instruments were violin and banjo, and he was exposed early on to music by the playing of his uncle A. J. Shipman, who played solo blues guitar in clubs like Ruff's/Magic Moment and whose picture appeared in *Life Magazine,* playing guitar on board his navy ship in 1947.[2] Lonnie learned from Shipman and took lessons on the trumpet, but recalls especially the work of a local musician who inspired him, at age nine, as a pianist. "Cow Cow Willie" used to come down and play piano for all the kids, and Lonnie copied his style and later received some pointers from Willie, a low-down blues pianist.

Lonnie played in bands with Big Ed, Reecy Matthews, and Benny Reynolds in Ted Turner's Wayne High School jazz band as well, which at times became the Lonnie Bennett Orchestra after school and took first place at the Ninth Street YMCA in 1952. This orchestra was later cut down and became the Rocks Orchestra, playing dates like the Amalgamated Dimwits Ball, a function related to DJ Bugs Scruggs's Amalgamated Order of Dimwits for Teens. At age sixteen Bennett also filled in for Jimmy Reed's drummer, who had been arrested, for two nights at the Ebony Club at Wayne and Simmons—a club that also booked such other blues stars as B. B. King and Big Maybelle. When Lonnie went into the service, the Rocks band continued with Big Ed, Harold Willingham, Rufus Irby, Landon Cos, and Paul Merle. After Bennett got out of the service, he played with Albert Washington for eight or nine years from 1964 on, recording about fifteen tunes with him in the mid-sixties, including "Ain't It a Shame," one of Albert's best. In 1970 he formed his own group, Lonnie and the Backbeats, performing at places like the Soul Lounge, and sometimes including horn man Harold Byrd, a music instructor at Lincoln Heights High School.

But Lonnie has always held down jobs and made music a sideline: he worked as a crane operator at Milacron for thirteen years, signed on as a police officer in Lincoln Heights in 1964, moving up to chief in 1969 and resigning in 1970, moved on to Western Electric as an installer, and finally took a job with Rodeway Express, which put him on the road much of the time and pretty much put an end to his regular performing as a musician in Cincinnati. However, Lonnie still found the time to put together a series of highly successful "Cavalcade of Blues" shows at the Apple nightclub, featuring such artists as Lonnie Bennett, Albert Washington, Ray Felder, Maurice Gipson, Virgil Schooler, Big Ed Thompson, myself, and others, which normally drew good crowds and provided a strong evening of blues performing in the city. Lonnie now prefers playing the organ to the piano, but continues his interest in various types of keyboard instruments. He no longer performs full-time, but, he declares, blues has been part of him all of his life: "It sort of relieves me," he told me, speaking seriously. "Music's still my life."

Pianist/organist Jon Thomas was born February 21, 1918, in Biloxi, Mississippi. His family moved to Cincinnati's West End in 1921, living at various locations on Wade, Betts, Fourteenth and Central, and Fifteenth and Central, and Thomas began beating on chairs to entertain the other kids. Eventually he graduated to the piano, learning to play by ear. He recalled the rub-board bands who used to play on the streets, and Little Joe the tap dancer, and formulated a dream: "That was my dream—to play music and get paid."[3] In the thirties he achieved that dream when he began playing for ten to twelve dollars a week. He had been in a band at Holy Trinity, where he learned to read big band music, and he observed pianist Blackjack and studied piano rolls to pick up other pointers. From weekend rent parties in the mid-thirties to jobs at the Green Lantern on Sixth Street and a stint with the Hopkins Melody Boys, Thomas moved on to a place in the segregated WPA band in 1941–43.

Thomas was drafted in 1945, but got out in 1946 and formed a band that played pop tunes like "Embraceable You." After they disbanded, he joined Popeye Maupin for a stretch, and then finally formed his own Hammond organ quartet in 1955, with Clifford Bush, Osborn Whitfield on sax, and Chick Farley on drums. In 1956 Thomas started his recording career, recording that year at King with Little Willie John (on "Fever") and the following year with Titus Turner, Earl Connelly King, and Tiny Topsy. King Records had been alerted to Thomas because of his local popularity; in his career he went on to back Cozy Cole, Rudy West, Tab Smith, Roy Brown, Earl Bostic (who wanted to take him on the road), Gene Redd, the Drifters, Otis Williams and the Charms, and the Five Keys.

But the big news that year for Thomas was the beginning of his own recording career as a headliner, starting with an LP and three or four singles, mostly blues, for Mercury Records. His biggest success came from a record he made in 1960: "I made my own record. That was 'Heartbreak.' [In] nineteen sixty I made my own record. You know, my label. I called it *Journey*. And I played around here and went to Cleveland and took it to the disc jockeys. While I was there ABC Paramount got interested in it. And they flew me up there to be on Dick Clark's show. . . . This was in May 1960." The same band that did his Mercury LP—Chick Farley, Osborn Whitfield, Charles Grayson, and J. T. on organ—did his "Heartbreak" single, but the subsequent LP substituted Otis French for Whitfield, and Chick Farley had departed by that time as well. Thomas "rode on that record for about four years," but eventually settled here in Cincinnati, gave up his band, and began working as a single, playing jazz, pop, and cocktail lounge music at the Travelodge, Revolving Restaurant, Loll 43, and other places. The days he played with Lula Reed at Ruff's and with Big Maybelle at the Sportsman Club were gone now. He played as a single from 1967 until January 1988. Since then he's been playing less often, but he still plays—and very well—and deserves another chance to demonstrate the talent that made him a fine session man and strong artist in his own right.

Another highly respected organist around Cincinnati is Boots Johnson, who was born (like Albert Washington) in Rome, Georgia, but a little earlier, on December 24, 1919. He moved to Springfield, Ohio, when he was two years old. There he first began playing in his teens, having been around musical relatives all his life, including an uncle "Fathead Leslie," who played Count Basie-type blues in Chattanooga. Over the years Johnson has played many local night spots, including Screw Andrews's Copa Club, the Sportsman's Club, Perkins's, the Travelodge, Babe Baker's Jazz Corner, and, booked by Universal Attractions, about the same circuit as Jon Thomas. Johnson claims to have recorded for Chess and Checker with his own group in the fifties, with Raymond Herring on sax and Johnny Lytle on vibes, but these sides haven't been traced. Johnson actually did a recording session for King Records in 1964, four years before he moved here permanently in 1968:

Hold Me Baby   King 6185
If I Had the Chance (to Love You)   ———

The sessions featured Billy Nelson on vocals, Johnson on organ, two unknown guitarists, Gene Redd on horns, and Don Litman on drums. Nelson, born August 28, 1927, in Cincinnati, was himself a popular local musican and vocalist. A pianist, flautist, and trombonist, Nelson spent time as a vocalist with the Ink Spots and did some recordings in Chicago in addition to his Cincinnati King recordings. When he died on August 25, 1984, from complications due to his having swallowed a toothpick, he was greatly mourned, and a benefit fund-raiser on September 5, 1984, at the Collage nightclub drew featured performers H-Bomb Ferguson, Big Ed Thompson, Albert Washington, Big Joe Duskin, the Skid Row Blues Band, and myself, in addition to other local blues and jazz performers.

At one point, Johnson was in line to take the favored organ spot vacated when Bill Doggett left King, but the position ultimately went to the other person being considered for the job, Hank Marr, so Johnson continued gigging, backing up stars like Laverne Baker, Gene Ammons, Jimmy Witherspoon, Otis Williams, Big

Maybelle, and Ray Charles, building a strong reputation as a top-notch organist along the lines of Jimmy McGriff, Wild Bill Davis, and Doggett. It is a reputation he maintains to this day, following him to places like Leo Lick's Home Like Inn in New Baltimore on Blue Rock Road.

One other group of musicans associated in the late fifties and early sixties with Cincinnati was a group called the Bees (on Finch) and the Blues Bees (on Boyd). Various musicians recall the Bees playing around Cincinnati: Ed Thompson remembered them playing the Wein Bar, Lonnie Bennett saw them at Ruff's, Albert Washington took over their spot at the Vet's Inn. They are, certainly, remembered as a hard-core blues band. "They was *stone* blues," Lonnie Bennett emphasized, and indeed they were. The lead vocalist was Robert "Cherokee" Singleton, backed ably on guitar by Leroy "Sugarfoot" Bonner, formerly with Robert Ward and the Ohio Untouchables out of Dayton, Ohio, a bass player named Rico (according to Vince Morton) or Dan (according to Albert Washington), a harmonica player named Chico, unknown keyboards, and Rufus on drums. At the Vet's Inn, according to Albert Washington, they were crowd pleasers: "They had them long chords you drag out the door then. Say they walked up and down Eastern Avenue singing the blues. They say Cherokee could get down. Say people was followin em up and down the street."[4]

John Finch and Vince Morton met the Bees, who operated out of Hamilton, Ohio, at a club called the Hippodrome and were instantly impressed with their style. Morton told me that the Bees cut two singles for Finch, but only one has turned up, recorded in Cincinnati in 1962, at Finch's recording studio:

7321	Oh Yes	Finch 7321/2
7322	Tough Enough	————

Unfortunately, Singleton died of a heart attack (or poisoning?) before the record was released and Bonner, who lived on Chestnut Street in Hamilton, was unable to satisfy the demand for the band that made the record, despite the fact that the record sold, according to Morton, over 25,000 copies. "But they wanted Singleton," Morton shook his head, "but he was dead."[5] According to Roosevelt Lee, Bonner left the Bees to join the Ohio Players, with whom he is reportedly still playing. Little Boyd mentioned in an interview with Mike Leadbitter that a "Cherokee Robert" (obviously Singleton) recorded a song, "So Jealous," with Boyd's help, and this may be the other single Morton mentioned—and it may also verify Boyd's presence on the sides.[6] According to Boyd, DJ Bugs Scruggs was involved with the Bees' recordings.

Boyd, possibly Louis Boyd, was born August 24, 1924, in Carthage, Mississippi. He fell under the influence of John Lee "Sonny Boy" Williamson's harmonica playing, and spent some time with bluesmen Elmore James and Rice Miller before coming to Cincinnati in the late fifties. Boyd claimed to have cut recordings for his Boyd label at a Fortune Studio (untraced) in Cincinnati around 1957–58 with the "Little Blue B's."[7] The sides, though, were likely cut closer to 1962 or 1963. He had recorded also four (rather undistinguished) sides backing Smokey Smothers at King in 1962, including "Way up in the Mountains of Kentucky," which names several Kentucky locations. After his Boyd releases, he left Cincinnati in 1964 or 1965 for Los Angeles, where he recorded for Singleton. So Boyd and the Blues Bees were around Cincinnati for a number of years in the late fifties and early sixties, but Singleton's death, and the departure of Bonner and Boyd, spelled the end of the Bees' popularity. Still, their big-selling record assured that they would be remembered as being among Cincinnati's best blues bands.

One of my most interesting but ultimately frustrating encounters began one day while I was walking down Madison Road in Oakley past Lloyd Hazelbaker's music store in the late seventies. As I glanced inside I saw a black man, about 6'2", 185 pounds, somewhere near eighty years old, buying guitar strings, and I couldn't resist going inside to ask him if he knew anything about the blues. Luckily I had a harmonica along, and I knew Mr. Hazelbaker, so breaking the ice was no trouble. And did the man know anything about the blues! Jack Richardson had been in Cincinnati about twenty or thirty years, and during that time his playing was confined to his apartment, which was now apartment 1407 at 534 Clark Street. He had been born, though, in Atlanta, spending his early years there and staying in Georgia until he came to Cincinnati. "Did you ever hear of a guy named Willie McTell?" I wondered, leadingly. "Oh yeah," he answered. "Willie McTell, Curley Weaver, Buddy Moss," he began, and five minutes later we were at my parents' home listening to a Curley Weaver recording of "Oh Lawdy Mama" from 1935. "Boots and Shoes. Meet me round the corner, bring me my boots and shoes. That's Curley Weaver," Mr. Richardson said, surprised, upon hearing the first few notes of guitar in the record. And he kind of *looked* at me. A white boy in his mid-twenties with a forty-year-old recording by a black blues singer from Georgia. He hitched his thumbs in the waist band of his overalls and listened to Weaver, Moss, McTell, Peg

Leg Howell, and others, just listening and laughing a bit, and then got out his guitar to play.

It became obvious to me that at one time he had been at least a good player in the raggy blues style found in parts of the Southeast. He still attempted the difficult fingerings, the flashy, syncopated picking, but he was able only to hint on occasion that he in fact could play them, though he could make some rudimentary chords and picking sound awfully good. He did come down to WAIF for my radio show once to play, but I heard him only three or four times, at his apartment, and usually his wife intervened, admonishing him not to play blues or talk about it. She would have him play church songs and break in on the vocals herself in a passable but hardly distinctive voice; Jack would just sigh and sit back and play. Although I rode them to church a time or two and gave her a solicited donation for her church, it became obvious that she didn't want the blues to be a subject in her presence, so I saw Jack no more.

Late in 1988 I checked the directories at the Cincinnati Historical Society and saw that Mr. Richardson was still listed on Clark Street, but at a different address, with his wife no longer listed as residing with him, so I headed back for Clark Street to get more of his story. When I knocked on his door a woman answered, telling me that no one named Jack Richardson lived there. As I was leaving, another woman in her thirties hung out her window and asked who I was looking for. "Oh, was he an old gentlemen? You mean the old man? Somebody told me he died a couple of months ago. Yeah, that's when I got his apartment."

James Jones contacted me through my show at WAIF, calling me on the phone occasionally and ultimately dropping off a tape for me at the station. Born in Alabama in the thirties, Jones had come to Cincinnati in the fifties, but he had learned guitar more recently. He had a one-key, one-chord, relaxed rural style, with a droning bass interspersing single string treble or bass runs, and he played mainly to accompaniment and sang only one slightly variable melody in a pinched vocal style. His style, though, was deceptively simple and sometimes hypnotic, possessing especially fine nuances and shadings when he got out his slide for some mean, low blues. He was a bit too humble about his own playing, but his love of the blues and his roots were evident:

So I know I wasn't the best, it was just somethin to let you know that I'm tryin to do somethin. I be sittin around listenin at that good blues each night durin the week. And so I said, "Well, I'll, alot of things I haven't heard, and I have tried to play a guitar a little bit myself, so I make up somethin, you know, nice, for my friends. . . ."

I likes the blues myself. I can't play that well, but I can think about somethin I heard played years ago, that I heard a man play guitar like that years ago. That other words, that he was hittin on a tub fixed where you kind of hit it heavy—like, somethin like a drum. So I heard him hit, play that. Other words, stand by here, with me, and so that's what make it go like that.[8]

Jones is apparently referring to the insistent beat in his own playing, a strong feature of his slow, sometimes measured style. Another influence on Jones was a guitarist in Alabama that Jones claimed was the best around. He played me a piece by Brother Norman Calhoun: "Here's a piece in 1937 that Brother Norman Calhoun was playin. But he wasn't singin, he was just only playin the guitar comin through the woods, and I was beginnin to hear it cause I was bound to the spring to get some water."

Also on his tape, Jones recorded a reworking of my song, "Going Down to the Graveyard," which nodded in my direction and then departed from my song almost totally! The same was true of his version of "Going Down Slow," a very loose and distinctive version of the St. Louis Jimmy Oden tune. Jones came to WAIF to play on the same date that Jack Richardson did, but soon after he moved from his apartment on Race Street, and all attempts to locate him have failed. He recorded on his tape a promo for a WAIF Blues Cruise, naming the three acts booked to perform on the cruise: "I wish somebody would tell me," he sang, "where is Albert Washington. I wish somebody would tell me, where is Steve Tracy. I wish somebody would tell me, where is Pigmeat Jarrett."

I wish somebody would tell me, where is James Jones.

There are, of course, other musicians I'd never heard, guitarists like Willie Hill and "Groundhog," and a man named Henry Walker, whose playing was described to me by white harmonica player Ron Tarter. Tarter had heard Walker one day as Tarter was walking down the street in Cumminsville. The playing was a cross between Lightnin' Hopkins and Elmore James, blaringly amplified through a tiny amplifier sitting next to the man as he sat playing on his front porch. It was raw, low-down gutbucket blues, according to Tarter, who knew it when he heard it. However, Walker remained elusive, and numerous attempts to meet him at his house, my house, the radio stations, or wherever, were unsuccessful. My last contact with his family in 1988 found him extremely ill and unable to do an interview.

Of course, many other black R&B and soul bands in town included blues in their repertoire. Lucky Carmichael, for example, who was born in Harrodsburg, Kentucky, on October 12, 1920, and died in Cincinnati on October 6, 1982, recorded three singles, the first in 1960, the second in 1960, and the third in 1961:

	Better Be with Me	Dillie 7750
	1109	——————
M-103	Lonesome and Lonely	Shar 4
M-104	I'm Coming Home	——————
LX-70010	Hey Girl	Loma 2006
LX-70011	Blues with a Feelin	——————

The Loma label produced singles by Smiley Lewis in New Orleans (1965), James Cotton in Chicago (1966), Barefoot Beefus in Los Angeles (1966), and Chuck Higgins, probably also in Los Angeles, and when I met Carmichael at a show I was playing at Gilly's in Dayton, he told me he had recorded in Chicago. He told me at that time he was still playing in clubs a bit, but he was obviously not as active musically as he would have liked.

Russell Givens, Jr., bassist at one time in the sixties for Howlin' Wolf in Chicago, also worked regularly in Cincinnati with a variety of bands, including Albert Washington, and with his brother, Donnie, on guitar, playing blues, R&B, and soul at places like the Soul Lounge on Madison Road. "Uncle Russell," as he is called, was bassist for Lonnie Bennett's successful series of blues shows, "The Cavalcade of Blues," in the eighties, and Russell recorded the session that Danny Adler did at Finch Recording Studios and attempted to release as Otis "Elevator" Gilmore. There is a very jazzy feel to Russell's playing, but he can dig in and play some fine blues, as could Walter Cash, who also played with Albert Washington and was noted for his habit of playing the bass with his left hand over the top of his fret board.

Guitarist "Big Red," who played his blues, among other things, on a "flying V" guitar, is another fine performer who is still around, as is pianist, guitarist, vocalist, Maurice Gipson. Gipson plays his blues and R&B in the Ray Charles vein, and is still performing blues, jazz, R&B, and standards with the Just Us Band at places like the Crystal Lounge on Gilbert Avenue. A younger man, Donnie Woods, is a Tennessee-born harp player in the Sonny Terry style and a staunch supporter of the performers on the Cincinnati blues scene. On the jazz-blues scene there was Popeye Maupin, whose vocal style veered toward Jimmy Witherspoon's. During his many years in Cincinnati, he sang a great deal around town before moving to the New York scene. Indeed, throughout the fifties, sixties, seventies, and eighties there were still a great number of places where one could go to hear black blues. Mention should also be made of Leslie Isaiah Gaines, Jr., local attorney at Gaines and Gaines, known also for his community involvement and flamboyant style. Gaines's "Reagonomics Blues" and "Jesse (Didn't Get No Justice)," both on his Justice Unlimited label, feature topical lyrics over a blues backing—the former even received a Handy Blues Award nomination as single of the year. A successful lawyer, now a municipal court judge, Gaines doesn't have a great deal of time to devote to blues performing, but he can be counted on for interesting blues releases. Cincinnati's most notable female blues singer today is Sweet Alice Hoskins, who was inspired by Albert Washington's performances at the Vet's Inn. She plays regularly around town with her group, the Unfinished Business Blues Band, and has built up quite a following for her live performances and interest in her recording "Different Shades of Blue." Her tight band has a strong contemporary feel, and she wails soulfully on versions of blues hits like "Down Home Blues" and "Steal Away."

In addition, there were increasing numbers of white blues performers popping up in town. One of the best was guitar hero Lonnie Mack, whose bluesy guitar playing is obviously drawn from black sources. Mack played in a number of black clubs in Cincinnati and on occasion with black musicians like Maurice Gipson and Albert Washington (with whom Mack recorded), and of course he cut his classic Fraternity sides and backed Freddy King and James Brown here. Blues like "Baby What's Wrong," "Down in the Dumps," "Mt. Healthy Blues," and "Cincinnati Jail" are unmistakably blues, but they bear just as unmistakably the stamp of a fine and individual performer. Another white perfomer, Bobby Van Hook, recorded two blues songs for Vince Morton's VLM label— "Down in Alabama" and "Baby One More Time"—after Morton heard Van Hook play on a gospel session. Danny Adler, a talented guitarist now residing in Europe, spent some time in black clubs in Cincinnati accompanying people like Slim Harpo and Jimmy Reed and recording an EP that included B. B. King's "Sweet Little Angel." Adler moved to London in 1972, where he formed the band Roogolator and played what he called "Gusha Gusha Music." He later went on to play with Rocket 88 and the Deluxe Blues Band as well as accompanying artists like Memphis Slim on recording sessions. In the sixties harmonica player Bill Lupkin played here with the Wells Street Blues Band before joining Chicago bluesman Jimmy

Rogers's band, recording with Rogers for Shelter Records (uncredited) and later playing in Los Angeles with blues shouter Jimmy Witherspoon.

Lupkin's fellow musician in the Wells Street Blues Band, Phil Buscema, went on to become a staple of the Cincinnati blues scene. Buscema was an important member of Big Joe Duskin's band for many years, and he has also enlivened many performances by Albert Washington at the Vet's Inn, at Gus's Place, and at the Sha-Rah Lounge. Indeed, Albert Washington rates him as the top blues guitarist in the city and has used him on recording sessions. Buscema has also backed pianist Pigmeat Jarrett as well. Happily, though, Buscema, who now lives in Dayton, Ohio, still finds the time to make it to Cincinnati to perform in his alternately slashing and fleet fingered and slow and sweet style.

Besides recording with Albert Washington, Buscema has also recorded with Steve Tracy and the Crawling Kingsnakes, a band whose reworkings of Walter Coleman's "I'm Going to Cincinnati" turned up on rock station WEBN's 1988 album project, and whose "Jordan River Blues" was released on soul station WBLZ's "Super Jam" LP—the only band of any kind to accomplish that feat. The Crawling Kingsnakes mix traditional blues elements with contemporary blues in their music, and have been seen around town opening up for the likes of B. B. King, James Cotton, Dr. John, Roy Buchanan, and others. Lead singer and harmonica player Steve Tracy has also opened up for Albert King, Sonny Terry and Brownie McGhee, Johnny Winter, and a host of others during his years on the blues scene, which really started for him when he won the 1971 National Harmonica Contest sponsored by Hohner Harmonicas and the National Candy Company and appeared on the Johnny Carson Show performing Little Walter's "Off the Wall." Subsequently Tracy began performing on radio, television, and around town with Albert Washington, Joe Duskin, Pigmeat Jarrett, the Kinfolks, and Lonnie Bennett, finally forming the Crawling Kingsnakes around 1985. The band recorded shortly thereafter, and that session and a subsequent one were issued on compact disc by Blue Shadow Records out of Amsterdam, Holland. Two cuts from that CD are scheduled to be used on the soundtrack of a French made-for-TV movie. Tracy also taped a performance and interview broadcast on the Nashville Network, and continues to perform around town and arrange dates for local blues performers around the country and overseas, including tours for his own band. The band completed a successful tour of the Netherlands in the summer of 1990.

Another longtime harmonica player on the Cincinnati scene is Phil Blank, whose band has held down the weekend spot at Cory's for some time. Blank, also a vocalist and guitarist, plays in a Chicago blues style that has kept his fans pleased for at least a decade in Cincinnati, minus a brief period when he left the city to work in California.

More recently vocalist-harmonica player Cincinnati Slim (real name K. C. Elstun, born March 12, 1955, in Cincinnati) has been gaining local attention, playing all over Ohio, early on especially at the Roosevelt Tavern, and opening up for the likes of Lonnie Mack. Slim was featured in *Cincinnati Magazine*'s "Best of Cincinnati" issue in 1987 as "Best R&B Band," producing a video for the TV special developed from the issue of the magazine. Slim also recorded a blues LP for a local jazz label, MOPRO, run by Helen Moor, a jazz enthusiast. He first came to the blues through James Brown, Ray Charles, and Little Richard, and names Little Walter, Big Walter, and William Clark among his influences and favorites.

Acoustic blues have been well served in the city by people like veteran performer Walter Craft, long popular on the city's folk circuit. Denny Buck, a blues DJ at WAIF in the mid-seventies, also played a number of clubs around town during that time, performing his repertoire of blues songs drawn from the likes of Bo Carter, Jim Jackson, and Robert Johnson. Ed O'Donal, who played both acoustic blues and Elmore James-style electric blues, was involved for a time with the Leo Coffeehouse circle of performers, representing the blues among their ranks. And while he wasn't a regular performer in clubs around town, Ron Tarter, an older, motorcyle-riding harp player and fan of Sonny Terry, made his presence felt in the city, though, unfortunately, he lost one of his lungs and had to give up playing a few years back.

In recent times a group called the Midnight Steppers brought acoustic country and blues and ragtime to the fore in clubs around Cincinnati. The group featured College Conservatory of Music grad and ragtime blues guitar virtuoso Bill Ellis, who draws his repertoire from the likes of Gary Davis, Leadbelly, Bukka White, and Casey Bill Weldon, ace rhythm guitarist Dudley Radcliff, and Larry Nager on bass, mandolin, and spirited washboard. Wherever the group played the stage was likely to be filled with an array of guitars, banjos, mandolins, basses, and almost anything else with strings, all expertly played in traditional style. Ellis had a cassette tape of his performances issued in the eighties, and recorded a second set of recordings in 1988 in North Carolina, which are scheduled for release as well. The band also took its music to National Public Radio, appearing on the bill with Duke Robillard and the Pleasure Kings on Larry Groce's "Mountain Stage" radio show in 1989, opened for such acts as the Bobs and Doc Watson, appeared at the Cuyahoga Folk Festival, and taped a blues segment for the Nashville Network. Unfortunately, this very promising band split up and both Ellis and Nager moved out of town.

Such performers have found warm audiences in a number of folk-oriented clubs around Cincinnati, including the Family Owl, in the late sixties a haven for folk-blues-jazz performers like guitarist Sandy Nassan, harmonica player Victor Van Buren, and many budding performers on open mike night; Arnolds; the Queen City Balladeers' shows; and the Blind Lemon Cafe, a folk club established in Mt. Adams in 1961 that even printed up matchboxes with Blind Lemon Jefferson's picture on them (inspired by his recording of "Matchbox Blues") to help advertise the club. One folk-oriented performer with Cincinnati connections who did not play in the clubs here, himself an admirer of Blind Lemon Jefferson as well as white country artist Jimmy Rodgers, was Harmonica Frank Floyd. Born in Mississippi, Floyd was a one-man band and comedian who worked in carnivals and medicine shows from the twenties on, finally landing a recording session released on Chess in 1951. Three years later he cut for Sam Phillips's Sun label in Memphis, but the recordings did not bring him the fame he desired. For years collectors thought that Floyd was black, but found out differently when he was rediscovered in the seventies. For a period in the seventies Floyd lived in Cincinnati, near Eighth and State, but his experience in the record business made him wary of both recording company executives and researchers, and his relative celebrity made him more of a candidate for festivals than local clubs. He recorded for both the Adelphi and Barrelhouse labels after he was rediscovered, but sadly died before he could capitalize on renewed interest in his work.

The club situation in Cincinnati, though, is much better now. With several clubs booking almost exclusively blues and a number of clubs featuring blues occasionally, there is obviously a demand for blues locally, and many groups have stepped forward to fill that demand, including, happily, veteran performers like Pigmeat, Joe Duskin, Albert Washington, H-Bomb Ferguson, and Big Ed Thompson.

As time went by the blues programming on black radio stations by such DJs as Ernie Waits, Babe Baker, and Bugs Scruggs gradually gave way to soul music, and the "blues revival," the focusing of attention on the blues by middle class and disenfranchised whites, brought blues programming to various white and "underground" stations.

Tom Knox was known to program some blues on WEBN, and jazz expert Oscar Treadwell made blues a part of his "Eclectic Stop Sighn." Later, when WAIF radio debuted with its alternative programming, a Sunday night blues show, "The Blue Jungle with Steve Tracy," was part of its original lineup, changing nights at several points but remaining on for nearly a decade, joined later by Denny Buck's blues show. WAIF made blues a part of its core programming, and prominently featured it in marathons and fund-raisers, helping to prove that a blues audience did indeed exist and giving many local blues artists the media exposure necessary to flourish. After some time off, I moved my blues show from WAIF to jazz station WNOP on Saturdays, and Downtown Scott Brown took my place when I left that station, which continues to serve the blues community with interviews, news, and current blues releases. The work of Ron Esposito on WVXU as both DJ and promoter was also a big boost to the blues community, as was the work of Kitty Carson at WAIF, Libby Remley at the Blues Hot Line, and the Greater Cincinnati Blues Society, which has been sponsoring benefits and activities and working on plans for a Cincinnati blues archive. I took over Ron's spot at WVXU when he moved on to Colorado in July 1992. It was this type of media activity, including TV appearances on shows like "The Nick Clooney Show," "New Faces," "MCM78," and cable, that made the blues revival a reality in Cincinnati and contributed to the present health of the blues in the city.

It has been a long time since Stovepipe recorded those fascinating glimpses of nineteenth-century black folk music that he performed regularly on Cincinnati streets, since Lonnie Johnson left his home on Rockdale for a session at King or a date at the Sportsman's Club, since Albert Washington stepped in front of a microphone and recorded "Sometimes I wonder what kind of city did I drift in?" What kind of city, indeed? A city, we might say, with a long history of blues, with all the ramifications of that statement. Segregation, racism, discrimination, exploitation, all of which gave birth to an enforced manner of living, and an ingenious manner of expression, a musical expression so undervalued in "official" Cincinnati histories that even King Records often does not show up in their pages, though it is recognized around the world as one of the most significant recording companies in the history of American music. It has been a long time coming, but as Albert Washington sings in his version of Sam Cooke's "A Change Is Gonna Come," he knows "a change is gonna come." Perhaps, though, it will be too late for too many. This book, even, comes too late to be able to report as much information as it could have if attention had been paid to Cincinnati blues earlier, and too late to offer Stovepipe the attention, and perhaps even royalties and bookings, he deserved. "And I swear you gon miss your Kid Cole," Cole sang in 1928, "baby, baby, when I'm gone." Well, a lot of blues performers have "been here and gone" without due notice, strangers, you might say, in their own hometown. Maybe we ought to say that it is the town that is strange for not embracing them, and it is the peculiar institution that kept them from achieving their fame. Let's hope that future histories don't ignore them. Let's make sure.

Notes

Introduction

1. Lyle Koehler, *Cincinnati's Black Peoples: A Chronology and Bibliography, 1787–1982* (Cincinnati: Cincinnati Arts Consortium, 1986), 1–2.

2. Jeffrey P. Brown, "Slavery in Northwest Territory," in *Dictionary of Afro-American Slavery*, ed. Randall M. Miller and John David Smith (New York: Greenwood, 1988), 547.

3. Ibid.

4. Koehler, *Cincinnati's Black Peoples*, 3–4.

5. Carter G. Woodson, "The Negroes of Cincinnati prior to the Civil War," *Journal of Negro History* 1, no. 1 (1916); rpt., *The Bobbs-Merrill Reprint Series in Black Studies*, 2.

6. Wendell P. Dabney, *Cincinnati's Colored Citizens* (1926; rpt., Cincinnati: Ohio Book Store, 1988), 49.

7. Koehler, *Cincinnati's Black Peoples*, 8.

8. Carol V. R. George, *Segregated Sabbaths: Richard Allen and the Rise of Independent Black Churches, 1760–1840* (New York: Oxford University Press, 1973), 122.

9. Gilbert Osofsky, ed., *Puttin' on Ole Massa: The Slave Narratives of Henry Bibb, William Wells Brown, and Solomon Northup* (New York: Harper and Row, 1969), 90.

10. Lafcadio Hearn, "Story of a Slave," *Cincinnati Commercial*, 2 Apr. 1876, 2.

11. Lafcadio Hearn, "Pariah People," *Cincinnati Commercial*, 22 Aug. 1875, 3.

12. Ibid.

13. Ibid.

14. Lafcadio Hearn, "Rat Row Ranches," *Cincinnati Enquirer*, 29 June 1874, 8.

15. Lafcadio Hearn, "Dolly: An Idyl of the Levee," *Cincinnati Commercial*, 27 Aug. 1876, 6.

16. Lafcadio Hearn, "Black Varieties: The Minstrels of the Row," *Cincinnati Commercial*, 9 Apr. 1876, 4.

17. Hearn, "Pariah People," 3.

18. Leon F. Litwack, *Been in the Storm So Long* (New York: Knopf, 1979), 223.

19. August Meier, *Negro Thought in America, 1880–1915* (Ann Arbor: University of Michigan Press, 1966), 10.

20. Zane L. Miller, *Boss Cox's Cincinnati: Urban Politics in the Progressive Era* (Chicago: University of Chicago Press, 1968), 30.

21. "Groan Comes from the South," *Cincinnati Enquirer*, 10 May 1917, 10.

22. WPA Writers Program, *Cincinnati: A Guide to the Queen City and Its Neighbors* (Cincinnati: Wiesen-Hart Press, 1943), 225–26.

23. "Studio for Negro Films Being Established Here," *Cincinnati Times-Star*, 4 May 1928, 18.

24. "Preservation of Stowe Home Urged," *Cincinnati Enquirer*, 1 July 1929, 7.

25. Ike Simond, *Old Slack's Reminiscence and Pocket History of the Colored Profession from 1865 to 1891* (1892; rpt., Bowling Green: Popular Press, 1974), 3, 7, 18, and 20.

26. "A Trip to Coontown," *Cincinnati Enquirer*, 14 Oct. 1900, 26.

27. "Uncle Tom's Cabin," *Cincinnati Enquirer*, 24 Mar. 1901, 4.

28. Lafcadio Hearn, "Levee Life," in *An American Miscellany*, vol. 1 (New York: Dodd, Mead and Co., 1925), 149. Further references to this article are given by page number in the text.

29. Tom Fletcher, *100 Years of the Negro in Show Business* (1954; rpt., New York: DaCapo, 1984), 213–14.

30. Ibid., 45.

31. "In Retrospect: Gussie Lord Davis, Tin Pan Alley Tunesmith," *Black Perspective in Music* 6, no. 2 (1978): 188.

32. Ibid., 190–91.

33. Gunther Schuller, "Rags, the Classics, and Jazz," in *Ragtime: Its History, Composers and Music*, ed. John Edward Hasse (New York: Schirmer, 1985), 85–86.

34. See reports in the *Cincinnati Times-Star* from 20 July 1938, 5; 7 Feb. 1940, 11; 31 Jan. 1941, 12; 6 Oct. 1941, 14; 28 Mar. 1942, 3; 29 May 1942, 5; 21 Nov. 1942, 5; and 8 June 1945, 6. Items were also reported in the *Cincinnati Post* and the *Cincinnati Enquirer* during those years as well. Matthews, also secretary-treasurer of Cincinnati Musicians Local 814 and church organist for twenty years at the Calvary Methodist Church, Seventh and Smith streets, died of a heart attack at the music school in October 1958 at the age of sixty-nine.

35. Frank Y. Grayson, *Pioneers of Night Life on Vine Street* (Cincinnati, 1924), 10.

36. Dabney, *Cincinnati's Colored Citizens*, 177. Dabney also reports that a prostitute named Clara Colville, who was white, was imprisoned in the workhouse for six months for kissing "Pork Chops" on Longworth Street near Vine at three o'clock in the afternoon. Subsequent to this, it is reported,

Negro musicians were forbidden to play music in the houses of prostitution, though surely they continued to do so, since local residents recall the practice continuing.

37. Barry Lee Pearson, *Sounds So Good to Me* (Philadelphia: University of Pennsylvania Press, 1984), 131.

38. Paul Oliver, *Meaning of the Blues* (New York: Collier, 1963), 332.

39. Franklin Rosemont, preface to *Blues and the Poetic Spirit*, by Paul Garon (London: Eddison Press Ltd., 1975), 7.

40. Bartlett Jere Whiting, *Early American Proverbs and Proverbial Phrases* (Cambridge, Mass.: Belknap, 1977), 37–38.

41. Son House, "Jinx Blues," *The Complete Library of Congress Recordings, 1941–42*, Travelin' Man, TM CD 02, 1990 [1942].

42. Albert King, "Blues Power," *Live Wire—Blues Power*, Stax LP 4128, n.d.

43. Alan Lomax, "The Homogeneity of African-American Musical Style," in *Afro-American Anthropology*, ed. Norman E. Whitten, Jr., and John F. Szwed (New York: Free Press, 1970), 197.

44. Kid Cole, "Niagara Fall Blues," *Down South*, Roots RL 313, n.d. [1928].

45. Jeff Todd Titon, *Downhome Blues Lyrics: An Anthology from the Post–World War II Era* (Boston: Twayne, 1981), 1.

46. Leroi Jones, *Blues People* (New York: Morrow, 1963).

47. Paul Oliver, *Conversation with the Blues* (New York: Horizon Press, 1965), 26.

48. Pearson, *Sounds So Good to Me*, 143.

49. Mark Humphrey, "I Am the Backbone of America: Interview with Johnny Shines," *Living Blues* 23 (1975): 29.

50. Janheinz Jahn, *Muntu: An Outline of the New African Culture* (London: Faber and Faber, 1961), 224.

51. Sam Charters, *The Bluesmen* (New York: Oak, 1967), 166.

52. Bruce Bastin, *Crying for the Carolines* (London: Studio Vista, 1971), 7–8.

53. Steven C. Tracy, *Langston Hughes and the Blues* (Urbana: University of Illinois Press, 1988), 89.

54. For a discussion of the characteristics of rural and urban blues, see David Evans, *Big Road Blues* (Berkeley: University of California Press, 1982); Jeff Todd Titon, *Early Downhome Blues* (Urbana: University of Illinois Press, 1978); and Charles Keil, *Urban Blues* (Chicago: University of Chicago Press, 1966).

55. Tony Russell, review of *Harlem Heavies*, *Blues Unlimited* 148/149 (Winter 1987): 30.

Chapter 1

1. William Collins, "The Negro of Cincinnati: A Study," *Cincinnati Enquirer*, 11 Nov. 1956, 72.

2. "This West End Problem: First Annual Report Shoemaker Health and Welfare Center" (Cincinnati: Community Chest and Council of Social Agencies, 1927).

3. Alfred Segal, "These Nostalgic Memories," *Cincinnati Post,* 4 June 1960, 4.

4. Alfred Segal, "In Which We Go Back 63 Years," *Cincinnati Post,* 17 Apr. 1965, 4.

5. "Opening the Doors of Opportunity: Annual Report of the Shoemaker Health and Welfare Center" (Cincinnati: Community Chest and Council of Social Agencies, 1928), 8–9.

6. "Tenth Annual Report of the Shoemaker Clinic" (Cincinnati, 1936), 1a.

7. Ibid., 6.

8. "Cincinnati Restricted District Is Abolished," *Cincinnati Enquirer,* 20 Nov. 1917, 7.

9. "Soliciting on the Streets Is Rampant," *Cincinnati Enquirer,* 13 Feb. 1918, 11.

10. " 'Hard Game' of Dice," *Cincinnati Enquirer,* 13 Dec. 1916, 8.

11. This date is reported in Sheldon Harris's *Blues Who's Who* ([New Rochelle, N.Y.: Arlington House, 1979], 472) as unconfirmed. The following report the 1883 date, but not the month and day: R. M. W. Dixon and John Godrich, *Recording the Blues* (London: Studio Vista, 1970); Derrick Stewart-Baxter, *Ma Rainey and the Classic Blues Singers* (New York: Stein and Day, 1970); and Samuel B. Charters and Len Kunstadt, *Jazz: A History of the New York Scene* (Garden City, N.Y.: Doubleday and Co., 1962).

12. Dixon and Godrich's *Recording the Blues* reports that these first two tunes were originally intended for Sophie Tucker (p. 9). However, Charters and Kunstadt report in *Jazz: A History of the New York Scene* (p. 85) that it was Mamie's second record, "Crazy Blues," for which Okeh was trying to secure Sophie Tucker, though Okeh was reluctant from the beginning to advertise a recording by a black singer.

13. Stewart-Baxter, *Ma Rainey,* 10.

14. Ibid.

15. Ibid., 15.

Chapter 2

1. Howard W. Odum, "Folk-Song and Folk-Poetry as Found in the Secular Songs of the Southern Negroes," *Journal of American Folklore* 24 (1911): 258–59.

2. Evans, *Big Road Blues,* 108.

3. Paul Oliver, *Songsters and Saints: Vocal Traditions on Race Records* (Cambridge: Cambridge University Press, 1984), 22.

4. James Mays, interview with author, 23 Nov. 1988. All references to comments or information provided by James Mays come from this interview.

5. Pigmeat Jarrett, interview with author, 6 Oct. 1988.

6. It has been suggested by an anonymous reviewer of this manuscript that the stovepipe served as a resonator for the kazoo.

7. Pigmeat Jarrett, interview with author, 18 Oct. 1988.

8. Steve Tracy, "Going to Cincinnati," *Living Blues* 38 (May–June 1978): 21.

9. Central Avenue was a particularly active thoroughfare in the early 1920s, the home of many bars and taverns and an active night life. In a letter to me dated 14 Nov. 1989, Zane Miller has termed it "the Lenox Avenue of the West End" in the early twentieth century.

10. All discographical details in this book are taken from R. M. W. Dixon and John Godrich's *Blues and Gospel Records, 1902–1943*, 3d ed. (London: Storyville, 1982), unless otherwise noted. The Stovepipe No. 1 discography is on pp. 709–10.

11. Titon, *Early Downhome Blues*, 46–47.

12. Laura Smith's version was released on Okeh 8246; Elzadie Robinson's was on Paramount 12420; Joe Linthecombe's version was on Gennett 7131; John Brim's version has been reissued on *On the Road Again*, Muskadine 100, 1971.

13. Dixon and Godrich, *Recording the Blues,* 21–22.

14. Tina McCarthy, letter to the author, 3 Apr. 1989.

15. David Pritchard, telephone conversation with author, 11 Apr. 1989.

16. Wilamae Minegan, telephone conversation with author, 11 Apr. 1989.

17. Chris Perkins, telephone conversation with author, 11 Apr. 1989.

18. It is not known why Stovepipe is called Stovepipe No. 1 on these sessions, since this designation did not appear on his earlier sessions. Possibly the existence of another "Stovepipe," Daddy Stovepipe, influenced him or the company to proclaim him as the first, in much the way that Rice Miller used to call himself the first Sonny Boy Williamson, the original, despite the fact that John Lee Williamson recorded under that name earlier than Miller.

19. Henry M. Belden and Arthur Palmer Hudson, eds., *North Carolina Folklore*, vol. 3 (Durham, N.C.: Duke University Press, 1952), 629–30.

20. Karnes's song has been reissued on *In the Spirit No. 1*, Origin OJL-12, n.d.; Blind Willie Johnson's is reissued on *Southern Sanctified Singers*, Roots RL 328, n.d.; Bo Weavil Jackson's can be found on *Ten Years of Black Country Religion*, Yazoo L-1022, n.d.; the New Gospel Keys' version is on *The Blues of Clarence Clay and William Scott*, Bluesville BV 1066, n.d.

21. Gary Davis's versions of these songs can be heard on *I Am a True Vine*, Heritage HT 307, 1985; *Reverend Gary Davis*, Yazoo L-1023, n.d.; and *When I Die I'll Live Again*, Fantasy 24704, n.d.

22. Tony Russell, *Blacks, Whites and Blues* (London: Studio Vista, 1970), 35.

23. Bo Weavil Jackson's version of "Saints" is on *Bullfrog Blues*, Mamlish, S 3809, n.d. Davis's version is on *Southern Sanctified Singers*, Roots RL 328, n.d. McTell's "Death Room Blues" is on *Atlanta Blues 1933*, JEMF 106, 1979. Charley Patton's "Oh Death," included on *Delta Blues*, Herwin

213, 1977, may be a version of "Soon One Morning." Clayborn's "Bye and Bye" was originally released on Vocalion 1097.

24. Daddy Stovepipe's "Sundown Blues" is reissued on *Alabama Country Blues*, Roots RL 325, n.d.

25. Samuel P. Bayard, ed., *Dance to the Fiddle, March to the Fife* (University Park: Pennsylvania State University Press, 1982), 145.

26. John A. Lomax and Alan Lomax, *American Ballads and Folk Songs* (New York: Macmillan, 1934), 258–59.

27. Ibid., 262.

28. See Furry Lewis, *In His Prime*, Yazoo L-1050, n.d.

29. Russell, *Blacks, Whites and Blues*, 26.

30. Ibid., 27.

31. Howard W. Odum and Guy B. Johnson, *The Negro and His Songs* (Chapel Hill: University of North Carolina Press, 1925), 227.

32. Alan Lomax, ed., *Folk Songs of North America* (Garden City, N.Y.: Doubleday and Co., 1960), 521.

33. Clayne R. Jensen and Mary Bee, *Square Dancing* (Provo, Utah: Brigham Young University Press, 1973), 69.

34. Margot Mays, *American Square Dance* (New York: Oak Publications, 1964), 48.

35. Lomax and Lomax, *American Ballads*, 269.

36. Bayard, *Dance to the Fiddle*, 334.

37. George Pullen Jackson, *White Spirituals in the Southern Uplands* (1933; rpt., New York: Dover, 1965), 168.

38. *The New Grove Dictionary of Music and Musicians*, ed. Stanley Sadie (London: Macmillan, 1980), vol. 8, p. 720.

39. George Williams's version was released on Columbia 14002-D; Edna Johnson's version was on Gennett 5367. It should be pointed out that the sheet music to this song was also published at the time as well.

40. Oliver, *Songsters and Saints*, 83.

41. See *The Best of Mississippi John Hurt*, Vanguard VSD 19–20, 1970 and *Frank Stokes*, Roots RL 308, n.d.

42. Clyde McCoy's version was issued on Columbia 2909-D; the Memphis Jug Band's was on Okeh 8956.

43. "It's Tight Like That" is reissued on Tampa Red's *Rare Blues of the Twenties*, Historical 1, n.d. The song was covered by numerous artists, including McKinney's Cotton Pickers, Irving Mills, Clara Smith, the Varsity Seven (with Coleman Hawkins and Benny Carter), and countless other blues and hokum singers who used the song as a basis for only slightly disguised "original" compositions.

44. Pigmeat Jarrett, interview with author, 18 Oct. 1988.

45. See Tampa Red's song on *Bottleneck Guitar 1928–1937*, Yazoo L-1039, n.d. Johnny Temple's version is on *Johnny Temple 1935–1939*, Document DLP-511, 1987.

46. "Beedle Um Bum" was released on Paramount 12714.

47. Eric Townley, *Tell Your Story* (Chigwell, Essex: Storyville, 1976), 21.

48. Ivy Smith, "Cincinnati Southern Blues," released on Paramount 12436.

49. The song is reissued on *Ishman Bracey (1928–30)*, Wolf WSE-105, n.d. Bracey's name was actually spelled Ishmon.

50. The opening line of stanza one was used by Blind Lemon Jefferson in his "Corinna Blues" reissued on *The Immortal Blind Lemon Jefferson*, Milestone MLP 2004, n.d. [1926].

51. Luke Jordan's "Cocaine Blues" was reissued on *The East Coast States Vol. 2*, Roots RL 326, n.d. [1927].

52. Fats Waller published a song entitled "Georgia Bo-Bo" in 1926, written in collaboration with Joseph Trent.

53. Tony Russell, review of *Give Me Another Jug*, Blues Unlimited 117 (Jan.–Feb. 1976): 28.

54. Pigmeat Jarrett, interview with author, 6 Oct. 1988.

55. The area around Rockdale and Reading in Avondale is another black neighborhood and the heart of Cincinnati's "second ghetto."

Chapter 3

1. Dixon and Godrich, *Blues and Gospel Records*, 50. The side by Virginia Lee is listed on p. 443.

2. See Dixon and Godrich, *Blues and Gospel Records*, 192, for the Walter Davis session, and 715 for the Sykes session. Walter Davis, *1930–1933*, Old Tramp OT-1213, n.d., includes some sides from the Davis session at the Sinton.

3. Tom Lord, *Clarence Williams* (Chigwell, Essex: Storyville, 1976), 28.

4. "By" here should be read as "by the way" or "because."

5. See *Charley Patton: Founder of the Delta Blues*, Yazoo L-1020, n.d., for Patton's song and Decca 7244 for the 78 release of Temple's "Louise Louise Blues."

6. Steve Tracy, "George Street Blues," Blues Unlimited 97 (Dec. 1972): 22.

7. Dabney, *Cincinnati's Colored Citizens*, 164.

8. Ibid., 167.

9. WPA Writers Program, *Cincinnati*, 236.

10. Pigmeat Jarrett, interview with author, 6 Oct. 1988.

11. Henry Vestine, jacket notes, *More of That Jug Band Sound*, Origin OJL 19, n.d.

12. The ad, originally in the *Chicago Defender*, 6 Apr. 1929, was reprinted in Max E. Vreede, *Paramount 12000/13000 Series* (London: Storyville, 1971), facing the page with number 12731 at the top.

13. The melody may in fact be based on Blind Lemon Jefferson's "Black Snake Moan."

14. Tony Russell, letter to the author, 25 Oct. 1972; Tony Russell, letter to the author, 29 Sept. 1972; Bob Eagle, letter to the author, 10 Oct. 1975.

15. Gary Katsel, letter to the author, 1 Feb. 1989.

16. If I am hearing these lyrics correctly—and they are very hard to understand—the verse refers to the prisoner's chagrin over not having anyone on the "outside" to run the still for him.

17. Three reissues of Frankie "Half Pint" Jaxon cover a selection of recordings from 1926 to 1933: *Saturday Night Scrontch*, Collector's Item 013, n.d.; *Can't Wait Till You Get Home*, Collector's Item 014, n.d.: and *The Remaining Titles*, Blues Documents 2049, n.d. Some of his vocal sides have been included on other reissued LPs, including Tampa Red's *Bottleneck Guitar 1928–1937*. An anonymous reader of this manuscript suggested that perhaps the song had been recorded previously by a woman, and that Tadpole had simply repeated her lyrics verbatim. That reader suggested no specific earlier version, and this writer knows of none.

18. Luke Jordan's version is reissued on *Virginia Traditions: Western Piedmont Blues*, BRI 003, 1978. Hattie Hart's version surfaced on *Memphis Blues 1928–1930*, RCA NL89276, n.d.

19. I have been unable to transcribe the lyrics of this stanza satisfactorily, and the stanza has resisted attempts by others as well.

20. Oliver, *Songsters and Saints*, 252.

21. "J. A. Whiteford Dies; Pearl Bryan Artist," *Cincinnati Post*, 12 Jan. 1966, 18.

22. Vance Randolph, coll. and ed., *Ozark Folksongs*, vol. 2 (Columbia: State Historical Society of Missouri, 1948), 44.

23. Bogan's two versions can be heard on *Bessie Jackson and Walter Roland*, Yazoo L-1017, n.d., and *Pot Hound Blues*, Historical HLP-15, 1970. Memphis Minnie's version was on 78 rpm Vocalion 1653.

24. Dabney, *Cincinnati's Colored Citizens*, 153–54.

25. Dixon and Godrich, *Blues and Gospel Records*, 166.

26. Dave Moore, letter to the author, 21 Oct. 1978.

27. Dixon and Godrich, *Recording the Blues*, 64, 104–5.

28. Willard Stargel, obituary, *Cincinnati Enquirer*, 3 Oct. 1968, 19:7.

29. "West End Sleuth to Retire," *Cincinnati Post*, 16 Apr. 1948, 26.

30. It should be pointed out that one could buy cocaine legally in drug stores early in this century.

31. Pigmeat Jarrett, interview, 18 Oct. 1988.

32. Jon Thomas, interview with author, 31 Oct. 1988.

33. Tracy, "Going to Cincinnati," 22.

34. Gilbert Bettman, telephone conversation with author, 9 Nov. 1988.

35. WPA Writers Program, *Cincinnati*, 493–94.

36. "Lockland," *Cincinnati Times Star*, 9 Jan. 1935, 6:6.

37. "Asserts Gaming 'Again Rampant' in Lockland," *Cincinnati Times Star*, 28 Dec. 1938, 1:6.

38. "Vice Conditions Intolerable in Lockland," *Cincinnati Times Star*, 26 Oct. 1942, 1:6

39. "Police Chief," *Cincinnati Enquirer*, 28 Oct. 1942, 24.

40. Pigmeat Jarrett, interview with author, 6 Oct. 1988.

41. Carr's first three (!) versions of "How Long—How Long Blues" are included on *Leroy Carr 1928*, Matchbox MSE 210, n.d.

42. The words are extremely difficult to understand here. "Roosevelt" may be incorrect.

43. A version by Fuller is included on each of the following two LPs: *Death Valley Blues*, Oldie Blues 2809, n.d., and *Shake That Shimmy*, Magpie 1807, 1979. Georgia White's version was on *The Blues Box*, MCA Coral (German) 6-30106, 1975. A version of "Mama Don't You Tear My Clothes" is on Snooks Eaglin, *Robert Pete Williams and Snooks Eaglin*, Fantasy 24716, 1973. Memphis Minnie's "Can I Do It For You" can be heard on *The Queen of Country Blues*, Old Tramp OT-1207, n.d.

44. Sykes's "Boot That Thing" is reissued on *Rare Blues 1927–1930*, Historical 5, n.d. Papa Charlie Jackson's "Shake That Thing" is included on *Fat Mouth 1924–1929*, Yazoo L-1029, n.d. Bob Eagle's "Controversies of the Blues—Pt. 1" (*Crazy Music* 10 [1977]: 11–14) discusses Eagle's view on this material.

45. Pigmeat Jarrett, interview with author, 6 Oct. 1988.

46. "Shake Mattie" is reissued on Jack Kelly, *Low Down Memphis Barrelhouse Blues*, Mamlish S-3803, n.d.

47. Karl Gert zur Heide, "Memphis Piano," *Blues Unlimited* 69 (Jan. 1970): 15.

48. Pigmeat Jarrett, interview with author, 18 Oct. 1988.

49. Ibid.

50. Reissued on Furry Lewis, *In His Prime*, and spelled on the original 78 "Kassie Jones."

51. Alan Lomax, ed., *Folk Song U.S.A.* (New York: Duell, Sloan, and Pearce, 1947), 250.

52. Tommy Johnson's song is included on *Tommy Johnson: Complete Recorded Works in Chronological Order*, Document DOCD 5001, n.d. *Mississippi and Beale Street Sheiks 1927–1932*, Biograph BLP-12041, 1972, includes the Sheiks' "New Stop and Listen." Ma Rainey's "Hear Me Talking To You" was recently reissued on *Ma Rainey*, Milestone M-47021, n.d.

53. David Evans, "Charley Patton: Conscience of the Delta," in *The Voice of the Delta*, ed. Robert Sacré (Liège: Presses universitaires de Liège, 1987), 182.

54. Paul Oliver, *Screening the Blues* (London: Cassell, 1968), 223.

55. Michael Stewart and Don Kent, jacket notes, *Low Down Memphis Barrelhouse Blues 1928–1935*, Mamlish, S-3803, n.d.

56. Will Batts, *Memphis Jamboree, 1927–1936*, Yazoo L-1021, n.d., includes Will Batts's version; Jack Kelly's versions are on *Low Down Memphis Barrelhouse Blues* and *South Memphis Jug Band*, Flyright LP 113, 1976.

57. Such artists as Clara Burston, Frances Wallace, James Cole, Tommie Bradley, Buster Johnson, and Sam Soward have been at times tentatively associated with Cincinnati. However, none of the local musicians with whom I am acquainted and none of my informants recall these names or

people at all. In addition, official records reveal no substantive evidence of their presences here and, significantly, the lyrics to their recordings do not mention Cincinnati locations or people either. It is not likely that these performers were Cincinnati residents, and therefore they fall outside the scope of this book. For those interested, *Tommy Bradley–James Cole Groups,* Matchbox 211, n.d., reissues fifteen recordings recorded between 1930 and 1932.

Chapter 4

1. Townley, *Tell Your Story,* 130.
2. Bruce Bastin, *Red River Blues: The Blues Tradition in the Southeast* (Urbana: University of Illinois Press, 1986), 54–55.
3. Dabney, *Cincinnati's Colored Citizens,* 100.
4. Pigmeat Jarrett, interview with author, 6 Oct. 1988. All quotes from Jarrett in this chapter are from this interview unless otherwise noted.
5. "Psycheye" is a phonetic spelling. Pigmeat says they called him this, but he never explained why except to say that there was something strange about one of his eyes.
6. Four recordings from 1924–26 by Jimmy Blythe are included on *Pitchin' Boogie,* Milestone MLP 2018, n.d.
7. Big Joe Duskin, interview with author, 23 Jan. 1988. The article by John M. Harris, "Cincinnati Blues—Attrition of Tradition," was published in the *Cincinnati Enquirer,* 15 July 1979, magazine section, 8–16. The quote comes from p. 16.
8. Duncan P. Schiedt, liner notes, *Blues before Sunrise,* Columbia CL 1799, 1962.
9. Carr's "George Street Blues" was reissued on *Leroy Carr 1930–35,* Magpie CD 07, 1990.
10. Information comes from Robert Bates, interview with author, 16 Oct. 1988; Big Joe Duskin, interview with author, 23 Jan. 1988; and Pigmeat Jarrett, interview with author, 18 Oct. 1988.
11. Paul S. Machlin, *Stride: The Music of Fats Waller* (Boston: Twayne, 1985), 5.
12. Charles Fox, *Fats Waller* (New York: A. S. Barnes and Co., 1961), 46.
13. Ibid.
14. Joel Vance, *Fats Waller: His Life and Times* (Chicago: Contemporary Books, 1977), 89.
15. Ibid., 88.
16. Maurice Waller and Anthony Calabrese, *Fats Waller* (New York: Schirmer Books, 1977), 107.
17. Ed Kirkeby, *Ain't Misbehavin': The Story of Fats Waller* (New York: Dodd, Mead, 1966), 163.
18. Mary Wood, "WLW Radio: The Early Years," *Cincinnati Enquirer,* 21 Mar. 1982, magazine section, 26.
19. Kirkeby, *Ain't Misbehavin',* 164.

20. See John Chilton's *Who's Who of Jazz* ([London: Bloomsbury Book Shop, 1970], 3, 75, 80, 87, 118, 120, 192, and 305) for references to Cincinnati. Chilton's *Sidney Bechet: The Wizard of Jazz* ([London: Macmillan, 1987], 102–3 and 106) also refers to experiences of Noble Sissle, Sidney Bechet, and Lena Horne in Cincinnati. Stephen Calt and Gayle Wardlow report in *King of the Delta Blues: The Life and Music of Charlie Patton* ([Newton, N.J.: Rock Chapel Press, 1988], 21) that Hacksaw Harney, who accompanied Pearl Dickson and Walter Rhodes, played in a jazz band in Cincinnati.

21. Tracy, "Going to Cincinnati," 25.

22. Roosevelt Lee, interview with author, 16 Oct. 1988.

23. Cissie Hill, "Remembering the Cotton Club," *Cincinnati Enquirer,* 19 Apr. 1981, magazine section, 8–12.

24. Big Joe Duskin, interview with author, 23 Jan. 1988; Pigmeat Jarrett, interview with author, 18 Oct. 1988.

25. Lonnie Bennett, interview with author, 18 Oct. 1988; Big Ed Thompson, interview with author, 26 Aug. 1988; Philip Paul, interview with author, 9 Nov. 1988.

26. Arnold's is located in downtown Cincinnati, and is noted for a relaxed, laid-back, sometimes folky atmosphere; Coco's is in northern Kentucky.

27. The version of the Scrap Iron Jazz Band was on 78 rpm Parlophone 6461; *Speckled Red,* Wolf 113, n.d., includes three versions of the song.

28. Priscilla Stewart's version was issued on 78 rpm Paramount 12224; Blythe's version is reissued on *Pitchin' Boogie.*

29. Fred Dellar, review of *Look at the People, New Musical Express,* 24 Jan. 1981; A. Coats, review of *Look at the People, Walnut Valley Occasional,* Sept. 1980; Gary Pitkin, review of *Look at the People, Rockingchair,* July 1980; Chris Lunn, review of *Look at the People, Victory Music,* July 1980; Leonard Duckett, review of *Look at the People, Beaumont Sunday Enterprise Journal,* 11 May 1980, 2C.

30. Britt Robson, "Pigmeat and Albert: Two Shades of Blues," *Cincinnati Magazine* 15, no. 6 (1982): 40.

31. Pigment Jarrett, *Snow on the Roof, Fire in the Furnace,* June Appal, 1979.

Chapter 5

1. James Mays, interview with author, 23 Nov. 1988. All quotes from James Mays in this chapter come from this interview unless otherwise noted.

2. Tracy, "George Street Blues," 22.

3. Steve Tracy, "Cincinnati Boogie Woogie," *Living Blues* 17 (Summer 1974): 18.

4. Tracy, "George Street Blues," 22.

5. A version of the song was recorded on 6 Dec. 1927 by William McCoy, released on 78 rpm on Columbia 14302. McCoy's complete recordings are

reissued on *Harmonicas Unlimited Vols. 1 and 2,* Document DLP 503/504, n.d., along with tracks by, among others, Daddy Stovepipe.

Chapter 6

1. Big Joe Duskin, interview with author, 23 Jan. 1988. All quotations from Duskin in this chapter are from this interview unless otherwise noted.

2. Joe has a tendency to embellish his stories, as many storytellers do, and it seems that some of his recollections, particularly of ages and dates, are faulty. For example, if Joe was 24 when his father was 104, Perry Duskin would have been 80 years old when Joe was born—that would certainly enhance the father's mythical status! That would have also meant that Joe was 9 years old when his father made him promise never to play boogie woogie and blues until the father was dead—and Joe tells stories, like the one below where he meets Freddy Slack, that presumably took place when he was around 18 years old. Enjoy the stories: whether things happened exactly this way or not, these stories are part of the persona of Big Joe Duskin.

3. Big Joe Turner, *Early Big Joe,* MCA-1325, 1980, contains one accompaniment by Slack to Turner. Freddy Slack and His Orchestra, *Riffette,* Big Band Archives LP-1202, n.d., contains five cuts with T-Bone Walker on guitar. Walker's *T-Bone Jumps Again,* Charly CRB-1019, n.d., contains Slack's two accompaniments to T-Bone. The cuts with Slack accompanying Walker are also out on Mosaic Records.

4. The original "Honky Tonk Train Blues" is included on Meade Lux Lewis, *Boogie Woogie Rarities 1927–1932,* Milestone MLP 2009, 1969.

5. Tracy, "Cincinnati Boogie Woogie," 18.

6. Actually, Fidelity Recording Co., at 121 E. Fourth Street where Wurlitzer was, did not go into business until 1949. It moved to 117 E. Fourth Street in 1958, and by 1962 was on the fifth floor at 129/131 W. Fourth Street. Joe, then, was definitely older than nineteen when he first recorded—he was at least twenty-eight.

7. Tracy, "Cincinnati Boogie Woogie," 18.

8. Bob Brumfield, "Back to the '40's with Big Joe," *Cincinnati Enquirer,* 22 May 1973.

9. Steven Rosen, "Sudsy Malone's: The Leader of the Laudromats," *Cincinnati Enquirer,* 28 Sept. 1986, 28.

10. Big Joe Duskin, postcard, Oct. 1988.

11. "News," *Blues Unlimited* 148/149 (Winter 1987): 5.

12. Denis Lewis, "The 1979 San Francisco Blues Festival," *Blues Unlimited* 137/138 (Spring 1980): 29, 31.

13. Bruce Bastin, review of *Cincinnati Stomp, Blues Unlimited* 135/136 (July–Sept. 1979): 47.

14. John Rockwood, review of *Don't Mess with the Boogie Man, Living Blues* 84 (Jan.–Feb. 1989): 60.

15. Dave Williams, review of *Don't Mess with the Boogie Man,"* Blues and Rhythm* 40 (Nov. 1988): 30.

16. Steven C. Tracy, "A *MELUS* Interview: Big Joe Duskin," *MELUS* 10 (Spring 1983): 71.

Chapter 7

1. "Phonograph Records to Be Made Here," *Cincinnati Times Star,* 1 Nov. 1944, 5.

2. Jon Hartley Fox, "King of the Queen City: The Story of King Records," transcripts of four programs, program 1, p. 5.

3. Jon Fox, program 1, p. 6.

4. Richard L. Gordon, "The Man Who Is King," *Saga* (Jan. 1950): 63. This article presented information on Sydney Nathan that formed a basis for subsequent discussions of him in print.

5. Ibid., 63.

6. "Shooting Gallery Head Held on False Pretense Charge," *Cincinnati Post,* 21 Aug. 1938.

7. "Two Charges Dismissed," *Cincinnati Post,* 9 Sept. 1938.

8. Gordon, "Man Who Is King," 64.

9. Jack Ramey, "Juke Box Operator," *Cincinnati Enquirer,* 6 Feb. 1949, sec. 3, 1.

10. "Two Corporations Replace King Record Company," *Cincinnati Post,* 8 Oct. 1946, 11.

11. Bill Millar, liner notes, *Big Fat Mamas Are Back in Style Again,* Route 66 KIX-4, 1977. Jackson died of cancer on 31 July 1989.

12. Bill Daniels, "Queen Records," *Whiskey, Women And* 10 (Nov. 1982): 10–14.

13. Jerry Ransohoff, "Record Firm Here Smashes Jim Crow," *Cincinnati Post,* 21 Mar. 1949, 6.

14. Arnold Shaw, *Honkers and Shouters* (New York: Macmillan, 1978), 278.

15. Ibid., 278–79.

16. Jon Fox, program 4, p. 14.

17. Ibid.

18. Steve Tracy, "King of the Blues Pt. 1," *Blues Unlimited* 87 (Dec. 1971): 4.

19. Shaw, *Honkers and Shouters,* 277.

20. Tracy, "King of the Blues Pt. 1," 4–5.

21. Ibid., 5.

22. Ibid.

23. Shaw, *Honkers and Shouters,* 277.

24. Ray Felder, interview with author, 10 Nov. 1988. All subsequent comments by Ray Felder are taken from this interview.

25. Ed Conley, interview with author, 14 Mar. 1989. All subsequent comments by Ed Conley are taken from this interview.

26. Shaw, *Honkers and Shouters,* 279.

27. Tracy, "King of the Blues Pt. 1," 4.

28. Norbert Hess, "I Didn't Give a Damn If the Whites Bought It," *Blues Unlimited* 119 (May–June 1976): 17–24.
29. Shaw, *Honkers and Shouters,* 240.
30. Daniels, "Queen Records," 10.
31. Tracy, "King of the Blues Pt. 1," 8.
32. John Broven, "Roy Brown, Pt. 1," *Blues Unlimited* 123 (Jan.–Feb. 1977): 8–9.
33. John Broven, "Roy Brown, Pt. 2," *Blues Unlimited* 124 (Mar.–June 1977): 14.
34. Per Notini and Bengt Weine, liner notes, *Mr. Blues Is Coming to Town,* Route 66 KIX-3, 1977.
35. Broven, "Brown, Pt. 1," 6.
36. Preston Love, liner notes, *Oh Babe!* Route 66 KIX-20, 1980. Subsequent quotes by Preston Love dealing with Wynonie Harris come from this source.
37. Philip Paul, interview with author, 9 Nov. 1988. All subsequent quotes by Philip Paul are taken from this interview.
38. Tracy, "King of the Blues Pt. 1," 8–9.
39. Waxie Maxie, liner notes, *Breakin' Up the House,* Charly CD 43, 1987.
40. Tony Burke, review of *Breakin' Up the House, Blues Unlimited* 147 (Spring 1986): 42.
41. Jon Thomas, interview with author, 31 Oct. 1988. All subsequent quotes by Jon Thomas come from this interview.
42. Danny Adler, liner notes, *Trading Licks,* Charly CD 51, 1987.
43. H-Bomb Ferguson, interview with author, 8 Feb. 1984. All subsequent quotes by H-Bomb Ferguson in this chapter are taken from this interview.
44. Adler, liner notes, *Trading Licks.*
45. Pigmeat Jarrett, interview with author, 6 Oct. 1988; Lonnie Bennett, interview with author, 18 Oct. 1988; Roosevelt Lee, interview with author, 16 Oct. 1988; Vince Morton, interview with author, 14 Mar. 1989. All subsequent quotes by these people in this chapter come from these interviews.
46. Peter Guralnik, liner notes, *Big Maybelle: The Okeh Sessions,* Epic EG 38456, 1983.
47. Ibid.
48. Norbert Hess, liner notes, *Bad Bad Girl!* Charly CD 47, 1987.
49. Bill Millar, liner notes, *Seventh Street Boogie,* Route 66 KIX-4, 1977.
50. John Lee Hooker, telephone conversation with author, 1985.
51. Jim O'Neal and Amy O'Neal, "Living Blues Interview: John Lee Hooker," *Living Blues* 44 (Autumn 1979): 16.
52. It is not known how Hooker worked with the Delta Big Four, a Mississippi-based group, and the Fairfield Four, based in Nashville, while he was in Cincinnati. Perhaps he appeared on the bill with them at a show on the radio.

53. Tracy, "King of the Blues Pt. 1," 6.

54. Steve Tracy, "King of the Blues Pt. 3," *Blues Unlimited* 89 (Feb.–Mar. 1972): 8.

55. Peter B. Lowry, liner notes, *Blues Go Away from Me*, Savoy Jazz SDL 1155, 1985.

56. Tracy, "King of the Blues Pt. 1," 6.

57. Steve Tracy, "King of the Blues Pt. 2," *Blues Unlimited* 88 (Jan. 1972): 7.

58. Mike Leadbitter, "Madison Nite Owl," *Blues Unlimited* 110 (Oct.–Nov. 1974): 5.

59. Ibid., 6.

60. Ibid., 7.

61. Tracy, "King of the Blues Pt. 2," 7.

62. Ibid.

63. Ed Conley, interview with author, 14 Mar. 1989.

64. "Cincinnati Firm Called In on Disc Jockey Payoffs," *Cincinnati Enquirer*, 20 Nov. 1959, 1.

65. "Local Firm to Give Data to Probers," *Cincinnati Post*, 20 Nov. 1959, 1.

66. "Local Firm Bows to FTC on Payola," *Cincinnati Post*, 18 Oct. 1960, 2.

67. "Tenn. Firm Buys King Records," *Cincinnati Post*, 22 Oct. 1968, 27.

68. "King Records Sold Again," *Cincinnati Post*, 14 Nov. 1968, 44.

69. "News," *Blues Unlimited* 105 (Dec. 1973/Jan. 1974): 30.

70. Big Ed Thompson, interview with author, 26 Aug. 1988.

71. Galen Gart, telephone conversation with author, 6 July 1989.

Chapter 8

1. H-Bomb Ferguson, interview with author, 8 Feb. 1984. All subsequent quotes by H-Bomb Ferguson come from this interview unless otherwise noted.

2. Lewis M. Wallace, "H-Bomb Goes Off," *Clifton* 17 (Summer 1989): 29.

3. Ibid.

4. Barry Lee Pearson, " 'One Day You're Gonna Hear about Me': The H-Bomb Ferguson Story," *Living Blues* 69 (1986): 16. All discographical details for Ferguson's recordings come from this source, with additions for the 1957–60 sessions by Ed Thompson.

5. Ibid.

6. Aaron Fuchs, liner notes, *The Shouters*, Savoy SJL 2244, 1980.

7. Pearson, "One Day," 19.

8. Charles Sawyer, *The Arrival of B. B. King* (New York: Da Capo, 1980), 69.

9. Pearson, "One Day," 21.

10. "Blues Estaffette '88," *Juke Blues* 15 (Spring 1989): 17–19.

Chapter 9

1. Albert Washington, interview with author, 23 Jan. 1989. All subsequent quotes by Albert Washington come from this interview. Also, all discographical details were provided by Albert Washington and Steve Tracy.

2. Bob Laughton and Cedric Hayes, "Post-War Gospel Records Discography," unpublished manuscript.

3. Bill Cummerow, "Albert Washington," *Living Blues* 9 (Summer 1972): 7.

4. Vince Morton, interview with author, 14 Mar. 1989. All subsequent quotes by Vince Morton come from this interview.

5. Cummerow, "Albert Washington," 7.

6. Ian Cull, review of "Turn on the Bright Lights," *Blues Unlimited* 68 (Dec. 1969): 22.

7. Keef Hartley, review of "Turn on the Bright Lights," *Blues Unlimited* 99 (Feb.–Mar. 1973): 23.

8. Mike Leadbitter, review of "Ain't It a Shame" and "Go On and Help Yourself," *Blues Unlimited* 87 (Dec. 1971): 24.

9. Jacques Demetre, review of "Betty Jane," *Blues Unlimited* 102 (June 1973): 22; Mike Leadbitter, review of "Betty Jane," *Blues Unlimited* 103 (Aug.–Sept. 1973): 19.

10. Leadbitter, review of "Ain't It a Shame," 24.

11. Ed Bedinghaus, "Legendary Caldonia Alone in Walnut Hills," *Cincinnati Enquirer*, 30 Sept. 1976, B2.

12. Steve Tracy, obituary for Caldonia Reynolds, *Living Blues* 60/61 (Summer–Fall 1984): 72.

13. Steve Tracy, "The Blues in Future American Literary Anthologies," *MELUS* 10 (Spring 1983): 15.

14. Down Home Music, review of *Sad and Lonely*, catalog for P-Vine Special, Japanese Chess, and Japanese Fire labels, 1985.

15. Steven Rosen, "Singin' the Blues at the Sha-Rah," *Cincinnati Enquirer*, 3 Aug. 1986, 12–13.

16. Bez Turner, review of "Matchbox"/"Nobody Knows," *Blues Unlimited* 146 (Autumn/Winter 1984): 52.

Chapter 10

1. Big Ed Thompson, interview with author, 26 Aug. 1988. All subsequent quotes from Ed Thompson come from this interview.

2. Lonnie Bennett, interview with author, 18 Oct. 1988. All subsequent quotes by Lonnie Bennett come from this interview.

3. Jon Thomas, interview with author, 31 Oct. 1988.

4. Albert Washington, interview with author, 23 Jan. 1989.

5. Vince Morton, interview with author, 14 Mar. 1989.

6. Mike Leadbitter, "Off the Wall," *Blues Unlimited* 107 (Apr.–May 1974), 12.

7. Ibid., 9.

8. James Jones, audiotape of recordings and commentary by Jones, n.d. The tape was sent to me by Jones at the WAIF-FM studios around 1975–76.

Bibliography

Adler, Danny. Liner Notes. *Trading Licks.* Charly CD 51, 1987.

"Appeal to State to Stop Negro." *Cincinnati Enquirer,* 8 May 1917, C11.

"Asserts Gaming 'Again Rampant' in Lockland." *Cincinnati Times-Star,* 28 Dec. 1938, 1.

Bainer, Maria. Review of *Going to Cincinnati. Blues Life* 50 (1990): 45.

Bastin, Bruce. *Crying for the Carolines.* London: Studio Vista, 1971.

———. *Red River Blues: The Blues Tradition in the Southeast.* Urbana: University of Illinois Press, 1986.

———. Review of *Cincinnati Stomp. Blues Unlimited* 135/136 (July–Sept. 1979): 47.

Bayard, Samuel P., ed. *Dance to the Fiddle, March to the Fife.* University Park: Pennsylvania State University Press, 1982.

Bedinghaus, Ed. "Legendary Caldonia Alone in Walnut Hills." *Cincinnati Enquirer,* 30 Sept. 1976, B2.

Belden, Henry M., and Arthur Palmer Hudson, eds. *North Carolina Folklore.* Vol. 3. Durham, N.C.: Duke University Press, 1952.

Bentley, Chris. "Chris's Curiosities: Oddball Blues Records—Roosevelt Lee." *Blues and Rhythm* 72 (1992): n.p.

"Blues Estaffette '88." *Juke Blues* 15 (Spring 1989): 17–19.

Broven, John. "Roy Brown, Pt. 1." *Blues Unlimited* 123 (Jan.–Feb. 1977): 4–11.

———. "Roy Brown, Pt. 2." *Blues Unlimited* 124 (Mar.–June 1977): 14–21.

Brown, Jeffrey P. "Slavery in Northwest Territory." In *Dictionary of Afro-American Slavery,* edited by Randall M. Miller and John David Smith. New York: Greenwood Press, 1988, 546–50.

Brown, Patrick W. Review of *Don't Leave Me. Living Blues* 99 (Sept.–Oct. 1991): 47.

———. Review of *Bad Times Blues. Living Blues* 92 (July–Aug. 1990): 55–56.

Brumfield, Bob. "Back to the '40's with Big Joe." *Cincinnati Enquirer,* 22 May 1973.

Burke, Tony. Review of *Breakin' Up the House. Blues Unlimited* 147 (Spring 1986): 42.

Calt, Stephen, and Gayle Wardlow. *King of the Delta Blues: The Life and Music of Charlie Patton.* Newton, N.J.: Rock Chapel Press, 1988.

Charters, Sam. *The Bluesmen.* New York: Oak, 1967.

Charters, Samuel B., and Len Kunstadt. *Jazz: A History of the New York Scene.* Garden City, N.Y.: Doubleday and Co., 1962.

Chilton, John. *Sidney Bechet: The Wizard of Jazz.* London: Macmillan, 1987.

————. *Who's Who of Jazz.* London: Bloomsbury Book Shop, 1970.

"Cincinnati Firm Called in on Disc Jockey Payoffs." *Cincinnati Enquirer,* 20 Nov. 1959, 1.

"Cincinnati Restricted District Is Abolished." *Cincinnati Enquirer,* 20 Nov. 1917, 7.

Coats, A. Review of *Look at the People. Walnut Valley Occasional,* Sept. 1980, n.p.

Collins, William. "The Negro of Cincinnati: A Study." *Cincinnati Enquirer,* 11 Nov. 1956, 72.

Cull, Ian. Review of "Turn on the Bright Lights." *Blues Unlimited* 68 (Dec. 1969): 22.

Cummerow, Bill. "Albert Washington." *Living Blues* 9 (Summer 1972): 6–7.

Dabney, Wendell P. *Cincinnati's Colored Citizens.* Cincinnati: Dabney Publishing Co., 1926; rpt., Cincinnati: Ohio Book Store, 1988.

Dahl, Bill. Review of *Down the Road Apiece. Living Blues* 97 (May–June 1991): 58.

————. Review of "Medicine Man"/"I Had a Dream." *Living Blues* 91 (May–June 1990): 49.

Daniels, Bill. "A Deluxe and Regal Feast." *Whiskey, Women And* 10 (Nov. 1982): n.p.

————. "Queen Records." *Whiskey, Women And* 10 (Nov. 1982): 10–14.

Darwen, Norman. Review of *Going to Cincinnati. Blues and Rhythm* 53 (July 1990): 33.

Dellar, Fred. Review of *Look at the People. New Musical Express,* 24 Jan. 1981, n.p.

Demetre, Jacques. Review of "Betty Jane." *Blues Unlimited* 102 (June 1973): 22.

Dixon, R. M. W., and John Godrich. *Blues and Gospel Records 1902–1943.* 3d ed. London: Storyville, 1982.

————. *Recording the Blues.* London: Studio Vista, 1970.

Down Home Music. Review of *Sad and Lonely.* Catalog for P-Vine Special, Japanese Chess, and Japanese Fire labels, 1985.

Duskin, Big Joe. Postcard. 27 Jan. 1988.

————. Postcard. Oct. 1988.

Eagle, Bob. "Controversies of the Blues—Pt. 1." *Crazy Music* 10 (1977): 11–14.

————. Letter to author. 10 Oct. 1975.

Epstein, Dena J. *Sinful Tunes and Spirituals*. Urbana: University of Illinois Press, 1977.

Evans, David. "Africa and the Blues." *Living Blues* 10 (1972): 27–29.

———. "African Elements in Twentieth-Century United States Black Folk Music." *Jazzforschung* 10 (1978): 85–110.

———. *Big Road Blues*. Berkeley: University of California Press, 1982.

———. "Charley Patton: Conscience of the Delta." In *The Voice of the Delta*, edited by Robert Sacré. Liège: Presses universitaires de Liège, 1987: 109–214.

Faxon, John D. "Big Ed Thompson Benefits Successful." *Blues Record* 1, no. 1 (1992): 1–2.

"Fifteen Hundred Negroes." *Cincinnati Enquirer*, 6 May 1917, 8.

Fletcher, Tom. *100 Years of the Negro in Show Business*. 1954; rpt., New York: Da Capo Press, 1984.

Fox, Charles. *Fats Waller*. New York: A. S. Barnes and Co., 1961.

Fox, Jon Hartley. "King of the Queen City: The Story of King Records." Transcripts of four radio programs.

Fuchs, Aaron. Liner notes. *The Shouters*. Savoy SJL 2244, 1980.

George, Carol V. R. *Segregated Sabbaths: Richard Allen and the Rise of Independent Black Churches, 1760–1840*. New York: Oxford University Press, 1973.

Gordon, Richard L. "The Man Who Is King." *Saga*, Jan. 1950: 63–65.

Grayson, Frank Y. *Pioneers of Night Life on Vine Street*. Cincinnati, 1924.

Grefenstette, Carl M. Obituary for Bull Moose Jackson. *Living Blues* 89 (Dec. 1989): 37–38.

"Groan Comes from the South." *Cincinnati Enquirer*, 10 May 1917, 10.

Guralnick, Peter. Liner notes. *Big Maybelle: The Okeh Sessions*. Epic EG 38456, 1983.

"Hard Game of Dice." *Cincinnati Enquirer*, 13 Dec. 1916, 8.

Harris, John M. "Cincinnati Blues—Attrition of Tradition." *Cincinnati Enquirer*, 15 July 1979, magazine section, 8–16.

Harris, Sheldon. *Blues Who's Who*. New Rochelle, N.Y.: Arlington House, 1979.

Hartley, Keef. Review of "Turn on the Bright Lights"/"I'm the Man"/"Woman Love"/"Doggin' Me Around." *Blues Unlimited* 99 (Feb.–Mar. 1973): 23.

Hearn, Lafcadio. "Black Varieties: The Minstrels of the Row." *Cincinnati Commercial*, 9 Apr. 1876, 4.

———. "Dolly: An Idyl of the Levee." *Cincinnati Commercial*, 27 Aug. 1876, 6.

———. "Levee Life." In *An American Miscellany*. Vol. 1. New York: Dodd, Mead and Co., 1925.

———. "Pariah People." *Cincinnati Commercial*, 22 Aug. 1875, 3.

———. "Rat Row Ranches." *Cincinnati Enquirer*, 29 June 1874, 8.

———. "Story of a Slave." *Cincinnati Commercial*, 2 Apr. 1876, 2.

Heide, Karl Gert zur. "Memphis Piano." *Blues Unlimited* 69 (Jan. 1970): 14, 15, 18.

Hess, Norbert. Liner notes. *Bad, Bad Girl!* Charly CD 47, 1987.

———. "I Didn't Give a Damn If the Whites Bought It." *Blues Unlimited* 119 (May–June 1976): 17–24.

Hill, Cissie. "Remembering the Cotton Club." *Cincinnati Enquirer,* 19 Apr. 1981, magazine section, 8–12.

Horst, Herman van der. Review of *Going to Cincinnati. Oor,* 17 Mar. 1990.

Hughes, Jon, ed. "Period of the Gruesome." Unpublished manuscript of a collection of writings by Lafcadio Hearn. University of Cincinnati, 1988. Photocopy.

Humphrey, Mark. "I Am the Backbone of America: Interview with Johnny Shines." *Living Blues* 23 (1975): 28–29.

"In Retrospect: Gussie Lord Davis, Tin Pan Alley Tunesmith." *Black Perspective in Music* 6, no. 2 (1978): 188–230.

"Influx of Negroes from South." *Cincinnati Enquirer,* 7 May 1917, 7.

Jackson, George Pullen. *White Spirituals in the Southern Uplands.* 1933; rpt., New York: Dover, 1965.

Jahn, Janheinz. *A History of Neo-African Literature.* New York: Grove Press, 1968.

———. *Muntu: An Outline of the New African Culture.* London: Faber and Faber, 1961.

"J. A. Whiteford Dies; Pearl Bryant Artist." *Cincinnati Post,* 12 Jan. 1966, 18.

Jensen, Clayne R. and Mary Bee. *Square Dancing.* Provo, Utah: Brigham Young University Press, 1973.

Jones, James. Audiotape of recordings and commentary by Jones, n.d.

Jones, Leroi. *Blues People.* New York: Morrow, 1963.

Kamins, Richard B. Review of *Going to Cincinnati. Cadence* 17 (Nov. 1991): 72.

Katsel, Gary E. Letter to author. 1 Feb. 1989.

Keil, Charles. *Urban Blues.* Chicago: University of Chicago Press, 1966.

Kindel, Mary Ann. "Pigmeat Jarrett at the Public Library." *Blues Record* 1, no. 1 (1992): 2.

"King Firm." *Cincinnati Enquirer,* 4 Mar. 1960, 7B.

"King Records Sold Again." *Cincinnati Post,* 14 Nov. 1968, 44.

Kirkeby, Ed. *Ain't Misbehavin': The Story of Fats Waller.* New York: Dodd, Mead and Co., 1966.

Kochakian, Dan. Letter to author. 28 June 1989.

Koehler, Lyle. *Cincinnati's Black Peoples: A Chronology and Bibliography, 1787–1982.* Cincinnati: Cincinnati Arts Consortium, 1986.

Kustner, Axel. "Living Country Blues." *Blues Unlimited* 142 (Summer 1982): 30–35.

Laughton, Bob. "The Gospelaires of Dayton, Ohio." *Blues Unlimited* 69 (Jan. 1970): 20.

Laughton, Bob, and Cedric Hayes. "Post-War Gospel Records Discography." Unpublished manuscript.

Leadbitter, Mike. "Madison Nite Owl." *Blues Unlimited* 110 (Oct.–Nov. 1974): 5–7.

——. "Off the Wall." *Blues Unlimited* 107 (Apr.–May 1974): 9, 12.

——. Review of "Ain't It a Shame" and "Go On and Help Yourself." *Blues Unlimited* 87 (Dec. 1971): 24.

——. Review of "Betty Jane." *Blues Unlimited* 103 (Aug.–Sept. 1973): 19.

Lewis, Denis. "The 1979 San Francisco Blues Festival." *Blues Unlimited* 137/138 (Spring 1980): 29–31.

Litwack, Leon F. *Been in the Storm So Long.* New York: Knopf, 1979.

"Local Firm Bows to FTC on Payola." *Cincinnati Post,* 18 Oct. 1960, 2.

"Local Firm to Give Data to Probers." *Cincinnati Post,* 20 Nov. 1959, 1.

"Lockland." *Cincinnati Times-Star,* 9 Jan. 1935, 6.

Lomax, Alan, ed. *Folk Song U.S.A.* New York: Duell, Sloan, and Pearce, 1947.

——, ed. *Folk Songs of North America.* Garden City, N.Y.: Doubleday and Co., 1960.

——. "The Homogeneity of African-American Musical Style." In *Afro-American Anthropology,* edited by Norman E. Whitten, Jr., and John F. Szwed. New York: Free Press, 1970: 181–220.

Lomax, John A., and Alan Lomax. *American Ballads and Folk Songs.* New York: Macmillan, 1934.

Lord, Tom. *Clarence Williams.* Chigwell, Essex: Storyville, 1976.

Love, Preston. Liner notes. *Oh Babe!* Route 66 KIX-20, 1980.

Lowry, Peter B. Liner notes. *Blues Go Away from Me.* Savoy Jazz SDL 1155, 1985.

Lunn, Chris. Review of *Look at the People. Victory Music* (July 1980). n.p.

Machlin, Paul S. *Stride: The Music of Fats Waller.* Boston: Twayne, 1985.

Man, Herrie. Review of Croco's Town Blues Festival. *Oor* 18 (8 Sept. 1990): 37.

Mays, Margot. *American Square Dance.* New York: Oak Publications, 1964.

McCarthy, Tina. Letter to author. 3 Apr. 1989.

McNutt, Randy, and Steve Rosen. "When King Was King." *Cincinnati Enquirer,* 5 July 1981, magazine section, 14–19.

Meier, August. *Negro Thought in America, 1880–1915.* Ann Arbor: University of Michigan Press, 1966.

Millar, Bill. Liner notes. *Big Fat Mamas Are Back in Style Again.* Route 66 KIX-14, n.d.

——. Liner notes. *Seventh Street Boogie.* Route 66 KIX-4, 1977.

Miller, John. Liner notes. *Twist It Babe.* Yazoo 1034, n.d.

Miller, Zane L. *Boss Cox's Cincinnati: Urban Politics in the Progressive Era.* Chicago: University of Chicago Press, 1968.

——. Letter to author. 14 Nov. 1989.

Moore, Dave. Letter to author. 21 Oct. 1978.

Murray, Karen. "Blues Lovers Get Special Treat as Four-Day Bonanza Begins." *Winnipeg Free Press,* 4 Feb. 1988, n.p.

Nager, Larry. "Ballard Owes Career to Nathan." *Cincinnati Post,* 17 Jan. 1990, 1C, 4C.

———. "The Birth of Rock 'n' Roll." *Cincinnati Post,* 17 Jan. 1990, 1C, 4C.

———. "Seymour Stein Learned the Ropes at King." *Cincinnati Post,* 17 Jan. 1990, 4C.

Nelson, David. Obituary for Bull Moose Jackson. *Living Blues* 89 (Dec. 1989): 36–37.

———. Obituary for Sonny Thompson. *Living Blues* 89 (Dec. 1989): 39.

The New Grove Dictionary of Music and Musicians. Edited by Stanley Sadie. 20 vols. London: Macmillan, 1980.

"New Warrant Names Sidney [*sic*] Nathan." *Cincinnati Enquirer,* 26 Aug. 1938, 28.

"News." *Blues Unlimited* 105 (Dec. 1972/Jan. 1974): 30.

"News." *Blues Unlimited* 148/149 (Winter 1987): 5.

Notini, Per, and Bengt Weine. Liner notes. *Mr. Blues Is Coming to Town.* Route 66 KIX-3, 1977.

Nudelman, Betty. Review of *Look at the People. Come for to Sing,* Spring 1981, n.p.

"Obituary: Willard Stargel." *Cincinnati Enquirer,* 3 Oct. 1968, 19.

Odum, Howard W. "Folk-Song and Folk-Poetry as Found in the Secular Songs of the Southern Negroes." *Journal of American Folklore* 24 (1911): 255–94.

Odum, Howard W., and Guy B. Johnson. *The Negro and His Songs.* Chapel Hill: University of North Carolina Press, 1925.

Oliver, Paul. "African Influence and the Blues." *Living Blues* 8 (1972): 13–17.

———. *Conversation with the Blues.* New York: Horizon Press, 1965.

———. "Echoes of the Jungle?" *Living Blues* 13 (1973): 29–32.

———. Liner notes. *Juke Joint Blues.* Blues Classics 23, 1970.

———. *Meaning of the Blues.* New York: Collier, 1963.

———. *Savannah Syncopators: African Retentions in the Blues.* New York: Stein and Day, 1970.

———. *Screening the Blues.* London: Cassell, 1968.

———. *Songsters and Saints: Vocal Traditions on Race Records.* Cambridge: Cambridge University Press, 1984.

O'Neal, Jim, and Amy O'Neal. "Living Blues Interview: John Lee Hooker." *Living Blues* 44 (Autumn 1979): 14–22.

Ongena, Berend. Review of Steve Tracy and the Crawling Kingsnakes at Croco's Town Blues Festival, Netherlands. *Block* 76 (Dec. 1990): 19.

———. "Blues Festival schiet in roos." *Twentsche Courant,* 27 Aug. 1990, 10.

"Opening the Doors of Opportunity: Annual Report of the Shoemaker Health and Welfare Center." Cincinnati: Community Chest and Council of Social Agencies, 1928.

Osofsky, Gilbert, ed. *Puttin' on Ole Massa: The Slave Narratives of Henry Bibb, William Wells Brown, and Solomon Northup.* New York: Harper and Row, 1969.

Ouwehand, Ton. "Prima Bluesklimaat op eerste Croco's Town." *Dagblad Van Het Oosten,* 27 Aug. 1990, 13.

The Paramount Book of the Blues. Port Washington, Wis.: New York Recording Laboratories, 1927.

Pearson, Barry Lee. *Sounds So Good to Me.* Philadelphia: University of Pennsylvania Press, 1984.

———. "One Day You're Gonna Hear about Me: The H-Bomb Ferguson Story." *Living Blues* 68 (1986): 15–26.

"Phonograph Records to Be Made Here," *Cincinnati Times Star,* 1 Nov. 1944.

Pitkin, Gary M. Review of *Look at the People. Rockingchair,* July 1980, n.p.

"Police Chief." *Cincinnati Enquirer,* 28 Oct. 1942, 24.

"Preservation of Stowe Home Urged." *Cincinnati Enquirer,* 1 July 1929, 7.

Ramey, Jack. "Juke Box Operator." *Cincinnati Enquirer,* 6 Feb. 1949, sec. 3, 1.

Randolph, Vance, coll. and ed. *Ozark Folksongs.* Vol. 2. Columbia: State Historical Society of Missouri, 1948.

Ransohoff, Jerry. "Record Firm Here Smashes Jim Crow." *Cincinnati Post,* 21 Mar. 1949, 6.

Robson, Britt. "Pigmeat and Albert: Two Shades of Blues." *Cincinnati Magazine* 15, no. 6 (1982): 40–43.

Rockwood, John. Review of *Don't Mess with the Boogie Man. Living Blues* 84 (Jan.–Feb. 1989): 59–60.

Rosemont, Franklin. Preface to *Blues and the Poetic Spirit,* by Paul Garon. London: Eddison Press, 1975.

Rosen, Steven. "Singin' the Blues at the Sha-Rah." *Cincinnati Enquirer,* 3 Aug. 1986, 12–13.

———. "Sudsy Malone's: The Leader of the Laundromats." *Cincinnati Enquirer,* 28 Sept. 1986, 28, 30.

Rowe, Mike. *Chicago Breakdown.* London: Eddison Press, 1973.

Ruppli, Michel, comp. *The King Labels: A Discography.* 2 vols. Westport, Conn.: Greenwood Press, 1985.

Russell, Tony. *Blacks, Whites and Blues.* London: Studio Vista, 1970.

———. Letter to author. 29 Sept. 1972.

———. Letter to author. 25 Oct. 1972.

———. Review of *Give Me Another Jug. Blues Unlimited* 117 (Jan.–Feb. 1976)

———. Review of *Harlem Heavies. Blues Unlimited* 148/149 (Winter 1987): 30.

Sacré, Robert, ed. *The Voice of the Delta.* Liège: Presses universitaires de Liège, 1987.

Sawyer, Charles. *The Arrival of B. B. King.* New York: Da Capo, 1980.

Schiedt, Duncan P. Liner notes. *Blues before Sunrise.* Columbia CL 1799, 1962.

Schuller, Gunther. "Rags, the Classics, and Jazz." In *Ragtime: Its History, Composers, and Music,* edited by John Edward Hasse. New York: Schirmer, 1985: 79–89.

Seroff, Doug. Letter to author. 23 May 1989.

Segal, Alfred. "In Which We Go Back 63 Years." *Cincinnati Post,* 17 Apr. 1965, 4.

————. "These Nostalgic Memories." *Cincinnati Post,* 4 June 1960, 4.

"78 Presents the Rarest 78s (C-D)." *78 Quarterly* 1, no. 4 (1989): 86–92 (includes listings for the Cincinnati Jug Band, Walter Cole, and Bob Coleman, with label photos of the CJB and Cole 78s).

Shaw, Arnold. *Honkers and Shouters.* New York: Macmillan, 1978.

————. *The World of Soul.* New York: Paperback Library, 1971.

"Shooting Gallery Head Held on False Pretenses Charges." *Cincinnati Enquirer,* 21 Aug. 1938, n.p.

Simond, Ike. *Old Slack's Reminiscence and Pocket History of the Colored Profession From 1865–1891.* 1892; rpt., Bowling Green: Popular Press, 1974.

Solding, Staffan. Review of *Look at the People. Jefferson,* 1980, n.p.

"Soliciting on the Streets Is Rampant." *Cincinnati Enquirer,* 13 Feb. 1918, 11.

Southern, Eileen. *Biographical Dictionary of Afro-American and African Musicians.* Westport, Conn.: Greenwood Press, 1982.

Steel, Suzanne. Letter to author. 27 June 1989.

Stewart, Michael, and Don Kent. Liner notes. *Low Down Memphis Barrelhouse Blues 1928–1935.* Mamlish S-3803, n.d.

Stewart-Baxter, Derrick. *Ma Rainey and the Classic Blues Singers.* New York: Stein and Day, 1970.

"Studio for Negro Films Being Established Here." *Cincinnati Times-Star,* 4 May 1928, 18.

"Tenn. Firm Buys King Records." *Cincinnati Post,* 22 Oct. 1968, 27.

"Tenth Annual Report of the Shoemaker Clinic." Cincinnati, 1936.

"This West End Problem: First Annual Report Shoemaker Health and Welfare Center." Cincinnati: Community Chest and Council of Social Agencies, 1927.

Titon, Jeff Todd. *Downhome Blues Lyrics: An Anthology from the Post-World War II Era.* Boston: Twayne, 1981.

————. *Early Downhome Blues.* Urbana: University of Illinois Press, 1978.

Townley, Eric. *Tell Your Story.* Chigwell, Essex: Storyville, 1976.

Tracy, Steven C. "Albert Washington." *Blues Unlimited* 83 (July 1971): 15.

————. "The Blues in Future American Literary Anthologies." *MELUS* 10 (Spring 1983): 15–28.

————. "Cincinnati Blues History Day." *Living Blues* 56 (Spring 1983): 25.

————. "Cincinnati Boogie Woogie." *Living Blues* 17 (Summer 1974): 18.

————. "Cincinnati Stomp." *Block* 75 (July–Sept. 1990): 19–21.

———. "George Street Blues." *Blues Unlimited* 97 (Dec. 1972): 22.

———. "Going to Cincinnati." *Living Blues* 38 (May–June 1978): 20–25.

———. "James Mays: Link with Bygone Blues." *Cincinnati Enquirer,* 11 Jan. 1976.

———. "King of the Blues Pt. 1." *Blues Unlimited* 87 (Dec. 1971): 4–8.

———. "King of the Blues Pt. 2." *Blues Unlimited* 88 (Jan. 1972): 7–10.

———. "King of the Blues Pt. 3." *Blues Unlimited* 89 (Feb.–Mar. 1972): 8–10.

———. *Langston Hughes and the Blues.* Urbana: University of Illinois Press, 1988.

———. "A *MELUS* Interview: Big Joe Duskin." *MELUS* 10 (Spring 1983): 65–85.

———. Obituary for Caldonia Reynolds. *Living Blues* 60/61 (Summer/Fall 1984): 72.

———. Review of *Sad and Lonely. Blues Unlimited* 108 (June–July 1974): 24.

———. "Steve Tracy and Big Joe Duskin." *Blues Unlimited* 101 (May 1973): 10–11.

"A Trip to Coontown." *Cincinnati Enquirer,* 14 Oct. 1900, 26.

Tsotsi, Tom. "Richmond, Indiana (1923–1934), Pt. 2." *78 Quarterly* 1, no. 4 (1989): 78–82.

Turner, Bez. Review of "Matchbox"/"Nobody Knows." *Blues Unlimited* 146 (Autumn/Winter 1984): 52.

"Two Charges Dismissed." *Cincinnati Post,* 9 Sept. 1938.

"Two Corporations Replace King Record Company." *Cincinnati Post,* 8 Oct. 1946, 11.

"Uncle Tom's Cabin." *Cincinnati Enquirer,* 24 Mar. 1901, 4.

Vance, Joel. *Fats Waller: His Life and Times.* Chicago: Contemporary Books, 1977.

"Vice Conditions Intolerable in Lockland." *Cincinnati Times-Star,* 26 Oct. 1942, 1.

Vreede, Max E. *Paramount 12000/13000 Series.* London: Storyville, 1971.

Wallace, Lewis M. "H-Bomb Goes Off." *Clifton* 17 (Summer 1989): 28–29.

Waller, Maurice, and Anthony Calabrese. *Fats Waller.* New York: Schirmer Books, 1977.

Warford, Dave. "Sweet Alice Hoskins: The Queen City's Queen of the Blues." *Blues Record* 1, no. 1 (1992): 2.

Washington, Kevin. "Berth of the Blues." *Cincinnati Enquirer Extra,* 15 Apr. 1986, 1–2.

Waterman, Richard Alan. "Comments on Paul Oliver's *Savannah Syncopators.*" *Living Blues* 6 (1971): 30–36.

Waxie Maxie. Liner notes. *Breakin' Up the House.* Charly CD 43, 1987.

"West End Sleuth to Retire." *Cincinnati Post,* 16 Apr. 1948, 26.

Whiting, Bartlett Jere. *Early American Proverbs and Proverbial Phrases.* Cambridge, Mass.: Belknap Press, 1977.

Williams, Dave. Review of *Don't Mess with the Boogie Man*. *Blues and Rhythm* 40 (Nov. 1978): 30.

Wood, Mary. "WLW Radio: The Early Years." *Cincinnati Enquirer*, 21 Mar. 1982, magazine section, 26.

Woodson, Carter G. "The Negroes of Cincinnati prior to the Civil War." *Journal of Negro History* 1, no. 1 (1916). Rpt., *The Bobbs Merrill Reprint Series in Black Studies*.

WPA Writers Program. *Cincinnati: A Guide to the Queen City and Its Neighbors*. Cincinnati: Wiesen-Hart Press, 1943.

Zijlstra, Don. Review of *Going to Cincinnati*. *Block* 75 (July–Sept 1990): 21.

Interviews

Bates, Robert. Telephone conversation with author. 16 Oct. 1988.
Bennett, Lonnie. Interview with author. 18 Oct. 1988.
Bettman, Gilbert. Telephone conversation with author. 9 Nov. 1988.
Conley, Ed. Interview with author. 14 Mar. 1989.
Duskin, Big Joe. Interview with author. 28 Sept. 1982.
——— . Interview with author. 23 Jan. 1988.
Felder, Ray. Interview with author. 10 Nov. 1988.
Ferguson, H-Bomb. Interview with author. 8 Feb. 1984.
Gart, Galen. Telephone conversation with author. 6 July 1989.
Hooker, John Lee. Telephone conversation with author. 1985.
Jarrett, Pigmeat. Interview with author. 6 Oct. 1988.
——— . Interview with author. 18 Oct. 1988.
Johnson, Boots. Interview with author. 30 Nov. 1988.
Lee, Roosevelt. Interview with author. 16 Oct. 1988.
Mays, James. Interview with author. 23 Nov. 1988.
Minegan, Wilamae. Telephone conversation with author. 11 Apr. 1989.
Morton, Vince. Interview with author. 14 Mar. 1989.
Paul, Philip. Interview with author. 9 Nov. 1988.
Perkins, Chris. Telephone conversation with author. 11 Apr. 1989.
Pritchard, David. Telephone conversation with author. 11 Apr. 1989.
Thomas, Jon. Interview with author. 31 Oct. 1988.
Thompson, Big Ed. Interview with author. 26 Aug. 1988.
Washington, Albert. Interview with author. 23 Jan. 1989.

Discography

Adler, Diz. *A Diz Adler Production*. No Label, 1971.
——— . *Otis "Elevator" Gilmore: Cincinnati's Finest*. Flyright 623, 1989.
Allen, Annisteen. *Give It Up*. Official 6051, 1989.
Arnold, Kokomo. *Blues Classics by Kokomo Arnold and Peetie Wheatstraw*. Blues Classics 4, n.d.
Baby Bonnie. *Female Blues Singers, Vol. B1*. Selmerphone SHN 4012, 1991 (6 cuts).
Ballard, Hank. *Dance Along*. King 759, n.d.
——— . *Hank Ballard and the Midnighters*. King 581, n.d.
——— . *Let 'Em Roll*. Charly CD 240, n.d.
——— . *The One and Only*. King 674, n.d.
——— . *Twenty Hits*. King 5003, n.d,
——— . *24 Hit Tunes*. King 950, n.d.
Batts, Will. *Memphis Jamboree, 1927-1936*. Yazoo L-1021, n.d. (includes "Highway Blues").
Big Maybelle. *Blues, Candy, and Big Maybelle*. Savoy SJL 1168, n.d.
——— . *Ladies Sing the Blues*. Savoy 2233, 1979 (8 cuts).
——— . *The Last of Big Maybelle*. Paramount 1011, n.d.
——— . *The Okeh Sessions*. Epic EG 38456, 1983.
Blind Blake. *Ragtime Guitar's Foremost Exponent*. Yazoo 1068, n.d.
Blythe, Jimmy. *Pitchin' Boogie*. Milestone MLP 2018, n.d.
Bogan, Lucille. *Bessie Jackson and Walter Roland*. Yazoo 1017, n.d.
——— . *Pot Hound Blues*. Historical HLP 15, 1970 (4 cuts).
Bostic, Earl. *All His Hits*. King 5010, n.d.
——— . *Alto Magic in Hi-Fi*. King 597, n.d.
——— . *Altotude*. King 515, n.d.
——— . *Blows a Fuse*. Charly CD 241, n.d.
Boyd, Little. *Southside Screamers! Chicago Blues 1948-1958*. St. George 1003, 1984 (2 cuts).
Bracey, Ishmon. *Ishmon Bracey (1928-30)*. Wolf WSE-105, n.d.
Bradley, Tommy. *Harmonicas, Washboards, Fiddles, and Jugs*. Roots RL 311, n.d. (1 cut).
——— . *More of That Jug Band Sound*. Origin OJL-19, n.d. (2 cuts).

Bradley, Tommy, and James Cole. *Tommy Bradley—James Cole Groups.* Matchbox 211, n.d.

Bradshaw, Tiny. *Breakin' Up the House.* Charly 1092, n.d.

———. *The Great Composer.* King 653, n.d.

———. *I'm a Hi-Ballin' Daddy.* JB 621, 1989.

Brim, John. *On the Road Again.* Muskadine 100, 1971 (2 cuts).

Brown, Buster. *Fort Valley Blues.* Flyright-Matchbox 250, 1973 (2 cuts).

———. *The New King of the Blues.* Fire (Japan) 6004, n.d.

Brown, Charles. *Please Come Home for Christmas.* Gusto 5019, n.d.

———. *Sunny Road.* Route 66 KIX-5, 1978.

Brown, James. *A CD of JB.* Polydor 825 714-2, 1985.

———. *A CD of JB II.* Polydor 831 700-2, 1987.

———. *Live at the Apollo.* Polydor 843 479-2, 1990.

———. *Messing with the Blues.* Polydor 847 258-2, 1990.

———. *Roots of a Revolution.* Polydor 817 304-2, 1989.

———. *Showtime.* Smash MGS 27054, n.d.

———. *Star Time.* Polydor 849 108-2, 1991.

———. *Super Bad.* King KS 1127, n.d.

———. *Thinking about Little Willie John and a Few Nice Things.* King 1038, n.d.

Brown, Roy. *Hard Luck Blues.* Gusto 5036X(2), n.d.

———. *Laughing but Crying.* Route 66 KIX-2, 1977. *See also* Wynonie Harris.

Carr, Leroy. *Blues before Sunrise.* Columbia CL 1799, 1962.

———. *Leroy Carr 1928.* Matchbox MSE 210, n.d.

———. *Leroy Carr 1930-1935.* Magpie CD 07, 1990 (includes "George Street Blues").

Carter, Bo. *Bo Carter's Greatest Hits.* Yazoo 1014, n.d.

———. *Twist It Babe.* Yazoo 1034, n.d.

Cincinnati Jug Band. *More of That Jug Band Sound.* Origin OJL 19, n.d. (1 cut).

———. *Tub Jug Washboard Bands.* BASF 1029848-5, n.d. (2 cuts). *See also* Various Artists, *Cincinnati Blues.*

Clay, Clarence, and William Scott. *The New Gospel Kings.* Bluesville 1066, n.d.

Clayborn, Edward. "Bye and Bye." Vocalion 1097, 1927.

Cole, Kid. *Down South.* Roots RL 313, n.d. (2 cuts).

———. *If Beale Street Could Talk.* Magnolia 501, n.d. (2 cuts). *See also* Various Artists, *Cincinnati Blues.*

Coleman, Bob. *Country Blues Obscurities Vol. 2.* Roots RL 340, n.d. (1 cut). *See also* Various Artists, *Cincinnati Blues.*

———. *Tub Jug Washboard Bands.* BASF 1029848-5, n.d. (2 cuts). *See also* Various Artists, *Cincinnati Blues.*

Coleman, Walter. *Blues Box 1.* MCA Coral 6, 30106, 1975 (2 cuts).

———. *Mama Let Me Lay It on You.* Yazoo 1040, n.d. (1 cut). *See also* Various Artists, *Cincinnati Blues.*

Crockett, David. *Give Us Another Jug.* Whoopee 102, n.d. (2 cuts).
———. *Harmonicas, Washboards, Fiddles, and Jugs.* Roots RL 311, n.d. (2 cuts).
———. *The Jug Bands.* RBF 6, 1963 (2 cuts).
———. *Stovepipe No. 1 and David Crockett.* Blues Documents BD 2019, 1988. *See also* Stovepipe No. 1.
Daddy Stovepipe. *Alabama Country Blues.* Roots RL 325, n.d. (2 cuts).
Davis, Blind Willie. *Southern Sanctified Singers.* Roots RL 238, n.d.
Davis, Gary. *I Am a True Vine.* Heritage HT 307, 1985.
———. *Reverend Gary Davis.* Yazoo 1023, n.d. (includes "I Am a True Vine").
———. *When I Die I'll Live Again.* Fantasy 24704, n.d. (includes "I Am the Light of This World").
Davis, Walter. *First Recordings, 1930-1932.* JSP CD 605, 1992.
———. *1930-1933.* Old Tramp OT-1213, n.d. (includes sides from Sinton Hotel session).
———. *Think You Need a Shot.* RCA 731015, n.d. (includes 1 cut from Sinton Hotel session).
Doggett, Bill. *Fourteen Hits.* King 5009, n.d.
———. *Leaps and Bounds.* Charly CD 281, n.d.
The Dominoes. *The Dominoes with Billy Ward.* King 5008, n.d.
———. *The Dominoes with Clyde McPhatter.* King 5006, n.d.
———. *The Dominoes with Jackie Wilson.* King 5007, n.d.
———. *14 Original Greatest Hits.* King 1005, n.d.
———. *Sixty Minute Man.* Charly CD 242, n.d.
Dupree, Champion Jack. *Blues for Everybody.* King 5037X (2), n.d.
———. *Sings the Blues.* King KCD 735, 1988.
Duskin, Big Joe. *Cincinnati Stomp.* Arhoolie 1080, 1979.
———. *Don't Mess with the Boogie Man.* Special Delivery 1017, 1988.
———. *Down the Road Apiece.* Wolf 120.609, 1991.
———. *San Francisco Blues Festival Vol. 2.* Solid Smoke 8010, 1981 (1 cut).
Eaglin, Snooks. *Robert Pete Williams and Snooks Eaglin.* Fantasy 24716, 1973 (includes "Mama Don't You Tear My Clothes").
Ferguson, H-Bomb. *Bad Time Blues.* Papa Lou 801, 1990.
———. *Boogie on Broadway.* Moonshine 119, n.d. (1 cut).
———. *"Don't Leave Me"/"She Don't Want Me."* Finch 701013, 1987.
———. *Life Is Hard.* Savoy SJL 1176, n.d.
———. *"Medicine Man"/"I Had a Dream."* Finch U-23811.
———. *More West Coast Winners.* Moonshine 115, n.d. (1 cut).
———. *New York Notables.* Moonshine 105, n.d. (1 cut).
———. *The Shouters.* Savoy SJL 2244, 1980 (8 cuts).
———. *Shouting the Blues.* Specialty SPCD 7028-2, 1992 (2 cuts).
The Five Keys. *14 Hits.* King 5013, n.d.
The Five Royales. *The Real Thing.* Dr. Horse 802, n.d.
———. *Roots of Soul.* Charly CRB 1096, n.d.
———. *17 Hits.* King 5014, n.d.

Fuller, Blind Boy. *Death Valley Blues*. Oldie Blues 2809, n.d.
——— . *Shake Your Shimmy*. Magpie 1807, 1979.
Gaines, Leslie Isaiah. "The Check Bouncing Congressman Blues." Cincy Sound CSR0292, 1992.
——— . "The Insane Hussein Blues." Cincy Sound CSR0191, n.d.
——— . "The Jesse Jackson Blues." Cincy Sound CSR0188, n.d.
——— . "The Reaganomic Blues." Cincy Sound CSR0181, n.d.
——— . "The Working Poor American Blues." Cincy Sound CSR 0192, n.d.
Green, Cal. "The Big Push"/"Green's Blues." Federal 12318, n.d.
Harris, Wynonie. *Good Rockin' Blues*. Charly CD 244, n.d.
——— . *Here Comes Mr. Blues*. Official 6024, n.d.
——— . *Mr. Blues Is Coming to Town*. Route 66 KIX CD-3, 1977.
——— . *Oh Babe!* Route 66 KIX-20, n.d.
——— . *Playful Baby*. Route 66 KIX-30, n.d.
Harris, Wynonie, and Roy Brown. *Battle of the Blues*. Charly CD 37, 1985.
——— . *Battle of the Blues*. King KCD 607, 1988.
——— . *Battle of the Blues Vol. 2*. King KCD 627, 1988.
Hart, Hattie. *Memphis Blues 1928-1930*. RCA NL89276, n.d. (2 cuts).
Hayes, Clifford. *Clifford Hayes and the Dixieland Jug Blowers*. Yazoo 1054, n.d.
Henry, Robert. *Detroit Ghetto Blues 1948-1954*. Nighthawk 104, n.d.
——— . *Down in Hogan's Alley*. Flyright 4073, n.d. (2 cuts).
Hooker, John Lee. *Don't You Remember Me*. Charly CD 245, n.d.
——— . *Moanin' and Stompin' Blues*. King 1085, n.d.
——— . *16 Selections: Every One a Pearl*. King 727, n.d.
Hope, Lynn. *Lynn Hope and His Tenor Sax*. Pathe 15-46661, n.d.
——— . *Morocco*. Saxophonograph CD 508, n.d.
Hoskins, Alice. *Different Shades of Blue*. Papa Lou 804, n.d.
House, Son. *The Complete Library of Congress Recordings*. Travelin' Man, TM CD 02, 1990.
Hunter, Ivory Joe. *I Had a Girl*. Route 66 KIX-25, n.d.
——— . *Jumping at the Dew Drop Inn*. Route 66 KIX-15, n.d.
——— . *Seventh Street Boogie*. Route 66 KIX-4, 1977.
Hurt, Mississippi John. *The Best of Mississippi John Hurt*. Vanguard VSD 19-20, 1970.
Jackson, Bo Weavil. *Ten Years of Black Country Religion*. Yazoo L-1022, n.d. (includes "I'm On My Way to the Kingdom Land").
Jackson, Bull Moose. *Big Fat Mamas Are Back in Style Again*. Route 66 KIX-14, n.d.
——— . *Moose on the Loose*. Saxophonograph BP 506, n.d.
Jackson, Papa Charlie. *Fat Mouth 1924-1929*. Yazoo L-1029, n.d.
James, Jesse. *Barrelhouse Blues*. Yazoo 1028, n.d. (1 cut).
——— . *Country Blues Classics Vol. 1*. Blues Classics 5, n.d. (1 cut).
——— . *Rugged Piano Classics*. Origin OJL 15, n.d. (1 cut).

Jarrett, Pigmeat. *Look at the People*. June Appal JA 035, n.d.
——— . *Snow on the Roof, Fire in the Furnace*. June Appal, no number, 1979 (2 cuts).
Jaxon, Frankie. *Can't Wait Till You Get Home*. Collector's Item 014, n.d.
——— . *The Remaining Titles*. Blues Documents 2049, n.d.
——— . *Saturday Night Scrontch*. Collector's Item 013, n.d.
Jefferson, Blind Lemon. *The Immortal Blind Lemon Jefferson*. Milestone MLP 2004, n.d.
John, Little Willie. *Fever*. Charly CD 246, n.d.
——— . *Free at Last*. King KS-5034X, n.d.
——— . *Mister Little Willie John*. King 603, n.d.
——— . *Sure Things*. King 739, n.d.
Johnson, Blind Willie. *Sweeter as the Years Go By*. Yazoo 1078, n.d. (includes "Go with Me to That Land").
Johnson, Lonnie. *Me and My Crazy Self*. Charly CD 266, 1991.
——— . *Originator of Modern Blues Guitar*. Blues Boy CD 300, n.d.
——— . *Tomorrow Night*. King KS 1083, 1976.
——— . *Twenty-Four Twelve-Bar Blues*. King 958, n.d.
Johnson, Robert. *The Complete Recordings*. Columbia C30034, 1990.
Johnson, Tommy. *Complete Recorded Works in Chronological Order*. Document DOCD 5001, n.d.
Jordan, Luke. *The East Coast States*. Roots RL 326, n.d. (includes "Cocaine Blues").
——— . *Virginia Traditions: Western Piedmont Blues*. BRI 003, 1978 (2 cuts—includes "Won't You Be Kind").
Karnes, Alfred G. *In the Spirit No. 1*. Origin OJL-12, n.d. (includes "I Am Bound for the Promised Land").
Kelly. Jack. *Low Down Memphis Barrelhouse Blues*. Mamlish S-3803, n.d. (3 cuts).
——— . *Memphis Blues Vol. 2*. Roots RL 329, n.d. (1 cut).
——— . *South Memphis Jug Band*. Flyright LP 113, 1976.
King, Albert. *The Big Blues*. King 852, n.d.
——— . *Live Wire—Blues Power*. Stax LP 4128, n.d.
——— . *Travelin' to California*. King KSD 1060, n.d.
King, Freddy. *Bossa Nova and Blues*. King 821, n.d.
——— . *Freddy King Sings*. Modern Blues Recordings MBCD 722, n.d.
——— . *Gives You a Bonanza of Instrumentals*. King 928, n.d.
——— . *Hideaway*. Gusto GD-5033X, n.d.
——— . *Just Pickin'*. Modern Blues Recordings MMBXLCD-721, 1989.
——— . *Vocals and Instrumentals*. King 964, n.d.
King, Freddy, Lula Reed, and Sonny Thompson. *Boy, Girl, Boy*. King 777, n.d.
Lee, Roosevelt. "Come Little Girl"/"Don't Leave Me Baby." Huber 1001, 1957.
——— . "Lazy Pete"/"I'm So Sad." Excello 2022, 1954.

Lewis, Furry. *In His Prime.* Yazoo 1050, n.d.

Lewis, Meade Lux. *Boogie Woogie Rarities 1927-1932.* Milestone MLP 2009, 1969 (2 cuts).

Littlefield, Little Willie. *K.C. Loving.* K.C. 101, 1977. *See also* Memphis Slim.

Marr, Hank. *Sounds from the Marr-ket Place.* King 1025, n.d.

McCoy, Clyde. "Tear It Down." Columbia 2909-D, 1933.

McCoy, William. *Harmonicas Unlimited Vols. 1 and 2.* Document DLP 503/504, n.d. (includes "Mama Blues").

———. "Mama Blues." Columbia 14302, 1927.

McNeely, Big Jay. *The Best of Big Jay McNeely Vol. 2.* Saxophonograph BP 1300, n.d.

———. *Big Jay in 3-D.* King CD 650, n.d.

McTell, Blind Willie. *Atlanta Blues 1933.* JEMF 106, 1979.

Memphis Jug Band. "Tear It Down Bed Slats and All." Okeh 8956, 1934.

Memphis Minnie. *The Queen of Country Blues.* Old Tramp OT-1207, n.d. (includes "Can I Do It for You Pt. 1").

———. "Tricks Ain't Walkin' No More." Vocalion 1653, 1931.

Memphis Slim. *Life Is Like That.* Charly CD 249, 1991.

Memphis Slim, Pete Lewis, Little Willie Littlefield. *Messin' Around with the Blues.* Gusto GD-5038X(2), 1976.

Milburn, Amos. *Blues and Boogie—His Greatest Hits.* NEXUS CD 132, 1990.

———. *Just One More Drink.* Route 66 KIX-7, 1978.

Millinder, Lucky. *Lucky Days.* MCA 1319, 1980.

Mississippi Sheiks. *Mississippi and Beale Street Sheiks 1927-1932.* Biograph BLP-12041, 1972 (4 cuts).

The New Gospel Keys. *The Blues of Clarence Clay and William Scott.* Bluesville BV1066, n.d.

The Ohio Untouchables. "Nobody Does Something for Nothing"/"Your Love Is Real." Thelma 601, n.d.

———. *Three Shades of the Blues.* Lupine 8003, n.d. (4 cuts).

Patton, Charley. *Charley Patton: Founder of the Delta Blues.* Yazoo L-1020, n.d.

———. *Delta Blues.* Herwin 213, 1977.

Peabody, Dave. *Americana.* Waterfront WF 033, n.d.

Phillips, Little Esther. *Bad Baad Girl.* Charly CRB 11OO, n.d. (released as Charly CD 47).

———. *The Best Songs Little Esther Ever Recorded.* King 622, n.d.

———. *Better Beware.* Charly CD 248, n.d.

Piano Red. *Happiness Is Piano Red.* King 1117, n.d.

The Platters. *19 Hits.* King 5002, n.d.

Rainey, Ma. *Ma Rainey.* Milestone M-47021, n.d.

Reed, Lula. *Blue and Moody.* King 604, n.d.

———. *I'm Gone Yes I'm Gone.* Sing 1157, n.d.

Rhodes, Todd. *Your Daddy's Doggin' Around.* Jukebox Lil 615, n.d.

Rogers, Jimmy. *Gold Tailed Bird.* Shelter SW 8921, 1973.

Scrap Iron Jazz Band. "The Dirty Dozens." Parlophone 6461, 1918.

Slack, Freddy. *Riffette.* Big Band Archives LP 1202, n.d.

Smith, Ivy. "Cincinnati Southern Blues." Paramount 12436, 1927.

Smith, Mamie. *Vol. 1.* Document 551, 1989.

———. *Vol. 2.* Document 552, 1989.

———. *Vol. 3.* Document 553, 1989.

———. *Vol. 4.* Document 554, 1989.

———. *Vol. 5.* Document 555, 1989.

Smothers, Smokey. *The Complete Sessions.* Krazy Kat 7406, 1982.

Speckled Red. *Speckled Red.* Wolf 113, n.d.

Stewart, Priscilla. "Mr. Freddie Blues." Paramount 12224, 1924.

Stokes, Frank. *Frank Stokes.* Roots RL 308, n.d.

Stovepipe No. 1. *Missouri and Tennessee.* Roots RL 310, n.d. (3 cuts).

———. *Rare Blues 1927-1935 Vol. 4.* Historical 5829-4, n.d. (1 cut).

———. *Skoodle Um Skoo: Early Blues Vol. 1.* Matchbox SDR 199, n.d. (4 cuts).

———. *Stovepipe No. 1 and David Crockett.* Blues Documents BD 2019, 1988.

Sweet Papa Tadpole. *Tampa Red 1928-1942.* Blues Documents BD 2001, 1983 (2 cuts). Released domestically on Story of Blues CD 3505-2, n.d.

———. *Tampa Red: Complete Recordings in Chronological Order, Vol. 4.* Document DOCD 5076, 1992.

Sykes, Roosevelt. *Rare Blues 1927-1930.* Historical 5, n.d. (includes "Boot That Thing").

———. "Tender Hearted Woman"/"I Wonder." Cincinnati 3500, n.d.

Tampa Red. *Bottleneck Guitar 1928-1937.* Yazoo L-1039, n.d.

———. *Rare Blues of the Twenties.* Historical 1, n.d. (includes "It's Tight Like That").

Temple, Johnny. *Johnny Temple 1935-1939.* Document DLP-511, 1987.

———. "Louise Louise Blues." Decca 7244, n.d.

Thompson, Big Ed. *Big Ed Thompson and the All Stars.* Papa Lou 802, n.d.

Tracy, Steve, and the Crawling Kingsnakes. *Going to Cincinnati.* Blue Shadow BSCD-4707, 1990.

———. "Going to Cincinnati"/"Jordan River Blues." Nothing But Cool NBCR 45-001, 1990.

———. *WBLZ Super Jam '87,* 1987 (1 cut).

———. *WEBN Album Project, 20th Anniversary Edition,* 1987 (1 cut). *See also* Albert Washington

Turner, Big Joe. *Early Big Joe.* MCA-1325, 1980.

Various Artists. *After Hours.* King 528, n.d.

———. *Cincinnati Blues.* Blues Documents BD 2021, 1988 (includes Kid Cole, Cincinnati Jug Band, Bob Coleman, Walter Coleman). Released domestically on Story of Blues CD 3519-2, n.d.

———. *Harmonicas Unlimited Vols. 1 and 2.* Document DLP 503/504, n.d.

———. *Ride, Daddy, Ride.* Charly CD 272, 1991.

————. *Risky Blues*. King KS-1133, 1976.

————. *Twenty-Five Years of Rhythm and Blues*. King 1004, n.d.

Vinson, Eddie. *Cherry Red Blues*. Gusto GD-5035X(2), n.d.

Walker, T-Bone. *The Complete Recordings of T-Bone Walker 1940-1954*. Mosaic MD6-130, 1990.

————. *T-Bone Jumps Again*. Charly CRB 1019, n.d.

Walker, Willie. *East Coast Blues 1926-1935*. Yazoo L-1013, n.d. (2 cuts).

————. *Mama Let Me Lay It on You*. Yazoo 1040, n.d. (1 cut).

Washboard Bill. "River Boat Dock"/"In the Morning." King 4783, n.d.

Washington, Albert. "Ain't It a Shame"/"Somewhere down the Line." Deluxe 45-135, n.d.

————. *A Woman's Love*. P-Vine PCD 2162, n.d. (several cuts).

————. "Betty Jane"/"If You Need Me." L and W 721102, n.d.

————. "Case of the Blues"/"One More Chance." Rye 954, n.d.

————. *Diamonds in the Rough*. P-Vine PLP 727/28, n.d. (5 cuts).

————. "Doggin' Me Around"/"A Woman Is a Funny Thing." Fraternity 982, n.d.

————. "God Is Good to Me"/"God Hear My Prayer." Preston 902014, n.d.

————. "Go On and Help Yourself"/"Loosen These Pains and Let Me Go." Jewel 946, n.d.

————. "Having a Good Time"/"Crazy Legs." M in the Street P 1114, n.d.

————. "Hold Me Baby"/"I'm Gonna Pour Me a Drink." Fraternity 1021, 1969.

————. "I Haven't Got a Friend"/"So Tired." VLM 1099-1100, 1964.

————. "I Want You Here with Me for Christmas Pts. 1 and 2." Included on *Merry Christmas, Baby*. Paula PCD-12, 1991.

————. "Love Is a Wonderful Thing"/"I Wanna Know How You Feel." Rye 21416, 1970.

————. "Matchbox"/"Nobody Knows What Tomorrow May Bring." Jewel 8145, 1985.

————. "Ninety-Nine Pair Shoes"/"What a Beautiful Day." M in the Street 553-20, 1972.

————. *Sad and Lonely*. Eastbound EB9007, 1973.

————. "So Good"/"Before the Sun Goes Down." L and W 491-15, n.d.

————. *Step It Up and Go*. IRIS ICD 1005, 1992.

————. "Taste of Chicago"/"Fat Rat." Westworld 708033, n.d.

————. "Tellin' All Your Friends"/"Rome Georgia." Fraternity 1002, n.d.

————. "Turn on the Bright Lights"/"Lonely Mountain." Fraternity 1016, 1969.

————. "Woman Love"/"Bring It on Up." Fraternity 1010, n.d.

————. "You Gonna Miss Me"/"Ramble." Finch 10990, 1962. This title was reissued on Bluestown 703, n.d., as "You're Gonna Miss Me"/"Ramble," and on the CD anthology *Bluestown Story Vol. 2*, Wolf WBJ 014, 1992.

————. "You're Messing Up My Mind"/"Do You Really Love Me." Preston International, no number, 1973.

Washington, Albert, and Steve Tracy. "I Walk a Long Way"/"Going Down to the Graveyard." Preston 3269, 1980.

Watson, Johnny. *I Heard That!* Charly CD 48, 1987.

——— . *Johnny "Guitar" Watson.* King 857, n.d.

White, Georgia. *The Blues Box.* MCA Coral (German) 6-30106, 1975 (2 cuts, including "Daddy Let Me Lay It on You").

Williams, Lee. "I'm Tore Up"/"They Told a Lie." Federal 12502, n.d.

Williams, Otis. *Sixteen Hits.* King 5015, n.d.

Willis, Ralph, and Country Paul. *Faded Picture Blues.* King KS1008, n.d.

General Index

Little Esther, 125, 126, 135–36, 160
Littlefield, Little Willie, 126
Little Jim's Cafe, 40, 96, 97
Little Joe, 12, 89, 191
Little Milton, 185
Little Richard, 145, 161, 200
Little Son Joe, 184
Little Walter, 200
Living Blues Magazine, 110, 112, 177
Lockland, 64–65, 187
Lockwood, Robert Jr., xxviii, 110, 143
Loma Records, 197
Lomax, Alan, xxv, 19, 21, 23, 75
Lomax, John, xxvi, 19, 23, 137
Longworth St., 4, 5
Lonzo, 85
Louis, Joe, 89
Louis, Joe Hill, 9
Louisville Jug Band, 52
Love, Preston, 126, 128, 129
Loveland, 15–16, 33
Loveland Historical Museum, 15
Lubinsky, Herman, 125
Lunceford, Jimmy, 123
Lupkin, Bill, 198, 199
Lyceum, The, xxi
Lynch, Frank, 183
Lyons, Cleveland, 160
Lytle, Johnny, 192

Mabon, Willie, 111
Mack, Clarence, 132, 148
Mack, Lonnie, 172, 173, 174, 175, 176, 180, 198, 200
Macon, Uncle Dave, 187
Madison Rd., 197
Madisonville, 172, 185, 197
Magic Moment, 188, 189
Magic Sam, 170
Magid, Lee, 157
Mahogany Hall, 100, 109
Main St., 62
Malone, Billy, 161, 188
Malone, Kid, 137, 146
Mann, Lois, 120
Manor Records, 116
Marable, Fate, 132
Marr, Hank, 135, 147, 192
Marvell, John, 160
Matthews, Artie, xxiii, 147

Matthews, Reecy, 190
Maupin, Popeye, 191, 197–98
Mays, James, xvi, 1, 9, 10, 11, 12, 27, 33, 40, 41, 42, 62, 63, 78, 85, 94–99, 114
McAllister St., xix
McCarthy, Tina, 15
McCoy, Clyde, 27
McDuff, Brother Jack, 147
McFarland St., 81
McGee, Sam, 187
McGhee, Brownie, 109, 125, 140, 141, 199
McGriff, Jimmy, 193
McLemore's, 65, 73
"MCM78" (television program), 182, 202
McMillan Ave., 170
McPhatter, Clyde, 144
McPherson, Joe, 168
McShann, Jay, 146
McTell, Blind Willie, 19, 194
McVea, Jack, 125
Memphis Horns, 181
Memphis Jug Band, 27
Memphis Minnie, 54, 67, 68, 71
Memphis Slim, 111, 142, 198
Mendelsohn, Bernie, 181
Mendelsohn, Fred, 135
Menke, William H., 89
Mercury Records, 116, 128, 191
Merle, Paul, 190
Meyer, William D. "Bang," 161
MGM Records, 137
Michelson, Nathan, 89
Midnight Steppers, 200
"Midwestern Hayride" (radio program), 117
Milburn, Amos, 147
Miley, Bubber, 7
Miller, George, 160
Millinder, Lucky, 7, 119, 123, 124, 128, 130, 133
Mill St., 5, 96
Milton, Roy, 128
Minegan, Wilamae, 15
M in the Street Records, 173, 179
Miracle Records, 116
Mississippi Sheiks, 76
Miss Kitty's, 91

Williams, George, 25
Williams, J. Mayo, 120, 123, 152
Williams, Joe, 152
Williams, Lee, 142
Williams, Otis, 145, 191, 192
Williams, Pinkie, 132, 157, 158
Williams, Ricky, 188
Williams, Willie B., 98
Williamson, Sonny Boy (John Lee
    Williamson), 100, 140, 194
Willingham, Harold, 190
Willis, Bill, 143, 147, 194
Willis, Ralph, 140
Wingfield, B. T., 30
Wings over Jordan Choir, 120
Winnipeg Folk Festival, 93
Winter, Johnny, 199
Wise, Jessie, 108
Witherspoon, Jimmy, 126, 142, 192,
    197, 199
WLW-AM, 87–88, 117
WNOP, 184, 202
Wolfe, John, 118

Wolf Records, 112
Wood, Mary, 88
Wood, Robin, 110
Woods, Donnie, 197
Woods, Henrietta, xviii
Woodson, Carter G., xvii
Worthington, Thomas, xvi
WPA Band, 191
Wright, Ruby, 148
Wright, Sam, 40, 85
WSAI-AM, 165
Wurlitzer, 108
WVXU-FM, 202
WZIP-AM, 187

Xavier University, 139

Yancey, Jimmy, 109
Yas Yas Girl (Merline Johnson), xxiv
YMCA, 190
York, Rusty, 173, 176, 183
York Brothers, 121, 123
Young, Ernie, 179

Song Index

STEVE TRACY received his doctorate in English from the University of Cincinnati in 1985. He is the author of *Langston Hughes and the Blues* and has contributed essays, articles, interviews, and reviews dealing with American and African-American literature and folklore to a variety of publications in literature and music. Tracy has been performing on and writing about the Cincinnati blues scene since 1971, working as a blues DJ and producing an LP by Pigmeat Jarrett for the June Appal label. His CD, *Going to Cincinnati,* was released in 1990, and he has opened for such blues artists as B. B. King, Muddy Waters, Sonny Terry and Brownie McGhee, Albert King, and Taj Mahal, and has recorded with Albert Washington, Joe Duskin, Pigmeat Jarrett, and the Cincinnati Symphony Orchestra.